ORACLE®   *Oracle Press*™

Oracle Big Data Handbook

Tom Plunkett

Brian Macdonald

Bruce Nelson

Helen Sun

Mark F. Hornick

Keith Laker

Khader Mohiuddin

Debra L. Harding

David Segleau

Gokula Mishra

Robert Stackowiak

Mc
Graw
Hill
Education

New York   Chicago   San Francisco
Athens   London   Madrid   Mexico City
Milan   New Delhi   Singapore   Sydney   Toronto

Cataloging-in-Publication Data is on file with the Library of Congress

Oracle Big Data Handbook

234567890   DOC DOC   10987654

ISBN   978-0-07-182726-3
MHID   0-07-182726-9

Sponsoring Editor
Paul Carlstroem

Editorial Supervisor
Janet Walden

Project Manager
Nidhi Chopra,
Cenveo® Publisher Services

Acquisitions Coordinator
Amanda Russell

Technical Editors
Jean-Pierre Dijcks and Dan McClary

Copy Editor
Margaret Berson

Proofreader
Claire Splan

Indexer
Claire Splan

Production Supervisor
Jean Bodeaux

Composition
Cenveo Publisher Services

Illustration
Cenveo Publisher Services

Art Director, Cover
Jeff Weeks

For our families

About the Authors

Big Data encompasses a wide variety of technologies and all of the authors have specific responsibilities with regards to Oracle's Big Data products. The team has extensive experience with Architecture Design, Big Data, Business Intelligence, Hadoop, Java, MapReduce, and Platform Design. Additional details on the authors' expertise are provided in the individual bios that follow.

Tom Plunkett is the lead author of several books, including *Oracle Exalogic Elastic Cloud Handbook*. In 2009, Tom led a team that won a Big Data research project for the Office of the Secretary of Defense. In 2010, Tom co-taught a semester-length graduate course that covered MapReduce and other Big Data topics for Virginia Tech's Computer Science Department. In 2012, Tom helped the Frederick National Laboratory for Cancer Research win several industry awards for analyzing relationships between genomes and cancer subtypes with the Oracle Big Data Appliance, including the 2012 Government Big Data Solutions Award (best big data project out of over eighty nominated projects), 2013 Excellence.Gov Finalist for Excellence in Innovation, and 2013 ComputerWorld Honors Laureate for Innovation. Besides his work for Oracle, Tom also teaches graduate-level computer science courses for Virginia Tech as an adjunct instructor and distance learning instructor. Tom has spoken internationally at over 40 conferences on the subjects of Big Data and Cloud Computing. Previously, Tom worked for IBM and practiced patent law for Fliesler Meyer. Tom holds a B.A. and a J.D. from George Mason University, an M.S. in Computer Science from Virginia Tech, and has taken graduate courses in Management Science and Engineering from Stanford University.

Brian Macdonald is a Distinguished Solution Consultant and certified Oracle Enterprise Architect with Oracle. Brian has over 20 years of experience creating architectures and implementing analytic platforms to address a wide range of customer needs including Data Warehousing, Business Intelligence, OLAP, Hadoop, Master Data Management, and ETL technologies. Brian has worked with hundreds of companies, including many of the top companies in the Fortune 500. Brian embraces new technologies to improve existing applications and provide innovative solutions for customers. Prior to Oracle, Brian worked for Information Resources Inc., implementing OLAP and data warehouse applications to perform complex mathematical algorithms for loan portfolio management. Brian enjoys using analytic techniques to analyze a wide range of sporting statistics.

Bruce Nelson is the Oracle Big Data lead for the western United States with a focus on Hadoop and NoSQL. He has over 24 years of experience in the IT industry with high performance database systems including Oracle, Oracle RAC, and Oracle Exadata. As the Director of Database Administration and Engineering at Bizrate, he redesigned and implemented the overall technology stack for Bizrate.com's data systems. Before Bizrate, Bruce was the VP of Data Systems Architecture at Countrywide Financial where he drove initiatives to bring Oracle and Linux on commodity hardware into Countrywide. He also led several initiatives around early Hadoop and commodity HPCC computing. At Yahoo, Bruce led several pioneering redesign and migration projects including migrating Yahoo's high performance Oracle RAC from SAN to NFS. In 1993 Bruce developed FileNet Corp.'s online presence on the Internet and created one of the first few thousand registered Web sites in the world. He went on to create one of the first database driven, interactive customer support Web site that allowed customers to follow their open service tickets on the Internet.

Helen Sun is a thought leader in Big Data and Information Architecture and a certified Oracle Enterprise Architect. Helen has over 15 years of business and technology leadership experience in a variety of industries including financial services, health care, market research, and supply chain management. Her main areas of experience include enterprise data management and information architecture including MDM, Data Integration, BI/DW, and Big Data. At Oracle, Helen assists large organizations through complex business and IT transitions. Helen is the lead author of Oracle Information Architecture Framework and Development Process and has published various white papers on Information Management, Data Governance, and Big Data. Helen has hosted a number of webinars on the same topics and has spoken at Oracle's Big Data Online Forum as well as conferences including Oracle OpenWorld. She was also a plenary speaker at The Open Group World Conference on Big Data.

Mark Hornick is a Director in the Oracle Database Advanced Analytics group, focusing on Oracle R Enterprise (ORE), Oracle R Connector for Hadoop (ORCH), and Oracle R Distribution (ORD). He also works with internal and external customers in the application of R for scalable advanced analytics applications in Oracle Database, Exadata, and the Big Data Appliance, also engaging in SAS-to-R conversion and performance benchmarking. Mark is coauthor of *Java Data Mining: Strategy, Standard, and Practice*. He joined Oracle's Data Mining Technologies group in 1999 through the acquisition of Thinking Machines Corp. Mark was a founding member of the IOUG Business Intelligence Warehousing and Analytics (BIWA) SIG and currently serves as an Oracle Advisor. He has conducted training sessions on R, ORE, and ORCH worldwide, and has presented at conferences including Oracle OpenWorld, Collaborate, BIWA Summit, and the R user conference useR!. Mark holds a Bachelor's degree from Rutgers University and a Master's degree from Brown University, both in Computer Science.

Keith Laker has been with Oracle for over 15 years and is currently a Senior Principal Product Manager for Data Warehousing and Big Data. He has extensive experience of the Big Data, data warehouse, and business intelligence markets, having worked in a variety of roles, including post-sales consultancy, customer support, and product management. Keith has spoken internationally at many Oracle user group conferences and delivered presentations worldwide on the subjects of data warehousing, data integration, multidimensional modeling, and Big Data. Prior to joining Oracle, Keith worked for Information Resources Inc. implementing OLAP and data warehouse systems for a wide variety of customers around the world.

Khader Mohiuddin is the Big Data Lead for North America's Central Region at Oracle. Khader worked at Oracle for six years, then Sun Microsystems for six years, three years at Accenture, and re-joined Oracle in 2010. In his current role, Khader applies his 20 years of enterprise software, hardware, and industry consulting expertise to architect Big Data solutions that solve the most complex business problems for customers. Khader is an expert in Information Architecture and has developed creative solutions for the oil and gas, utilities, telecom, finance, and auto industries in the areas of Data Warehousing, Advanced Analytics, and high-concurrency online systems. Khader first joined Oracle in 1996, as part of Oracle Consulting in New York, where he solved scalability issues for complex database systems at major telecom companies. He transferred to Oracle Database development in Redwood Shores, CA in 1997, where he engineered and won several competitive benchmarks for customers worldwide. He joined Sun Microsystems in 2002 as a Staff Engineer leading the effort of optimizing Oracle Database and Oracle Enterprise Applications on the Sun platform at the kernel level. He played a key role proving out Exadata Architecture as a concept during the initial stages of the development of the product, combining Sun and Oracle technologies. Khader worked at Accenture as a Business Transformation Architect and designed data systems for Fortune 100 customers using private/public clouds, DbaaS, IaaS, and so on. He helped companies achieve operational excellence by applying modern technologies to solve business problems resulting in savings of millions of dollars. In addition, Khader has authored white papers and given presentations at major conferences and local Hadoop user groups.

Debra Harding is a technologist with over 20 years of field experience successfully working with Fortune 500 companies as they evolve their core foundations for execution. As an Oracle Business Architect and Big Data Evangelist, Debra works with executive management teams as they transform their environments for competitive advantage while maintaining costs and reducing complexity. As an avid traveler, Debra has accomplished the Bridge Climb over Sydney Harbor and enjoyed skiing on the French Alps, and both she and her young daughter recently hiked to the Harding Ice Fields in Alaska. Debra's most successful journey, however, is as a Stage IV cancer survivor, and it is the driving force behind her involvement with Big Data analysis for the Life Sciences industry. In 2008, only 2 percent of the population had ever been diagnosed with this type of cancer; which meant very little information had been acquired and investigated on how to fight it. Debra believes that by harnessing the power of Big Data to analyze larger data sets in a cost-effective manner, scientists will be able to identify these smaller patterns of anomalies and work together to change lives.

David Segleau is the Director of Product Management for the Oracle NoSQL Database, Oracle Berkeley DB, and Oracle Database Mobile Server. He joined Oracle as the VP of Engineering for Sleepycat Software (makers of Berkeley DB). He has over 30 years of industry experience, leading and managing technical product teams. He has worked extensively with database technology as both a customer and a vendor. David has held management positions at many technology companies, including Britton-Lee, ShareBase, Teradata, Illustra, Informix, ANTs Software, Sleepycat Software, and now Oracle. David has spent most of his career working with leading and innovative technologies. What he enjoys most is merging customer and business requirements with product development expertise, thereby generating products and technology that solve real-world problems.

Gokula Mishra is Vice President and leader of the Advanced Analytics and Big Data team for Global Market Development, IBU, at Oracle. Gokula has over 25 years of experience in designing, developing, and managing implementation of business-driven IT strategy, Enterprise Information Management, Big Data, DW and BI, Big Data and Advanced Analytics architectures and solutions. His industry expertise includes retail, CPG, oil and gas, energy, financial services, healthcare and life sciences, and manufacturing. He is a practitioner and thought leader in Advanced Analytics and Big Data, MDM, Data Quality, and Data Governance. He has spoken at many conferences in these subject areas. Prior to Oracle, Gokula worked for Sears Holdings, HP, TransUnion, EW Solutions, Sierra Atlantic, Booz & Co., and ZS Associates. Gokula holds a B.E. (Honors) in Electrical & Electronics Engineering from BITS Pilani, and an M.S. in Computer Science from Northwestern University.

Robert Stackowiak is Vice President of Information Architecture and Big Data in Oracle's Enterprise Solutions Group. He is recognized worldwide for his expertise in Oracle data warehousing, Big Data strategy, and business intelligence technologies and solutions. He has spoken at worldwide conferences and has authored many books and articles on business intelligence and database technology including *Achieving Extreme Performance with Oracle Exadata* (Oracle Press), five editions of *Oracle Essentials* (O'Reilly Media), and *Oracle Data Warehousing and Business Intelligence Solutions* (Wiley). Follow him on Twitter @rstackow.

About the Technical Editors

Jean-Pierre Dijcks is a Senior Principal Product Manager in Oracle's Server Technology division focusing on Big Data. After earning a degree in industrial engineering from the University of Twente in the Netherlands, Jean-Pierre joined Oracle Netherlands as a data warehouse consultant working on data warehouse implementations throughout Europe. In late 2000 he moved to Oracle product development as a Product Manager for Oracle Warehouse Builder. Since 2008 Jean-Pierre has been a database product manager focusing on parallel computing. Big Data and Hadoop, including Oracle Big Data Appliance, are now Jean-Pierre's main focus.

Dan McClary currently serves as Principal Product Manager for Big Data and Hadoop at Oracle. Prior to joining Oracle he served as Director of Business Intelligence at Red Robot Labs in Palo Alto, CA. He previously was a Visiting Scholar at Northwestern University and the Howard Hughes Medical Institute, where his research in Complex Systems focused on applying Hadoop to large-scale graph problems. Dr. McClary received his Ph.D. in Computer Science from Arizona State University, where his work centered on adaptive optimization of mobile and ad-hoc networks. He holds an M.S. in Computer Science from Arizona State University focused on hard real-time schedulability in distributed systems and was founder of imgSurf, a biometrics and electronic medical record company.

Contents at a Glance

Contents

PART I
Introduction

PART II
Big Data Platform

PART III
Analyzing Information and Making Decisions

Acknowledgments

This project has taken considerable effort. We would like to thank our families for putting up with the extra burden above and beyond our normal work responsibilities. We would like to thank Oracle and the members of the Big Data mailing list for their support of this project. We would like to thank our technical editors, JP and Dan, for their many comments. We would like to thank everyone on the Oracle Press and McGraw-Hill editorial and production team, especially Paul Carlstroem and Amanda Russell. We would like to thank Doug Cutting, Margo Seltzer, Melliyal Annamalai, Peter Jeffcock, and many others who have made suggestions, given feedback, and provided content for this book. Finally, there are far too many people to thank everyone individually, so we would like to thank everyone that we have not mentioned yet.

Additional Acknowledgments from Tom Plunkett

I would like to thank Laura, Daniel, Daphne, my parents, and my other family members for putting up with this additional drain on my time. I would also like to thank my coauthors, my technical editors, my coworkers, my management team, my editors, and everyone else who assisted with this effort. In particular, I would like to thank Rizwan Jaka, Mark Comishock, Ken Currie, Peter Doolan, Mark C. Johnson, Lauren Farese, Mark A. Johnson, and Franco Amalfi for their support and encouragement.

Additional Acknowledgments from Brian Macdonald

I would like to thank Yvette, Julianna, and Jazzy for their understanding and excitement in this project. I couldn't have done this without your support. I would especially like to thank Melliyal Annamalai for her technical expertise and willingness to help with all my detailed questions. I would like to thank all my coworkers and coauthors who provided insight and a sounding board to bounce lots of good and bad ideas off; specifically, Jim Fisher, Bruce Nelson, and Marty Gubar. I want to thank Nuge Ajouz and Craig Lockwood for their support over the years, which provided me the opportunity to follow my passions, which led to this book. And finally, I would like to thank Tom Plunkett for his expertise and guidance in the process of creating this book.

Additional Acknowledgments from Bruce Nelson

I would like to acknowledge my appreciation to my wife Hilary Nelson and son Zachary for their unwavering support and understanding of my chosen path and obsession in the world of information technology. I want to thank Brian Macdonald and Tom Plunkett for encouraging me to get involved with this book project.
I also want to acknowledge the help and many hours of discussions from Jeff Needham and Ed Gasiorowski, who provided the sounding board and inspiration for a lot of the insights that ultimately went into this book. Lastly, we all owe a huge debt of gratitude to the men and women who are the unsung heroes of the open source community who make Hadoop live and breathe.

Additional Acknowledgments from Helen Sun

I would like to acknowledge my grateful appreciation to my husband William Smith, my son Nathaniel Smith, and my other family members for their continuous support and understanding as I worked on writing this book.
Also to my parents, my father Huazhi Sun and my beloved late mother Hongyuan Lin, who instilled in me a zest for learning and a spirit for success that will continue to propel me to pursue higher goals in life and career.

Additional Acknowledgments from Khader Mohiuddin

I give grateful appreciation to my parents and siblings for their hard work in providing me with a sound foundation and guidance that has led me to this stage in my life and career. Thanks to my wife and children for putting up with the additional drain on my time spent in writing this book, sacrificing vacations and free time, in general. I also want to acknowledge Jacco Draaijer, Jean-Pierre Dijcks, Dan McClary, and Brian Macdonald for technical reviews of my content, and Tom Plunkett, the man who encouraged me to be a part of this pioneering effort. My thanks are due also to Nidhi Chopra at Cenveo Publishing Services and the staff of Oracle Press at McGraw-Hill Professional who had to manage deadlines as we incorporated into the book the latest innovative product feature changes from Oracle engineering.

Additional Acknowledgments from David Segleau

I would like to thank my wife Lynn for her ongoing support during the extra hours that it took to write the chapter on Oracle NoSQL Database. Lynn was also my first reviewer and editor. Many thanks to Tom Plunkett, Dan McClary, and J.P. Dijcks for their support and technical review. Finally, thanks to the entire Oracle NoSQL Database engineering team for giving me such an excellent product to write about.

Additional Acknowledgments from Gokula Mishra

I would like to thank my wife Ratna and my children Seetal, Jyoti, and Samir for their support, encouragement, and understanding during many weekends I worked on writing the chapter on governance. I also want to thank my coauthors and my coworkers for their encouragement and support. My special appreciation goes to Tom Plunkett for his help and guidance, to my chapter reviewers J.P. Dijcks and Dan McClary for great feedback and comments, and to Sunil Soares for being the inspiration to write this chapter.

Introduction

T his book describes Oracle's approach to Big Data. The *Oracle Big Data Handbook* is intended as a handbook for anyone with an interest in Big Data, including architects, administrators, and developers. As a broad overview, this book will remain relevant for future versions of Oracle products. Although there are other books on Big Data and Apache Hadoop, this is the first book to focus on Oracle's approach to Big Data. This is a technical book that does not assume any prior knowledge of Oracle's approach to Big Data. This book includes screenshots, diagrams, and photographs when relevant.

Big Data itself is the hottest technical topic of the past several years (2010 through 2013). Data is growing extremely rapidly (over 60 percent compound annual growth according to some analysts; over 100 percent according to others). More information is being created than traditional information technologies can store and process. New technologies based on Apache Hadoop are essential to enable businesses to analyze a variety of different types of information. Businesses need to be able to combine unstructured information such as Facebook posts, Twitter sentiment, sensors, traffic information, and so on, with structured information such as online transaction processing information and traditional data warehouses, and then be able to make competitive decisions based on that information.

Oracle has recently announced a number of new and important products related to Big Data. The Oracle Database, the Oracle Exadata Database Machine, the Exalytics Machine, Endeca Information Discovery, Oracle NoSQL Database, and the Advanced Analytics Option for the Oracle Database have capabilities related to Big Data. The Oracle Big Data Appliance includes Oracle hardware, Oracle NoSQL, and Cloudera's Distribution of Hadoop. The Oracle Big Data Connectors provide the ability to connect the Hadoop Distributed File System (HDFS) to an Oracle database among other capabilities. All of these products, and more, are discussed within this book.

Part I: Introduction

Chapter 1: Introduction to Big Data describes why Big Data is important, why it is hot now, and where it fits with other Oracle technologies.

Chapter 2: The Value of Big Data describes the value proposition for Big Data. This chapter also provides an in-depth list of Big Data use cases that can be referred to in later chapters.

Part II: Big Data Platform

Chapter 3: The Apache Hadoop Platform describes the software and hardware foundations of Hadoop and its capabilities on a commodity Linux platform.

Chapter 4: Why an Appliance? provides a comparison between the Oracle Big Data Appliance and a build-your-own Apache Hadoop cluster on commodity hardware. This chapter provides Total Cost of Ownership (TCO) calculations and also discusses implications for different types of analysis.

Chapter 5: BDA Configurations, Deployment Architectures, and Monitoring describes architectural configuration options including Hadoop only, NoSQL only, Hadoop and NoSQL combined, multiple BDAs, and interconnecting BDA racks with Exadata. Also described are memory options, capacity on demand, NameNode High Availability, and multitenancy. This chapter also covers managing and monitoring jobs on Hadoop clusters.

Chapter 6: Integrating the Data Warehouse and Analytics Infrastructure to Big Data describes connecting a Big Data environment to a traditional Data Warehouse in order to expand who can get access to the information and how they can get access to the information.

Chapter 7: BDA Connectors describes what the connectors are and how to use them. This chapter includes code examples, configuration options, and performance comparisons. Topics will include but are not limited to connector architecture, benefits/ use cases for Oracle SQL Connector for HDFS, and Oracle Loader for Hadoop.

Chapter 8: Oracle NoSQL Database provides an introductory overview of NoSQL technology and NoSQL applications in general, as well as a NoSQL use case. Topics covered include the Oracle NoSQL Database architecture, its APIs, the operational features and options, as well as installing, configuring, and running Oracle NoSQL Database.

Part III: Analyzing Information and Making Decisions

Chapter 9: In-Database Analytics: Delivering Faster Time to Value provides an introduction to In-Database Analytics and Predictive Analytics. Topics covered include Oracle Data Mining, Oracle Data Miner, text and data mining algorithms, and Oracle's statistical functions; introduction to ORE; Oracle OLAP; spatial analytics; semantic/graph analytics; and integrating in-database analytics into data transformations.

Chapter 10: Analyzing Data with R provides an introduction to open source R, the R environment, IDE, ecosystem of packages from the Comprehensive R Archive Network (CRAN), trends and limitations; an anatomy of an R script; an introduction to Oracle R Enterprise (ORE) and the limitations it addresses to open source R; ORE architecture and packaging; ORE install and configuration steps (brief); examples of using various ORE features including the transparency layer and embedded R execution; Oracle R Connector for Hadoop—its benefits and features; and ORCH examples.

Chapter 11: Endeca Information Discovery provides a history of Endeca, the Endeca product suites, and their various capabilities and key features at a high level; an introduction to the Endeca Information Discovery platform; Endeca and Business Intelligence complementary technologies; architecture of Endeca Information Discovery—Studio, MDEX engine, and Information Integration suite; and unifying diverse content sets, with an emphasis on Apache Hadoop data.

Chapter 12: Big Data Governance provides an overview of Enterprise Data Governance, discusses the benefits of Big Data, describes how Big Data has created new challenges for data governance, and provides guidance on how one should approach governance for Big Data and make it an integral part of overall Enterprise Data Governance.

Chapter 13: Developing Architecture and Roadmap for Big Data provides a practical approach on how to develop Big Data architecture in an incremental manner. It talks about the impact of Big Data on an organization's Information Architecture, the development process of establishing the Big Data future state architecture, the new governance process, skill sets required to enable the new architecture, and some of the best practices.

Intended Audience

This book is suitable for the following readers:

- Developers and architects who wish to understand Oracle's Big Data strategy and product offerings

- Database administrators who want to understand how Big Data can integrate with a database

- Business users who want to understand what capabilities are offered by the combination of Big Data and Oracle's products

- Technical managers or consultants who need an introduction to Big Data

PART
I

Introduction

CHAPTER
1

Introduction to
Big Data

Thisbook covers many topics related to Big Data from an Oracle perspective, including the Oracle Big Data Appliance, the Big Data Connectors, Exadata, Exalytics, R, Oracle NoSQL, and other topics. Big Data is an emerging technology that will be discussed at length in this chapter, particularly the value of engineered systems to Big Data. This chapter serves as an introduction to the rest of the book, as many of these topics are described in greater detail throughout the book.

Big Data

Organizations increasingly need to analyze information to make decisions for achieving greater efficiency, profits, and productivity. As relational databases have grown in size to satisfy these requirements, organizations have also looked at other technologies for storing vast amounts of information. These new systems are often referred to under the umbrella term "Big Data."

Gartner has identified three key characteristics for big data: Volume, Velocity, and Variety.[1] Traditional structured systems are efficient at dealing with high volumes and velocity of data; however, traditional systems are not the most efficient solution for handling a variety of unstructured data sources or semistructured data sources. Big Data solutions can enable the processing of many different types of formats beyond traditional transactional systems. Definitions for Volume, Velocity, and Variety vary, but most big data definitions are concerned with amounts of information that are too difficult for traditional systems to handle—either the volume is too much, the velocity is too fast, or the variety is too complex.

A fourth V, Value, might also be useful in discussion of Big Data characteristics, since information in unstructured data sources may be low in value when isolated, whereas information in traditional structured systems may be high in value when isolated. Unstructured information may be "low density"; that is, a single observation on its own may not add value. However, when this data is aggregated, valuable trends may be identified.

It is possible to identify other V's (Veracity, and so on), but our analysis will focus on these four (Volume, Velocity, Variety, and Value).

Web logs and application logs are often described as Big Data. The increasing demands for digital video and music, handheld devices, and the Internet are causing an incredible increase in the amount of data to be stored. Examples include clickstream data, social networks, smartphone location-based services, Web server logs, data streams from instruments, real-time trading data, blogs, and social media such as Twitter and Facebook.

---

[1] See http://blogs.gartner.com/doug-laney/deja-vvvue-others-claiming-gartners-volume-velocity-variety-construct-for-big-data/

Our society is becoming increasingly inundated with digital information. Today, information is broadcast from satellites and transmitted over the airwaves, cables, fiber networks, and through other means. In 2004, monthly Internet traffic exceeded 1 exabyte, the equivalent of 1000 petabytes. In 2011, monthly Internet traffic exceeded 27 exabytes. An exabyte is a unit of information or computer storage equal to one quintillion bytes. One kilobyte equals 1000 bytes. One megabyte equals 1000 kilobytes. One gigabyte equals 1000 megabytes. One terabyte equals 1000 gigabytes. One petabyte equals 1000 terabytes. One exabyte equals 1000 petabytes.

Google's MapReduce Algorithm and Apache Hadoop

In the late 1990s, there were numerous search engines in the marketplace: Alta Vista, the predecessors to Microsoft's Bing, DirectHit, Inktomi, Yahoo, and many others. There were even meta-search engines, such as MetaCrawler, that would combine search results from multiple search engines.

Most search engines attempted to analyze Web pages for textual meaning, and then created an index of Web pages that could be searched against using key words. Some search engines were directories based on human analysis, such as Yahoo.

Google overtook all of its competitors in the search engine market and became the dominant player for search engines. Google gained market share by providing better search results than its competitors could provide.

There were millions of Web pages in the world, and more being created by people all over the world. The Google founders recognized that traditional approaches were inadequate for identifying relevant documents in the World Wide Web. Human-based directories could not scale to the size of the Web; even Yahoo had to make arrangements with an automated search engine to provide additional search results to its directory results. Traditional automated algorithms were also inadequate. Focusing on key words and how often a particular word is used in a document was not sufficient to provide documents with the desired level of relevancy.

The Google founders recognized that most hyperlinks in the 1990s were created by human beings while creating or updating a Web page. The text near a hyperlink is often used to describe the page that is being linked to. The Google founders realized that this text would give them a description of the Web page that they could use in their search engine as a textual meaning for the page. They further realized that therefore they didn't need to process the entire World Wide Web in their search engine; all they needed to process was the hyperlinks and the text associated with hyperlinks, thereby significantly reducing the amount of information they needed to process and store.

The search results Google was able to produce were better than the results produced either by human-based directories such as Yahoo or automated search engines such as Alta Vista. In a way, Google was the first Web 2.0 application, as Google effectively crowd-sourced the meaning of Web pages for their search engine by relying on how other people described Web pages with hyperlinks.

Google has subsequently made many other innovations in the field of search retrieval in order to scale their search engine to the massive growth rate of the World Wide Web. One of their most important innovations was on how to scale their search index to cover the massive size of all of the Web pages in the World Wide Web. Instead of using a relational database, Google invented a technology called MapReduce, which they described in a paper published in 2004.[2] Subsequent papers described the Google File System, BigTable, Dremel, Spanner, and other advances.

In 2006, Doug Cutting was working on Apache Lucene, an open source search engine, and realized that he needed a capability similar to that provided by Google's MapReduce technology. Unfortunately, Google does not make its MapReduce technology available to others. Therefore, Doug Cutting started work on an open-source MapReduce implementation, which later became the Apache Hadoop project. Yahoo quickly recognized the value of Apache Hadoop, and hired Doug Cutting to lead their efforts in this area. Facebook, government intelligence agencies, and other organizations have adopted Apache Hadoop as well.

After Apache Hadoop was successful as an open source project providing MapReduce capabilities, the open source community created additional open source projects based on other Google research papers. These projects included HBase (based on BigTable), Pig and Hive (based on Sawzall), and Impala (based on Dremel).

Apache Hadoop is a technology that is the foundation for many of the Big Data technologies that will be discussed at length in this book. Today, Apache Hadoop's capabilities are being used in a variety of ways to store information with efficiency, cost, and speed that was not possible previously. Hadoop is being used for far more than simply performing analysis on Web information.

Existing data warehouse infrastructure can continue to provide analytics, while new technologies, such as Apache Hadoop, can provide new capabilities for processing information.

Apache Hadoop contains two main components: the Hadoop Distributed File System (HDFS), which is a distributed file system for storing information, and the MapReduce programming framework, which processes information. Hadoop enables parallel processing of large data sets because HDFS and MapReduce can scale out to thousands of nodes. Apache Hadoop is described in greater detail in Chapter 3.

---

[2] http://static.googleusercontent.com/external_content/untrusted_dlcp/research.google.com/en/us/archive/mapreduce-osdi04.pdf

Oracle's Big Data Platform

Oracle has created a Big Data platform that can analyze all of an organization's information, including their structured information, semistructured information, and unstructured information. The components of the Big Data platform are shown in Figure 1-1.

As shown in Figure 1-1, unstructured and semistructured data can be transformed into structured data before storing it in a traditional data warehouse along with the rest of an organization's structured data. After semistructured data has been stored in HDFS or a NoSQL database on the Oracle Big Data Appliance, it can be preprocessed for loading into an Oracle Database running on the Oracle Exadata Database Machine. Once the information is stored in a data warehouse on Exadata, business intelligence applications such as Oracle Business Intelligence EE, Endeca, and Exalytics can perform analytics on the information.

The Oracle Big Data Appliance (BDA) is Oracle's first engineered system for Big Data. Hardware and software are engineered together to optimize extreme performance for Big Data applications. The BDA is designed to revolutionize Big Data application development, enabling enterprises to increase their speed in deploying new Big Data applications. The BDA includes Cloudera's distribution for Hadoop and

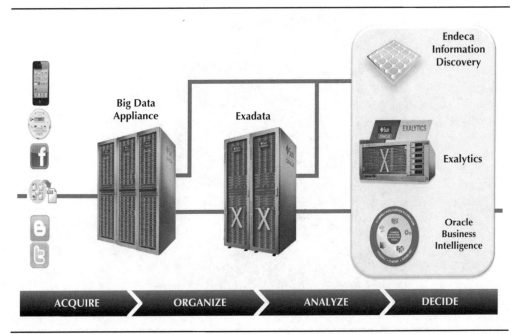

FIGURE 1-1. *Oracle Big Data platform*

the Oracle NoSQL Database on Sun hardware. InfiniBand is used for high-performance networking. Chapter 4 discusses the benefits that an organization can obtain by using the BDA over a commodity infrastructure. Chapter 5 discusses configuration and monitoring for a BDA. Figure 1-2 shows the Oracle Big Data Appliance deployed in the Oracle Solution Center in Santa Clara, California.

Cloudera's Distribution for Hadoop (CDH) is the market-leading Hadoop distribution. Chapter 3 describes CDH in detail.

The Oracle NoSQL Database can quickly acquire and organize schema-less, unstructured, or semistructured data. It is an "always available," distributed key-value data store with predictable latency and fast response to queries, supporting a wide range of interactive use cases. It has a simple programming model, making it easy to integrate into new Big Data applications. Oracle NoSQL is ideal for Big Data applications that require a fast data store that supports interactive queries and updates with a large volume of data. The Oracle NoSQL Database is discussed in detail in Chapter 8.

The Oracle Big Data Connectors enable access to the Hadoop Distributed File Systems (HDFS) from an Oracle Database and data loading to an Oracle database

FIGURE 1-2. *Oracle Big Data Appliance*

from Hadoop. There are also connectors to provide native R interface to HDFS and the MapReduce framework. Finally, there is a graphical connector for Oracle Data Integrator to generate Hadoop MapReduce programs. Chapter 7 discusses the Oracle Big Data Connectors in detail.

The Oracle Exadata Database Machine is an integrated software and hardware platform that has been designed for data warehouses, On-Line Transaction Processing (OLTP), and database consolidation. The Exadata Machine's InfiniBand fabric enables extremely fast Input/Output (I/O) communication between the storage server and the database server (Infiniband is also used within the BDA). Oracle Exadata includes intelligent storage server software that considerably increases the performance of data warehouses by reducing the amount of information that needs to be communicated between the data warehouse server and the storage server. Chapter 6 discusses how to integrate your traditional data warehouse with Big Data.

The Oracle Exadata Database Machine and the Oracle Big Data Appliance are two of the main engineered systems that Oracle offers. Some of the other engineered systems include the Oracle Exalogic Elastic Cloud machine for running application workloads and the SPARC Super Cluster Machine, which can host both databases and application workloads in a Solaris environment. There is a YouTube video showing an engineered system being deployed in a data center in a single day (contrast that with the typical new platform deployment in an IT environment requiring weeks or months). Figure 1-3 shows four engineered systems next to each other in the Oracle Solution Center in Santa Clara, California.

Oracle Advanced Analytics combines the capabilities of Oracle Data Mining with Oracle R Enterprise, an enhanced version of the open source R statistical programming language. Oracle Advanced Analytics allows analytics to be performed in the database, as opposed to moving massive quantities of information into an analytics environment, eliminating network latency. This can produce a 10× to 100× improvement in performance compared to processing outside the database. This also allows the organization to take advantage of the database's security model to protect their analytics information. Chapter 9 describes Oracle Advanced Analytics. Chapter 10 describes Oracle's R products.

Oracle Endeca Information Discovery is a data discovery platform for exploration and analysis of data with multiple schemas. Information is loaded from source systems and stored in a data model that supports changing data. Endeca can be deployed on the Oracle Exalytics In-Memory Machine, an engineered system that provides in-memory analytics for rapid decision making. Exalytics can be linked by a high-speed InfiniBand connection to a data warehouse on Oracle Exadata providing analytics for business intelligence applications accessing data warehouses. Oracle Endeca Information Discovery is described in Chapter 11.

Combining these many products with rapidly changing technologies can result in stress on an organization's traditional governance methodology and approach to enterprise architecture. Chapter 12 discusses Big Data governance. Chapter 13 discusses how to incorporate Big Data into an information architecture.

FIGURE 1-3. *Engineered systems in the Oracle Solution Center*

Organizations need the right tools to capture and organize a variety of data types from different sources, and to be able to analyze it within the enterprise. Oracle's engineered systems and software provide a Big Data platform to help organizations unlock the value of Big Data.

Summary

This chapter provided an introduction to Big Data. This chapter also served as a technical introduction to the rest of the book, as many of these topics are described in greater detail throughout the book.

CHAPTER

2

The Value of Big Data

D o you know Anonymous?

- They do not have a Facebook account.

- They do not tweet, blog, upload to Pinterest or Instagram, search StumbleUpon, download from Hulu or Netflix, nor utilize an iPod, iPad, or a Bluetooth headset.

- Their mobile number is on the "Do Not Call" list and they do not exchange their address information to get a coupon, register a product for warranty, or get a discount on magazine subscriptions.

- They prefer books over Nooks, DVDs over TV, phone calls instead of e-mails, and they block texts from senders not in their contact list.

Who are Anonymous and why should you care?

Anonymous are your customer, they represent possible revenue to your company, and they are one of many. I know this first hand, because to some businesses, I am Anonymous.

Am I Big Data, or Is Big Data Me?

As a technologist, I do understand the value of using different devices to communicate: my stepdad is 81 years old and an actor. He uses a Bluetooth headset, to stay connected when he is working on a film; my mom uses her iPad to study connective tissues and skeletal structures for her certification; and my daughter is getting an iPhone for her birthday for a multitude of uses beyond telephone calls.

As a parent, I am aware there is a trade-off between convenience and privacy. Our dependence on daily access to online information is astounding—even causing withdrawal symptoms for heavy Internet users comparable to those of substance abusers. We go online to "quickly" check the weather, news, or to send an e-mail, and an hour later, many of us are still connected; the thought of disconnecting for one day raises anxiety levels in the most casual user. Try it.

As a consumer, I am proactive in restricting access to my information from many marketing channels because the deluge of unsolicited offerings has little value to me. What does have value to me is the flexibility to choose where, when, and how to search for your product or service; if you can deliver the same consistently positive experience with every interaction, and protect my transaction, there is little incentive for me to take my business elsewhere. I am loyal.

Consider the value of having customers like me: discretionary income to spend on your product or service, and not distracted by multiple competitive offers. There is also a competitive advantage because you can correlate hard-to-obtain customer information (for example, e-mail address, cell phone number) with buying history and location. However, if your view of the customer is based on the product or service you offer, you are only seeing a part of the picture, and that weakens the connection.

Consider the challenge of attracting customers like Anonymous—because that is what your competition is doing. Some use a "shotgun" marketing strategy, blasting a message to a broad audience and hoping to reach their target. Weekly mailings addressed to *Resident*, and pop-up ads on frequently accessed sites are the reasons customers "opt-out" of having their address on national mailing lists and being contacted by an "affiliate" of the company they do business with; and pop-up blockers are common features on all their Web browsers. Your competition only has a sketch of Anonymous, not even part of a picture—for now.

Effective communication with customers requires a level of understanding that goes beyond the fields queried in your data warehouse. Capturing and keeping the customers' attention is becoming reliant on understanding the sentiment behind their actions—or perceived inactions. For example, there is a high probability that 80 percent of customer service calls are generated by 20 percent of your customers, which means you have captured a lot of data on customers who are costing you money. Many organizations include this universe for marketing decisions, but it represents an out-of-focus portrait of their customer profile.

Many of your customers are low-maintenance customers, after the initial negotiation for your product or service; they often delegate one-time payments to a credit card and automate recurring payments with their bank account. While there are definite cost savings in online versus paper billing, it also reduces the opportunity for companies to get the customer's attention. As aggregators of all my transactions, my credit card company and my bank have my attention on a monthly basis, and they know me very well. I only have one of each, and have been with both for over 20 years. They show me they value my business by respecting my privacy and learning from my actions to offer services that interest me. They have my loyalty.

Of the few times over the years when I have had to contact either one to question a transaction, or to report a lost card, I spoke directly with a representative. Each time they responded to the issue as if it was the most important one they had to resolve that day—which they did. More importantly, they did not use my time to try to upsell or cross-sell me; they stayed focused on what they could do for me, instead of what I could do for them. Every time we interact, they provide a positive customer experience, and they have my attention. When I am online to check accounts for either company, I am willing to click a link to learn about their latest offering; no pop-ups necessary.

There are hundreds of companies who thought they knew me because we had done business together once or twice. They could have my name, address, and e-mail information, but it has as much value as someone "liking" your business on Facebook just to get a coupon. There are dozens of companies who have considered me their customer because of a long history together; often it was a matter of convenience, such as the local grocery store, or resulted from limited choices—there are not a lot of options when you need electricity, gas, and water. There are a only a handful of companies I would recommend in person if asked my opinion.

Many customers would be comfortable going online and expressing this type of positive sentiment publicly if they had the time. However, if they have an unpleasant experience with your customer service with no resolution, then many of them would find the time to post a negative review.

Gone are the days when an organization could generate an automated e-mail response and expect a 48-hour window for a personalized customer service response to an unhappy customer.

Instead of fuming in silence, many customers find support from friends, both in person and online. The illusion of anonymity on popular social networking sites such as Facebook and Twitter, and the documented sense of immediate gratification in response to an online post, have shifted the balance of power from company to consumer. A negative review is estimated at having five times as much impact as a positive review—and infinitely more value for your competition.

Even more alarming to some organizations is the realization that many comments are not stored solely on their Web site; consumers are posting questions, complaints, and reviews on a variety of social networks, which are replicated across servers and across the globe—and they are expecting a timely response.

With an estimated average of one hundred "friends" for each Facebook and Twitter account, the exponential reach of one negative post, replicated globally across multiple servers, can challenge your long-term growth by the loss of potential customers.

There are unforeseen operational costs as well; if an unhappy customer provides their work e-mail as primary contact for a response by customer service, and their personal e-mail to post a negative review, not only does it appear to your internal metrics as if there are twice the number of complaints, but duplicate resources could be assigned to resolve the same issue.

Many businesses attempting to provide "social care" by creating customer service accounts on popular social networking sites are struggling because they are not prepared to handle the high volume of dynamic data coming in from so many different sources in unstructured formats. The pressure continues to increase because every misstep is public.

Organizations today need to evolve their existing analytical processing capabilities before they can translate data into emotions (likes, dislikes) from social networks or electrical signals from a variety of devices (for example, sensors, smartphones) and respond in a timely fashion without taxing their existing infrastructure or reducing their quality of service.

The combination of the three "V's," high Volume, Variety of formats, and uncontrolled Velocity, defines Big Data. The elusive fourth "V" for Value is derived from the exploration of the Big Data combination of source and content as it applies to what is being investigated.

Big Data offers strong competitive value for those who can harness it. There are millions of businesses worldwide who are waiting for the opportunity to have Anonymous as their customer; and it only takes one unpleasant encounter with your company to give them that chance.

Big Data, Little Data—It's Still Me

Coming back to where you started is not the same as never leaving.
                                                —Terry Pratchett, *A Hat Full of Sky*

History has an annoying habit of repeating itself.

The Big Data whirlwind is reminiscent of the rapid expansion of online activity in the 1990s. We have new terminology ("dot.com" versus "social network"), new skill sets (HTML versus MapReduce) and new roles (Web designer versus data scientist); and once again, you have a steep learning curve to understand how to obtain value from a global phenomenon.

This is in addition to the compounded complexity resulting from reactive versus strategic responses to the dot.com fallout.

The technical evolution from mainframe to client server to a multitier architecture enabled companies to offer products and services via Web portals to compete with the availability of a global online marketplace. However, the competitive intensity of the "Internet bubble" forced many businesses to create a Web presence too quickly and with very little thought of how this activity would integrate into their existing infrastructure.

It was once considered less expensive and faster to separate environments by communication channels (catalog, call centers, Web site, and so on). Now, millions of dollars are spent yearly on consolidation and subsequent deduplication of customer data, which skews analysis and results in some questionable marketing choices.

For example, this past December, I opened a DVD case containing three popular Christmas movies and found a coupon for baloney. It had a festive picture of reindeer flying over a sandwich, and offered a dollar in savings, which I could use at my leisure within the next 13 months.

I am a vegetarian. No matter how long the coupon was valid, it was of no value to me; there was, however, a cost to the company to develop this marketing campaign, print the coupons, and insert them into the manufacturing process. Somewhere, there is a lot of data suggesting the combination of Christmas and lunch meat would be successful.

Maybe someone on Facebook "liked" baloney on one of their posts, and then "liked" a Christmas movie on another; then their friends responded with their favorite Christmas movies and it "snowballed" from there (pun intended).

It is certain that someone made a decision to finance this shotgun approach to marketing and hoped they would find their target customer.

Before we can find the value in Big Data, we need to ensure we do not repeat the mistakes of the past and end up in the same place 20 years from now, with a chasm between customers and business that has reduced the amount and quality of customer information, and restrictive capabilities for expansion within enterprise infrastructures due to complexity and cost.

What Happened?

When we analyze the evolution of technical advancements in circuitry from the 1970s to today, we discover a correlation of new capabilities for both business and consumers. Miniaturization of components combined with increased memory and processing power continues to impact how we interact with each other socially, as business owners and as customers on a daily basis. It became a cautionary tale when automation and digital devices not only changed the way we communicated, but were substituted for personal interaction. The result is where many companies are today; they have a lot of "Little Data" on unhappy or neutral customers.

The term "Little Data" was coined in the media to represent information currently stored inside the enterprise and to differentiate it during discussions about "Big Data." It is the correlation of the two where an organization can uncover new customer dimensions for analysis. Once this goal has been realized, it is essential to use the results of this analysis to strengthen customer relationships. If not, then Big or Little, the data could become worthless.

Consider the technology choices implemented 20 years ago to reduce costs by automating the interaction between customer and customer service representative (CSR). In a technology ironically named Interactive Voice Response systems (IVRs), the caller is forced to listen to a litany of options, press a variety of digits, be put on hold multiple times, and made to listen to muzak or sales pitches—and more often than not, be hung up on and forced to do it again. No need to guess the customer sentiment when they have to call back a second time.

Instead of feeling valued as customers, many people would at first feel "lucky" when they did reach a CSR—and then the feeling usually melted into frustration and impatience after being passed to multiple people in different departments, forced to give the same information, and once again be placed on hold. Even if each CSR provided quality service, spending a half hour on the phone to obtain basic information, or make account changes, diminishes any interest in adding new services. Many people used to remain as customers because there were not a lot of options. Things have changed.

The meteoric rise of the dot.com bubble in the 1990s and the combination of its crash with rampant Merger and Acquisition (M&A) activity in the early twenty-first century forever changed the balance of power from business to customer on a global scale. As the lines have blurred between "foreign" and "domestic" competition, so has the picture many companies once had of their customer.

Being globally responsive and offering local personal service is a strong competitive differentiator. Unfortunately, not many businesses have the capabilities to take advantage of it.

As a technologist, I understand that the complexity of combining customer data from an M&A, with existing customer data stored throughout the enterprise, and updates captured from multichannel activity (call centers, e-mail, postal mail, Web site, and so on) often results in CSRs having to access multiple systems—each with their own security profile—to respond to a basic customer query about account balances.

As a customer, however, I do not understand why it takes so long to answer a basic question about my account. I am not alone, and as loyal as many customers can be to certain companies, if you waste their time you lose their business. It is that simple.

Now What?

In the same way the wind existed before the windmill was built to harness its power, Big Data has been a part of the business world for many years. Just think of the Web and server logs generated and wiped each week.

This data was often considered *low-density* with little value; it was not cost-effective to capture and store this uncontrollable jumble of bits and bytes at the same time an organization continued to struggle with transforming and integrating *high-density* high-value structured data into their enterprise systems.

Today, the proprietary technology designed to extract specific value from Big Data has become mainstream—but the adoption rate for many organizations is slow because of the perceived complexity and inflexibility of their environment. Perception is not reality.

As more analysts give credibility to Big Data's significance across industries, businesses are once again reacting to the pressure instead of strategizing how these powerful sources of information will impact their existing capabilities. Creating a company Facebook account without defining the value of a "like" for your business is the same as deploying a static Web site displaying your address and contact number. It checks the box for the analysts rating your company, but it does nothing for your customers.

Organizations who assume they need to provision a separate Big Data environment similar to their Web site infrastructure with little consideration of future impact, or try to repurpose their existing environment to capture this data, are doomed to receive the same results as before: less customer awareness, more complexity, and higher costs.

The experienced IT professionals who support today's enterprise infrastructure have set the bar for success high because of their proven ability to manage and respond to each of the Big Data trifecta: Velocity, Volume, and Variety, for example:

- **Velocity** Web site traffic (online sales, app downloads), streaming video

- **Volume** Terabytes stored in data warehouses combined with multiple disparate systems across the enterprise regularly queried for reports

- **Variety** Flat files, EDI, PDF, MS Office applications, text, images, audio

However, new skills and business processes are necessary to manage all three parameters for the same source at the same time, while still maintaining the quality of service of the existing environments.

As daunting as this may appear, Big Data has become widely adopted because it offers more than additional revenue. As we continue to digitize our environment, we have an opportunity to improve operations and reduce costs through the capture and analysis of data generated from the execution of strategic business processes. Consider the ability to analyze a business process in flight and develop an algorithm to respond to variations in expectations. The sooner the business is aware of a possible challenge, the greater the opportunity to resolve it prior to affecting service levels.

Every industry is affected by Big Data, and because of its very nature, it demands a flexible infrastructure to adapt and respond to a consistently changing model of our world. Big Data—when done well—enables you to sharpen the picture by understanding different facets of your customers.

The journey to finding the value within Big Data starts with a question you need to answer and will be different for each company. As you gain more experience, the process will become easier to manage.

History has an annoying habit of repeating itself. The good news is that now we are ready.

Reality, Check Please!

If we knew what it was we were doing, it would not be called research, would it?
–Albert Einstein

Was Albert Einstein angry when he said this? Was it said sternly, with the emphasis on *"would it"*? Or was it said in a sing-song way as if to a small child, "would it"?

If only they had emoticons back then, one smiley face or frownie face would make all the difference in our interpretation. Or would it?

Without facial expressions, gestures, or voice modulation, it is challenging to deduce the tone of a message. When the words are jumbled together inside a data cloud, stripped of punctuation, and peppered with misspellings and trendy words, it is easy to misinterpret the true meaning.

Since Big Data can be language-, industry-, and process-specific, the context of the information—knowing where, when, why, and how it was created—is as essential to its value as the content itself. Just as you need the right technology to acquire and store the information, you also need the right skill set to develop hypotheses based on the multiple facets of data, and the right governance to ensure the choices made from the results of the analysis fit with your strategy.

Changing our intent from narrowing the questions asked to widening the questions explored with Big Data opens up opportunities for value that might not have been previously considered. Concurrent with the new role of a data scientist is the creation of extraordinary hypotheses based on internal and external sources of Big Data:

- ■ **Internal**   If you knew this measurement (how often, how long, how much) about this thing (person, situation, place), it would show this pattern and then you would be able to take this action (reduce costs, save time, and so on).

- ■ **External**   If you did not have limitations related to the data's form (Word, PDF, and so on), then you can obtain this information from this new source (internal repositories, social media, blogs, information brokers, and so on) and then you can take this action (reduce costs, save time, and so on).

Consider the following Big Data examples of each scenario.

One of the more famous cases of finding value within Big Data was demonstrated by MCI in the early 1990s analyzing their massive amounts of internal data.

- ■ *If you knew the number and length of calls for each customer account, it would provide insight into their calling patterns and you could offer targeted services based on their level of activity to increase revenue.*

While the hypothesis itself was probably more complex than this statement, MCI's legendary "Friends and Family Campaign" resulted from the analysis of millions of historical customer call records, which identified social calling patterns among certain groups. Since federal privacy restrictions prevented MCI from contacting individuals within a customer's group directly, they incentivized each customer to self-identify their contacts to obtain discounts, and were able to substantially increase revenue.

They innovatively anchored the loyalty of their customers by associating an action with a sentiment—belonging to someone's friends and family circle was associated with an intimate connection that not many wanted to break.

As previously mentioned, the Big Data source is relevant to the question you are trying to solve. In the previous example, internal data was analyzed to increase revenue; the next example demonstrates the use of external Big Data sources to improve quality of life.

Twenty years after the MCI campaign, Big Data was used to analyze genome diagnostic capabilities and translated into life-altering results. It also started with a basic hypothesis:

- *If you did not have technical limitations related to the complexity of clinical data, then you could combine and analyze patterns from millions of patients and build diagnostic algorithms for physicians to identify patients at risk.*

  The breakthrough by medical diagnostic company CardioDX enabled the first nonintrusive test predictor for heart disease, and was named one of the "Top Ten Medical Breakthroughs of 2010" by *Time* magazine.

So what?

If you are not in the telecom or healthcare industry, the value of Big Data sources containing call patterns and patient data might not interest you. Unless you have customers who use the phone, and want to remain healthy throughout their lives, then maybe you do. For example:

- Insurance companies—risk analysis of texting while driving and disability claims

- Retailers—sales of cell phones, types of vitamins, medical supplies

- Media—mobile phone application usage, delivery of fitness apps, and so on

Using Big Data technology with advanced analytics, organizations can correlate internal customer data and external behavioral data to develop and test hypotheses predicting responses to specific events.

While global responsiveness and local personal service are the new competitive differentiators, innovative analyses of uncommon data sources are the enablers.

What Do You Make of It?

What do you make of this map? This? Well, I can make a hat; I can make a brooch; I can make a pterodactyl...

–from the movie, *Airplane*

Ironically, despite all attempts at privacy from customers like Anonymous, their daily habits generate volumes of identifiable digital footprints that can be used to re-create a trail of activity. These universes of Big Data are recognizable by their common names: electric, phone, credit card, and cable bills.

The threat of new competitors into the utility and credit card marketplaces has been greatly diminished by the massive infrastructures necessary to manage and store the volume of data generated at an uncontrollable velocity. Adding the complexity of a variety of devices (for example, smartphones, smart meters), and correlating this information to generate monthly billing statements was an expensively prohibitive process. Things have changed.

The common analytical advantage for utility and credit card companies is the combination of their customer's location and activity. They know where their customers are—or maybe only where the bills are sent—and the generation of Big Data by location is used to develop algorithms to predict behavior and generate alerts for anomalies.

If a customer downloads a prospectus from an investment firm, then purchases a toy from a retailer, and then donates to an online charity, each organization captures only the action performed on their own site. The utility and credit card companies will have more information on the customer because they capture when, where, and how each action was performed. They can only hypothesize about "why." Remember, that customer might be your customer as well, and you can also hypothesize the "why."

If you want to find Anonymous, you no longer need a massive infrastructure to acquire and process the volume and variety of information arriving with such velocity; all you need is the right technology, the intent to provide a positive customer experience, and an understanding of the process.

Information Chain Reaction (ICR)

Similar to a chemical chain reaction, Big Data is a byproduct of each stage in an *Information Chain Reaction (ICR)*, a series of rapidly occurring events where the output of one stage produces a response in the next. The three primary events are: *communicate*, *connect*, and *change*.

As shown in Figure 2-1, an ICR is triggered by the intent to *communicate* by a member within a community. Loosely defined as groups with a common focus, a community can represent either human interests (for example, family, work, hobbies) or machine signals (for example, smartphones, heart monitors, smart meters). The category of Big Data generated is relative to the community, which means choosing the right sources is essential for your competitive analysis.

Intent to *communicate* without the ability to *connect* turns a tweet on the customer's smartphone into stored text. In addition to the content of the message itself, turning on the phone and sending the message generates a volume of measurable Big Data signals containing information such as the device, time, and location, which can be used to hypothesize on the customer's intent and predict the customer's next step.

If you know where the customer is going, you can capture their attention.

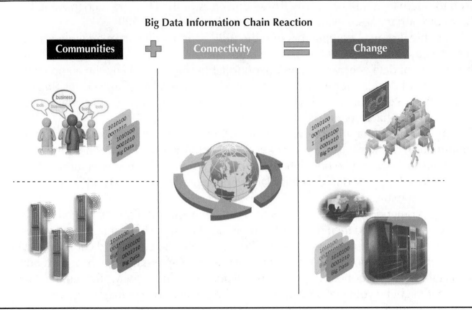

FIGURE 2-1. *Information chain reaction*

Every time there is a connection, there is a measurable *change* that is captured; turning a phone on but not making a call automatically sends a signal to the nearest cell tower, opening a browser window but working on an Excel spreadsheet locally adds a line to a Web log, browsing a site and abandoning the cart affects the server cache—each nonaction leaves a digital footprint as part of a Big Data universe and has the potential to deliver value, but it has been consistently ignored.

Historically, businesses respond to cyclical activity such as stocking for holiday sales or increasing server capacity for online trading when the market opens, and rarely analyze lulls in activity.

When things are going well, we look to future prospects; when things are going badly, we focus on what happened to customers in the past. With Big Data, organizations have the opportunity to look to what is happening with their customers today and respond automatically based on predictive analysis of this information.

Big Data, Big Numbers, Big Business?

The temptation to form premature theories upon insufficient data is the bane of our profession.

–Sherlock Holmes

No discussion of Big Data is complete without including astronomical calculations of the trigger event in the Information Chain Reaction: the intent to *communicate.*

Consider the Infographics created every few months to showcase the intensity of Big Data by displaying how much processing occurs every 60 seconds. Different companies choose different metrics based on current trends. Comparing this information provides insight into the complexity of analyzing information in the era of Big Data and the instability of the environment. For example, search online and compare the 2011 Infographic from Go-Globe with the 2012 Infographic from DOMO. Both of the graphics represent online activity occurring every 60 seconds.

Viewed separately, each image appears to indicate phenomenal growth and opportunity for different sectors. However, the true value of any measurement is relative, and comparing the two images actually illustrates the variety and volatility of the online ecosystem.

For example, despite phenomenal activity in 2011, Pandora (13,000 music streams/minute), Skype (500 million voice calls/minutes), and Craigslist (12,000 ads posted/minute) are conspicuously missing from the 2012 snapshot.

If these companies had been a strategic source of information for your business—and the partnership actively marketed—their absence could raise market concerns about your company's stability. We need to remember the lessons learned from the dot.com crash, or we are doomed to repeat our mistakes: Online activity is not an accurate measurement of stability, and growth does not necessarily equal revenue.

Overnight, shoe manufacturers have become information brokers—valuable if you share the same customer base and your product/service is associated with footwear. Otherwise, you are working with a data set filtered by someone else's criteria—and it might not work for your market.

Understanding what and how we want to measure is as important as having the right data to measure.

Traditional questions used to assess a company's viability need to evolve in alignment with new online opportunities, and the parameters will continue to change based on the Big Data sources being considered. For example:

■ Google experienced 188 percent growth between 2011 and 2012—what percentage resulted in click-through to your business and generated additional revenue? Was the expense for your company to be displayed in the first five search results less than the profit received?

■ Does Apple's 262 percent increase in downloads from 2011 to 2012 correlate to the release of the latest iPhone and represent new users setting up their system or experienced users increasing activity? If you contract with Apple to include your mobile application as part of a core download, but it is not accessed by the user, how much is it costing you?

■ How many Instagram users also have Twitter accounts? If you contract with both companies, are you paying for duplicate information?

■ With tabbed browsing capabilities, are users logged into both Pinterest and Twitter at the same time and switching back and forth? Does this mean your ads are being viewed by half as many users appearing as twice as many accounts?

■ If 500 users had three different Facebook profiles, do they count as 500 or 1500 users?

Conversion of online activity into revenue demands detailed clarity about what is being measured and why it is of value; otherwise, it can appear to be of value simply because it is being measured.

While online companies are private, the number of users can be "estimated," but once the companies are public, they are subject to the same rules and regulations as the brick-and-mortar companies.

Two of the most popular social networking sites today provide examples we can learn from when analyzing a company as a source of Big Data: Twitter and Facebook.

Twitter

Based on the media's accepted reliance of Twitter's capabilities to quickly *communicate* and *connect* users with information such as storm warnings and safety instructions during power outages, Twitter has evolved into a type of informal emergency broadcast system. It has gained such credibility, even powerful business magnate Warren Buffet created a Twitter account in 2013.

However, there have been very public incidents of false postings that have been detrimental to public safety. Also, depending on whom you ask (or rather which Web site you browse), the number of Twitter accounts and the number of tweets change daily. Because this information is "reported" by different blogs, they are given an inflated air of accuracy.

Until there are safeguards in place to prevent the impact of false postings and the clarity of tweet value, organizations need to be cautious before positioning any private social networking site as a core source to their Big Data strategy.

It is only if your messages reach the right users at the right time that this becomes of value; if your tweet is one of the many "hash tags" flooding the consumer's view, it reduces its effectiveness.

And remember—Anonymous likely does not have a Facebook or Twitter account, which means you are effectively anonymous to them.

Facebook

Prior to its public launch in 2012, Facebook increased the limit on its status page from 500 to 63,206 characters. After the launch, Facebook claimed they were collecting 500 terabytes (TB) of data a day. Since the information posted is "private," there is currently no way of knowing if the 500TB is information, noise, or includes counts of allocated space per user regardless of the actual status update. A basic "TTFN" (Ta Ta For Now) could be counted as over 63,000 characters instead of 4.

Later in 2012, Facebook announced approximately 8 percent of their 955 million active users were duplicate or false accounts, between 150 to 300 employees were needed to weed out the fraud, and there were noticeable reductions in the percent of likes on certain sponsors' Web sites. Before the sponsors could determine lost revenue, they had to measure what a "like" is worth to them. Most could not do it.

This should be an ongoing concern. Just as the costs of billboards and flyers are factored into your marketing budget, the return on investment from both marketing and obtaining information, each sponsor will have to determine if the value of a "like" is overpriced. The value of Facebook as an outlet to reach customers is only effective if your customers use it.

Before negotiation with any external Big Data source, consider if your business needs to know what is written, who writes it, the number of characters used, how it is communicated, and so on, because these new parameters will affect the value you receive for your investment.

You also have another powerful option: Be your own source of Big Data.

Internal Source

Once you start to store and analyze the Big Data generated by your customers every time they interact with your business, you will uncover patterns of activity that will drive the creation of new hypotheses and algorithms. You also have an untapped source of value within your four walls—your employees.

As the lines blur between employee and consumer, many people use their smartphones, laptops, and tablets for both personal and business use. As social networking becomes mainstream, the processes learned on external sites can be leveraged to create your own internal social network. Unlike collaborating through e-mail or the cumbersome tools of the past, which forced users to learn a new application, because of the familiarity of a social network, users can easily transfer their knowledge from external to internal. The benefit of having this internal test ground is the ability to learn the technology in a cost-effective manner and begin to generate and test hypotheses on content ("likes," "clicks," and so on), and extrapolate on what you find internally into developing assumptions about your customers.

It also offers a way for your employees to connect as a team and share information. Internally, at Oracle we use Oracle Social Network to collaborate and communicate easily. Each group is a "conversation," and within your profile you can select documents and have a list of documents from *all* the conversations you are involved with. This saves a tremendous amount of time in e-mail and reliance on access to a specific device (for example, a laptop) to locate a document.

There is another advantage to blurring the lines internally; the interaction of different groups within your company without being separated by business function. On a global scale, the ability for IT and the business to *communicate* their views on a joint topic can enable greater change. Just as a technologist and a finance manager can exchange ideas on LinkedIn, your internal team can exchange ideas while abstracted from their role.

Enabling them to *connect* through a variety of devices to make *changes* mimics the Information Chain Reaction and the Big Data "digital exhaust" created by your customers and can provide as powerful insights as any external community.

ICR: Connect

On a highway a single driver may own three different cars (SUV, station wagon, pickup truck), but they can only drive one at a time. On the *information highway*, a single user can have multiple devices connected simultaneously, with each performing different functions such as streaming music, downloading an app, uploading a picture, or receiving a text.

Smartphones, laptops, tablets, health monitors; the list of devices we use every day keeps growing, as does the Big Data universe generated by their usage. Correlating location and time parameters with the device used to access your site provides insight into the users themselves.

While the company providing *connect* capabilities would have the broadest view of a customer's actions, you can grow your own Big Data universe by capturing additional facets of the contact and analyzing responses for better service.

The generation of *connect* Big Data from the automation of Machine to Machine (M2M) devices also provides opportunities for operational improvements and cost reductions. Similar to a battery-powered smoke detector continually monitoring the environment but sending out an intermittent chirp as it starts to lose power, there are identifiable patterns of signals prior to a system failure within your enterprise. Signals that might appear random could be correlated into a pattern of decline and then used to predict and prevent a costly system failure—or an intruder.

In addition to phones is another common tool used daily, that capture snapshots of customers' activity and can be used to predict people's actions—credit cards.

Consumers use credit cards in all facets of their lives, to pay for groceries and entertainment, to shop, and to donate—even parking meters now accept credit cards. Combined with the 2D readers in smartphones to scan boarding passes, coupons, and so on, the convenience of swiping a card has replaced the anonymity of currency—and it is a continuous stream of Big Data.

Being aware of changes in your customers' daily routines enables you to take action rather than react.

ICR: Change

Similar to colors generated from streaming a beam of light through a prism, streaming Big Data through the right infrastructure will display *changes* in customers' perspectives.

Sentiment, like machine signals, is measureable; there is a change of state between an event and an action. The challenge is to have a large enough universe of the right information to test your hypothesis correlating the change to your action.

Traditionally, organizations execute a variety of applications; each with a finite number of options when dealing with input data: accept, transform, or reject. Once the quality of the data is confirmed, the data is transformed and a routine is executed based on the input, resulting in one of the following: change, addition, update, deletion-error. Processing time required for input files can be influenced by the availability of technical resources.

Extraordinarily, the very existence of Big Data itself represents a *change* and any transformation into a structured format reduces the quality of the data for analysis.

Online sentiment, unlike machine code, is not deterministic; the same conditions will not consistently result in the same output. However, similar to a social scientist analyzing societal relationships to detect patterns of behavior, your data scientist can analyze Big Data to detect patterns of online activity and then develop algorithms to predict actions.

For example, as customers update their contact information, either online or over the phone, the old information is often deleted. Yet keeping historical records enables an organization to develop a hypothesis regarding their customers' lifestyle and predict their choices. Analyzing a change in e-mail from a free e-mail service ("@gmail.com"), to a school domain ("@harvard.edu") to a business ("@oracle.com") offers insight into the customer's journey from student to employee, associated financial status, and ability to purchase your product or services.

With Big Data you can start to frame the picture you have of your online customers, which was previously inaccessible. Before online shopping, many people were restricted to products that were locally available; their form of transportation—bus, minivan, and convertible—was a factor in their shopping patterns and offered insight into consumer choices. Now, there are thousands of global options.

If the customer lands on your Web site, it is an active choice, and you have the customer's attention, so it would make sense to capture information about the customer's form of connectivity and their actions to learn more about them.

Suppose that once on your Web site, the customer goes to your Contact page, enters a few lines, then discards or scrolls down a lengthy article in seconds but then closes out. The customer might have felt satisfied if they found what they needed, or they might have been unhappy with the complexity of the information, or they might have had to leave because dinner was ready. Having large amounts of multi-faced data enables many hypothesis to test.

Every complementary action to being online, switching on lights, activating a device (for example, laptop, tablet, smartphone), or opening a browser, is captured within a Big Data universe with others performing *the same actions*. The information you have access to depends on where you are in the Information Value Chain.

In addition to providing opportunities for revenue, *changes* from Big Data can be analyzed to obtain operational efficiencies and enable a new level of testing existing processes for effectiveness.

Every time we use a device to replace paper, we are creating a digital representation of our actions, which generates an exponential amount of information for analysis. We not only receive cost savings through automation, but also generate information that could have been lost or misplaced, and can be used to offer future insights for our customers.

For example, many companies have replaced their expense reimbursement process from mailing in receipts to demanding that each one be scanned in and submitted with the expense report. This reduces the cost of manually preparing and acting on the expense report, provides an audit trail of submission and receipt, and enables analysis of both the transmission, sender, and expense amounts, which can be correlated across the enterprise to identify extravagant expenses and certain extras that might have previously fallen under the radar.

This internal information can then be combined with Big Data from external travel sites to assess the effectiveness of your travel policy in saving money or correlated with data from Human Resources to hypotheses on employee retention.

Another area for cost savings is within your document management process. The number of documents people send each day is compounded by the different versions and formats that can be generated for each one. Many people perform manual versioning by changing the file name (v1, v2), but rarely do they delete the previous versions once the final copy has been edited and approved. Add on the capability of transforming a Word document into a PDF, a PowerPoint into a jpeg, and a large number of duplicates can be quickly amassed in multiple formats.

The time spent trying to locate information increases in length and complexity when the different search tools are implemented on different systems, or the data is stored in Outlook files that can only be viewed within the application itself. The cost associated with the time to locate documents by one person each day is substantial when multiplied by each employee in your organization.

When you consider the time associated with providing collateral for lawsuits and audits, the benefit of being able to process large amounts of data in a variety of formats within a short timeframe becomes clearer.

Big Data technology enables organizations to remove the barriers created by the variety of formats by extracting the information while maintaining the integrity of the source. As a result, each organization can simultaneously analyze existing document management capabilities without disrupting existing business processes.

The possibilities for finding Value in Big Data are only limited by what you think you cannot find.

Wanted: Big Data Value

We are stuck with technology when what we really want is just stuff that works.
                                                    –Douglas Adams, *The Salmon of Doubt*

Driver, patient, investor—a customer by any other name still generates revenue.

Big Data offers more than a way to generate revenue or improve operational efficiencies. It can become a strategic part of your business by widening your options for exploration.

Starting with a clear customer definition is essential for strategizing how to cost-effectively increase your traditional data universe with Big Data, and engage the right resources to answer questions relevant to your business model.

Because of the existing complexity resulting from linking customers by channel instead of the reverse, we have to be cautious about repeating history using sources of Big Data. Instead of assuming that a majority of your customers are on one specific social network, analyze the probability of your customer being interested in multiple sites—or not being online at all.

One Big Data universe can represent a variety of customers across industries that are linked together for a common reason. Perhaps they were all on the same canceled flight and blogged about it, or they all uploaded pictures of the same event to a central site for review.

The beauty of Big Data technology is that the source is not damaged in the filtering process; unlike the time-consuming process to rerun and transform traditional structured data, you can rerun a Big Data universe with the same information, or wait for the next wave.

Unique to Big Data technology is the opportunity to receive different types of information from the same source and apply it to the same traditional data for innovative analysis. We can also measure and influence a variable that has been previously elusive—customer sentiment.

Competitors select specific focus areas to differentiate their product or service, and the choices vary depending on the industry. Processing speed is a consideration for a laptop, but is not relevant when buying a refrigerator.

Despite the anonymity of personal e-mail identifiers and federal privacy restrictions to protect customer information, there are many public sources of information that can be used to test how your customers "feel," not only about your company, but about many things.

Big Data takes cross-selling to a whole new level by linking companies across industries. While it might make sense for an airline to partner with a hotel chain, it is the out of the ordinary collaboration that catches our attention nowadays. For example, I recently received an offer from a new energy provider in my area offering reward points to my favorite hotel chain as an incentive to become their customer as well. Although I did not make the change, it had enough of a positive impact on me that I not only read the brochure, but remembered the campaign and included it here as a reference.

However, the most effective way to understand the sentiment expressed by your customer is to "become" your customer. If just once, every person in your organization acted as a prospect in search of information on your product or service, and then anonymously posted how they felt about the process and the results inside your social network, you would capture a perspective of your business unlike any analyst report. It becomes even more interesting when they perform the same analysis on your competition.

The intent to *communicate* sentiment using a specific device to *connect* resulting in a *change* of state for the target site is the same process your customers go through to evaluate your product or service. By performing the analysis first, you have an opportunity to strengthen your connection by improving the customers' online experience, and reducing the risk of negative reviews.

The following examples represent other avenues to cost-effectively gather public Big Data to formulate and test your hypothesis. Each item can be tweaked to represent the facets of data that are relevant to your model, but all are created in response to finding information on a specific topic.

Big Data Example 1: Clinical Trial Research Within the Healthcare Industry

In critical care situations, doctors and nurses are often delayed in updating information because their primary focus is on the patient instead of trying to locate and sign into a laptop. From a patient perspective, struggling with serious illnesses and the effects of treatment can make even small tasks seems insurmountable.

Both medical staff and patients involved in clinical trials need to be able to easily *communicate* information quickly; a long response time from the site or a complicated intake process not only increases the rate of abandonment but diminishes the efficacy of the trial.

The rollout of the mHealth (mobile health) platform has enabled the medical community to *connect* using mobile technology and positively impact data capture during clinical trials. The Big Data generated as a byproduct of the *communicate-connect-change* process also provides additional insights that might not have been captured, such as the length of time between taking medication and entering a response, or the location of the patient during the trial.

By using hand-held devices such as smartphones and tablets to connect, the involvement of both participants and doctors is increased, which is crucial to the success of the trial.

Complementary to the Big Data captured from the clinical trial process are auxiliary actions that can be taken to provide additional insights:

- Perform trend analysis on popular sites such as Google, WebMD.com, or DrOz.com for search terms correlated to recent drug tests, and geospatial data over a period of time to uncover patterns of activities.

- Capture increased searches of certain side effects such as "insomnia" within a specific online community (for example, MSActiveSource.com, PatientsLikeMe.com, Inspire.com) or questions about interrupted sleeping patterns five months after the clinical trial is completed to identify long-term side effects not previously considered.

- Identify increases in the number of complaints about the medical device used for administering the drug to alert the clinical trial investigators of possible problems.

- Utilize sites such as Archives.com, Ancestry.com, and Census.gov to hypothesize on migratory patterns and environmental factors on health issues.

Example 2: Improvements in Car Design for Driver Safety Within the Automotive Industry

It is not an easy task to change a driver's behavior.

Over the years, it has been the auto industry that has first taken action to protect drivers from themselves through the development of safety features such as air bags and engineering redesigns to absorb crashes.

In 2013, studies by the National Highway Traffic Safety Administration (NHTSA) uncovered the fact that usage of mobile phones for texting while driving has become the number one distraction, endangering drivers, passengers, other commuters, and bystanders.

Although many new vehicles have engineering devices to automatically reduce the risk of accidents by taking control from the driver in certain situations, addressing the distracted driving issue is still in the design phase.

Using Big Data technology, the auto industry has an opportunity to reduce the estimated five-to-seven-year average design time and deliver safety features faster.

New models are composed of thousands of parts and tested for over 30 different crash conditions with sensors used to capture impact data from multiple perspectives. Additionally, up to 25 crash test dummies can be used per model, and each generates an estimated stream of 4,000 data sets in two-fifths of a second.

As a result, it takes thousands of engineers and scientists weeks of analysis for each sensor to ensure high performance and safety under a variety of conditions and to meet thousands of regulatory standards.

Implementation of Big Data technology within the car manufacturing process has the potential to enable powerful cost savings in terms of analysis time and time to market.

Incorporating complementary Big Data sources into their analysis process enables additional opportunities to respond faster to changes in driving habits, identify patterns of defects to increase safety considerations, and reduce the number of recalls. These are some of the possible collaborative opportunities:

- Combine recorded human driving behavior from the NHTSA with sensor data from crash test dummies to calibrate responses and uncover additional insights.

- Cost-effectively run additional tests after delivery of car to market, subjecting it to similar driving conditions as drivers to identify possible points of failure.

- Analyze current and historical R&D information by car family.

- Incorporate state police accident reports by vehicle type.

- Partner with the Motor Vehicle Registry to identify recurring areas of problems with yearly vehicle inspection across the manufacturers' product line.

- Engage with the telecommunications industry to jointly understand the impact of cell phone usage and "vehicle-to-vehicle" communication capabilities.

- Use information from sites such as CarFax.com, which contains accident information, and Safercar.gov, which contains safety information combined with sentiment analysis, for further design analysis.

Summary

The value of Big Data for your organization will be realized by the reliability of its source, its relevance to your existing customer data, and your ability to evolve the infrastructure necessary to acquire, organize, analyze, and store the results.

For organizations to successfully engage with customers online, they must demonstrate a commitment to customer service by being globally responsive and locally attentive. Big Data offers organizations an opportunity to gain perspective on what is relevant to their customers now and prioritize their efforts to produce the strongest competitive advantage.

The combination of internal and external Big Data sources enables a unique, multi-faceted perspective both in the information itself, and the measurement of the response to the information.

At the end of the day, most customers may forget some details, but they are likely to remember the feeling generated from interacting with your company.

By delivering a positive experience across all channels, you will generate positive sentiment—which does translate into revenue and true value.

PART II

Big Data Platform

CHAPTER
3

The Apache
Hadoop Platform

I f you are new to Hadoop, you probably have been overwhelmed by the sheer number of different utilities, processes, and configuration files in the Hadoop ecosystem. It's very easy to lose sight of the core Hadoop platform and its significance as a unique, extremely powerful, and—believe it or not—uncomplicated distributed compute and storage platform. A lot of us tried out Hadoop for the first time in late 2007. Grid computing systems and database systems on commodity hardware were already becoming commonplace.

In those days we hadn't yet heard the term Big Data, but building systems that could scale across hundreds of gigabytes or terabytes of disparate data sets was a daily challenge that many of us in banking, Internet, and healthcare were faced with. In the database world we had already learned how to harness commodity hardware and take advantage of advances in storage, compute, and network to build systems that rivaled anything the big iron servers of the day could do. At that time Hadoop was relatively simple; its compelling attribute was its distributed file system and integration with MapReduce, a distributed computing methodology from Google. It was very raw, and with Java at its core, it made everyone think twice about what we felt comfortable with.

We had been living with systems written in C and C++ that were the product of years of development and were fast, efficient, but slow to adapt to changing hardware and operating system standards. With Hadoop, we had an open source system written in Java that we could easily understand and adapt to our evolving commodity hardware. Many of the advancements in RDBMS optimizers, I/O, and parallel computing developed in C and C++ are being replaced by these new open source technologies written purely in Java, posing new challenges to the platform architect, who has to go back to the basics as far as learning to make the Hadoop system perform and scale.

Today Hadoop, operating systems, processors, storage, and networking have matured significantly. In some ways Hadoop has strongly influenced the platform and vice versa. At the time of writing this chapter, Java-based systems can now perform at almost wire speed with Linux kernels able to handle what were once exotic network topologies such as Infiniband or 10GBE networks, or improved page cache and file systems that make Java file I/O fast and efficient, local storage systems that can take full advantage of inexpensive 2TB and 3TB disks. Java running in 64-bit Linux is now the norm, with more and more improvements coming to the JVM and Hadoop core every day.

Hadoop now boasts many innovative tools and subsystems. The level of abstraction away from writing very complicated MapReduce jobs and the black art of managing the parallel computing environment is making it easier for more and more people to start working with Hadoop. We are now seeing real-time processing with in-memory databases, sophisticated interfaces, and easy-to-care-for deployment and monitoring. But at the end of the day Hadoop is about the distributed file system and MapReduce at its processing core. In this chapter I will dig into the software and hardware foundations of Apache Hadoop and the commodity Linux platform.

Software vs. Hardware

The Hadoop technology stack is modular and socket-based. Every software service of Hadoop relies on the kernel and hardware platform (CPU, RAM, disk, and network) to communicate and distribute I/O and messaging.

Understanding Hadoop at the level of its software and hardware foundation is still important. Knowing how the core platform works and why can inform you about the best path to take for your first Hadoop project and also protect you from making assumptions about the Hadoop platform or worse. Not respecting the capabilities and limitations of Hadoop could lead you to make a very expensive or disastrous mistake.

The Hadoop Software Platform

When we talk about Hadoop, what do we really mean? Hadoop is a growing number of tools, apps, and utilities, but at its core, once you take all of those things away, when is it still Hadoop? The core platform of Hadoop is a collection of services connected by network sockets (see Figure 3-1). Namenode, Datanode, and HDFS along with the scheduling and process management services of JobTracker and TaskTracker—all can live on one node (as a single-node Hadoop pseudo-cluster) or can be distributed across many separate nodes.

This is what makes Hadoop so unique and such a game changer. You can remove everything, including MapReduce, and still you have the core distributed file system, the heart and soul of Hadoop. From the file system the default compute architecture has been MapReduce. MapReduce is a set of modular components that talks to the

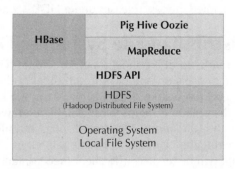

FIGURE 3-1. *Hadoop logical stack*

Hadoop Distributed File System (HDFS) via a socket-based API. Interestingly enough, MapReduce was not a native Hadoop component, but was originally created by Google for their proprietary distributed file system. MapReduce on its own can talk to other file systems, databases, and noSQL databases. New compute architectures are starting to come on the scene. YARN (Yet Another Resource Negotiator) is a perfect example of a new compute module; the underlying HDFS does not change and you can freely flip back and forth at will. What makes this all possible is the fact that with a socket-based technology, you just need the port and the API description and you can plug into the file system and could even write your own scheduler.

Hadoop Distributions and Versions

Apache Hadoop is an open-source Apache project that is freely downloadable from the Apache Web site. If you go the open source route, what you will find is not one but several different branches of Hadoop. In the early days of Hadoop, version incompatibilities were always an issue because different projects depended on different versions of Hadoop. Today we have 0.20.x legacy Hadoop and 0.23.x YARN. Apache 1.2 is the current stable release as of this writing, which traces its lineage back to the 0.20.x release. Apache 2.x, next generation (or MR2), is still considered a nonproduction release for the most part because it is still acquiring features and functionality for YARN, federation and name space, and traces its lineage to the 0.23.x release.

There are several commercial distributions that include the Apache Hadoop stack and related projects; they include Cloudera, Hortonworks, and Intel, to name a few.

They are significant because they both contribute a large part of their integration and development back into the Apache source tree. At a core Hadoop level they are relatively the same in feature and function. The main technical differences are subtle but significant. Cloudera has opted to blend the 1.x and 2.x within their CDH distributions, allowing the user to run in production the stable 1.x MapReduce while also being able to start testing out the 2.x features in the same software stack. Since HDFS is the same underneath, a Cloudera user can turn off 1.x and turn on 2.x. Hortonworks, on the other hand, has separated the two releases under HDP 1.x and 2.x.

The Hadoop Distributed File System (HDFS)

The HDFS file system is made up of a collection of large data blocks distributed across one or more physical disks on one or more physical nodes utilizing the operating system kernel and file system. HDFS is made up of a block registry (Namenode) and the block containers themselves (Datanode). If we want to talk to the file system, we talk to the Namenode. Directory listings and file operations all start with the client contacting the Namenode, which will tell us on what Datanode and which blocks our data will be located. The client then contacts the Datanode(s) directly and read or writes blocks of data. All of these interactions are socket-based and modular. Since there usually will be multiple copies of the data blocks due to replication, blocks are selected by locality and load on Datanodes and availability.

Unlike the traditional file systems (EXT3 or EXT4) where block sizes are a few KB, and disk blocks are 512 bytes, Hadoop data blocks can range in size from 64MB minimum to 128MB or 256MB, but data blocks can be configured to 1GB or larger. Typically, 128MB or 256MB is the norm. When data scales into the petabyte range, replicating small blocks is inefficient, so HDFS maintains much larger blocks than a traditional file system.

Each Map process in MapReduce attempts to correspond to an HDFS data block (see Figure 3-2). Data block sizes are configurable by the Hadoop admin for defaults and also by the application developer at run time.

When we consider the Hadoop platform, OS, HDFS, and hardware (CPU, disk, and network), you need to be aware that HDFS is sitting on top of the traditional file system and has to live with the rules, performance capabilities, and limitations of that file system. The file system I/O underneath HDFS utilizes the kernel and its mechanisms for caching and block handling.

Data Replication

One of the reasons that Hadoop and its HDFS file system have been so successful is that HDFS is highly fault-tolerant; you can lose an entire node in the cluster and the file system will keep working with no data loss. Hadoop achieves high ability by replicating copies of data blocks to other nodes. By default Hadoop generally has three replicas of every data block. In practice this means that for every 100MB that is ingested into Hadoop, you are actually consuming 300MB. Replication defaults are set by the Hadoop admin, but the user can select a replication factor at run time for writing data. Also replication can be changed as well for blocks that are already written to the HDFS file system. Replication can be set to 0, no copies, or set to 4, 5, or more.

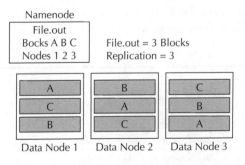

FIGURE 3-2.   *Namenode Datanode interaction*

Blocks are replicated using a pipelining system. Assuming our replication count is 3, the client write operation (DataStreamer) requests a list of Datanodes and locations to write to from the Namenode and streams packets to the first node (see Figure 3-3). That Datanode then sends those packets on to the second, which in turn sends them on to the third. If any of the nodes were to fail during this operation, the pipeline is closed and the write operation is recovered and resumed transparently to the user.

Performance Considerations for Replication   Block replication can be also used for more than high availability. On data ingest, as the replication factor increases, the rate at which data can be loaded decreases. This is due to the time it takes to transfer the data block down the pipeline and receive acknowledgement of the write. It is not uncommon to set replication to 1 or 0 copies on large data ingest tasks to increase the rate at which data can load. Replication can be changed later on as needed. Hardware plays a significant role in how large of a performance hit replication will take. Disk and network speeds, capacity, and utilization all are factors, along with the number of disks on the Datanode. This will be covered in detail later in the hardware section.

Replication and Read Operations   Having multiple copies of a data block allows for the Namenode to have more choices to select from when a read operation or MapReduce job is being set up. For some data sets that have a high concurrency rate such as a common file that is used by many MapReduce jobs or a common dimension table in Hive, it may be advisable to increase the replication factor.

Namenode Service

The Namenode service is the key to making the HDFS file system work. It is the in-memory registry that keeps track of the blocks allocated to a file on the data nodes along with file and directory metadata, and is persisted to local disk for safekeeping. When we read or write data to or from HDFS, we contact the Namenode, and when a MapReduce job is submitted, the Namenode is contacted to locate data blocks that map processes will use. Because of its role as the block registry, if it fails the

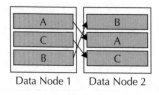

Data Node 1   Data Node 2

FIGURE 3-3.   *Block replication*

Hadoop cluster cannot read or write data or run MapReduce jobs. Until recently, the Namenode was considered as a single point of failure (SPOF). The single point of failure has been addressed by keeping a synced replica managed by a system called Zookeeper, known as a secondary name node. If the primary Namenode fails, the secondary can take over.

The Namenode service can manage an enormous amount of HDFS storage. Again, this is one of the reasons HDFS block sizes are so big. The Namenode service gets block data from regular heartbeats from the Datanode service. It also keeps track if blocks are under-replicated or if a Datanode service has failed.

Here's a configuration and performance consideration: If our Hadoop cluster is using 128MB blocks, for every 1GB of RAM that Namenode uses, it can manage about 800,000 objects (blocks, files, directories). If the Namenode service is running on a server with 64GB of RAM, it can manage roughly 50 million objects or approximately 6 petabytes raw. A new feature in Hadoop called HDFS Federation also allows you to run multiple Namenode services, with each service managing a volume or namespace. This can extend the Namespace service capability and capacity.

Datanode Service

The Datanode service is the business end of the HDFS file system. It stores and retrieves blocks when instructed by the client or Namenode, and informs the Namenode periodically of the blocks it is storing. The Datanode also is the workhorse behind forwarding blocks for replication to other Datanode services on other nodes.

Scheduling, Compute, and Processing

Even though MapReduce is not really HDFS-specific, it has become the "lingua franca" of almost all Hadoop processing. It was developed by Google to schedule and distribute batch processing across a cluster of servers. It brings the process to the data on the HDFS file system, which is what makes Hadoop so innovative and is a core Hadoop advantage. In truth, MapReduce can run against any data or no data at all. It can be pointed to noSQL DBs, relational databases, and in-memory caches.

The platform of MapReduce and the services that support it are very different than what is often referred to as a MapReduce job program. The Java code that makes up a MapReduce is just software and libraries that interact with the MapReduce services. In theory, the MapReduce job code that is written can run on both frameworks. In the latest versions of Hadoop, this framework (YARN) is even designed to allow for other distributed processing tasks such as MPI to be managed. The MapReduce framework even allows for non-Hadoop-specific code to be run in a pipeline using Hadoop Streaming. When we look at Hadoop today, we are faced with two separate systems to process our data. The original framework known as MapReduce V1 is commonly linked to the 0.20 version of Hadoop. The new YARN (or MapReduce V2) framework is tied to the 0.23 version. The scheduling and processing platforms for each of these frameworks are very different and have distinct advantages and disadvantages. The YARN framework was created to solve a number of the disadvantages of the 0.20 MapReduce platform services.

JobTracker, TaskTracker Services, and MapReduce V1

The original MapReduce system (see Figure 3-4) consisted of a JobTracker and TaskTracker services. The JobTracker's purpose was to be the point of submission of a job and then parcel out, distribute the work to individual TaskTrackers on separate nodes. The TaskTracker usually lives with the Datanode service since this is where we want the work to take place. Like all of the services in Hadoop, it is socket-based and like the Namenode service, there is only one JobTracker service and it can be a single point of failure. The V1 framework can scale up to about 4000 nodes. The amount of intercommunication between the TaskTracker and JobTracker, along with messaging and data movement between TaskTrackers, can be a resource bottleneck, especially in poorly written MapReduce code.

Anatomy of a MapReduce Job

The anatomy of a job in Hadoop starts with a client requesting a job ID from the JobTracker service and then checks the file system for the necessary file and directory paths, computes the number of input splits (job slices) needed and then copies the job

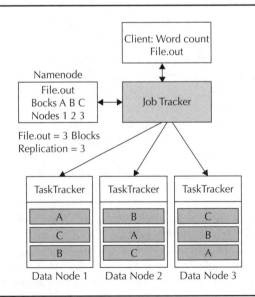

FIGURE 3-4. *MR1 framework*

jar file and configuration data to the JobTracker job folder under the job ID, copies the job jar file to the TaskTrackers, and finally submits the job to the JobTracker.

The JobTracker looks for available and appropriate TaskTrackers and creates and dispatches one map task for every input split and creates a number of reduce tasks as defined by the job configuration to the TaskTracker services. It also creates a setup and cleanup task for every TaskTracker assigned to run this job to set up the job and clean up after execution or a job fault.

The TaskTrackers now run the Java process and communicate their progress to the JobTracker. The JobTracker deals with concurrency and scheduling conflicts using either a FIFO or Fair Scheduler Job Scheduler. FIFO is a straightforward first on the queue and is the first to run. Fair Scheduler attempts to balance short and long resource-heavy jobs across the Hadoop cluster nodes.

Resource Manager, Node Manager Services, and YARN

The new YARN (Yet Another Resource Negotiator) framework attempts to solve some of the shortcomings in the MapReduce V1 framework by breaking the responsibilities of the JobTracker into separate daemons, the Resource Manager to manage the cluster resources and the Application Master to manage the individual running applications running on the cluster. Instead of TaskTrackers that are tied to the JobTracker service, YARN makes use of NodeManager containers that are spawned to handle the distributed tasks from the Application Master.

Operating System Choices

Since Hadoop is written in Java, in theory it can be considered as operating system–agnostic. Linux, Windows Server, and Windows desktop, Solaris, or AIX are all operating systems that have support for Java. But Apache Hadoop was created on Linux, and tested and developed on Linux by the open source community. Because of that distinction, operating system choice is important. The default operating system for running Hadoop is 64-bit Linux, usually RedHat or some variant of RedHat Linux such as Centos or Oracle Enterprise Linux. Also SLES, Ubuntu, and Debian are supported as well. For RedHat variants, versions 5.x or 6.x 64-bit is recommended. You can run Hadoop in a 32-bit Linux environment, but it isn't recommended and really only should be used for development and testing.

Microsoft has created a commercial port of Hortonworks Hadoop that can be run on 64-bit Windows operating systems by allowing native support of Java and modifying some of the Linux-specific conventions found in Hadoop. As of this writing this port is still in beta but is worth mentioning.

The Java version is also important for the same reasons as OS. Even though Java 7 has been out for some time, the Hadoop core has been developed and tested on 64-bit Java 6 and generally, the supported version as of writing this chapter has been JDK 1.6.0_8 minimum and the recommended version is 1.6.0_31 64-bit. The Linux operating system and Java JVM work together to provide the operating environment for Hadoop. Keeping that in mind, Java takes full advantage of the services the operating system has to offer. This makes it easy to develop and maintain but also has performance and stability consequences. Everything Hadoop is going to do is going to touch the kernel. In turn, having a stable OS that is configured properly with correct drivers and patches is critical along with the correct JVM settings to allow Java to work at its best. Out of the box, both Linux and Java are able to support Hadoop in a wide range of workloads; any tuning or configuration changes are workload- and environment-specific and beyond the scope of this chapter.

I/O and the Linux Kernel

Because of Hadoop's extensive use of Java socket I/O for all of its services, there are some interesting developments as far as performance considerations for HDFS disk I/O. The Linux kernel up to version 2.6.18 (RedHat 5) used pdflush to manage the kernel page cache for flushing blocks to disk. Pdflush is a set of kernel threads that are responsible for writing the dirty pages to disk. The kernel page cache contains in-memory copies of data blocks belonging to files kept in storage on disk or disks. Pages that are written to by a process, but not yet written to disk, are accumulated in cache and are known as "dirty" pages. Pages in the cache are then flushed to disk after an interval of 30 seconds.

As servers gained a larger number of disks and the size of the disks increased to 1, 2, or 3TB, pdflush started to become a serious bottleneck for I/O processes that used the kernel, such as Java and Hadoop, because pdflush threads are common to all block devices and caused contention under load. If one disk was slow or very busy, the kernel would have to wait, causing writes to disk to slow to a crawl.

In the 2.6.32 kernel for RedHat 6 variants and Oracle OEL 5.8 unbreakable Linux, a new mechanism for flushing dirty blocks to disk was created called BDI. The BDI flusher dedicated threads to individual spindles so that a busy operation on one disk will not affect the others. The improvement in performance went from writing 30MB/sec to 90 to 100MB/sec under load.

Another performance consideration is that since every service is socket-based and can generate significant network traffic, especially for block movement, using larger packet sizes to reduce the load on the kernel or use network hardware that offloads from the kernel such as some newer 1GBE and 10GBE NICs or QDR Infiniband can make a significant difference in performance. Remember that every I/O for disk or network has to go through the kernel.

The Hadoop Hardware Platform

Hadoop's genius and fundamental driver was that you could do supercomputing on commodity hardware. Hadoop was developed at Yahoo where the prevailing culture during the 2000s, when Hadoop was created, was to do as much as you could on inexpensive commodity server and networking hardware. The same can be said for other innovators of projects for Hadoop: Facebook, Google, and eBay. This was a function of Internet-scale computing where it was impractical to have a data center of enterprise class servers all the same age with fully redundant power and network. To that end, Hadoop demands only that you have enough memory for your chosen workload and that your servers should have similar software versions, disk capacities, and disk counts. Hadoop is designed to run in heterogeneous environments where nodes can be purpose-built in the cluster for certain tasks such as Namenode, JobTracker, or management and monitoring.

Hadoop will run on almost any hardware, from old laptops to custom-built, high-performance servers. It's a tradeoff between the four pillars of price, function, supportability, and performance.

CPU and Memory

Most modern Intel- and AMD-based servers have multiple cores and sockets. The old architecture of a single CPU on a bus with a few GBs of RAM is ancient history. Today the CPU has given way to as many as eight or more CPU cores per socket, and servers with two or four sockets are common. Memory capacities are commonly starting at 32 or 64GB of RAM and can go up to 128GB of RAM or more. Server hardware choices today are pushing the user toward the multicore, large-memory servers because they are affordable and powerful. The computing power needed for most Hadoop operations is minimal to the computing power delivered by most modern servers. Because compute power is getting cheaper and more powerful, we are seeing a move toward new uses of Hadoop and also specialty Hadoop systems that can do genetic mapping or extreme number crunching of weather data for NASA, all on commodity hardware.

Network

Network choices for Hadoop are driven by workloads, price, and data center standards. Hadoop was designed to be used with commodity 1GBE networks in mind and can perform reasonably well with this kind of network. 10GBE networks are slowly becoming the standard in some data centers, and hardware and Linux OS improvements have made 10GBE more and more a standard. 10GBE networks are still very expensive over 1GBE, but as servers increase in power and storage capacity, 1GBE networks can be a bottleneck in Hadoop because of the ever-increasing amount of data movement between nodes in the cluster. Infiniband came before 10GBE, but as a socket-based network on its own, it is not usable for Java and Hadoop. Infiniband IP over IB, on the other hand, can deliver as much as 4x capacity as 10GBE at one-third of the cost. Infiniband is a network technology that is known for high speed and low latency in grid and HPCC computing. Since Hadoop depends on TCP/IP sockets for communication, IP protocols can be layered on top of

Infiniband. The main issue with Infiniband is that the IT skill set in the data centers to support this protocol is lacking. But for systems that are prebuilt like an appliance, Infiniband has a huge advantage over 10GBE in cost and performance.

Network bonding for Hadoop to increase throughput on 1GBE networks can help with performance issues, but bonding for redundancy is not really critical because of Hadoop's ability to deal with node or network failure gracefully. Running Hadoop on its own network, on the other hand, is something that you will want to do. Hadoop fully supports running dual-homed networks. Most Hadoop systems in production today allow clients to access and interact with one network that is on the company network, and the intercommunication between Hadoop nodes is done on a private network and is isolated.

Disk

Maximum disk capacity has increased eight-fold in the last few years from 500GB, 1TB, 2TB, 3TB, and now 4TB drives with little change in price. Disk drive performance often exceeds over 110MBs/second. Server hardware can now have as many as 12 or more drives installed. Disk drives, like CPUs, have become commodity hardware. The only rule of thumb to go by is that you should have a balance between spindles and CPU cores. Having too many cores and one disk is a waste because disk I/O is still a critical function of Hadoop and the disk will be a bottleneck. Having too many disks with a few CPU cores will cause CPU loading issues and bottlenecks.

SAN and NAS (Network File System or iSCSI) as a storage option for Hadoop is not a good option. SANs and NAS are designed to centralize the management and control the risk of storage management. But both types of storage perform poorly under heavy loads because they share the storage across a system managed by a controller. Because the Hadoop HDFS file system can tolerate faults and outages and because its storage is federated with no need to share files, a SAN or NAS appliance is not needed.

Putting It All Together

Today, Big Data projects are being initiated with the business, marketing, and BI segments of companies because there is a demand for deeper and more comprehensive analytics. The impetus to use Hadoop as a response to take advantage of years of "throwaway" raw data to mine to gain a competitive edge has taken hold. Hadoop is becoming a critical system in IT and the days of DIY systems with hundreds of nodes are giving way to concerns for security, support, and TCO. IT departments are now facing the challenge to build and maintain large clusters of Hadoop and are struggling to standardize and get a handle on the extreme growth and scale these systems represent, without the skill sets to make it happen.

Throughout this chapter I have tried to show that the Hadoop platform is a modular set of socket-based services, connected by network on commodity hardware and OS. Most IT departments are not geared to running at Internet scale like Yahoo or Google. The DIY cluster that ran in someone's cubicle for $400 or $500 per TB is in the spirit of Hadoop. The Hadoop platform has matured way beyond stringing a few old servers together. Today a DIY cluster of a hundred nodes could cost your company's IT organization as much as $4 million to build in server hardware and network infrastructure, plus the costs of building the system and maintaining it. Hadoop has become big business and, if you are not careful, a very lucrative business for your hardware and network vendors.

The future of the Hadoop platform as it moves into traditional IT will have to be a prebuilt system, appliance, or engineered system. To meet the skill set challenges and combat the enterprise cost of bringing in Hadoop, we will see a fundamental change in how Hadoop will be deployed.

CHAPTER
4

Why an Appliance?

C hapter 3 discussed what Hadoop is, its components, and some of the decisions that need to be made to build a cluster. With this in mind, Oracle could have published reference architectures based on its Sun servers to address the needs of their customers. Instead, in January 2012 Oracle released Oracle Big Data Appliance as an engineered system to run Hadoop and the Oracle NoSQL database. But why create an appliance? After all, the foundation of Hadoop and NoSQL databases is to create a platform for distributed computing using commodity hardware. But distributed computing is more complex than simply connecting a bunch of cheap servers together. While it may be simple to get a small cluster up and running, it requires expertise to get a production cluster up and running and working effectively.

This chapter will describe why Oracle created Oracle Big Data Appliance, why it was designed the way it was, and what expertise Oracle incorporated into Oracle Big Data Appliance.

Why Would Oracle Create a Big Data Appliance?

Many people ask "Why should any organization buy a Hadoop appliance?" While this is a valid question at first glance, the question should really be "Why would anyone want to build a Hadoop cluster themselves?" Building a Hadoop cluster for anything beyond a small cluster is not trivial. If a cluster of four or five nodes is needed, it can be built on commodity servers, or old hardware can be salvaged to get the cluster up and running quickly. Another option is to start off with virtual machines that have Hadoop installed and are readily available from many of the Hadoop distribution vendors as well as Oracle. Many organizations do just this when they are evaluating Hadoop and trying to determine if they have a good use case. But as soon as the cluster needs to be grown to scale, it becomes clear that building a large production cluster is quite different than building a small test cluster. As with so many things in this world, it is easy to create something at small scale. As children, many of us built club houses or tree houses. As we get older, we even envision how we could build a small house. But we are smart enough to know that we would have no idea where to start if we wanted to build a multistory building or even a skyscraper. The same can be said for building a large Hadoop cluster. It is easy to build a small one, but building a large cluster is not so easy.

This leads to the fundamental question: Why do we as an industry always want to write our own code or build our own solutions from scratch? Is it because we enjoy doing it and we have the basic know-how? While this may be true, this isn't a good enough reason. We certainly wouldn't want our local transportation department building buses from scratch. Is it because a technology is new and there are no other options? Perhaps this is a valid option if there really are no better options. If an organization wants to go down the build-it-yourself route, they must be comfortable with being a leader who develops new technologies, as Google and Yahoo have done with Hadoop.

However, most companies adopt new technologies when others have figured out how to leverage them efficiently. Very few companies build their own enterprise resource planning (ERP) applications any more. Why should they? Others have developed solutions based on a broad base of expertise. Most organizations end up building their own system because they feel that they can do it cheaper than buying a solution, assuming it exists. In practice, this is very rarely the case unless the organization has employees with deep expertise to do the job right the first time. Just ask any home owner if they saved money when they had to call a plumber, electrician, or tradesman after they tried to fix the "easy" problem themselves. In reality, people end up spending a lot more money and time learning what not to do.

However, it is easy to fall into the trap of do-it-yourself for various reasons. Unless an organization has the deep expertise required or they are building something that is unique that provides a differentiated competitive advantage, it is rarely worth doing. While it is easy to get a small cluster up and running, going big is more difficult. And that is why Oracle decided to create an appliance to make it easy for their customers to deploy Big Data solutions at production scale. Simplicity is the driving force behind the Big Data Appliance.

What makes Oracle Big Data Appliance so easy to deploy? Simply put, it was designed that way from the start. This simplicity is achieved by adhering to several key principles about what an appliance should deliver. These principles are that Oracle Big Data Appliance should

- Be optimized

- Provide the shortest time to value

- Reduce risk

- Be cost-effective

The rest of this chapter discusses how Oracle Big Data Appliance achieves these benefits.

What Is an Appliance?

An appliance can be defined in many ways, but the most basic definition is: an appliance is something that is designed to do specific task. That's quite a simple definition at first glance, but an appliance is more than just a device designed for specific tasks. An appliance takes vast experience about performing that task and encapsulates it into something that makes it unnecessary for the user to have that same knowledge. An appliance comes prebuilt with this knowledge so it can be plugged in and used for its intended purpose. That is the primary goal of Oracle Big Data Appliance. It is to provide a distributed computing platform that gives organizations the ability to address Big Data problems, without having to know how to set up, configure, acquire, and deploy a distributed computing cluster.

An appliance for Big Data technologies must address everything needed to run the appliance. It must include the hardware, the software, and support. The hardware should be selected and configured to optimize processing by eliminating as many bottlenecks as possible. It should be balanced for the task at hand, which is distributed computing to address a wide range of problems. The software should be configured to take advantage of the hardware configuration. This means setting parameters so that they can leverage the CPU, memory, storage, and networking capabilities. These parameters should also be tested across many workloads so that the performance is optimized for the greatest number of applications. And most importantly, the appliance should be able to be brought into a company's environment without them having to know all the details of how the appliance is configured. All they should need to do is unpack the machine, plug in the power, and connect it to their network. From a software configuration perspective, all they should need to do is supply information about their environment, such as IP address ranges, and the rest should be handled without deep knowledge about how the software works. That is the simplicity of an appliance.

Oracle Big Data Appliance was purposely designed and built to be an appliance with simplicity at the heart of its value. Oracle does not provide a choice of distributions or a multitude of hardware configuration options. Nor is Oracle Big Data Appliance a reference architecture. If Oracle provided many choices, it wouldn't be an appliance and it would not be simple to deploy.

What Are the Goals of Oracle Big Data Appliance?

Oracle Big Data Appliance was created as a platform to address the largest number of use cases possible. It can be thought of as an optimized Big Data machine to run Hadoop and NoSQL databases for a broad spectrum of data processing, statistical, and analytical workloads. It was created to make the adoption of these Big Data technologies easy, without the need to understand the intricacies of building a balanced distributed computing environment.

Oracle realized that Oracle Big Data Appliance would not exist as a standalone data processing environment. Data silos exist all over organizations, which adds significant complexity and cost whenever users need to perform data analysis.

Oracle Big Data Appliance was designed to be connected to other data systems rather than being just another data silo. Oracle realized it would need to work with and share data with these other data repositories. With this in mind, Oracle developed other technologies that enabled Oracle Big Data Appliance to connect with other components that are used to address Big Data problems. This includes integration with the R statistical language, the Oracle Database, and the Oracle Exadata Database Machine. Oracle views all of these technologies as complementary. Each component performs specific tasks that the other components will leverage. So let us explore how Oracle Big Data Appliance delivers an *optimized* appliance with the *quickest time to value* while *reducing risk* at a *cost-effective* price.

Optimizing an Appliance

What does it mean to optimize an appliance? An appliance can be optimized for very specific use cases or to address a wide range of applications. As the use cases are narrowed, it becomes easier to optimize the appliance, but in that process functionality is limited. Let us consider a toaster, perhaps the most common and underappreciated of all appliances. If the purpose of the toaster was to always toast a single piece of white bread to be a light golden brown color, it would be straightforward to design one to accomplish that task. The toaster would be designed so that the heating elements would stay on for a predetermined amount of time at a specific temperature. The design would create a slot so that the bread fit exactly in the middle and the heating elements would be placed on each side at a specific distance from the bread. Someone would simply turn on the toaster and out comes the perfect piece of toast. However, in doing this, no control for different-sized bread or darker or lighter toast would be provided. What would happen if the bread was removed from a freezer and is not fully defrosted? These variations limit the toaster's usefulness. So in designing a toaster, manufacturers add a dial to adjust the heat. This introduces some user controls and gives the appliance more functionality, but still maintains control over how the appliance functions. The appliance now allows for flexibility while retaining its core ability to perform its function optimally.

Even with this flexibility, it is still optimized for a single purpose, which is making toast. Oracle Big Data Appliance is also optimized and preconfigured for specific functions. These functions are Hadoop and NoSQL applications.

Any distributed computing platform needs to have software and hardware. So Oracle needed to determine what software to utilize and what the hardware components and configuration would be. Each of these components needs to be considered as a system to ensure an optimized engineered system.

Oracle Big Data Appliance Version 2 Software

Oracle Big Data Appliance comes with several pieces of open source software installed on the machine:

- Oracle Linux with Unbreakable Enterprise Kernel

- Oracle Hotspot Java Virtual Machine

- Cloudera's Distribution including Apache Hadoop

- Cloudera Manager

- Oracle Big Data Appliance Enterprise Manager Plug-In

- Oracle R Distribution

- Oracle NoSQL Database Community Edition

The software components were chosen to provide the most robust capabilities supporting a wide variety of use cases. Oracle had many options for the different software components but decided to choose an open source platform for Oracle Big Data Appliance. By utilizing an open source model, Oracle Big Data Appliance can adopt the latest improvements more quickly by leveraging the open source community. This is especially important since Big Data technologies are relatively young and evolving quickly.

Let's take a look at why Oracle chose each of the individual components.

Linux is the de facto standard for Hadoop processing, so using Linux was an obvious decision. Oracle chose to use Oracle Linux for Oracle Big Data Appliance as it is the standard operating system for all of the Oracle Engineered Systems. While Oracle could have chosen any of the other leading Linux distributions, by using Oracle Linux, Oracle has the flexibility to make optimizations to the OS that would specifically help Oracle Big Data Appliance. Using Oracle Linux also helps reduce the support and configuration costs, which reduces the total cost of ownership for Oracle Big Data Appliance.

Hadoop and the Oracle NoSQL database both require a Java Virtual Machine (JVM) to run, so Oracle selected their Hotspot JVM for Java 1.6 because it is the standard JVM for Hadoop and it worked extremely well out of the box. The choice of operating system and JVM are fairly obvious choices since they are Oracle products and Oracle would want to include their own components. What is more interesting are the other software components that are included.

The most interesting component, and the one people ask about most frequently, is related to Cloudera. Why did Oracle choose Cloudera? This question really has two more interesting aspects to it. Why did Oracle choose an existing distribution as opposed to creating their own? And since they decided to not create their own, then why Cloudera?

First, let's talk about why Oracle did not create their own distribution. The simplest answer is it was a time-to-market decision. Big Data and Hadoop opportunities are of great interest to many organizations and Oracle wanted to take advantage of this opportunity. As in any organization, R&D dollars are limited and Oracle felt it would be better to use its resources to focus on integrating Hadoop and R with the Oracle Database as opposed to creating its own distribution. Oracle could have devoted resources to develop its own Hadoop distribution, but that would have taken significant time and would have delayed its ability to deliver the Big Data Appliance. Hadoop is also still evolving rapidly and there is little benefit for Oracle to create its own forked distribution. IBM and Microsoft each started to build their own distribution and ultimately gave up before they gained any traction in the market. The best approach is to leverage the leading distribution and contribute to the open source community to improve this distribution. This allows Oracle to focus on delivering the appliance and adding value by integrating the appliance and its software with other components. Oracle believes that they can add more value by building an appliance than by developing yet another Hadoop distribution.

Since Oracle decided to go with an existing distribution, they needed to decide which one. To select the distribution, Oracle needed to consider many factors. These included

- Open source vs. proprietary

- Apache vs. vendor supported

- Market share of vendor

- Maturity of the management framework and the GUI tool

- Maturity of vendor

- Completeness of distribution

Oracle chose the Cloudera Distribution including Apache Hadoop (CDH) as the foundation for Oracle Big Data Appliance for many reasons. The most important consideration is that Cloudera is the clear leader for Hadoop. Cloudera has more customers than any other distribution. It's also the leading contributor to Apache Hadoop, which means that any critical bugs can be fixed quickly and accepted by the community. This is true for all components that are in the distribution, not just HDFS or MapReduce, but Oozie, Zookeeper, HBase, and so on. Cloudera also has the most nodes under management, has robust training programs for Hadoop, and has the only certification program. So it makes perfect sense to include the Cloudera Distribution including Apache Hadoop on Oracle Big Data Appliance. Cloudera did not just provide the distribution to Oracle; they also are working closely with

Oracle, developing new capabilities to enhance Hadoop. This partnership not only leads to a more robust solution for Oracle Big Data Appliance customers, but these enhancements benefit the whole Hadoop community.

While Oracle Big Data Appliance is designed as an appliance, that doesn't mean it should be plugged in and left unmonitored. A Hadoop cluster still needs to be managed to keep track of available space, add users, and monitor CPU and memory usage by MapReduce jobs. So deciding on management software is a critically important consideration. The availability of Cloudera Manager is an additional benefit that was important in the selection of Cloudera. Cloudera Manager provides extensive management capabilities that do not come with the Apache distribution. Management is a key requirement for enterprise customers, which Oracle considers its primary customer base.

While Cloudera Manager provides a rich management tool for the Hadoop platform, it does not extend to the hardware platform. Oracle thus developed additional capabilities with its Enterprise Manager plug-in. Oracle Enterprise Manager is a robust management platform that now has the ability to monitor Oracle Big Data Appliance and is integrated with the Cloudera Manager to provide complete management capabilities for the Hadoop cluster.

But Big Data is more than Hadoop. Many people consider NoSQL databases as a key technology and performing statistical analysis on the data as a key requirement for many Big Data projects. With these requirements in mind, Oracle has added two other software components to Oracle Big Data Appliance. These are the Oracle NoSQL database and R. These components are discussed in more detail in Chapters 8 and 10 respectively. The Oracle NoSQL database and R are installed, configured, and optimized so that they can be run in conjunction with Hadoop.

Oracle Big Data Appliance X3-2 Hardware

The software was the first part of the decision on what to include in Oracle Big Data Appliance. Now Oracle actually had to build the appliance. Oracle had to make the same decisions that anyone who is going to create a Hadoop cluster or a NoSQL cluster would make. Only Oracle had a few other questions to consider that are different from those of most other companies. First, Oracle was creating a multipurpose machine that could do Hadoop processing, NoSQL processing, or both. Second, Oracle didn't have a specific use case that they were designing for. Oracle Big Data Appliance should be able to run a wide range of workloads and run them efficiently.

So how would an appliance be designed that has two major software components on it that have different performance characteristics? If it was designed to be optimized for a NoSQL workload, then will Hadoop processing suffer? Or if optimization is for Hadoop, will NoSQL applications not perform well? Since both components are distributed platforms, Oracle decided that both components should leverage all nodes of Oracle Big Data Appliance. In doing so, Oracle needed to make sure the hardware should support these configurations.

Oracle thus needed to pick its hardware so that it would be optimized for the largest number of configurations. Oracle needed to decide what each node configuration would be and how these nodes would be networked. Since Oracle was designing this as an appliance for enterprise customers, they also need to take into consideration other aspects. Oracle decided to make sure that the appliance was highly available by removing as many single points of failures as possible. Oracle needed to ensure that the cluster can be easily expanded and that Oracle Big Data Appliance can connect to other systems in their customers' data centers.

Oracle currently uses the Sun X3-2L servers as the building blocks for the cluster. The Sun X3-2L are designed for clustered environments while providing flexibility needed for Hadoop and NoSQL clusters. Oracle also decided to offer Oracle Big Data Appliance in a full 42U rack that would include the compute nodes and switches in one configuration.

Oracle Big Data Appliance has the following specifications as described in Tables 4-1 and 4-2.

Node Configuration	2 x Eight-Core Intel Xeon E5-2660 Processors (2.2 GHz)
	64GB Memory (expandable to 512GB)
	Disk Controller HBA with 512MB Battery–backed write cache
	12 x 3TB 7,200 RPM High Capacity SAS Disks
	2 x QDR (40Gb/s) Ports
	4 x 10 Gb Ethernet Ports
	1 x ILOM Ethernet Port
Leaf Switch and Data Center Connectivity	2 x 32 Port QDR Infiniband Switch
	32 x Infiniband ports
	8 x 10Gb Ethernet ports
Spine Switch for Expansion	1 x 36 Port QDR Infiniband Switch
	36 x Infiniband Ports
Cabinet and Additional Hardware Components	Ethernet Administration Switch
	2 x Redundant Power Distributions Units (PDUs)
	42U rack packaging
Spares Kit	2 x 3 TB High Capacity SAS disk
	Infiniband cables

TABLE 4-1. *Oracle Big Data Appliance X3-2 Hardware Specifications (Full Rack Configuration, 18 Nodes)*

	Maximum		Typical
Height	42U, 78.66" - 1998 mm		
Width	23.62" - 600mm		
Depth	47.24" - 1200 mm		
Weight	909.5 kg (2005 lb)		
Power	10.0KW		7.0 KW
Cooling	34,142 BTU/hour		23,940 BTU/hour
Airflow	1,573 CFM		1,103 CFM

TABLE 4-2. *Selected Oracle Big Data Appliance Full Rack Environmental Specifications*

NOTE
At the time this book was published, the current generation of the Big Data Appliance was the X3-2. Please refer to the Oracle Big Data Owner's Guide for more detailed hardware and environmental specifications as well as the most current hardware configurations.

Oracle realized that not all customers are ready for a full rack cluster. Many customers are just getting started with Hadoop and are looking to test out a few use cases before they invest fully. To address the needs of customers who want to start with a small cluster, Oracle offers Oracle Big Data Appliance X3-2 Starter Rack, which can be expanded to a full rack by adding Oracle Big Data Appliance X3-2 In-Rack Expansions. The Oracle Big Data Appliance X3-2 Starter Rack is a 6-node configuration that is delivered in a full rack chassis with all the networking, power, and other components of a full rack Oracle Big Data Appliance. This makes expansion simple since customers only need to add additional nodes. To increase the capacity of the cluster, customers would purchase Oracle Big Data Appliance X3-2 In-Rack Expansion, which is simply 6 additional nodes that will be added to a Starter Rack. These configurations allow customers to grow their clusters from 6 to 12 to 18 nodes as required by specific use cases. The Oracle Big Data Appliance X3-2 family is shown in Figure 4-1.

| Oracle Big Data Appliance X3-2 Starter Rack 6 Nodes | Oracle Big Data Appliance X3-2 In-Rack Expansion 12 Nodes | Oracle Big Data Appliance X3-2 Full Rack 18 Nodes |

FIGURE 4-1.   *Oracle Big Data Appliance family*

Where Did Oracle Get Hadoop Expertise?

Why would an organization buy a Hadoop appliance from Oracle? After all, Oracle is best known for its flagship relational database product, which has a different data management paradigm compared to Hadoop. This is not where Oracle has historically been focused, so where did Oracle get its expertise for building Oracle Big Data Appliance?

Oracle is the leader in relational database management systems with a 48.3 percent share of the market according to Gartner[1]. IDC[2] shows Oracle as the leader in the data warehouse platform with a 42.0 percent market share. Many of these systems contain large amounts of data that have grown into the hundreds of terabytes and petabyte range. This leadership position demonstrates that Oracle has vast experience with creating software and hardware platforms to manage large volumes of data. However, Big Data is more than just pure data volumes, as discussed in previous chapters. There are significant quantities of additional information that does not reside in relational databases that needs to be analyzed.

---

[1] Source: Gartner report entitled, "Market Share, All Software Markets Worldwide 2012," March 29, 2013

[2] Source: IDC report entitled "Worldwide Business Analytics Software 2012–2016 Forecast and 2011 Vendor Shares," July 2012, section "Worldwide Data Warehouse Management Software Revenue by Leading Vendor"

According to an IDC study,[3] data stored in relational databases, called structured data, represents about 10 percent of all data. The rest is unstructured data that can provide a tremendous amount of useful information. This 90 percent of data represents an incredible data management market that Oracle would like to help customers manage. And with Oracle's leading place in the data management market, Oracle has created an offering to complement its data warehousing platform led by Oracle Exadata Database Machine.

When Oracle acquired Sun in 2010, Oracle announced a clear intention to create systems that are designed and engineered to leverage the hardware and software in a way that couldn't be done independently. This is called their Engineered Systems strategy. Oracle's first Engineered System was announced in 2008 and was designed to provide optimal performance for the Oracle database for data warehousing applications. This engineered system is now called Oracle Exadata Database Machine. Over the years, Oracle has taken the experience of designing high-performing, easy-to-manage systems and built out a family of Engineered Systems to address many specific tasks. There are engineered systems for Business Intelligence, Middleware, and even an Oracle Database Appliance. Through the development of these systems, Oracle has learned how to efficiently build a task-specific appliance that is easy to deploy. So building a Hadoop appliance was a natural step.

Oracle also brings significant experience in developing large-scale data processing systems. While Hadoop has tremendous capabilities, it still has a ways to go to address many of the needs of large enterprise customers who are concerned with managing these systems. Capabilities like security, backup, auditing, disaster recovery, and others are either immature or missing from the Hadoop platform. These are areas where Oracle has vast experience and is contributing to the community via its partnership with Cloudera. Oracle was a driving force in improving the high availability of the NameNode in CDH4. While the active/passive paradigm became available in CDH4, there were still some limitations in that both the active and standby NameNodes needed access to a shared storage device. The limitations required the storage device to be on an additional file server, which made the whole concept of an appliance suboptimal. Oracle helped design improvements that allowed the shared directory to be in the appliance, further simplifying deployments of Hadoop.

But Oracle did not just rely on its experience in large-scale data processing in designing Oracle Big Data Appliance. While it would have been very easy to create an appliance based on their knowledge, Oracle realized they could learn quite a bit from the Hadoop community to ensure that Oracle Big Data Appliance met customers' needs. Oracle spent significant time talking with the leading and largest users of Hadoop to understand how they configured and manage their clusters.

---

[3] www.idc.com/getdoc.jsp?containerId=prUS23177411#.UQu31PvUweN

Oracle discussed ideas about how an appliance should be configured with these companies so that Oracle could validate and conform to industry best practices. And when Oracle decided to go with Cloudera, discussions continued on what the best way to configure Oracle Big Data Appliance would be. All of this experience has led to a Hadoop appliance that is packed with industry best practices.

Configuring a Hadoop Cluster

Oracle had to go through the same steps that anyone building a Hadoop cluster needs to go through. This involves making informed choices on a wide range of topics, which are discussed in Chapter 3. The following list, while not exhaustive, includes common questions that you need to consider when building a Hadoop cluster:

- What distribution of Hadoop will be used?

- How many compute nodes will be needed?

- Will the nodes be bought or will they be custom built?

- How much RAM per node will be needed?

- What CPU manufacturer and version will be used?

- What clock speed?

- How many CPUs/cores/node?

- How much storage per node will be used?

- Will direct attached storage or a storage farm designed for Hadoop be leveraged?

- What networking protocol will be installed?

- What switches will be needed?

- How will the system be balanced to eliminate bottlenecks?

- What OS will be used?

- What level of redundancy will be needed?

- What Hadoop parameter settings will need to be modified?

- What file system underneath HDFS should be used?

- What block size should be used as default?

- How many mappers and reducers should there be?

These are all important decisions that need to be made, and these decisions can have a significant impact on the performance and reliability of the cluster. Without experience in building Hadoop clusters, there are many points where a bad decision can have crippling effects on the system.

As discussed, Oracle has thought through, analyzed, discussed with experts, and tested Oracle Big Data Appliance to address these issues. Oracle has leveraged their experience with building Exadata and other Engineered Systems and applied them to Oracle Big Data Appliance. Let's take a look at three core components of the cluster and why Oracle chose each one. We will consider node configuration, network choice, and redundancy.

Choosing the Core Cluster Components

The first item to consider is how the nodes should be configured. As listed previously in Table 4-2, Oracle uses the same configuration for all of the nodes. For Oracle Big Data Appliance X3-2, Oracle is using the Sun X3-2L servers as this is the standard X86 server that Oracle offers for distributed computing. This is a commodity server that can be configured to meet many workloads. This server provides a perfect platform for configuring a Hadoop node. When customers start learning about Hadoop, they often hear about Hadoop being designed to run on cheap, commodity hardware. So while an employee can run down to the local big box store and buy a very cheap server, this isn't an optimal strategy for most companies. Cheap servers fail often. And while Hadoop has been designed with this in mind; if a node fails, it should be replaced. The total cost of replacing nodes will add up over time when the hardware and personnel costs are considered. The fact that someone needs to be paid to procure the machines, configure them, and make sure everything is set up correctly is often overlooked when considering the total cost of the cluster. If an organization is running extremely large clusters and their business is based on Hadoop, like Google, then this is a good strategy. But for the typical corporation, this will just add to the total cost without adding any business benefit.

Oracle configured the Sun X3-2L to be close to industry best practices as far as core/RAM/spindle ratios. Each node has 64GB of RAM, 16 cores, and 12 3TB drives. This maps to a ratio of 4GB/core and 1.25 cores/spindle. This core-to-spindle ratio is slightly higher than is often recommended, but with the introduction of the 16-core chips and the existing hard drive configurations, getting to a one-to-one ratio wasn't feasible.

Oracle also decided to use the same node configuration for the master and data nodes. This seems to contradict many best practices at first glance, but is not a big deal when the reasons why Oracle made this decision are understood. Oracle Big Data Appliance was built with large clusters in mind where node uniformity allows for a cluster that is easier to grow and manage. If Oracle had created different configurations for the different node types, then expansion and configuration options would have become more difficult. Uniformity allows Oracle to offer a single-rack configuration where additional racks can be added to the cluster easily because they are the same configuration. Customers can just order a new rack of Oracle Big Data Appliance and they do not need to worry whether the nodes will be master or data nodes. More importantly, node uniformity allows services to be moved around without being limited to master nodes only. Suppose the NameNode fails. On failure, any other node can be used as the NameNode and the same performance characteristics will be in place. Additionally, in multiple rack configurations, the primary and secondary name nodes can be placed on separate racks, offering additional levels of availability protection. If Oracle Big Data Appliance did not use uniform nodes, then every cluster would need to be ordered and configured for the specific requirements of that cluster. And these requirements may change as the cluster grows. This would not be an appliance approach and would introduce additional cost and risk to the cluster.

Using the same node configuration leaves room for additional configuration options for any node. One option is to increase the memory on the NameNode. This is often necessary for large clusters with a very large number of files when a custom cluster is built. Since each block requires approximately 150 bytes of RAM, the more files that are loaded on the cluster, the more memory will be needed. Oracle Big Data Appliance uses a default of 256MB as its block size, so assuming 48GB of the 64GB is available to the NameNode, Oracle Big Data Appliance can handle dozens of petabytes of data before additional RAM is needed for the NameNode. Any node on Oracle Big Data Appliance can have its memory upgraded up to 512GB. So if a data node needs additional memory, it can be increased as needed to meet specific data processing requirements.

Since the master nodes have the same configuration as the data nodes, the master nodes can also be used as data nodes. While most clusters would not be configured this way, some organizations may want to leverage the extra capacity if there is a small number of users or a relatively small number of files on the cluster. This reuse leads to cost savings and the ability for Oracle Big Data Appliance to provide more value. Uniformity also makes node replacement on failure easier. As part of support for Oracle Big Data Appliance, Oracle will come on site and replace any node that fails. Since Oracle Big Data Appliance configuration is based on a single node type, replacement is easier with less risk of having the wrong replacement part. Oracle can thus reduce its cost, which results in a lower cost appliance for customers.

One final benefit of node uniformity is the ability for Oracle Big Data Appliance to support multiple Hadoop clusters. This allows a customer to essentially partition Oracle Big Data Appliance into distinct clusters to meet specific needs. A customer may configure 6 nodes for a development cluster and then use the remaining 12 nodes for production. Or a customer can build three separate 6-node clusters to support a multitenant configuration. Each one of these clusters will have master nodes and DataNodes. If more DataNodes are needed, expansion would occur in the same way as if only one cluster was being configured. The additional DataNodes would be assigned to one or all of the clusters, providing extensive configuration and extensibility flexibility. This would not be possible if master nodes and data nodes had different configurations. The Mammoth configuration tool, which is used to configure Oracle Big Data Appliance, can simply pick a node, assign it a function, and then configure that node.

Oracle included 3TB drives on all nodes, which tends to be on the high side of best practices. The risk of having large drives is that the probability of passing multiple blocks to other nodes in the Hadoop cluster during a MapReduce job will increase. Oracle has addressed this risk and minimized its effects by its choice of the network configuration.

Oracle has taken a bold step on its choice of a networking backbone. Oracle has included the InfiniBand network as the backbone of Oracle Big Data Appliance. Oracle uses the InfiniBand network to connect all the nodes in the cluster as well as externally to other systems like the Exadata Database Machine. Oracle chose InfiniBand since networking tends to become the bottleneck in many clusters. This bottleneck will occur if there are many users running concurrent jobs or when the shuffle/sort ends and data is passed to reducers. This step is where data can be flying between all the data nodes. By using InfiniBand, Oracle has dramatically reduced the bottlenecks that will come with smaller network speeds. Reducing network bottlenecks is critical since Oracle Big Data Appliance is designed to handle a wide range of workloads. If a typical use case will not stress the network, then there will be lots of excess capacity, which isn't a problem. But if there is not enough bandwidth, then the cluster can come to a compete crawl, essentially killing the whole value of Hadoop. InfiniBand is a key addition to the platform to support the majority of workloads that customers will need.

Assembling the Cluster

The final consideration is how to assemble the cluster to address the needs of enterprise-scale customers. While an organization can easily stack a series of nodes and wire them together, building a production quality cluster in a data center to support many users requires some extra thought. Oracle has a long history of developing data solutions and Engineered Systems that can easily be integrated into a data center to address the requirements of the most demanding customers. So while the goal of the Oracle Big Data Appliance is simplicity, reliability is also very important.

How did Oracle design Oracle Big Data Appliance so that it maximizes up time? Choosing a reliable node configuration in the Sun X3-2L was the first step. However, there are other decisions that Oracle made to ensure that Oracle Big Data Appliance stays up and running. Oracle added redundancy in several places to address the common reasons for outages. Let's take a look at two of the most common single points of failure that the Hadoop software does not address: power failure and network failure.

Power failure can impact a Hadoop cluster in two ways depending on whether a master node or data node goes down. If any of the master nodes go down, then the cluster will not be available for its designed purpose. This is critical if the NameNode goes down, especially if the high-availability capabilities have not been enabled and configured correctly. In the event of power failure, one of two options can be taken: Either replace the power supply or replace the whole node itself. The biggest issue is whether there are replacement parts on hand. In most cases, they will not be available and thus an organization will have to wait until the new part arrives and then start the cluster up again. Care will also have to be taken to ensure that there were no data corruption issues when the power went out. Losing a data node is not as damaging since Hadoop is designed to handle these errors. The cluster will lose a proportional amount of compute power, though. So if the cluster has ten data nodes and one is lost, the cluster will be down 10 percent. If the cluster is smaller, then the percentage loss will be higher. The DataNodes can be replaced when convenient.

Since Oracle Big Data Appliance has dual power supplies, the cluster is protected against one of the PDUs going down. While this is likely to be a rare event, it is much better to be safe than sorry as you never know when Murphy's Law will strike.

The other type of failure is a network failure, which can kill the cluster instantly. If data can't be transferred in or out of the cluster or users cannot connect to it, the cluster isn't very useful. Or if the networking connecting all the nodes fails, the cluster is essentially shot. If the internal network fails, a user could certainly submit a job, but the job tracker will not be able to talk to the task tracker, so the job will eventually fail. To account for this, Oracle has added two Sun Network QDR InfiniBand Gateway Switches to Oracle Big Data Appliance, providing redundant networking. If one of the switches fails, Oracle Big Data Appliance will keep on processing. Each node on the cluster also has two ports to provide a backup in case one of them fails. By providing redundancy in the network, Oracle Big Data Appliance limits the number of scenarios where the cluster will be taken off-line.

What About a Do-It-Yourself Cluster?

The "do it yourself" or "build your own" approach to Hadoop is very compelling since that is how Hadoop was originally developed. And since many engineers have heard this story and are confident in their abilities, it sounds appealing to want to build your own cluster. But a Hadoop cluster is not a simple system when it grows beyond anything more than a few nodes. Does anyone still build their own PCs? Would most people build their own house? While each of these tasks are doable in that a person can buy blueprints for a house or they can read any of the many Web sites dedicated to building PCs, in the end, it is not a good proposition for most people or corporations. To perform these tasks, companies will need expertise, time, and money. The build-your-own approach is always a trade-off on these three constraints. Unless someone is an expert, they will definitely spend more time and more money building the cluster. And even if they have the expertise, is that where company resources should be spent?

Building a custom Hadoop cluster will not give any organization a competitive advantage. The applications and analysis developed on the cluster will, but just having a box of blinking lights in of itself will not. So resources should be dedicated to the activities that are most valuable. Getting the cluster up and running in the fastest amount of time while ensuring that it remains up and running is critical. This is ultimately the value of Oracle Big Data Appliance.

What if despite the advantages of purchasing an appliance, someone really wanted to custom build a large Hadoop cluster? Would they be prepared to answer the Hadoop cluster configuration questions that we listed earlier, under the heading "Configuring a Hadoop Cluster"? They should ask themselves if they have the expertise to make the correct decisions across all of these topics. What would happen if they made a wrong choice on one or more of these questions? Would they know the impact on the organization? Would it be a minor configuration issue that some tuning could fix to get the cluster performing well? Or would it be a major design issue that would create a need to re-architect the whole cluster? What impact would it have on the business? How much time would they have to fix the problem while keeping the business users on hold? These are real questions that need to be considered before going down the build-your-own path, and they are not trivial.

There are many sources of information to assist organizations in building their own cluster and numerous Web sites that describe best practices for building a cluster. Even Hadoop distributors, including Cloudera, provide best practices for how to build a custom cluster. A simple Web search for best practices will display many links explaining how Hadoop works, and what the best ratio of CPUs to RAM and CPUs to disk ratios should be. There is plenty of information about how the networking works and suggestions on the configurations that should be used. Anyone can go to a hardware vendor and they will tell them the exact servers they should buy for their cluster. In fact, there is so much information out there and at times conflicting best practices, that anyone contemplating building a custom cluster will need to spend significant time figuring out what to believe.

If someone wanted to take the easy way out, they could look at the specifications of Oracle Big Data Appliance and just build the cluster using the same hardware and configure it in a similar manner. But if they were going to go down this path, why not just buy the machine instead of building it? In the end, experience is the key to understanding how to build a cluster and acquiring that experience takes time, effort, and money. Oracle has already packaged up all of the expertise and put it in Oracle Big Data Appliance. This sentiment was expressed by one CIO when he stated that even if building their own cluster was cheaper, it wouldn't be worth the extra time it would take to get it up and running and working optimally.

Another case in point is a large data processing company who was looking at Oracle Big Data Appliance compared to a custom-built cluster using nodes from a leading hardware vendor. This customer decided to build the cluster first and then bring in Oracle Big Data Appliance. They planned a few weeks to get the cluster up and running and then another couple of weeks to perform some Hadoop test. They experienced all the common problems people face while building a cluster. The wrong cables were shipped, packing all the hardware took longer than expected, the cluster didn't start up right away, and they couldn't figure out why. So after two months of trial and error, they still did not have the cluster up and running. In this two-month period, they could have had the Oracle Big Data Appliance delivered and installed and completed their testing. Additionally, they could have put the Oracle Big Data Appliance into production.

Let us revisit networking as this is the most challenging aspect of a Hadoop cluster. It is critical to understand what the workloads are going to be so that there will be adequate networking for the cluster. Many estimates state that networking costs will be 20–25 percent of the cost of the whole cluster covering networks cards, switches, cables, and so on. Ideally there should be just enough capacity to cover the needs so that too much is not spent on networking. However, if user demands change and excess capacity is needed, changing the whole network is not easy and can significantly increase the costs of the cluster. So getting this right in the first place is critical. This is why Oracle chose InfiniBand to ensure that the network will not be a bottleneck.

This raises the final reason companies will try to build a cluster on their own. They think it is cheaper to do it themselves compared to buying an appliance. When consideration is given to how much a cluster will cost, there are two broad topics that need to be considered: how much the hardware, software, and support will cost and how fast the cluster can be set up and put into production. This is sometimes referred to as the time to value.

Total Costs of a Cluster

Determining how much a hypothetical Hadoop cluster will cost is a difficult task as there are so many configuration choices that can be made. These choices can be broken into four general categories:

- Hardware
- Software and support
- Operational costs
- Labor

The total cost of a Hadoop cluster will always be a trade-off among these costs. If an organization goes with the Apache version of Hadoop to save on software support cost, they will need to spend more on labor to support the cluster. If they use smaller-sized nodes, they will end up with more nodes and thus require more data center space. If they build a system themselves, they will require more operational costs to design and physically build the cluster. Additional opportunity costs will be incurred as it will take longer to build the cluster. Essentially, this is a cost optimization problem where an organization wants to get the best cluster for the least total cost in the shortest amount of time. A sample of the distribution of costs across these four categories comparing a do-it-yourself cluster compared to Oracle Big Data Appliance is shown in Figure 4-2.

Let's consider what it would cost to build a similarly configured cluster as Oracle Big Data Appliance. This example will focus on the hardware costs since they are the easiest to quantify. The additional benefits of included support, reduced labor, and operating costs will just be additional benefits over a build-your-own system.

One challenge in performing a price comparison is that every vendor has different prices and every customer will receive different discounts. For the purpose of this comparison, prices will be based on list pricing of Hewlett-Packard hardware (as of December 2012) as it is a popular platform for many enterprise customers as well as list pricing for the Oracle Database Appliance. Included in the price comparison will be the cost of hardware and Linux support as it is a core component to getting the hardware platform up and running. Included are the servers used for the nodes, similar memory and storage configurations, as well as the InfiniBand network switches. Items like cables, a rack cabinet, and other smaller priced components are not included as they will represent a small percentage of the total cost. The specifications we will consider are listed in Table 4-3.

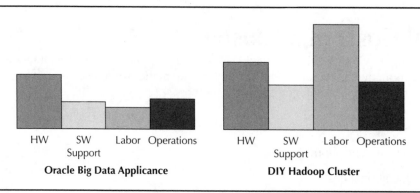

FIGURE 4-2.   *Oracle Big Data Appliance cost distribution compared to a custom cluster*

Number and processor type of nodes	18 nodes (2x eight-core Intel Xeon E5-2660 processors (2.2 GHz)
Memory per node	64GB
Storage per node	36TB (12x3) per node
Networking components	3 InfiniBand switches

TABLE 4-3.   *Oracle Big Data Appliance Key Configuration Specifications*

HP ProLiant DL380p Gen8 Server

Product Description	SmartBuy DL380p Gen8 E5-2660 (2P)
Processor Name	Intel Xeon E5-2670 (8 core, 2.60 GHz, 20MB, 115W)
Standard Memory	32GB
Hard Drives Installed	None ship standard; supports up to 8 SFF
Power Supply	2 × 750W
Cost	$6,979

TABLE 4-4.   *HP Comparable Specifications*

According to HP Solutions for Hadoop,[4] HP is recommending using their HP ProLiant DL380p Gen8 Server family for Hadoop clusters. The model that most closely resembles Oracle Big Data Appliance is the SmartBuy DL380p Gen8 E5-2660 (2P), which comes with the specifications in Table 4-4.[5]

Now we need to price out the key components of the cluster. The cost for each component and total cost are listed in Table 4-5.

To build a similar-sized cluster to Oracle Big Data Appliance, it will cost $445,491 plus a little extra for the rack, cables, hard drive cages, and so on, and this does not include support for Hadoop.[6] This price does not include all the soft costs of research and planning of the cluster, assembling, configuration, tuning, and

---

[4] http://h71028.www7.hp.com/enterprise/us/en/partners/hadoop.html

[5] http://h10010.www1.hp.com/wwpc/us/en/sm/WF25a/15351-15351-3328412-241644-241475-5177957 .html?dnr=1

[6] Oracle also has a detailed price comparison in its blog (https://blogs.oracle.com/datawarehousing/entry/ price_comparison_for_big_data), which shows a three-year total cost of ownership advantage of Oracle Big Data Appliance of 13 percent.

Component	Quantity	Unit Price	Extended Price
HP ProLiant DL380p Gen8 Server	1	$6,979	$6,979
Additional 32GB RAM HP 8GB (1x8GB) single-rank x4 PC3-12800 (DDR3-1600) registered CAS-11 Memory Kit	4	$756	$3,024
HP 3TB 6G SAS 7.2K rpm LFF (3.5-inch) Midline 1-year warranty hard drive	12	$859	$10,308
Cost per Node			**$20,311**
Cost per server	18	$20,311	$365,598
Voltaire InfiniBand 4X QDR 36-port Reversed Air Flow Managed Switch	3	$12,999	$38,997
Total Cluster Hardware Cost			**$404,595**
Red Hat Enterprise Linux Server Standard (up to 1 guest) per socket pair (3 years)	18	$2,277	$40,896
Total Cost for Hardware and OS Support			**$445,491**

TABLE 4-5.   *HP Hadoop Cluster Cost*

testing of the cluster. All of these steps will require Hadoop expertise, which can be difficult to find and is often expensive. The cost of Oracle Big Data Appliance is much simpler to determine. Oracle Big Data Appliance has a list price of $450,000 with maintenance of 12 percent or $54,000 per year. Oracle will typically discount Oracle Big Data Appliance, which would lower both the hardware and support costs. Included in the price of Oracle Big Data Appliance is all the hardware specified in Table 4-2 as well as support for the complete software stack. And Oracle Big Data Appliance is preconfigured and optimized, and it just needs to be plugged in to the corporate data center.

This is a simple comparison to show that from a pure cost perspective, Oracle Big Data Appliance is very competitive on price. A company can always get cheaper hardware, but with that they would incur the risks discussed earlier in this chapter and their labor costs will rise. They also have other concerns if they go with less expensive nodes related to the capacity that these nodes will provide.

Less expensive nodes will have less processing power and storage, which will require more nodes in the cluster. More nodes mean there will need to be more racks and thus there will be a need for more space in the data center. With data center space being at a premium and the additional cost for power, cooling, and facility costs, more nodes are not an optimal design goal.

Oracle Big Data Appliance also optimized its configuration for the high-availability capabilities of Hadoop that comes with CDH4. This eliminates the need for an external shared filesystem, which is not included in the cost comparison, but would increase the cost of a DIY cluster.

While we have only been considering hardware costs until now, Oracle Big Data Appliance also comes with Cloudera support included. This will significantly sway the cost benefit in favor of Oracle Big Data Appliance since most organizations will license some distribution of Hadoop. With a single call, customers get support for all the nodes, networking, operating system, and CDH4. There is no fingerpointing as to who is responsible for the problem. Oracle support will look at the whole system. Oracle also includes Auto Service Requests alerts on Oracle Big Data Appliance. In the event of any hardware issue that triggers an alert, Oracle Big Data Appliance will create a service request and send it to Oracle. Oracle will then not only send a field engineer to replace the faulty hardware, but will also make sure the cluster is up and running and recognizes the new hardware. One special consideration from a software support perspective is that Oracle includes HBase as part of the Cloudera Distribution included on Oracle Big Data Appliance. Cloudera has a separate subscription for CDH4 and HBase; thus, Oracle provides extra value if applications are going to include HBase.

Since every Oracle Big Data Appliance is configured the same, Oracle can resolve issues quickly. This is because every customer's system is the same as what Oracle develops and tests on. If a custom cluster is built, it is likely no one will have the exact same configuration that was built. This makes problem resolution extremely difficult. It requires significant amounts of time and money in labor cost and business delays. The human costs rise since full-time employees are needed who are familiar with Hadoop, networking, Linux, and Java and are ready to resolve these problems at any time. And there is not a large supply of these people available today. Thus the people who are available can demand significant salaries.

There is one last benefit to consider, and that is how fast business benefits of the Hadoop cluster can be realized. This is where Oracle Big Data Appliance offers tremendous time-to-value benefits.

Time to Value

Hadoop offers tremendous opportunities to solve many new analytical problems while providing a more cost-effective platform for many data processing problems. Organizations are coming up with a wide variety of use cases that promise to provide them with competitive advantages and operational efficiencies. So what should a company do when they have a use case that can have a major impact on the organization and they have business users asking when can they get a cluster up and running? What is the path that will provide the quickest time to value, or in other words, how can a cluster be set up and running in the shortest amount of time? There is a choice: Build your own cluster or buy one. There is no question that an appliance approach will provide the fastest time to value for getting a Hadoop cluster up and running.

Oracle Big Data Appliance is simple to get up and running and users can be developing on the appliance in approximately two days after delivery. This is because Oracle Big Data Appliance is preassembled and is ready to be plugged in to any data center on delivery. Customers who purchase Oracle Big Data Appliance have very few steps in order to get started.

1. Order an Oracle Big Data Appliance.

2. Fill out Oracle Big Data Appliance configuration template.

3. Take delivery.

4. Provide power, networking, and floor space.

5. Have Oracle install and configure the machine.

6. Start analyzing Big Data.

It really is that simple! When the time that it will take to build your own cluster is compared to the time it takes to deploy Oracle Big Data Appliance, there really is no comparison. Building a large cluster requires a significant amount of time to unbox all the servers, stack them in the rack, connect all the power, connect all the network cables, install the servers, and configure all the nodes—not to mention the delays if any mistakes are made. And mistakes are common, especially if the people developing the cluster are not networking experts. Errors like connecting cables to the wrong port or misconfiguring a node by a simple typo are very common. Debugging these issues can take a significant amount of time. Careful planning needs to take place to ensure that the correct length cables are ordered and that all the right parts are ordered. If a critical component is forgotten, the cluster may not be able to get up and running. And don't forget getting access to the data center. Many data center managers have strict rules on access. There may only be a small window during the day to do the install. Many data centers lock down access at certain points of the month or year. All of this increases the risk that the cluster will not be up and running in the time frame expected.

Oracle Big Data Appliance eliminates many of these concerns because Oracle has a well-defined, repeatable process that every customer utilizes. Oracle has a standard installation and configuration process that customers should leverage. If a hardware component fails, Oracle will come in and replace the component. They will also ensure that the cluster recognizes the new component and is back up and running as it should be. If an organization builds their own cluster, the support contract with the chosen hardware vendor will provide a replacement for any failed part, but they will not be able to make sure the Hadoop cluster is running fine. This is the Hadoop administrator's responsibility. Troubleshooting problems will also be handled more quickly since Oracle has the exact same configuration at Oracle that the customer has. Therefore, it is very easy to replicate errors, which leads to quicker resolution. In a build-your-own cluster, it is very likely that no one will have the same exact configuration. So finding the root cause of errors can be significantly more difficult.

The elimination of all the issues involved in building a custom Hadoop or NoSQL cluster is perhaps the most important benefit of an Engineered System delivered as an appliance.

How to Build Out Larger Clusters

Oracle Big Data Appliance was designed so that expanding the cluster as demand increases is easy. Multiple Oracle Big Data Appliances can be connected together using the InfiniBand network by simply wiring the new machine to the existing switches in each rack. Oracle Big Data Appliance comes with all the network switches and cables needed to expand the cluster to 18 racks. This would result in a cluster of 324 nodes, 5,184 cores, 20.736TB of RAM, and 11.664 petabytes of raw storage. If additional racks are needed, additional switches would be required to support the extra racks. Oracle has design specifications for larger racks, so the configuration is straightforward.

As part of the Oracle Big Data Appliance installation service, Oracle will install the hardware and add the new rack to the cluster. Expanding the cluster is just as easy as installing the first Oracle Big Data Appliance. This is dramatically different from a build-your-own cluster, where adding additional nodes and racks become very complex if the cluster was not designed for the required size up front. The most common issues arise from networking at scale. As more nodes are added, more switches are needed, increasing the complexity of the network. If all network components are not correctly designed, connected, and configured correctly, the cluster will either not work efficiently or not work at all. The resulting delays will be costly in terms of dollars and business impact.

Can I Add Other Software to Oracle Big Data Appliance?

Oracle Big Data Appliance is designed as an appliance to run specific software components using an optimal configuration. But the Big Data software ecosystem is large and Oracle has included only specific software components. Many Big Data applications may require other software components that interact with the software on Oracle Big Data Appliance. Suppose a customer wanted to run Solr and wanted to put it on Oracle Big Data Appliance for searching files that are stored on HDFS.

Where should Solr be installed? Could a customer install it on Oracle Big Data Appliance? The simple answer is yes, it can be installed on Oracle Big Data Appliance and Oracle will continue to support Oracle Big Data Appliance and all preinstalled software components. But just because it can be done, that doesn't necessarily mean it should be done. Oracle has optimized Oracle Big Data Appliance to ensure that each node is optimized for addressing the workload of Hadoop or NoSQL. This means that the amount of CPU, memory, storage, and networking is balanced to minimize bottlenecks anywhere in the system. If additional software is added that alters that balance, then the system may be suboptimized.

What an Oracle Big Data Appliance customer should think about is: what effect will the new software have on the system? Will it be memory-intensive or CPU-intensive? Will it require a significant amount of storage? What OS or other dependencies does it require? If the software that will be installed will have minimal impact, then it is acceptable to include the software on Oracle Big Data Appliance. This is very common for management and other types of agents that corporate clients want on all their computer systems. If there will be significant resource usage, then one must ask if the software should be installed on Oracle Big Data Appliance. If there is excess capacity on any nodes, then one can consider installing the software on that node. This should be done with the knowledge that this will limit an organization's ability to meet demand if it increases in the future.

With this in mind, including extra software on Oracle Big Data Appliance should be done cautiously. Oracle Big Data Appliance has been designed to scale out easily, but if other components were included, the administrators will need to take on extra responsibility as well. Remember that one of the key V's for Big Data is volume and Big Data systems are designed to add more data over time. Ultimately, capacity limits will be encountered on Oracle Big Data Appliance as demand increases. Therefore, it is highly recommended that any significant additional software should be installed on its own dedicated hardware platform.

Drawbacks of an Appliance

By now it should be apparent that the appliance approach that Oracle has taken offers many advantages. With all these advantages, why would anyone who is serious about building a Hadoop or NoSQL cluster not go with Oracle Big Data Appliance? The one reason that an appliance is not the right choice is complete flexibility. Oracle Big Data Appliance only allows growth in six-node increments and the only modification to the hardware allowed is increasing the RAM on each node. But what if a use case dictates a very specific workload and the cluster needs to be optimized for this workload?

This would be a valid reason to build a custom cluster, but whoever builds it must have deep expertise to design the cluster to meet this specific need. The cluster will also not be available for other workloads. It is therefore important to make sure that the value received from the use case is worth the cost of customization. The risk of building custom clusters for every use case is that eventually an organization will end up with many clusters that cannot share data or processing. This will result in excess capacity and cost compared to using Oracle Big Data Appliance.

This chapter discussed why Oracle developed Oracle Big Data Appliance as an Engineered System for Hadoop and NoSQL databases. When all the variables that go into creating a distributed computing platform are considered, simplicity should always be the focal point for any enterprise. The more deviation from simplicity, the greater the risk to the organization to meet user needs and the more the cluster will cost. This will ultimately reduce the ability to deliver powerful results—which is the whole point of using Hadoop or NoSQL in the first place.

CHAPTER
5

BDA Configurations, Deployment Architectures, and Monitoring

Big Data deployments can consist of several racks of server/storage nodes with many components, including Hadoop/HDFS, Hive, HBase, Oozie, Flume, Oracle NoSQL DB, and so on. Architecture of a Big Data deployment will vary from user to user depending on the use case and workload requirements. It is critical to have the right integration of Big Data into the existing data warehouse, data processing, and analytics architecture. The integration must also extend to existing operations and management. The Oracle Big Data Appliance (BDA) provides optimized configurations suitable for building many different deployments as shown in Figure 5-1. This chapter describes the different BDA configurations, deployment architectures, connecting BDA to relational database systems like Exadata and the Data Center LAN, multitenancy, scalability, high availability, data center connectivity, management, and monitoring.

Introduction

A very basic Hadoop cluster configuration looks like the one shown in Figure 5-2. Each square box is a node (a physical server with local CPU, memory, and disk). The two high-level categories of nodes in a Hadoop cluster are "master nodes" and

Starter Rack   Starter Rack +   Full Rack
                      In-Rack Expansion

FIGURE 5-1. *Oracle Big Data Appliance—flexible and scalable architecture*

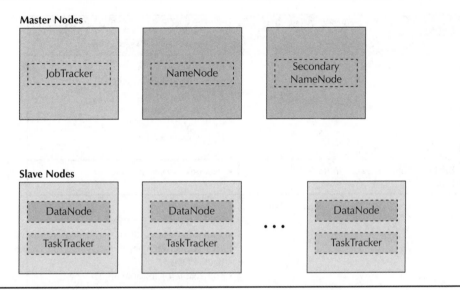

FIGURE 5-2. *Basic Hadoop cluster configuration*

"slave nodes." Each of the nodes runs services called JobTracker, NameNode, and so on. These are software daemon processes. Hadoop consists of several daemons—NameNode, DataNode, JobTracker, JournalNode, and TaskTracker are the core daemons. Each daemon runs in its own JVM (represented by a dotted line in Figure 5-2). Although technically it is possible to run all these daemons on the same physical node, in real production clusters this is never done. The services are distributed on different physical nodes of the Hadoop cluster. The decision on what daemon or service runs on which node in a Hadoop cluster is made based on several factors:

- The workload
- Processing capability of each node
- Overall scalability, reliability, and high availability

Oracle Big Data Appliance has been designed and optimized for Big Data processing taking into consideration scalability, availability, and reliability, both from a hardware (rack, disk, memory, networking) and software (Hadoop daemons, monitoring agents, NoSQL DB, and so on) perspective. The Big Data Appliance is offered in three sizes, listed next.

Product Name	Hardware BOM
Big Data Appliance X3-2 Starter Rack	• 6 Nodes • 2 InfiniBand Leaf Switches • 1 InfiniBand Spine Switch • 1 Cisco Management Switch • Rack, PDUs • Fully cabled + full spares kit
Big Data Appliance X3-2 In-Rack Expansion	• 6 Nodes (No switches etc)
Big Data Appliance X3-2 Full Rack	• 18 Nodes • 2 InfiniBand Leaf Switches • 1 InfiniBand Spine Switch • 1 Cisco Management Switch • Rack, PDUs • Fully cabled + full spares kit

FIGURE 5-3. *Big Data Appliance hardware configurations*

■ Big Data Appliance X3-2 Full Rack (18 nodes)

■ Big Data Appliance X3-2 Starter Rack (6 nodes)

■ Big Data Appliance X3-2 In-Rack Expansion (6 nodes)

This architecture enables you to expand your system as requirements grow—while minimizing cost and complexity. Oracle Big Data Appliance Full Rack is an 18-node configuration. The full rack can be divided into multiple clusters using the configuration software (Mammoth) delivered with the system. Alternatively, you can leverage the Oracle Big Data Appliance Starter Rack—a 6-node cluster. The starter rack has been conveniently packaged in the full rack chassis—allowing you to easily grow the system over time with Oracle Big Data In-Rack Expansion.

The differences between the three sizes are shown in Figure 5-3.

Big Data Appliance X3-2 Full Rack (Eighteen Nodes)

Full Rack (42U) configuration (see Figure 5-4) contains 288 processing cores and 648TB of raw storage in the following components.

FIGURE 5-4. *Big Data Appliance X3-2 Full Rack*

Eighteen Compute and Storage nodes, which include the following per node:

■ 2 × Eight-Core Intel Xeon E5-2660 processors (2.2 GHz)

■ 64GB memory (expandable to 512GB)

■ 12 3TB 7.2K RPM SAS disks preconfigured as 12 HW RAID 0 volumes with OS disks in SW RAID 1 volume on disk slot 0/12 × QDR (40Gb/s) ports

■ Disk controller HBA with 512MB battery-backed write cache (LSI Niwot)

■ Dual-port QDR (40Gb/s) InfiniBand Host Channel Adapter (HCA) (qMirage CX2)

- 4 × 10Gb Ethernet ports (Intel Kawela)
- 1 Ethernet port for Sun Integrated Lights Out Manager (ILOM) for remote management

2 × 32-port QDR InfiniBand switches (NanoMagnum2 Gateway NM2-GW):

- 32 × InfiniBand ports
- 8 × 10GigE ports

1 × 36-port QDR InfiniBand switch (NanoMagnum2 NM2):

- 36 × InfiniBand ports

Additional hardware includes

- 1 48-port Ethernet Administration Switch (Cisco 4948)
- 2 redundant 15 kVA PDUs (single-phase or three-phase, high voltage, or low voltage)
- 42U rack packaging

Spares Kit includes

- 2 × 3TB high-capacity SAS disk
- InfiniBand cables

A picture of a single node that is used inside the 18-node BDA cluster is shown in Figure 5-5.

Figure 5-6 shows the rack layout of a BDA full rack; both the rear and front views are shown side by side. Notice that the top two slots are empty (labeled 1U Solid Filler); these slots can be used for a top-of-rack (TOR) switch. Typically, a TOR switch is needed if the customer's data center does not support 10GbE. Since the BDA needs

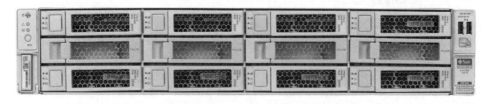

FIGURE 5-5. *A single node of the 18-node BDA full rack*

Rear View

U#	PDU B	Big Data Appliance	PDU A	U#
42		1U Solid Filler		42
41		1U Solid Filler		41
40	INP0	BDA Server 18	INP2	40
39				39
38		BDA Server 17		38
37				37
36		BDA Server 16		36
35				35
34		BDA Server 15		34
33				33
32		BDA Server 14		32
31				31
30		BDA Server 13		30
29				29
28	INP1	BDA Server 12	INP1	28
27				27
26		BDA Server 11		26
25				25
24		BDA Server 10		24
23				23
22		Sun Network QDR Infiniband GW Switch		22
21		Cisco Ethernet "Admin" Switch		21
20		Sun Network QDR Infiniband GW Switch		20
19		BDA Server 9		19
18				18
17		BDA Server 8		17
16				16
15		BDA Server 7		15
14				14
13	INP2	BDA Server 6	INP0	13
12				12
11		BDA Server 5		11
10				10
9		BDA Server 4		9
8				8
7		BDA Server 3		7
6				6
5		BDA Server 2		5
4				4
3		BDA Server 1		3
2				2
1		Sun Datacenter QDR Infiniband Switch		1
		Power Distribution Unit-A		
		Power Distribution Unit-B		

Front View

U#	PDU B	Big Data Appliance	PDU A	U#
42		1U Solid Filler		42
41		1U Solid Filler		41
40	INP0	BDA Server 18	INP2	40
39				39
38		BDA Server 17		38
37				37
36		BDA Server 16		36
35				35
34		BDA Server 15		34
33				33
32		BDA Server 14		32
31				31
30		BDA Server 13		30
29				29
28	INP1	BDA Server 12	INP1	28
27				27
26		BDA Server 11		26
25				25
24		BDA Server 10		24
23				23
22		1U Vented Filler		22
21		1U Vented Filler		21
20		1U Vented Filler		20
19		BDA Server 9		19
18				18
17		BDA Server 8		17
16				16
15		BDA Server 7		15
14				14
13	INP2	BDA Server 6	INP0	13
12				12
11		BDA Server 5		11
10				10
9		BDA Server 4		9
8				8
7		BDA Server 3		7
6				6
5		BDA Server 2		5
4				4
3		BDA Server 1		3
2				2
1		1U Vented Filler		1
		Power Distribution Unit-A		
		Power Distribution Unit-B		

FIGURE 5-6.   *Big Data Appliance X3-2 Full Rack layout*[1]

	BDA Full Rack - Hadoop+No SQL
Node18	No SQL Admin, No SQL Storage Agent, 12 shards (replication nodes)
Node17	No SQL Admin, No SQL Storage Agent, 12 shards (replication nodes)
Node16	No SQL Admin, No SQL Storage Agent, 12 shards (replication nodes)
Node15	DataNode, TaskTracker, Cloudera Mgr Agent, Puppet Agent
Node14	DataNode, TaskTracker, Cloudera Mgr Agent, Puppet Agent
Node13	DataNode, TaskTracker, Cloudera Mgr Agent, Puppet Agent
Node12	DataNode, TaskTracker, Cloudera Mgr Agent, Puppet Agent
Node11	DataNode, TaskTracker, Cloudera Mgr Agent, Puppet Agent
Node10	DataNode, TaskTracker, Cloudera Mgr Agent, Puppet Agent
Node9	DataNode, TaskTracker, Cloudera Mgr Agent, Puppet Agent
Node8	DataNode, TaskTracker, Cloudera Mgr Agent, Puppet Agent
Node7	DataNode, TaskTracker, Cloudera Mgr Agent, Puppet Agent
Node6	DataNode, TaskTracker, Cloudera Mgr Agent, Puppet Agent
Node5	DataNode, TaskTracker, Cloudera Mgr Agent, Puppet Agent
Node4	Standby JobTracker, Failover Controller, Hue, Hive, Oozie, ODI Agent, DataNode, TaskTracker, Cloudera Mgr Agent, Puppet Agent
Node3	Active Job Tracker, JournalNode, DataNode, TaskTracker, ZooKeeper, Failover Controller, CM Server Agent, MySQL Master, Puppet Agent
Node2	Standby NameNode, JournalNode, DataNode, ZooKeeper, Failover controller, MySQL backup Server, CM Agent, Puppet Agent
Node1	Active NameNode, JournalNode, DataNode, ZooKeeper, Failover controller, Balancer, CM Agent, Puppet Master & Agent

FIGURE 5-7. *BDA Full Rack software configuration*

10GbE, a switch like the Sun Network 10GbE switch 72p, which supports both 10GbE and 1GbE, can be installed in that empty slot.

Figure 5-7 illustrates a typical configuration of full rack BDA, where 15 nodes are dedicated to Hadoop and 3 for NoSQL DB. The figure also shows which service is running on each of the 18 nodes. Nodes 1 to 4 are the master nodes or special nodes, since they run the critical services in the cluster. Nodes 5 to 15 in full rack are data nodes. Nodes 16, 17, and 18 are dedicated NoSQL DB nodes. If you hook up another rack and dedicate all the nodes to Hadoop, most of the new 18 nodes are data nodes that join the cluster. Mammoth automatically moves the second name node to the second rack to ensure higher fault tolerance to hardware failures. As Hadoop is designed for scale-out, adding nodes is very easy. Data automatically rebalances itself in Hadoop.

Big Data Appliance X3-2 Starter Rack (Six Nodes)

Oracle Big Data Appliance is designed to serve all your workloads, starting with PoC and pilot projects, and it expands as your data and requirements grow. Initial Big Data pilots could start with the Big Data Appliance Starter Rack. This rack, which contains 6 nodes, comes fully equipped with switches and power distribution units (PDUs), so that it can be easily and quickly expanded as needed to 12 nodes and then to the full rack of 18 nodes by using Oracle Big Data Appliance In-Rack Expansions.

Configuration contains 96 processing cores and 216TB of raw storage in the following components.

Six compute and storage nodes, which include the following per node:

- 2 × Eight-Core Intel Xeon E5-2660 processors (2.2 GHz)

- 64GB memory (expandable to 512GB)

- 12 3TB 7.2K RPM SAS disks preconfigured as 12 HW RAID 0 volumes with OS disks in SW RAID 1 volume on disk slot 0/12 × QDR (40Gb/s) ports

- Disk controller HBA with 512MB battery-backed write cache (LSI Niwot)

- Dual-port QDR (40Gb/s) InfiniBand Host Channel Adapter (HCA) (qMirage CX2)

- 4 × 10Gb Ethernet ports (Intel Kawela)

- 1 Ethernet port for Sun Integrated Lights Out Manager (ILOM) for remote management

2 × 32-port QDR InfiniBand switches (NanoMagnum2 Gateway NM2-GW)—both leaf switches are provided in the starter rack:

- 32 × InfiniBand ports

- 8 × 10GigE ports

1 × 36-port QDR InfiniBand switch (NanoMagnum2 NM2):

- 36 × InfiniBand ports

Additional hardware includes

- 1 48-port Ethernet administration switch (Cisco 4948 or CU-supplied)

- 2 redundant 15 kVA PDUs (single-phase or three-phase, high voltage, or low voltage)

- 42U rack packaging

Spares Kit includes

- 2 × 3TB High Capacity SAS disk

- InfiniBand cables

Figure 5-8 shows the rack layout of a BDA starter rack. Both the rear and front views are shown side by side. Only 6 of the 18 nodes are populated. The same number of switches and PDUs are present in the starter rack as the full rack.

Rear View

U#	PDU B	Big Data Appliance	PDU A	U#
42		1U Solid Filler		42
41		1U Solid Filler		41
40		1U Solid Filler		40
39		1U Solid Filler		39
38		1U Solid Filler		38
37		1U Solid Filler		37
36	INP0	1U Solid Filler	INP2	36
35		1U Solid Filler		35
34		1U Solid Filler		34
33		1U Solid Filler		33
32		1U Solid Filler		32
31		1U Solid Filler		31
30		1U Solid Filler		30
29		1U Solid Filler		29
28		1U Solid Filler		28
27		1U Solid Filler		27
26		1U Solid Filler		26
25		1U Solid Filler		25
24		1U Solid Filler		24
23		1U Solid Filler		23
22	INP1	Sun Network QDR Infiniband GW Switch	INP1	22
21		Cisco Ethernet "Admin" Switch		21
20		Sun Network QDR Infiniband GW Switch		20
19		1U Solid Filler		19
18		1U Solid Filler		18
17		1U Solid Filler		17
16		1U Solid Filler		16
15		1U Solid Filler		15
14		1U Solid Filler		14
13	INP2	BDA Server 6	INP0	13
12				12
11		BDA Server 5		11
10				10
9		BDA Server 4		9
8				8
7		BDA Server 3		7
6				6
5		BDA Server 2		5
4				4
3		BDA Server 1		3
2				2
1		Sun Datacenter QDR Infiniband Switch		1
		Power Distribution Unit-A		
		Power Distribution Unit-B		

Front View

U#	PDU B	Big Data Appliance	PDU A	U#
42		1U Solid Filler		42
41		1U Solid Filler		41
40		1U Solid Filler		40
39		1U Solid Filler		39
38		1U Solid Filler		38
37		1U Solid Filler		37
36	INP0	1U Solid Filler	INP2	36
35		1U Solid Filler		35
34		1U Solid Filler		34
33		1U Solid Filler		33
32		1U Solid Filler		32
31		1U Solid Filler		31
30		1U Solid Filler		30
29		1U Solid Filler		29
28		1U Solid Filler		28
27		1U Solid Filler		27
26		1U Solid Filler		26
25		1U Solid Filler		25
24		1U Solid Filler		24
23		1U Solid Filler		23
22		1U Vented Filler		22
21	INP1	1U Vented Filler	INP1	21
20		1U Vented Filler		20
19		1U Solid Filler		19
18		1U Solid Filler		18
17		1U Solid Filler		17
16		1U Solid Filler		16
15		1U Solid Filler		15
14		1U Solid Filler		14
13	INP2	BDA Server 6	INP0	13
12				12
11		BDA Server 5		11
10				10
9		BDA Server 4		9
8				8
7		BDA Server 3		7
6				6
5		BDA Server 2		5
4				4
3		BDA Server 1		3
2				2
1		1U Vented Filler		1
		Power Distribution Unit-A		
		Power Distribution Unit-B		

FIGURE 5-8. *Oracle Big Data Appliance X3-2 starter rack layout*[2]

Figure 5-9 illustrates where each service runs on a starter rack BDA configured for Hadoop only. The starter rack BDA has four master nodes: Nodes 1, 2, 3, and 4. On the starter rack, the TaskTracker process runs on all nodes except Node 4. Since the starter rack has six nodes, it can be configured to run either Hadoop or NoSQL.

---

[2] Oracle Big Data Appliance Owner's Guide Release 2 (2.1) E36962-04, page 227

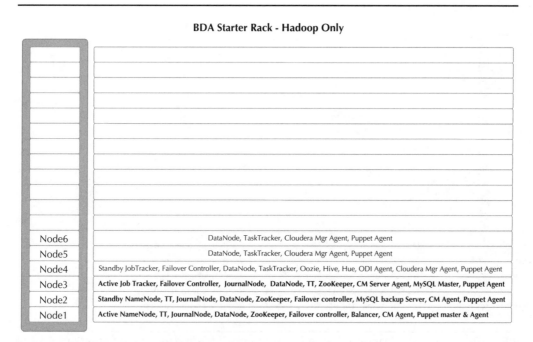

BDA Starter Rack - Hadoop Only

Node6	DataNode, TaskTracker, Cloudera Mgr Agent, Puppet Agent
Node5	DataNode, TaskTracker, Cloudera Mgr Agent, Puppet Agent
Node4	Standby JobTracker, Failover Controller, DataNode, TaskTracker, Oozie, Hive, Hue, ODI Agent, Cloudera Mgr Agent, Puppet Agent
Node3	**Active Job Tracker, Failover Controller, JournalNode, DataNode, TT, ZooKeeper, CM Server Agent, MySQL Master, Puppet Agent**
Node2	**Standby NameNode, TT, JournalNode, DataNode, ZooKeeper, Failover controller, MySQL backup Server, CM Agent, Puppet Agent**
Node1	**Active NameNode, TT, JournalNode, DataNode, ZooKeeper, Failover controller, Balancer, CM Agent, Puppet master & Agent**

FIGURE 5-9. *Oracle Big Data Appliance X3-2 Starter Rack software configuration*

The blank boxes shown in the upper half of Figure 5-9 represent the empty slots in a starter rack. These slots will be used to expand from six nodes to 12 and then to 18, until the rack reaches capacity. It's not possible to have both Hadoop and NoSQL on it due to the lower number of nodes. Two starter racks can be had, one running Hadoop only and the other running NoSQL DB only (see Figure 5-10).

Big Data Appliance X3-2 In-Rack Expansion (Six Nodes)

Oracle Big Data Appliance X3-2 In-Rack Expansion includes a set of six additional servers to expand the starter rack configuration to 12 nodes and then to a full rack of 18 nodes. It helps customers easily and cost-effectively scale their footprint as their data grows. This configuration does not contain a rack, it contains the nodes (or servers) only, which are supposed to be installed in the empty slots of a starter rack to expand it. It does not come with any switches, because the existing switches in a starter rack will be used.

Hardware Modifications to BDA

The minimal options to vary the BDA from standard hardware configurations are listed next.

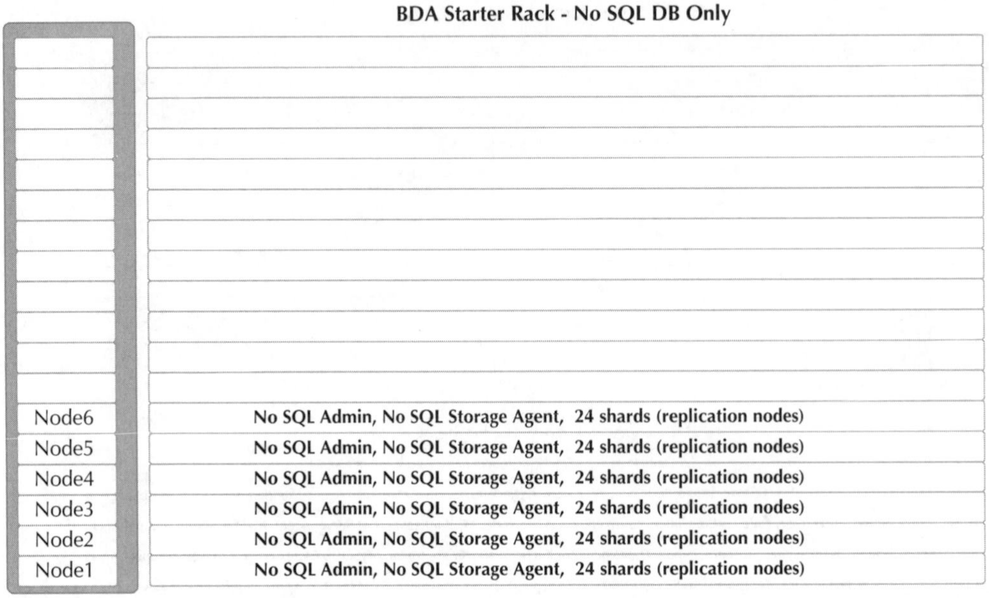

BDA Starter Rack - No SQL DB Only

Node6	No SQL Admin, No SQL Storage Agent, 24 shards (replication nodes)
Node5	No SQL Admin, No SQL Storage Agent, 24 shards (replication nodes)
Node4	No SQL Admin, No SQL Storage Agent, 24 shards (replication nodes)
Node3	No SQL Admin, No SQL Storage Agent, 24 shards (replication nodes)
Node2	No SQL Admin, No SQL Storage Agent, 24 shards (replication nodes)
Node1	No SQL Admin, No SQL Storage Agent, 24 shards (replication nodes)

FIGURE 5-10. *Oracle Big Data Appliance X3-2 Starter Rack software configuration—NoSQL DB only*

■ Four options for power distribution units (PDUs) for different country/region needs (single-phase or three-phase; low voltage or high voltage).

■ Customer-supplied option to swap Cisco switch with another 1U 48-port equivalent replacement of their own make/model.

■ Multiple BDAs can be connected together via InfiniBand to create a larger BDA configuration.

Oracle does not allow major changes to the BDA. If major changes are made, then the BDA would lose its "appliance"-like capabilities. These appliance benefits are explained in detail in Chapter 4 of this book.

Software Supported on Big Data Appliance X3-2

Following is the complete list of software that is included and supported on the Big Data Appliance. The latest versions of software will be used.

■ Oracle Linux

■ Java HotSpot Virtual Machine

- Cloudera's Distribution including Apache Hadoop

- Cloudera Manager

- Oracle Loader for Hadoop

- Oracle SQL Connector for Hadoop Distributed File System (OSCH)

- Oracle NoSQL Community Edition

- Oracle Data Integrator Agent

- Oracle R Connector for Hadoop

- R distribution

- Oracle Instant Client

- MySQL Database

Oracle Big Data Appliance Management Software

The software components are installed on all 18 servers in an Oracle Big Data Appliance rack. Oracle Linux, required drivers, firmware, and hardware verification utilities are factory installed. Among them are the following tools:

- Oracle Integrated Lights Out Manager (Oracle ILOM) consists of preinstalled, dedicated hardware and software that you can use to manage and monitor the servers and switches in an Oracle Big Data Appliance rack.

- The setup-root-ssh utility sets up passwordless SSH for the root user among all the servers in an Oracle Big Data Appliance rack.

- The DCLI utility executes commands across a group of servers on Oracle Big Data Appliance and returns the output.

- The bdacheckcluster utility checks the health of the cluster.

- The bdacheckib utility checks the private InfiniBand network.

- The bdachecknet utility checks the network configuration.

- The iblinkinfo utility lists the connections in the InfiniBand network.

- The listlinkup utility identifies the active Ethernet ports.

- The showvlan utility lists the virtual local area networks (VLANs) configured on a Sun Network QDR InfiniBand Gateway switch.

- The showvnics utility lists the virtual network interface cards (VNICs) created on a Sun Network QDR InfiniBand Gateway switch.

■ The bdaupdatefw utility updates the firmware. This should only be used if a disk or memory module has been replaced with one with an older firmware version.

■ All end-user software is installed on-site using the Mammoth utility.

BDA Install and Configuration Process

The BDA uses an efficient and error-proof process for installation. Installation and configuration of BDA is done using these two utilities:

■ BDA configuration

■ Mammoth

The BDA configuration utility is implemented as a series of spreadsheets (this will change in the near/medium future to a Java application). These spreadsheets can be found along with the documentation on BDA from Oracle. Once these spreadsheets have been filled out based on the customer-specific use case, then the utility validates the information entered and if the information is found correct, generates three files. The Mammoth utility installs and configures the software on Oracle Big Data Appliance using the files generated by the Oracle Big Data Appliance Configuration utility.

The Oracle Big Data Appliance Configuration utility generates the following files[3] to use when you configure the system. They are stored in a directory named *cluster_name-customer_name/rack_name*, such as bda-Example Inc/bda1. These files are automatically generated and are sensitive, so customers are advised not to edit these files directly, because that would lead to install issues, and it will then be difficult to find the root cause of those issues.

■ **BdaDeploy.json**   Contains the network configuration, which is used to configure the administrative network and the private InfiniBand network.

■ **BdaExpansion.json**   Contains the network configuration for one or two expansion kits. It contains information about all the servers, but no information about the switches and PDUs.

■ **mammoth-*rack_name*.params**   Contains all information for a server group provided in the spreadsheet, including the network configuration, port numbers, default user names, and passwords. The spreadsheet creates a separate parameter file for each cluster. If several clusters are being configured, then each parameter file is located in a separate subdirectory named config/cluster_name.

---

[3] Oracle Big Data Appliance Owner's Guide Release 2 (2.1) E36962-04, page 53

- ■ ***rack_name*-bda-install-template.pdf**   Reproduces the Installation Preview page of the spreadsheet in a printable format. The network administrator and others can use this Installation Template to verify the settings and make any last-minute corrections.

- ■ ***rack_name*-hosts**   Lists the IP addresses and domains for all hosts on all networks:

  - ■ Servers on the public (client) network

  - ■ Servers on the administrative network

  - ■ Servers on the private (InfiniBand) network

  - ■ Oracle ILOMs on the administrative network

  - ■ Switches and PDUs on the administrative network

- ■ ***rack_name*-preinstall-checkip.sh**   Runs a series of tests to ensure that the specified names and IP addresses for Oracle Big Data Appliance were added correctly to the name server, and they do not conflict with the existing network configuration.

Software components are classified into two categories on the BDA based on when they are installed:

- ■ Base Image software

- ■ Mammoth installation software

The Base Image software is installed in the factory prior to delivery, and the Mammoth installation software is installed at the customer site after delivery, based on the information entered in the BDA configuration utility.

The Base Image software consists of the following components:

- ■ Oracle Linux

- ■ Java HotSpot Virtual Machine

- ■ Oracle R Distribution

- ■ MySQL Server Advanced Edition

- ■ Puppet, firmware, utilities

The Mammoth installation software includes

- ■ Cloudera's Distribution including Apache Hadoop (CDH)

- ■ Cloudera Manager Enterprise

- ■ Oracle Database Instant Client

- Oracle NoSQL Database Community Edition (optional, no license required)

- Oracle Big Data Connectors (optional, requires a license):

  - Oracle SQL Connector for Hadoop Distributed File System (HDFS)

  - Oracle Loader for Hadoop

  - Oracle Data Integrator Agent

  - Oracle R Connector for Hadoop

NOTE
By default a BDA installation installs NoSQL DB Community Edition, which is open source and not supported by Oracle Support. NoSQL DB Enterprise Edition comes with support from Oracle, and it can be installed on the BDA. A license needs to be purchased from Oracle separately.

Critical and Noncritical Nodes

Critical services including the NameNode service and the JobTracker service are required for the cluster to operate normally and provide all services to users. Active and standby critical nodes are responsible for providing these services. If both the active and standby nodes fail, the cluster will suffer a loss of service. The cluster can continue to operate with no loss of service when a noncritical node fails.

The critical services are installed initially on the first four nodes of the primary rack. Table 5-1 identifies the critical services that run on these nodes. The remaining

Node Name	Node Position	Critical Functions
Active NameNode	Node01	Active NameNode, JournalNode, DataNode, ZooKeeper, Failover controller, Balancer, CM Agent, Puppet Master, and Agent
Standby NameNode	Node02	Standby NameNode, JournalNode, DataNode, ZooKeeper, Failover controller, MySQL Backup Server, CM Agent, Puppet Agent
Active JobTracker Node	Node03	Active Job Tracker, JournalNode, DataNode, TaskTracker, ZooKeeper, Failover Controller, CM Server Agent, MySQL Master, Puppet Agent
Standby JobTracker Node	Node04	Standby JobTracker, Failover Controller, Hue, Hive, Oozie, ODI Agent, DataNode, TaskTracker, Cloudera Mgr Agent, Puppet Agent

TABLE 5-1. *Critical Nodes*

nodes (initially node05 to node18) only run noncritical services. If a hardware failure occurs on one of the critical nodes, then the services can be moved to another, noncritical server. For example, if node02 fails, its critical services might be moved to node05. Table 5-1 provides names to identify the nodes providing critical services.

Moving a critical node requires that all clients be reconfigured with the address of the new node. The other alternative is to wait for the repair of the failed server. You must weigh the loss of services against the inconvenience of reconfiguring the clients.

Automatic Failover of the NameNode

The NameNode is the most critical process because it keeps track of the location of all data. Without a healthy NameNode, the entire cluster fails. Apache Hadoop v0.20.2 and earlier are vulnerable to failure because they have a single NameNode. There was a node called "Secondary NameNode," but it did not take over the duties of the primary NameNode in case the primary NameNode failed. By its name, it gives a sense that it's a backup for the NameNode, but in reality it's not. The function of the secondary NameNode was to merge the fsimage and the edits log files periodically and keep the edits log size within a limit. It's just a helper node for NameNode. That's why it's also known as CheckPoint node.

In clusters that are used exclusively for ETL or batch-processing workflows, a brief HDFS outage may not have immediate business impact on an organization; however, in the past few years we have seen HDFS begin to be used for more interactive workloads or, in the case of HBase, used to directly serve customer requests in real time. In cases such as this, an HDFS outage will immediately impact the productivity of internal users, and perhaps result in downtime visible to external users. For these reasons, adding high availability (HA) to the HDFS NameNode became one of the top priorities for the HDFS community.

The goal of the HA NameNode project is to add support for deploying two NameNodes in an active/passive configuration. This is a common configuration for highly available distributed systems, and HDFS's architecture lends itself well to this design. Even in a non-HA configuration, HDFS already requires both a NameNode and another node (Secondary NameNode) with similar hardware specs, which performs checkpointing operations for the NameNode. The design of the HA NameNode is such that the passive NameNode is capable of performing this checkpointing role, thus requiring no additional Hadoop server machines beyond what HDFS already requires.

The HA NameNode project that was included in Hadoop 2.0 maintains redundant NameNodes as shown in Figure 5-11. The data is replicated during normal operation as follows:

1. CDH maintains redundant NameNodes on the first two nodes. One of the NameNodes is in active mode, and the other NameNode is in hot standby mode. If the active NameNode fails, then the role of active NameNode automatically fails over to the standby NameNode.

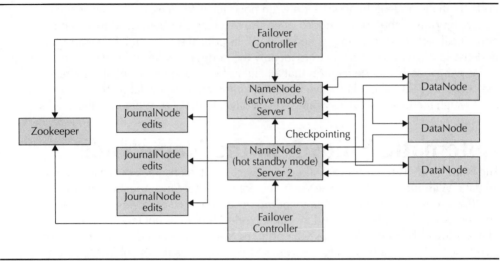

FIGURE 5-11. *Automatic failover of the NameNode on Oracle Big Data Appliance[4]*

2. On the BDA, the NameNode data is written to a mirrored partition so that the loss of a single disk can be tolerated. This mirroring is done at the factory as part of the operating system installation.

3. The active NameNode records all changes in at least two JournalNode processes, which the standby NameNode reads. There are three JournalNodes, which run on node01 to node03.

NOTE
Oracle Big Data Appliance 2.0 and later releases do not support the use of an external NFS filer for backups.

BDA Disk Storage Layout

Each node on the BDA has 12 physical disks of 3TB capacity each. Table 5-2 shows how the 12 disks are used when all nodes in a rack are dedicated to Hadoop. Disks 1 and 2 are used for the Operating System and possibly additional applications or files can be placed on the remaining 5TB of space.

In an 18-node full rack, if you chose 3 nodes for NoSQL DB and 15 nodes for Hadoop, then you get 3 nodes dedicated to NoSQL DB consisting of one node per disk for a total of 12 shards. Then the remaining 15 servers in a full rack BDA would be dedicated to Hadoop/HDFS. If you decide you want 6 servers dedicated to NoSQL DB, you'll get 24 shards. The storage layout for NoSQL DB with 3 dedicated nodes will look like the example shown in Figure 5-12.

---

[4]Oracle Big Data Appliance Software User's Guide Release 2 (2.1) E36963-03, page 27

Disks	Description
1 and 2	150 gigabytes (GB) physical and logical partition, mirrored to create two copies, with the Linux operating system
	All installed software
	NameNode data
	MySQL Database data
	The NameNode and MySQL Database data are replicated on two servers for a total of four copies
	2.8 terabytes (TB) HDFS data partition
3 to 13	Single HDFS partition

TABLE 5-2. *BDA Storage Layout—When Using HDFS Only*

Standard Disk Drive Mappings

Table 5-3 shows the mappings between the RAID logical drives and the operating system identifiers, and the dedicated function of each drive in an Oracle Big Data Appliance server.

Symbolic Link to Physical Slot	Initial Operating System Location	Dedicated Function
/dev/disk/by-hba-slot/s0	/dev/sda	Operating system
/dev/disk/by-hba-slot/s1	/dev/sdb	Operating system
/dev/disk/by-hba-slot/s2	/dev/sdc	HDFS
/dev/disk/by-hba-slot/s3	/dev/sdd	HDFS
/dev/disk/by-hba-slot/s4	/dev/sde	HDFS
/dev/disk/by-hba-slot/s5	/dev/sdf	HDFS
/dev/disk/by-hba-slot/s6	/dev/sdg	HDFS
/dev/disk/by-hba-slot/s7	/dev/sdh	HDFS
/dev/disk/by-hba-slot/s8	/dev/sdi	HDFS
/dev/disk/by-hba-slot/s9	/dev/sdj	HDFS
/dev/disk/by-hba-slot/s10	/dev/sdk	HDFS
/dev/disk/by-hba-slot/s11	/dev/sdl	HDFS

TABLE 5-3. *Mapping Between RAID Logical Drives and the Dedicated Function of Each Drive per Node*

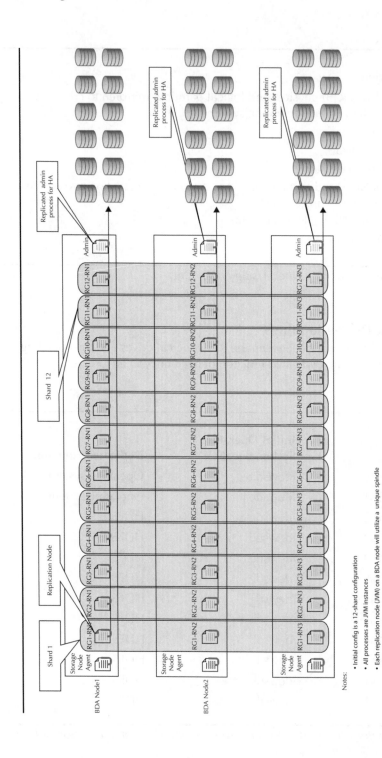

FIGURE 5-12. Dedicated NoSQL DB nodes storage layout

Symbolic Link to Physical Slot and Partition	HDFS Partition	Mount Point
/dev/disk/by-hba-slot/s0p4	/dev/sda4	/u01
/dev/disk/by-hba-slot/s1p4	/dev/sdb4	/u02
/dev/disk/by-hba-slot/s2p1	/dev/sdc1	/u03
/dev/disk/by-hba-slot/s3p1	/dev/sdd1	/u04
/dev/disk/by-hba-slot/s4p1	/dev/sde1	/u05
/dev/disk/by-hba-slot/s5p1	/dev/sdf1	/u06
/dev/disk/by-hba-slot/s6p1	/dev/sdg1	/u07
/dev/disk/by-hba-slot/s7p1	/dev/sdh1	/u08
/dev/disk/by-hba-slot/s8p1	/dev/sdi1	/u09
/dev/disk/by-hba-slot/s9p1	/dev/sdj1	/u10
/dev/disk/by-hba-slot/s10p1	/dev/sdk1	/u11
/dev/disk/by-hba-slot/s11p1	/dev/sdl1	/u12

TABLE 5-4. *Mappings Between HDFS Partitions and Mount Points*

Standard Mount Points

Table 5-4[5] shows the mappings between HDFS partitions and mount points.

Adding Storage to a Hadoop Cluster

Hadoop is designed for directly attached disks, and you scale both compute and storage at the same time by adding nodes into the Hadoop cluster. You don't add storage by itself. SAN or NAS devices are typically not added to Hadoop clusters to scale storage.

Hadoop-Only Config and Hadoop+NoSQL DB

The amount of usable storage on a BDA rack depends on the software configuration. There are two possible methods of configuring a BDA full rack, which affect storage capacity and also service configuration per node:

■ Hadoop and NoSQL DB: Use the BDA Rack for both HDFS and NoSQL DB

■ Hadoop/HDFS only

[5] Oracle Big Data Appliance Owner's Guide Release 2 (2.1) E36962-04, page 140

Currently, it is not supported to have a NoSQL DB Only appliance, meaning you cannot dedicate all of the storage on a full rack BDA to NoSQL DB. The appliance has to have Hadoop/HDFS along with NoSQL DB nodes.

This configuration choice is made while completing the spreadsheets of the BDA configuration utility. There are two questions in the BDA configuration utility that determine if NoSQL DB will be installed and if YES, how many nodes will be dedicated to NOSQL DB. The questions are

- Question 1: Install Oracle NoSQL Database Community Edition?

- Question 2: Total # of nodes to allocate for Oracle NoSQL Database?

If you choose NO for the first question, then no nodes are allocated to NoSQL DB and the BDA becomes a "Hadoop/HDFS" only appliance. If you choose YES for the first question, then you have to choose the number of nodes to be dedicated to NoSQL DB. The answer to the second question can *only* be in multiples of 3, because the minimum configuration of NoSQL DB is 3 nodes. If you choose 3, then you get 3 nodes dedicated to NoSQL DB consisting of 1 node per disk for a total of 12 shards. Then the remaining 15 servers in a full rack BDA would be dedicated to Hadoop/HDFS. If you decide you want 6 servers dedicated to NoSQL DB, you'll get 24 shards. Now the BDA becomes a "Hadoop and NoSQL DB" appliance. In the case of starter rack, you cannot configure it as a Hadoop+NoSQL DB appliance, because there are only 6 nodes in a starter rack and that's not sufficient to run both. The specifics of each type of appliance are explained in the following sections.

Hadoop-Only Appliance

In this configuration NoSQL DB will not be installed, so all of the nodes in a BDA full rack will be configured for HDFS as shown in Figure 5-13.

A full rack BDA has 18 nodes with 12 disks of 3TB each. So the raw storage capacity is 648TB. By default, Hadoop's replication factor for data is 3, so this reduces the usable capacity to 216TB. For the first rack, you typically will not use the 4 master nodes (Node 1, 2, 3, and 4) as Hadoop data nodes. So the usable storage for HDFS on the first BDA rack in a cluster will be 168TB (with replication 3).

Hadoop and NoSQL DB

In this configuration, the nodes in the BDA will be configured dedicated for Hadoop or NoSQL DB. For a full rack a typical configuration will be 15 nodes of Hadoop and 3 nodes of NoSQL DB. The services that will run on each node will be as shown in Figure 5-14. NoSQL storage is different from Hadoop storage and does *not* leverage HDFS for its storage system.

BDA Full Rack - Hadoop only

Node18	DataNode, TaskTracker, Cloudera Mgr Agent, Puppet Agent
Node17	DataNode, TaskTracker, Cloudera Mgr Agent, Puppet Agent
Node16	DataNode, TaskTracker, Cloudera Mgr Agent, Puppet Agent
Node15	DataNode, TaskTracker, Cloudera Mgr Agent, Puppet Agent
Node14	DataNode, TaskTracker, Cloudera Mgr Agent, Puppet Agent
Node13	DataNode, TaskTracker, Cloudera Mgr Agent, Puppet Agent
Node12	DataNode, TaskTracker, Cloudera Mgr Agent, Puppet Agent
Node11	DataNode, TaskTracker, Cloudera Mgr Agent, Puppet Agent
Node10	DataNode, TaskTracker, Cloudera Mgr Agent, Puppet Agent
Node9	DataNode, TaskTracker, Cloudera Mgr Agent, Puppet Agent
Node8	DataNode, TaskTracker, Cloudera Mgr Agent, Puppet Agent
Node7	DataNode, TaskTracker, Cloudera Mgr Agent, Puppet Agent
Node6	DataNode, TaskTracker, Cloudera Mgr Agent, Puppet Agent
Node5	DataNode, TaskTracker, Cloudera Mgr Agent, Puppet Agent
Node4	Standby JobTracker, Failover Controller, Hue, Hive, Oozie, ODI Agent, DataNode, TaskTracker, Cloudera Mgr Agent, Puppet Agent
Node3	Active Job Tracker, JournalNode, DataNode, TaskTracker, ZooKeeper, Failover Controller, CM Server Agent, MySQL Master, Puppet Agent
Node2	Standby NameNode, JournalNode, DataNode, ZooKeeper, Failover controller, MySQL backup Server, CM Agent, Puppet Agent
Node1	Active NameNode, JournalNode, DataNode, ZooKeeper, Failover controller, Balancer, CM Agent, Puppet Master & Agent

FIGURE 5-13. *BDA Full Rack—Hadoop only*

Checking for Use by Oracle NoSQL Database

Oracle Big Data Appliance can be configured to allocate the last 0, 1, or 2 disks for the exclusive use of Oracle NoSQL Database. HDFS data does not reside on the same disks.

To find out which disks are being used by Oracle NoSQL Database in a BDA full rack:

1. Open an SSH connection to the first server in the rack and log in as the root user.

2. Obtain the value of NOSQLDB_DISKS from the mammoth-*rack_name*. params configuration file:

   ```
   # cat /opt/oracle/BDAMammoth/mammoth-rackname.params | grep NOSQL
   ```

3. Use the value of NOSQLDB_DISKS to determine whether the replacement disk is allocated to Oracle NoSQL Database:

   ■ 0: No disks are allocated to Oracle NoSQL Database.

   ■ 1: The /dev/sdl disk is allocated to Oracle NoSQL Database.

   ■ 2: The /dev/sdk and /dev/sdl disks are allocated to Oracle NoSQL Database.

BDA Full Rack - Hadoop+No SQL

Node18	No SQL Admin, No SQL Storage Agent, 12 shards (replication nodes)
Node17	No SQL Admin, No SQL Storage Agent, 12 shards (replication nodes)
Node16	No SQL Admin, No SQL Storage Agent, 12 shards (replication nodes)
Node15	DataNode, TaskTracker, Cloudera Mgr Agent, Puppet Agent
Node14	DataNode, TaskTracker, Cloudera Mgr Agent, Puppet Agent
Node13	DataNode, TaskTracker, Cloudera Mgr Agent, Puppet Agent
Node12	DataNode, TaskTracker, Cloudera Mgr Agent, Puppet Agent
Node11	DataNode, TaskTracker, Cloudera Mgr Agent, Puppet Agent
Node10	DataNode, TaskTracker, Cloudera Mgr Agent, Puppet Agent
Node9	DataNode, TaskTracker, Cloudera Mgr Agent, Puppet Agent
Node8	DataNode, TaskTracker, Cloudera Mgr Agent, Puppet Agent
Node7	DataNode, TaskTracker, Cloudera Mgr Agent, Puppet Agent
Node6	DataNode, TaskTracker, Cloudera Mgr Agent, Puppet Agent
Node5	DataNode, TaskTracker, Cloudera Mgr Agent, Puppet Agent
Node4	Standby JobTracker, Failover Controller, Hue, Hive, Oozie, ODI Agent, DataNode, TaskTracker, Cloudera Mgr Agent, Puppet Agent
Node3	Active Job Tracker, JournalNode, DataNode, TaskTracker, ZooKeeper, Failover Controller, CM Server Agent, MySQL Master, Puppet Agent
Node2	Standby NameNode, JournalNode, DataNode, ZooKeeper, Failover controller, MySQL backup Server, CM Agent, Puppet Agent
Node1	Active NameNode, JournalNode, DataNode, ZooKeeper, Failover controller, Balancer, CM Agent, Puppet Master & Agent

FIGURE 5-14.   *BDA Full Rack—Hadoop+NoSQL DB*

4. To verify that the disks are part of a logical volume, you can run either pvscan or pvdisplay. All disks allocated for use by Oracle NoSQL Database are presented to it as a single logical volume named lvg1.

5. The following commands[6] verify that /dev/sdl1 is part of lvg1:

```
# pvscan
.
.
.
PV /dev/sdl1 VG lvg1 lvm2 [1.82 TB / 93.09 GB free]
Total: 1 [1.82 TB] / in use: 1 [1.82 TB] / in no VG: 0 [0
]
# pvdisplay
--- Physical volume ---
PV Name /dev/sdl1
VG Name lvg1
.
```

---

[6] Oracle Big Data Appliance Owner's Guide Release 2 (2.1) E36962-04, page 146

Memory Options

To add memory to a BDA, a customer can either choose to upgrade a few nodes (typically the name nodes for the Hadoop cluster) or all nodes in the Hadoop cluster. Typical memory upgrades would move a node from 64GB to 128GB (add 8 × 8GB DIMMs) or to 256GB (16 × 16GB DIMMs). The customer can upgrade to nonsymmetrical memory configurations, but Oracle does not recommend this. The maximum memory per node is 512GB. The procedure to add memory to a BDA node is explained in the BDA Owners guide.[7]

Deployment Architectures

A new system being introduced into the Data center has to integrate well with existing systems. This is a critical requirement in today's complex architectures, where Enterprise Data management is key. The Oracle BDA has been designed with these capabilities in mind. This section discusses the "deployment architectures" of the BDA in different customer situations. Each customer has unique requirements in terms of deploying the Oracle BDA; the requirements vary based on usage of Hadoop clusters.

Multitenancy and Hadoop in the Cloud

For the purpose of this book, we define *multitenancy* as the ability to deploy, co-locate, or co-host multiple Hadoop clusters or applications within the same BDA cluster, where different deployments may have different security and resource requirements and/or distinct sets of end users.

Traditionally, each organization has its own private set of computer resources that have sufficient capacity to meet the organization's SLA under peak or near-peak conditions. This generally leads to poor average utilization and the overhead of managing multiple independent clusters, one per each organization. Sharing clusters between organizations is a cost-effective manner of running large Hadoop installations since this allows them to reap benefits of economies of scale without creating private clusters. However, organizations are concerned about sharing a cluster because they are worried about others using the resources that are critical for their SLAs. Right now it takes a significant upfront investment in hardware and IT know-how to provision the hardware and the necessary IT admin skills to configure and manage a full-blown Hadoop cluster for any significant operation. Cloud services like Amazon Elastic Map Reduce will help reduce some of this, but they can quickly become costly if you need to do seriously heavy processing and especially if you need to manage data in HDFS as opposed to constantly moving it between your HDFS cluster and S3 in order to shut down data nodes to save cost, as is the standard with Amazon EMR. Utilities like Whirr

---

[7] Oracle Big Data Appliance Owner's Guide Release 2 (2.1) E36962-04, page 136

also help push the infrastructure management onto the EC2 cloud, but again, for serious data processing this can quickly become cost-prohibitive.

Hadoop already has various capacity management scheduling algorithms, but what is needed is higher-order resources management that can fully isolate between different organizations for security and data processing purposes to support true multitenant capability.

Hadoop jobs consist of a number of map and reduce tasks. These tasks run in slots on the nodes on the cluster. Each node is configured with a number of map slots and reduce slots based on its computational resources (typically one slot per core). The role of the scheduler is to assign tasks to any slots that are free.

Types of Schedulers

There are three types of schedulers:

- FIFO
- Fair Share
- Capacity

FIFO is the default scheduler, First In First Out. It does support job priorities; however, all work in each queue is processed before moving on to the next.

Fair Share scheduler organizes jobs into pools, unlike Hadoop's built-in FIFO scheduler; Fair Share scheduler lets small jobs make progress even if a large job is running, without starving the large job. It supports job priorities.

The Capacity scheduler assigns jobs to queues. Queue resource capacity can be configured, resource-based scheduling can be done, and it also supports job priorities.

It is designed to allow sharing a large cluster while giving each organization a minimum capacity guarantee. The central idea is that the available resources in the Hadoop MapReduce cluster are partitioned among multiple organizations that collectively fund the cluster based on computing needs. There is an added benefit that an organization can access any excess capacity not being used by others. This provides elasticity for the organizations in a cost-effective manner.

Which Scheduler to Use?

Use the Fair Share scheduler or Capacity scheduler rather than the FIFO scheduler. This allows you to provide SLAs and guaranteed resource availability to tenants appropriately. Using the FIFO scheduler runs the risk of blocking a small or critical job with an enormous ad-hoc job. Which scheduler you use depends on what features you want and what makes sense to you. They both have their pros and cons, but both are production quality. Establish appropriate users and groups and plan data layout based on required privileges. Unlike with relational databases, you do not get fine-grained privilege systems in Hadoop. The layout of files and directories dictates privileges and delegation. Have a known, documented directory structure where users can infer intentions based on where datasets live. This helps users understand what directories and datasets are considered ephemeral and what's guaranteed to persist indefinitely. Enable Kerberos security to ensure that people are who they say they are, if that's necessary in your environment. Document data retention policies and attach policies to directory trees; for example, all data under /user/<username> older than 180 days is pruned. Understand who's doing what, when, what resources they're consuming, and so on by using a solid monitoring mechanism.

Multitenant clusters provide many benefits due to sharing few centrally managed clusters instead of a siloed approach; however, sharing clusters does create some complexities.

There are several reasons to provide the capability of carving out multiple clusters from a single BDA. Development and testing environments are always needed; their resource (CPU cores/Memory/disk) needs are much smaller than those of a full rack BDA and are required to be isolated from the production environment. Hence Oracle has provided the capability to be able to configure multiple Hadoop clusters within a single rack of BDA as of Big Data Appliance Release 2 (2.1). Using this capability, an 18-node BDA rack can be split into three clusters of six nodes each.

Scalability

It is very easy to grow a Hadoop cluster using BDAs. Oracle Big Data Appliance deployments can be scaled by interconnecting multiple BDA systems. In addition to upgrading within a rack, multiple racks can be connected using the integrated InfiniBand fabric to form even larger configurations; up to 18 racks can be connected in a nonblocking manner by connecting InfiniBand cables without the need for any external switches (see Figure 5-15). Larger nonblocking configurations are supported with additional external InfiniBand switches, and larger blocking network configurations can be supported without additional switches. When expanding the number of nodes in the system, the software can be automatically configured to suit the requirements. New nodes can either form a separate Hadoop cluster, or can be automatically added into an already existing Hadoop cluster.

Big Data Appliance Full Rack can be configured as a single cluster as well as a set of clusters. The supported cluster sizes are a split of 6 and 12 nodes, a split of 9 and 9 nodes, or a split of 6, 6, and 6 nodes. Each of these clusters can grow by adding hardware and expanding the cluster separately with additional Big Data Appliances. The configuration can be grown in increments of full racks.

Furthermore, the Oracle Big Data Appliance can be connected to other Oracle engineered systems such as Exadata, Exalogic, or Exalytics using InfiniBand. At 40Gb/sec, InfiniBand provides more bandwidth as well as lower latency than Ethernet-connected systems. An example architecture of connecting a BDA rack to an Exadata rack is shown later in this chapter in Figure 5-18.

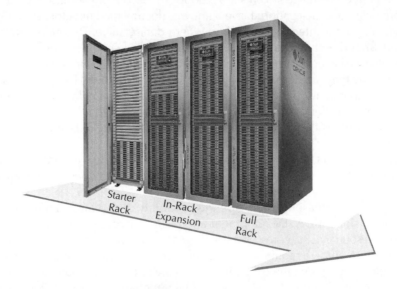

FIGURE 5-15. *Big Data Appliance internal network architecture*

Multirack BDA Considerations

When creating a multirack Hadoop cluster or providing access to Oracle Big Data Appliance from an Oracle Exadata Database machine, you must connect multiple racks to each other. Racks can be cabled together with no downtime.

During the cabling procedure, note the following:

■ There is some performance degradation while you are cabling the racks together. This degradation results from reduced network bandwidth, and the data retransmission due to packet loss when a cable is unplugged.

■ The environment is not a high-availability environment because one leaf switch must be off. All traffic goes through the remaining leaf switch.

■ Only the existing rack is operational, and any new rack is powered down.

■ The software running on the systems must not have problems related to InfiniBand restarts.

- The new racks must be configured with the appropriate IP addresses to be migrated into the expanded system before any cabling, and duplicate IP addresses are not allowed.

- The existing spine switch is set to priority 10 during the cabling procedure. This setting gives the spine switch a higher priority than any other switch in the network fabric. The spine switch is first to take the Subnet Manager Master role whenever a new Subnet Manager Master is set during the cabling procedure.

Installing Other Software on the BDA

Various components can be added onto BDA as long as they are compatible with underlying versions. Because BDA allocates the disks to HDFS and possibly NoSQL DB, additional components typically run on top of these storage systems. Examples are Apache Giraph, Apache Hama, and other Apache projects. For NoSQL DB, an example could be Blueprint (https://blogs.oracle.com/datawarehousing/entry/blueprints_for_oracle_nosql_database).

Customers can load additional software on Oracle Big Data Appliance servers. Oracle does not support questions or issues with the nonstandard modules. If a server fails, and Oracle suspects that the failure may have been caused by a nonstandard module, then Oracle Support may refer the customer to the vendor of the nonstandard module or ask that the issue be reproduced without the nonstandard module. Modifying the server operating system other than by applying official patches and upgrades is not supported. InfiniBand-related packages must always be maintained at the officially supported release.

BDA in the Data Center

To deploy Oracle Big Data Appliance, ensure that your network meets the minimum requirements. Oracle Big Data Appliance uses three networks. Each network must be on a distinct and separate subnet from the others. The following sections explain the network descriptions.

Administrative Network

This 1-gigabit Ethernet (GbE) network connects to your existing administrative network and is used to administer all components of Oracle Big Data Appliance. It connects the servers, Oracle ILOM, and switches connected to the Ethernet switch in the rack.

There are two uplinks to the administrative network:

■ From the Ethernet switch in the rack

■ From the KVM switch in the rack (Sun Fire X4270 M2-based racks only)

Each server has two network interfaces for administration. One provides administrative access to the operating system through the eth0 Ethernet interface, and the other provides access to the Integrated Lights Out Manager through the Oracle ILOM Ethernet interface. Oracle Big Data Appliance is delivered with the eth0 and ILOM interfaces connected to the Ethernet switch on the rack. Do not use the eth0 interface on the servers for client network traffic. Cabling or configuration changes to these interfaces are not permitted.

Domain Name System (DNS) servers are not required on the administrative network, although Oracle Big Data Appliance uses them if they are available. At least one Network Time Protocol (NTP) server must also be available. The NTP server for the administrative network can be different from the NTP server for the client network.

Client Access Network

This 10GbE network connects the servers through the gateway switches to your existing client network and is used for client access to the servers. Client applications access the software through this network by using the client network host names of the servers.

There are two Sun Network QDR InfiniBand Gateway switches in the rack. Each switch supports 1 to 8 connections for client access for a total of up to 16 client network connections. For failover, you must have at least one connection from each switch and scale up according to your requirements for loading data and providing client access.

At least one DNS server must be accessible on the client network. At least one NTP server must also be available. The NTP server for the client network can be different from the NTP server for the administrative network.

InfiniBand Private Network

This network connects the servers by using the InfiniBand switches on the rack and the bondib0 interface. This nonroutable network is fully contained within Oracle Big Data Appliance and any other Oracle engineered systems that are connected to it with InfiniBand cables. This network does not connect to your existing network. It is automatically configured during installation.[8]

---

[8]Oracle Big Data Appliance Owner's Guide Release 2 (2.1) E36962-04, page 42

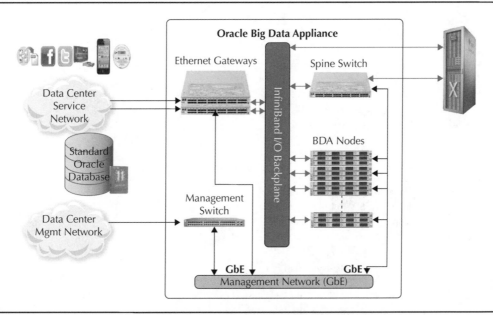

FIGURE 5-16. *Big Data Appliance internal network architecture*

The BDA utilizes 40Gb InfiniBand (shown in Figure 5-16). Ethernet connections are carried over InfiniBand. BDA server nodes are not individually connected to a 10Gb Ethernet infrastructure, but rather share connections provided through the Ethernet ports on the InfiniBand gateways.

Network Requirements

Before installation, network cables must run from your existing network infrastructure to the installation site. The requirements to connect Oracle Big Data Appliance to your existing network infrastructure are as follows:

- Management network connection requirements:
  - One 1Gbps Ethernet connection for the management switch in the rack
  - One 1Gbps Ethernet connection for the KVM switch in the rack (Sun Fire X4270 M2-based racks only)
- Client access network connection requirements:
  - Two (minimum) to 16 (maximum) 10Gbps Ethernet connections split between the two Sun Network QDR InfiniBand Gateway switches in the rack. The exact number of connections depends on your bandwidth requirements.

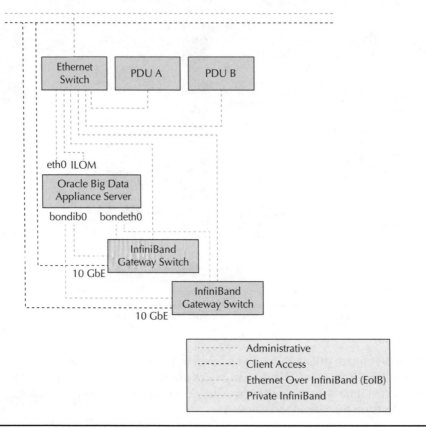

FIGURE 5-17. *Network diagram for a Sun Server X3-2L-based rack[9]*

The servers are configured on the network as follows (see Figure 5-17):

- **eth0**   Provides access to the operating system using the administrative network.

- **bondeth0**   Provides access to the server using the client access network.

- **ILOM**   Provides access to Oracle Integrated Lights Out Manager (ILOM) using the administrative network.

---

[9]Oracle Big Data Appliance Owner's Guide Release 2 (2.1) E36962-04, page 43

Connecting to Data Center LAN

BDA has two Gateway switches. These Gateway switches have 10Gb Ethernet to connect to the data center. This is considered the client network. If a customer does not have 10Gb Ethernet in their data center, it is possible to use a 1Gb to 10Gb switch.

Example Connectivity Architecture

Figure 5-18 illustrates how a BDA can be included into an existing architecture in the data center. The use case shown here consists of an existing Exadata. The data center does not support a 10GbE network. The BDA requires 10GbE to connect to a client network. Hence the switch "Sun Network 10 GbE Switch 72p" that supports both 10 GbE (or 40 GbE) and 1 GbE is being used between customer LAN and the BDA. A single 72p switch is shown here; for redundancy, two switches are recommended. The Exadata and BDA are interconnected using InfiniBand, in this example, 16 InfiniBand cables are connecting each Leaf switch to every Spine switch between the Exadata and BDA systems.

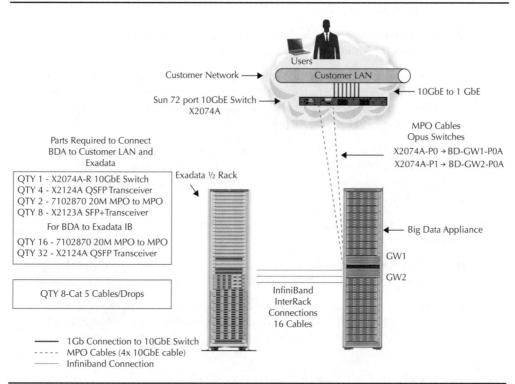

FIGURE 5-18.   *Interconnecting BDA to Data Center LAN and Exadata*

Oracle Big Data Appliance Restrictions on Use

The following restrictions apply to hardware and software modifications to Oracle Big Data Appliance. Violating these restrictions can result in the loss of warranty and support. This section draws heavily from the Oracle Big Data Appliance Owner's Guide.[10]

- Oracle Big Data Appliance hardware cannot be modified or customized, with three exceptions:

    - Replace the administrative 48-port Cisco 4948 Ethernet switch with an equivalent 1U 48-port Gigabit Ethernet switch that conforms to their internal data center network standards.

    - In a Sun Server X3-2L–based BDA rack, install a top-of-rack (TOR) switch that supports both 10 GbE (or 40 GbE) and 1 GbE, such as the Sun Network 10GbE Switch 72p, in rack slots 41 and 42. These slots are empty in the factory configuration.

    - Increase the memory per node from the default that Oracle Big Data Appliance X3-2 ships from the factory of 64GB to 512GB.

- Customers cannot update the firmware directly on Oracle Big Data Appliance servers. Oracle Big Data Appliance patches update the firmware of the server ILOM/BIOS, InfiniBand Host Channel Adapters (HCA), disk controller host bus adapters (HBA), and hard drives (HDD).

- The only exception is if the customer replaces a faulty server component (such as a disk drive) with a unit installed with firmware at a lower version than the faulty component. The upgrade must be performed using the bdaupdatefw utility.

- Customers can update the firmware of the other components of Oracle Big Data Appliance:

    - Customers can update the IOS and firmware versions on the Cisco 4948 Ethernet switch to meet their data center requirements.

    - Customers can update the firmware of the InfiniBand switches provided that they comply with the validated versions documented in My Oracle Support ID 1445762.2 and its related notes.

---

[10] Oracle Big Data Appliance Owner's Guide Release 2 (2.1) E36962-04, pages 24–26

- Customers can update the firmware of the power distribution units (PDUs) provided that they comply with the validated versions documented in My Oracle Support ID 1445762.2 and its related notes.

- Customers can update the firmware of the KVM switch and the KMM (keyboard, monitor, mouse) as needed (Sun Fire X4270 M2-based rack only).

- Customers can load additional software on Oracle Big Data Appliance servers. Oracle does not support questions or issues with the nonstandard modules. If a server fails, and Oracle suspects that the failure may have been caused by a nonstandard module, then Oracle Support may refer the customer to the vendor of the nonstandard module or ask that the issue be reproduced without the nonstandard module. Modifying the server operating system other than by applying official patches and upgrades is not supported. InfiniBand-related packages must always be maintained at the officially supported release.

- Customers can use Cloudera Manager to stop and start services, but cannot use it to move services from one server to another. The Hadoop services such as NameNode and JobTracker must remain on the servers where they were installed by the Mammoth utility.

- The network ports on the servers can connect to external non-Sun servers using Internet Small Computer System Interface (iSCSI) or Network File System (NFS) protocols. However, the Fibre Channel over Ethernet (FCoE) protocol is not supported.

- Only switches specified for use in Oracle Big Data Appliance, Oracle Exadata Database Machine, and Oracle Exalogic Elastic Cloud can be connected to the InfiniBand network. Connecting third-party switches and other switches not used in these engineered systems is not supported.

BDA Management and Monitoring

Hadoop, like most distributed systems, constitutes a monitoring challenge because the monitoring system must know about how the multiple services interact as a larger system. When monitoring HDFS, for example, we may want to see each daemon running, within normal memory consumption limits, responding to RPC requests in a defined window, and other "simple" metrics, but this doesn't tell us whether the entirety of the service is functional (although one may infer such things). Instead, it can be necessary to know that a certain percentage of data nodes are alive and communicating with the NameNode, or what the block distribution is across the cluster, to truly know the state of the system. Zooming in too close on a single daemon or host, or too far out on the cluster, can both be equally deceptive when trying to get a complete picture of performance or health of a service like HDFS.

Worse still, we want to know how MapReduce is performing on top of HDFS. Alert thresholds and performance data of MapReduce are inherently coupled to those of HDFS when services are stacked in this manner, making it difficult to detect the root cause of a failure across service and host boundaries. Existing tools are very good at identifying problems within localized systems (those with little to no external dependency), but require quite a bit of effort to understand the intricacies of distributed systems. These complexities make it difficult to ascertain the difference between a daemon being up and responding to basic checks and whether it is safe to walk away from a computer.

Hadoop has built-in support for exposing various metrics to outside systems. There are several open source tools available that represent these metrics in a graphical manner. Ganglia is a performance monitoring framework for distributed systems. Ganglia provides a distributed service that collects metrics on individual machines and forwards them to an aggregator, which can report back to an administrator on the global state of a cluster. Ganglia is designed to be integrated into other applications to collect statistics about their operation. While Ganglia will monitor Hadoop-specific metrics, general information about the health of the cluster should be monitored with an additional tool.

Nagios is a machine and service monitoring system designed for large clusters. Nagios will provide diagnostic information for tuning your cluster, including network, disk, and CPU utilization across machines.

The Big Data Appliance is designed to provide correlated end-to-end provisioning, monitoring, and management of hardware, software, and networking using a single monitoring tool. The Big Data Appliance plugin for Enterprise Manager delivers the first end-to-end management of the Hadoop cluster from hardware metrics to software and Hadoop metrics. To achieve the end-to-end management of the system, Enterprise Manager delivers all the system metrics users are accustomed to, using the Exadata plugin for Enterprise Manager. Enterprise Manager enables a seamless transition between the hardware and high-level software monitoring and the expanded Hadoop monitoring and diagnostics from Cloudera Manager. For Hadoop-related monitoring, EM enables a clickthrough into Cloudera Manager. This combination of functionality makes operations for a BDA simpler and allows operations staff to seamlessly switch between their Exadata, Big Data Appliance, and other Oracle engineered systems.

The Oracle Enterprise Manager Big Data Appliance plugin provides a common interface and leverages the following tools that are installed on the BDA to provide a deeper drill-down into various parts of the entire stack.

- Cloudera Manager

- Oracle Integrated Lights out Manager (ILOM)—Web and CLU interfaces

- Hadoop Monitoring Utilities—default Web GUI tools

- Hue
- Distributed Command Line Interface (DCLI)

The following sections provide a brief explanation of each of these utilities and its purpose.

Enterprise Manager

Using the Oracle Enterprise Manager Big Data Appliance plugin, you can

- Manage the hardware and software components that make up a Big Data Appliance Network as a single target or as individual targets (see Figure 5-19).
- Discover the components of a Big Data Appliance Network and add them as managed targets.

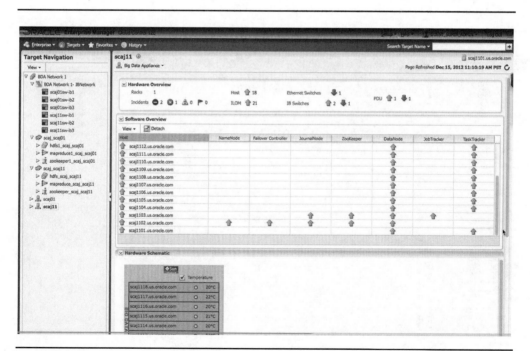

FIGURE 5-19. *Enterprise Manager can manage both BDA hardware and software.*

- Get a correlated view of Hadoop clusters and other systems that the Hadoop clusters are feeding or receiving data from, for example, Oracle Database or Exadata. (This is shown in Figure 5-20.)

- Study collected metrics to analyze the performance of the network and each Big Data Appliance component.

After selecting a target cluster, you can drill down into these key areas:

- **InfiniBand network**   Network topology and status for InfiniBand switches and ports

- **Hadoop cluster**   Software services for HDFS, MapReduce, ZooKeeper, Journal managers, TaskTrackers, and so on

- **Oracle Big Data Appliance rack**   Hardware status including server hosts, Oracle Integrated Lights Out Manager (Oracle ILOM) servers, power distribution units (PDUs), and the Ethernet switch

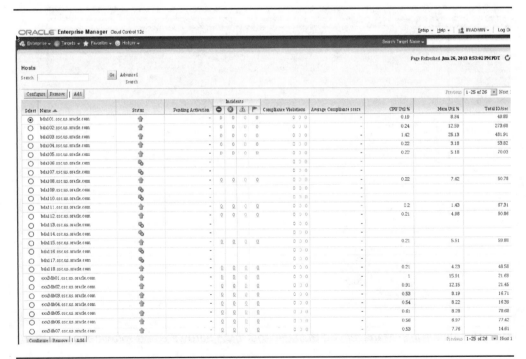

FIGURE 5-20.   *Correlated view of data being loaded into Oracle Database using Big Data Connectors from a BDA*

Cloudera Manager

Cloudera Manager is installed on Oracle Big Data Appliance to help you with Cloudera's Distribution including Apache Hadoop (CDH) operations. Cloudera Manager provides a single administrative interface to all Oracle Big Data Appliance servers configured as part of the Hadoop cluster.

Cloudera Manager simplifies the performance of these administrative tasks:

- Monitor jobs and services

- Start and stop services

- Manage security and Kerberos credentials

- Monitor user activity

- Monitor the health of the system

- Monitor performance metrics

- Track hardware use (disk, CPU, and RAM)

Cloudera Manager Server runs on the JobTracker node (node03) of the primary rack (BDA) and is available on port 7180. This is the default port. Cloudera Manager agents run on all the nodes of the BDA.

Cloudera Manager provides the interface for managing these services as shown in Figure 5-21:

- HDFS

- Hue

- MapReduce

- Oozie

- ZooKeeper

- Hive (since Cloudera Manager Version 4.5)

You can use Cloudera Manager to change the configuration of these services, stop, and restart them.

Hadoop Monitoring Utilities: Web GUI

Hadoop provides some basic tools by default for monitoring JobTracker and TaskTracker status. Users can monitor MapReduce jobs using these admin tools.

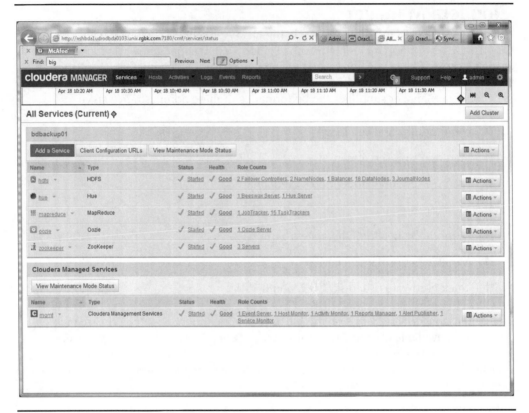

FIGURE 5-21. *Cloudera Manager Services Page*

Monitoring the JobTracker

Hadoop MapReduce Administration (see Figure 5-22) monitors the JobTracker, which runs on port 50030 of the JobTracker node (node03) on Oracle Big Data Appliance. In the example shown in Figure 5-22 the JobTracker service was running on hostname bda102.osc.us.oracle.com.

To monitor the JobTracker, open a browser and enter a URL like the following:

http://bda1node03.example.com:50030

In this example, bda1 is the name of the appliance, node03 is the name of the server, and 50030 is the default port number for Hadoop MapReduce Administration.

0.0.0.0 Hadoop Map/Reduce Administration - Mozilla Firefox

File Edit View History Bookmarks Tools Help

http://bda103.osc.us.oracle.com:50030/jobtracker.jsp

Most Visited ▾ Getting Started Latest Headlines ▾ Login - Oracle Enterp... Login - Cloudera Man... Hue Login 0.0.0.0 Hadoop Map/...

mapreduce - Cloudera Mana... ✖ 0.0.0.0 Hadoop Map/Reduce... ✖ ✚

0.0.0.0 Hadoop Map/Reduce Administration

State: RUNNING
Started: Fri Jun 14 13:47:57 PDT 2013
Version: 2.0.0-mr1-cdh4.2.0, Unknown
Compiled: Fri Feb 15 11:52:08 PST 2013 by jenkins from Unknown
Identifier: 201306141347

Cluster Summary (Heap Size is 86.17 MB/3.96 GB)

Running Map Tasks	Running Reduce Tasks	Total Submissions	Nodes	Occupied Map Slots	Occupied Reduce Slots	Reserved Map Slots	Reserved Reduce Slots	Map Task Capacity	Reduce Task Capacity	Avg.
0	80	17	15	0	80	0	0	180	90	18.0

Scheduling Information

Queue Name	State	Scheduling Information
default	running	N/A

Filter (Jobid, Priority, User, Name)
Example: 'user:smith 3200' will filter by 'smith' only in the user field and '3200' in all fields

Running Jobs

Jobid	Priority	User	Name	Map % Complete	Map Total	Maps Completed	Reduce % Complete	Reduce Total	Reduces Completed	Job Scheduling
job_201306141347_0017	NORMAL	oracle	IRI Hyper MR Harness - 1_queries/80week/xl/qs3	100.00%	480	480	68.12%	80	0	NA

Completed Jobs

Jobid	Priority	User	Name	Map % Complete	Map Total	Maps Completed	Reduce % Complete	Reduce Total	Reduces Completed	Job Scheduling
job_201306141347_0015	NORMAL	oracle	IRI Hyper MR Harness - 1_queries/80week/xl/qs3	100.00%	480	480	100.00%	80	80	NA
job_201306141347_0016	NORMAL	oracle	IRI Hyper MR Harness - 1_queries/80week/xl/qs3	100.00%	480	480	100.00%	80	80	NA

Retired Jobs

Jobid	Priority	User	Name	State	Start Time	Finish Time	Map % Complete	Reduce % Complete	J

FIGURE 5-22.   *Hadoop MapReduce Administration*

Monitoring the TaskTracker

The TaskTracker Status interface (see Figure 5-23) monitors the TaskTracker on a single node. It is available on port 50060 of all noncritical nodes (node04 to node18) in Oracle Big Data Appliance.

To monitor a TaskTracker, open a browser and enter the URL for a particular node like the following:

http://bda1node13.example.com:50060

In this example, bda1 is the name of the rack, node13 is the name of the server, and 50060 is the default port number for the TaskTracker Status interface.

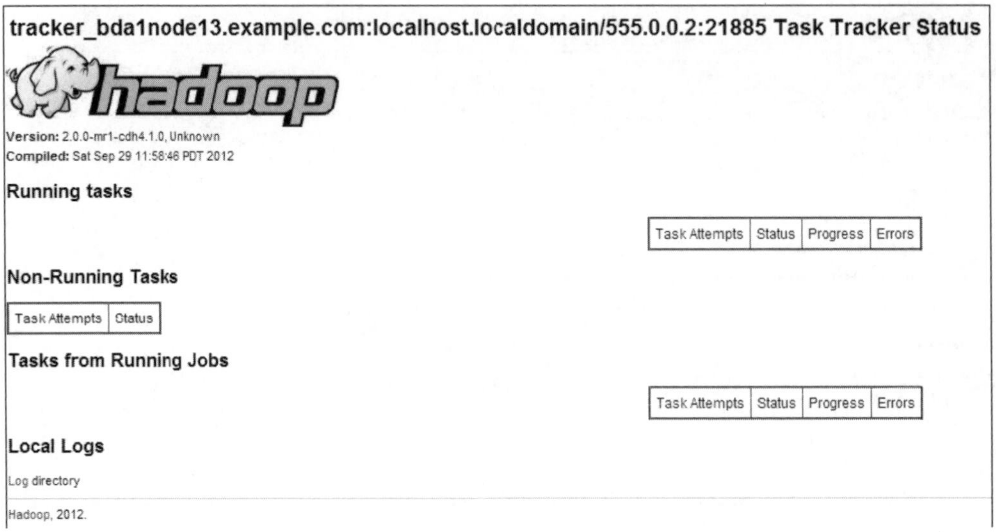

FIGURE 5-23. *TaskTracker status interface*

Oracle ILOM

Oracle Integrated Lights Out Manager (Oracle ILOM) provides advanced service processor (SP) hardware and software that you can use to manage and monitor the servers and switches in an Oracle Big Data Appliance rack. Oracle ILOM dedicated hardware and software is preinstalled on these components. It automatically initializes as soon as power is applied. Major parts of this section are taken from the Oracle Big Data Appliance Owner's Guide.[11]

Oracle ILOM enables you to actively manage and monitor servers in Oracle Big Data Appliance regardless of the operating system state, providing you with a reliable lights-out management (LOM) system.

With Oracle ILOM, you can proactively:

- Learn about hardware errors and faults as they occur

- Remotely control the power state of a server

- View the graphical and nongraphical consoles

- View the current status of sensors and indicators on the system

- Determine the hardware configuration of your system

- Receive generated alerts about system events in advance

---

[11] Oracle Big Data Appliance Owner's Guide Release 2 (2.1) E36962-04, Section 13

The Oracle ILOM service processor runs its own embedded operating system and has a dedicated Ethernet port, which together provide out-of-band management capability. In addition, you can access Oracle ILOM from the server operating system (Oracle Linux). Using Oracle ILOM, you can remotely manage Oracle Big Data Appliance as if you were using a local KVM.

Oracle ILOM Interfaces

Oracle ILOM supports two interfaces for accessing its features and functions. You can choose to use a browser-based Web interface or a command-line interface.

Web Interface   The Web interface enables you to use a browser to log in to the BDA server using the Service processor IP or the ILOM IP, and then perform system management and monitoring. Figure 5-24 shows the web interface of ILOM on a Oracle BDA X3-2 Server.

Command-Line Interface   The command-line interface (CLI) enables you to operate Oracle ILOM using keyboard commands. It adheres to industry-standard DMTF-style CLI and scripting protocols. Oracle ILOM supports SSH v2.0 and v3.0 for

FIGURE 5-24.   *Oracle ILOM Web interface on an Oracle Big Data Appliance X3-2 Server*

secure access to the CLI. From the CLI, you can reuse existing scripts and automate tasks using familiar interfaces.

Administrative Network Diagram

Figure 5-25 illustrates the administrative Oracle ILOM network. It shows two of the 18 servers and the two Sun Network QDR InfiniBand Gateway switches. The Cisco Ethernet management switch is connected to the servers and the InfiniBand switches.

Connecting to Oracle ILOM Using the Network

You can typically access Oracle ILOM using the network over an Ethernet connection. You must know the Oracle ILOM Ethernet address. Before system configuration, the address is the factory IP address setting. After system configuration, you can use either the component name or the IP address listed in the Installation Template. You can use either the CLI or the browser interface to access Oracle ILOM. Alternatively, you can launch a remote KVM session.

Hue

Hue runs in a browser and provides an easy-to-use interface to several applications to support interaction with Hadoop and HDFS. You can use Hue to perform any of the following tasks:

- Query Hive data stores

- Create, load, and delete Hive tables

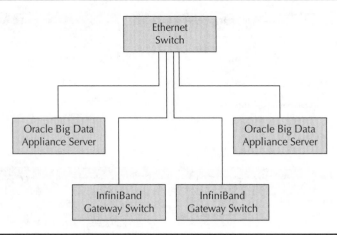

FIGURE 5-25. *Administrative network in Oracle Big Data Appliance*

- Work with HDFS files and directories

- Create, submit, and monitor MapReduce jobs

- Monitor MapReduce jobs

- Create, edit, and submit workflows using the Oozie dashboard

- Manage users and groups

Hue runs on port 8888 of the JobTracker node (node03) by default. A view of Hue is shown in Figure 5-26.

DCLI Utility

The DCLI utility allows you to execute commands on multiple Oracle Big Data Appliance servers in parallel. You can run the utility from any server. The DCLI utility can be run on the local server, and the commands specified in DCLI execute on the target servers. This allows administrative and monitoring tasks from one server for ease of management.

FIGURE 5-26.   *Hue*

CHAPTER
6

Integrating the Data Warehouse and Analytics Infrastructure to Big Data

B ig Data initiatives often start as experiments or research and development projects in IT or the lines of business to determine potential business value in analyzing such data.

Once the initial value of the solution is proven, organizations plan full-scale deployment and commonly include the existing data warehouse infrastructure as part of the Big Data infrastructure for several important reasons.

The data warehouse often serves as the home of the historic database of record within an organization. Existing, understood, and well-utilized business intelligence tools for reporting, querying, and analysis serve as the means for extracting business value from this database of record. The data warehouse is typically designed to facilitate navigation of the data by business analysts and to meet service level agreements (SLAs) for performance and availability. In addition, data warehouses based on a relational database provide levels of access and data security not achievable in a Hadoop cluster today. It should therefore come as no surprise that in organizations that have mature Hadoop clusters, data that is deemed valuable in Hadoop usually makes its way to the data warehouse.

We'll begin by describing the role of data warehouse and business intelligence infrastructure. We'll also look at how related Oracle products help complete the Big Data infrastructure. Finally, we'll revisit building out the infrastructure.

The Data Warehouse as a Historic Database of Record

Many organizations have established the need for a historic database of record, a place where data that dates back many years is available for historical reporting and for comparative analysis with current data. The timeframe the data represents and the granularity of the data available are often driven by legal compliance regulations and business analysis requirements. Historically, sources of such data have primarily come from relational databases, though other data sources are now becoming quite common. The kinds of reporting and analysis that occur in this historic database of record also lent themselves to deployment of a relational database.

When data is stored at its most granular level in the data warehouse, it is usually stored in what is called a *third normal form* (3NF) schema, designed to reduce data anomalies and redundancies. Such a 3NF schema generally serves as the basis of what is frequently described as an enterprise data warehouse. Of course, data in source systems that is to be loaded in the data warehouse is very often not consistently defined or validated. In such cases, the data must be cleansed or transformed when it is extracted from the sources and loaded into the target data warehouse. The need for this extraction, transformation, and loading (ETL) process gave rise to tools and utilities to define and interactively design the process, and generate code for the ETL scripts.

The data transformations can introduce time delays, also known as latency, during the ETL process. For near-real-time data feeds, replication solutions are sometimes selected as alternatives to ETL. However, these are intended to work primarily as store-and-forward mechanisms, so the key to such an approach is usually to ensure that data is clean and consistent at the source.

Data in 3NF is fine when business analysts are using reports that have been generated by an IT person familiar with this type of schema. However, for ad-hoc queries and drill-downs initiated by business analysts, the data should be presented in a more intuitive fashion for exploration. Initially, IT organizations built views on top of 3NF schema, but the maintenance of views proved to be problematic and difficult to modify in timely response to business requests. So the star schema emerged as an approach in data warehouses to enable business analysts to more easily navigate through the data themselves. A star schema stores the data in large transaction or fact tables and is surrounded by lookup or dimension tables. Today, most large-scale Oracle-based data warehouses are deployed as a hybrid mixture of 3NF for base data and star schema that include summary-level hierarchies.

The Oracle Database as a Data Warehouse

Oracle relational databases have served as "decision support systems," later called data warehouses, almost from their inception. In the mid-1990s, Oracle Parallel Server and Oracle7 became engines for terabyte-sized data warehouses. Today Oracle-based data warehouses have grown into the petabytes thanks to many further improvements in the Oracle Database and the introduction of engineered systems such as the Oracle Exadata Database Machine.

As organizations often rely on their historic database of record to make critical "just-in-time" business decisions, the data warehouse must exceed both high service levels for performance and demanding availability requirements. Oracle has addressed performance needs in the Oracle Database by providing increasing sophistication in its optimizer and improved self-tuning and management over the years. The Database feature list only continued to grow for supporting data warehousing workloads. Some of the key innovations introduced in the Oracle Database along the way to improve query performance include

- Bitmap indexes for optimally storing and retrieving low-cardinality data

- Parallel bitmap star joins for higher-speed joins

- Materialized views and summary tables for facts and dimensions

Smart scans and other performance optimizations unique to Exadata Storage Servers Analytics performance and capabilities have improved in the Oracle Database through support of SQL analytic functions, embedded online analytical processing

(OLAP), and embedded data mining and R support in the Advanced Analytics Option. ETL performance improved through introduction of embedded ETL functions.

As the data warehouses scaled into the petabytes in size, manageability and availability improvements were made through added functionality in Oracle Database releases, often also benefiting performance of queries. Some of these include the Partitioning Option, Automatic Storage Management providing striping and mirroring, Real Application Clusters (RAC) for scaling multiple nodes and instance failover, and Data Guard to propagate data from primary to secondary sites in case of failure.

Making sure data is available to the right business analysts at the right level of detail also leads to data security considerations. Key security functionality in the Oracle Database relevant in data warehousing includes

- Virtual Private Database (VPD) data access based on user roles

- Advanced security supporting multiple levels of access on a need-to-know basis

- Audit Vault providing the ability to understand who accessed data and what they did

We discuss some of these capabilities elsewhere in this book in more detail. However, as entire books have been written on this subject, you will want to explore those as well.

Why the Data Warehouse and Hadoop Are Deployed Together

Many of the features mentioned in the previous section provide capabilities not offered by Hadoop today. This is partly due to the maturity of relational database technology since it has a much longer history than Hadoop and partly due to the very different roles for each as originally intended. Remember, relational databases are optimized for structured high-density data that lends itself to storage in rows and columns. Hadoop is optimized for storing and processing large volumes of high-granularity data in a distributed file system regardless of data relationships. Each Oracle-engineered system (for example, the Oracle Exadata Database Machine and Oracle Big Data Appliance) is an optimized combination of hardware and software for the workloads to be run on the platform.

Of course, when a Hadoop programmer finds valuable data in their analysis, the data is often propagated to the data warehouse for the following reasons:

- The output from Hadoop is used to augment other data in the warehouse for analysis.

- Data in the data warehouse can be more easily navigated by business analysts.

- Data in the data warehouse is better secured for broader user communities.

- The data warehouse has well-defined business SLAs for performance and availability.

- Archival policies are well-tested, proven, and enforced for data in the data warehouse.

When data flows from the Hadoop cluster to the Oracle Database, valuable information is exposed to a wider set of consumers. Oracle offers a high-speed loader to facilitate data movement in this direction, Oracle Loader for Hadoop (OLH), which is part of the Oracle Big Data Connectors offering. Given that ETL tools are commonly used for defining loading processes into Oracle data warehouses, OLH is supported as an object in Oracle's Data Integrator tool (ODI). The Oracle Data Integrator Application Adapter for Hadoop enables ODI to generate optimized HiveQL code. The Oracle SQL Connector for Hadoop Distributed File System (OSCH) provides SQL access to HDFS for querying Hive tables and delimited text files and is supported in ODI.

If the destination for data is a non-Oracle data warehouse, the data is typically loaded into a generic data warehouse using standard Hadoop utilities (for example, Sqoop) or by using high-performance loaders offered by third parties. In some situations, Hadoop itself is made part of custom ETL processes to speed transformations, given its highly parallel nature and its support for advanced statistical analysis useful in building out transformations.

There are also situations where it makes sense for data to flow from the data warehouse into the Hadoop cluster. If most of the data to be analyzed lends itself better to analysis in Hadoop, it can make better sense to load reference data from the data warehouse into the Hadoop cluster. For such situations, you would likely use standard Hadoop Sqoop import capabilities.

The direction in which you choose to move data should match business requirements and functionality provided by the relational database engine and Hadoop cluster. Over time, the functionality mix will increasingly overlap in each as more Hadoop capabilities appear in relational databases and more relational database capabilities appear in Hadoop. For example, the Oracle Database has featured documented support of MapReduce-like functionality through the use of table functions going back many releases, and Oracle Database 12c features improved MapReduce-like functionality. That is not to say that you would use the Oracle Database as a substitute for Hadoop when you investigate the data structures in play and optimizations, the relative costs of the platforms, and other aspects, but you might use this capability where a blended approach is required and heavily tilted toward analysis of data residing in the Oracle Database. Similarly, if the blended approach is heavily tilted toward analysis of data in Hadoop, you might lean toward also loading data from the Oracle Database into Hadoop for analysis.

It is also worth noting in this section that you might want to build applications that can filter your data in an event-based fashion before it arrives in Hadoop or your data warehouse. Oracle Event Processing (OEP) includes an event visualization console useful in setting up ongoing queries of live data streams for such filtering.

Completing the Footprint: Business Analyst Tools

Most business analysts access their Big Data and data warehousing infrastructure using a variety of tools. Data discovery tools can provide an initial starting point where data can be gathered from structured and/or semistructured sources, and the path needed to gain value from the data is initially uncertain. Oracle's Endeca Information Discovery provides such a tool and includes the Endeca Server, which provides multiple drill paths through these types of data.

When building a schema makes sense, structured data typically is stored as previously mentioned in relational database schema, while semistructured data might be logically defined through Hive in Hadoop. Access to such data is commonly available through business intelligence tools that provide dashboards, reporting, and ad-hoc query capabilities. Oracle's Business Intelligence Foundation Suite is a typical example of a suite of tools providing access to a variety of data. At the time this book was being published, most major business intelligence tools vendors for relational databases were either supporting Hive or had plans to do so in the future via Open Database Connectivity (ODBC).

There are a growing number of statisticians who are now using the R statistical packages to analyze data residing in relational databases and in Hadoop clusters. Oracle provides support to run R programs without moving data out of an Oracle database as part of its Advanced Analytics Option. The Oracle Big Data Connectors enable R programs to be run against data residing in a Hadoop cluster using Oracle R Connector for Hadoop.

Data mining provides a means to determine and fine-tune mathematical algorithms that will predict the outcome of an event where there are a large number of contributing factors. Oracle provides in-database data mining algorithms as part of its Advanced Analytics Option and also offers a Data Mining Workbench for building out the data mining process flow. Hadoop distributions include Mahout, a programming library for data mining.

Some organizations incorporate a real-time recommendation engine as part of their deployment solution. For example, when someone is navigating a Web site, based on their profile, it might make sense to present them with a special sales offer or point them toward other products they might want to look at or other people they might want to connect with. Real-time recommendation engines are often custom built for this purpose. They are periodically updated using data and mathematical

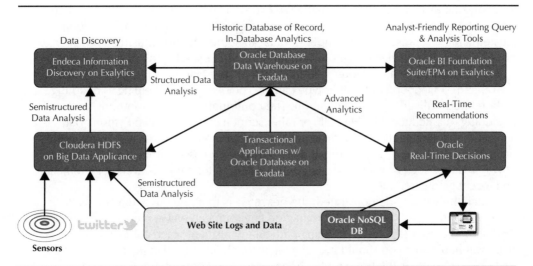

FIGURE 6-1. *Simplified view of an all-Oracle Big Data infrastructure and components*

models in the Hadoop cluster and/or data warehouse. Though the back-end infrastructure operates in batch mode, the recommendations appear to be made in real time. Oracle offers a recommendation engine that is called Oracle Real-time Decisions (RTD) for enabling such business rules.

Figure 6-1 illustrates an all-Oracle version of this complete footprint. Obviously, many organizations mix technology footprints from a variety of vendors in building out a footprint like this. Some are finding management, cost, and time-to-market benefits by consolidating the number of vendors involved as they decrease the number of support points and gain better out-of-the box integration.

Building Out the Infrastructure

There is no single right answer as to how you should go about building a complete infrastructure that includes Big Data. Organizations start with unique analytics footprints they've established and have differing business requirements they need to solve. Most organizations taking on a Big Data project have a data warehouse (or at least departmental data warehouses called data marts) and some sort of business intelligence tools.

It should be apparent that Hadoop will not replace a relational database data warehouse. However, many organizations previously were not able to analyze data from sensors, social media, and similar sources because of technical limitations in their relational databases. Hence, establishing and proving a new business use case for analyzing this type of data is usually the first step an organization will take when embarking on a Big Data project. A prototype is typically built on a small Hadoop cluster using a representative sample of data. In some situations, using a data discovery tool like Endeca might speed the process in establishing the potential value of analyzing semistructured data and deploying a Hadoop cluster.

Building a Hadoop cluster prototype can also be beneficial in helping to build Big Data related skills in your organization. The combination of programming skills (including MapReduce, Pig, HiveQL, or other scripting languages like Python), data analysis and distributed data optimization, data integration, and business skills is often difficult to find. Many organizations use a prototype effort as a learning experience for how to manage such projects and develop skills among their junior-level programmers and recent graduates.

Once the value is demonstrated, the next step is to move beyond a Big Data prototype and to size the Hadoop production environment. As we mentioned earlier, the Hadoop cluster is not seen as being particularly resilient when compared to the data warehouse, but you should take advantage of Hadoop availability characteristics that do exist, such as the triple replication of data and configuration of multiple highly available name nodes. By the very nature of Big Data, the storage required will grow quickly and incrementally and likely will quickly exceed the size of your data warehouse.

At this point, you should also have determined *who* will get business value from this data and *how* it should be accessed and further analyzed. You should then consider how you'll integrate the Hadoop cluster into your existing analytics footprint and any integration software you might need in addition to what is provided by Hadoop and your existing software. You'll also need to evaluate the impact on data warehouse availability and management procedures that may be of little interest to your prototype developers, but which likely will be critical to the overall success of the infrastructure in your business.

Further data and Hadoop cluster growth will likely be driven by business needs that mandate that longer periods of data will be kept in the cluster and new demand for storing data from additional sources. At each step of the way, you should be prepared to build more business cases justifying additional expansion of the overall infrastructure. Of course, it won't hurt to have proof points that validate earlier business cases that were presented as well.

CHAPTER
7

BDA Connectors

A s Hadoop takes on a more significant role as a data management and processing platform, it becomes important that other tools and databases can interact with Hadoop efficiently and leverage its robust capabilities. Oracle views Hadoop and the Oracle Database as complementary technologies that comprise a comprehensive data management platform for all data. While both technologies provide unique capabilities for data processing and analytics, it is important that data can be shared between the two systems efficiently and transparently. In Chapter 4 the benefit of InfiniBand to connect the Oracle Big Data Appliance and Exadata is discussed, but having a fast network between the two systems will only facilitate fast transfer. Software is still needed to efficiently transfer data over the network.

Apache Sqoop, which is bundled with Cloudera's Distribution including Apache Hadoop and is included on Oracle Big Data Appliance, is a tool that is designed to move data between Hadoop and relational databases. It is a generic tool, and while it is very useful for accessing any JDBC-compliant database, it is not optimized for the Oracle database. Oracle decided that they could create a set of high-performance tools that are optimized to move data into the Oracle database as well as providing additional capabilities that are not included with Apache Sqoop.

As mentioned in previous chapters, Oracle included Oracle R Distribution on Oracle Big Data Appliance to enhance the analytical capabilities that can be run on the appliance. There are a few points to consider when running R on the Oracle Big Data Appliance. First, R will only leverage the processing power of the node it resides on. And while this is more powerful than the typical workstation, it is only a fraction of the computing power of the whole cluster. Secondly, a statistician or analyst would need to log on to the node to use R. This creates security issues and the potential to overload a single node in the cluster. R users generally would rather use their workstation with R tools and then connect to a remote R server from their workstation. There is a better way to take advantage of R on the Oracle Big Data Appliance that allows users to continue to use their workstations.

In order to address these issues and create a more robust platform, Oracle created the Oracle Big Data Connectors. This chapter will discuss what the Big Data Connecters are, how they work, and the benefits they provide.

Oracle Big Data Connectors

Oracle Big Data Connectors are a suite of four connectors bundled together to enable high-performance data movement, real-time query capabilities, a GUI tool to make this all more usable, and statistical analysis between Hadoop and the Oracle database. The components included are

- Oracle SQL Connector for Hadoop Distributed File System (HDFS)
- Oracle Loader for Hadoop

■ Oracle Data Integrator Application Adapter for Hadoop

■ Oracle R Connector for Hadoop

Oracle bundles all four of the connectors into a single licensable package that can be used with the Oracle Big Data Appliance or any Hadoop cluster using Cloudera's Distribution for Apache Hadoop or Apache Hadoop. Specific versions are listed in the *Oracle Big Data Connectors User's Guide*.

The Oracle Big Data Connectors address three categories of functionality as described in Table 7-1.

This chapter will discuss version 2.0.1 of the Oracle Big Data Connectors.

Category	Connector	Function
Oracle Database Integration	Oracle Loader for Hadoop	Provides optimized loading of an Oracle database by generating specific data formats, leveraging Oracle-specific metadata, and leveraging MapReduce.
	Oracle SQL Connector for HDFS	Provides SQL access to HDFS and Hive from within the Oracle database without data being materialized in the Oracle database.
Statistical Analysis	Oracle R Connector for Hadoop	Provides the ability to use R client tools to submit R scripts on an entire Hadoop cluster leveraging MapReduce.
Developer Productivity	Oracle Data Integrator Application Adapter for Hadoop	Provides data integration developers using Oracle Data Integrator a set of Hadoop Knowledge Modules. Knowledge Modules are reusable code templates that encapsulate specific functionality to be included in integration or ETL workflows.

TABLE 7-1. *Big Data Connector Descriptions*

Oracle Loader for Hadoop

Oracle Loader for Hadoop is a high-speed loader for moving data from Hadoop into the Oracle database. It is invoked from the command line or via the Oracle Data Integrator Application Adapter as either a standalone process or part of a data integration workflow. Since Hadoop is an ideal platform for batch processing of data, it is frequently used for ETL-like processing and crunching on large data sets. Oracle Loader for Hadoop is typically invoked as the last stage of a MapReduce process after data preparation or analytics are performed on the Hadoop cluster. Oracle Loader for Hadoop is designed to leverage the parallel processing architecture of Hadoop and to move data-loading processing cycles from the Oracle Database platform to Hadoop. Oracle Loader for Hadoop takes into account the complete process of loading data into a database, so that it can leverage both platforms and take advantage of all the computing capacity available.

One of the key benefits of the Oracle database is high-speed queries. Oracle achieves this by providing fast access to data using a variety of access paths. These include indexes, partition pruning, hash joins, caching, Exadata Smart Scan, and so on. This is important when data that has been generated on Hadoop needs to be shared with many users on an ad-hoc basis using various tools such as Business Intelligence tools. Hadoop, and more specifically MapReduce, does not deliver the consistent, speed-of-thought access required by these users, and thus the capabilities of Oracle are required.

Therefore, if more data-loading task processes, like sorting and partitioning, can be offloaded from the database, then more resources can be applied to queries. Oracle Loader for Hadoop takes into consideration the definition of the target table by looking at the partitioning strategy on the table. The output of Oracle Loader for Hadoop will prepartition and optionally sort the data based on primary keys or other user-defined columns. This ensures that the data will be loaded into individual partitions of the database table and improves compression when a table uses Exadata Hybrid Columnar Compression.

Oracle Loader for Hadoop also handles data skew by balancing the data coming from the mappers to the reducers. Oracle Loader for Hadoop will evenly distribute the data so that no single reducer takes a disproportionate amount of processing time. This helps eliminate the possibility of any one reducer running longer than the others and thus extending the amount of time needed to load the database. This is accomplished by sampling the keys at the start of the job. Oracle Loader for Hadoop will then balance the keys to the reducers considering the number of partitions, the size of each partition, and the number of reducers. If a single partition needs to be split up to help balance the load, Oracle Loader for Hadoop will make the appropriate adjustments to make sure the load is balanced.

Whenever data is loaded into an Oracle database from an external source in a nontransactional model, it will go through a standard set of discrete steps. This process is often called the ETL (Extract-Transform-Load) process. While it is often debated which ordering of the transform and loading steps is more efficient, we will describe how this process applies to the use case of the Oracle Loader for Hadoop. Data will go through the following steps:

1. Ingestion to Hadoop as files on HDFS or a Hive table

2. Transformational processing of data

3. Loading of data into the Oracle database

Oracle Loader for Hadoop handles the last two steps of this process while the Oracle Data Integrator Application Adapter for Hadoop can additionally help with the first step. To accomplish this, Oracle Loader for Hadoop executes a MapReduce application that handles the following steps for the each phase of the MapReduce program.

■ **Mapper** This step will read the metadata about the target database table that resides in the Oracle database, read the InputSplits, convert data to Oracle data types, and send rows to the next step.

■ **Shuffle/Sort** This step will sort the data based on the target partitioning schema and balance the data to remove skew. This will ensure that the reducers are balanced.

■ **Reducer** This step will either connect to the Oracle database and load the data into the target table or it will create data files on HDFS.

Oracle Loader for Hadoop works in either an online or offline mode. The online mode will load data directly into the Oracle database via OCI direct path or JDBC. Offline mode will create files of either delimited text format or an Oracle Data Pump format. The primary use case of each output type is listed in Table 7-2.

Online Mode

The online mode of Oracle Loader for Hadoop provides for the direct loading of an Oracle target table without having to write the data out to HDFS. This increases operational efficiencies by creating a single job on Hadoop that preprocesses the data and then loads the data directly into the target table in parallel if appropriate. Therefore, when using the online mode, having the most efficient pathway between Hadoop and the Oracle database is critical. The optimal platform to achieve maximum throughput from Hadoop to Oracle is the Oracle Big Data Appliance and the Oracle Exadata Database Machine connected by the InfiniBand fabric. Other

Mode	Output Type	When to Use
Online	OCI Direct Path	Primary online option.
		Preprocessing of data and insertion into table in one step.
		Fastest online mode.
		Loading Oracle Partitioned Table.
	JDBC	Loading nonpartitioned Oracle tables.
		Non-Linux platforms.
		Target tables use composite interval partitions with a subpartition key column of CHAR, VARCHAR2, NCHAR, or NVARCHAR2.
Offline	Oracle Data Pump	Fastest load method.
		Lowest CPU utilization on database.
		Widest range of input formats.
		Distinct preprocessing and loading steps are required.
		Ability to query files via external tables.
	Delimited Text	Files need to be used for other purposes.
		Distinct preprocessing and loading steps are required.
		Ability to query files via external tables.

TABLE 7-2. *Output Type Capabilities*

configurations are supported, but performance characteristics will depend on the specifics of the hardware and software configuration.

Since the online mode allows for developers on Hadoop to initiate data loads on the Oracle database, the possibility exists that excessive load can be placed on the database at unexpected times. While the Oracle resource manager can manage resources, a better strategy is to load data when database resources are available. Therefore the online option is best used when there is excess capacity on the Oracle database or the Hadoop developer has no restrictions on when to insert data; in other words, during a regular, scheduled batch window.

The general flow of an online mode job is shown in Figure 7-1.

Oracle Loader for Hadoop provides two options for loading data into an Oracle database when using online mode.

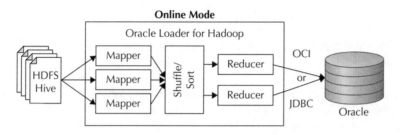

FIGURE 7-1. *Online mode*

Oracle OCI Direct Path Output

The OCI Direct Path option is the faster of the two online modes. In this mode Oracle Loader for Hadoop creates an OCI connection for each reducer task to perform parallel loads into each partition. By loading directly into each partition, bypassing SQL, concurrency increases and performance is improved.

This option should be used when Hadoop developers have free range to insert data into Oracle tables without concern for impacting other database jobs. This option is also useful for ETL type processes when the unpredictability of the preprocessing step can be afforded. This uncertainty can arise when the Hadoop cluster is used for many different use cases. If multiple Hadoop jobs are running, then the time it takes to run any one job can vary depending on the load on the cluster.

The OCI Direct Path output option does have some restrictions that need to be considered. They are

- The Oracle target table must be partitioned.

- Composite Interval portioned tables with subpartition keys of CHAR, VARCHAR2, NCHAR, or NVARCHAR2 are not supported.

- OCI Direct Path must be on a Linux x86.64 platform.

JDBC Output

The JDBC output option issues SQL INSERT statements to load data into the Oracle database and thus needs to go through the SQL layer. This adds an extra processing layer compared to the OCI Direct Path option, which results in a less performant option. The JDBC option uses the batching function of JDBC to bundle the INSERT statements. This can lead to partial loads of data that must be handled by the developer to ensure that all data is loaded. If an insert fails part way through the process, causing a job to fail, then some rows will be loaded and committed into the database, while the remaining rows will not. The developer will need to determine how to resolve this inconsistency. Since JDBC does not track individual insert failures, debugging requires up-front design considerations, which increase the overhead of using this option.

This option must be used when loading nonpartitioned tables. It is recommended that this option only be used on small data volumes as the OCI Direct Path option will provide superior performance.

Offline Mode

The offline mode of Oracle Loader for Hadoop will preprocess data that resides in Hadoop for loading into the Oracle database at a later time on demand. This can be done via command-line scripts or in an ETL flow. Oracle Data Integrator can be used to create the output file and then kick off the external table load. When using an offline mode, the output will most commonly be loaded into the Oracle database via external tables. This can be accomplished via Oracle SQL Connector for HDFS without moving data or by copying the output files to the Oracle database server and then loading into the database. Since the data is already preprocessed and ready to be loaded, timing of the loads is more predictable, assuming the data volumes stay consistent across loads. Data files created in offline mode can also be queried without loading the file into the database. While the offline mode will create files on HDFS and not load the data into an Oracle table at execution time, the target table still must exist at the time Oracle Loader for Hadoop is executed. Oracle Loader for Hadoop needs to read the metadata for the table, and thus if the table does not exist, Oracle Loader for Hadoop will fail.

The general flow of an offline mode job is shown in Figure 7-2.

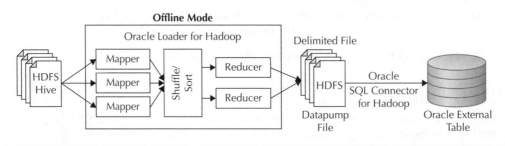

FIGURE 7-2. *Offline mode*

Oracle Data Pump Output

In Oracle Data Pump output mode, Oracle Loader for Hadoop produces binary files that are compatible with the ORACLE_DATAPUMP access driver. This output format provides the fastest mechanism for loading data into the Oracle database from a pure ingestion perspective. Performance is optimized since the file already contains data in an Oracle-ready format. Formatting happens in the preprocessor stage of the MapReduce job. Therefore, on ingestions, no data type conversions or other processing needs to occur. Data can be directly added into the table partition.

To access this file an external table must be created. If the data is going to remain on HDFS, then the ExternalTable tool as part of Oracle SQL Connector for HDFS should be used to create the external table in Oracle. If the file is going to be copied to the Oracle database, then Oracle Loader for Hadoop will create several scripts that will create the necessary objects to access the file on the Oracle database server. Oracle Loader for Hadoop will create

- An Oracle external table definition

- An Oracle directory object that is referenced in the external table definition

- A script to insert the data from the external table into the target table

These files can be found in the _olh directory of the Oracle Loader for Hadoop MapReduce jobs output directory.

The Oracle Data Pump output options should be used when the fastest ingestion speeds are needed and there is a need to minimize the amount of CPU cycles used on the Oracle database. This option reduces the CPU requirements since a regular insert is not made. The import does not go through all the SQL layers and thus will avoid the overhead of a conventional insert.

NOTE
Oracle Data Pump files created with Oracle Loader for Hadoop cannot be loaded into the Oracle database with the `IMPDP` *command.*

Delimited Text Output

In Delimited Text Output mode, Oracle Loader for Hadoop produces a delimited text file that is specified when the Oracle Loader for Hadoop command is executed. Like the Oracle Data Pump Output option, this option provides very fast load performance but requires more CPU resources on Oracle. This is due to data type checking that happens through a regular insert into the RDBMS and other processing that must occur for each record.

To access this file an external table should be created. If the data is going to remain on HDFS, then the ExternalTable tool as part of Oracle SQL Connector for HDFS should be used to create the external table in Oracle. If the file is going to be copied to the Oracle database, then Oracle Loader for Hadoop will create two files that can be used to load the data in to the target table. These files are

- Oracle SQL*Loader control files for each of the output tasks. If the table is not partitioned, a single control file will be created.

- A SQL script to load the file into the target table, called oraloader-csv.sql.

Since this option creates a comma-delimited text file, the file can be used for any other purpose desired.

Installation of Oracle Loader for Hadoop

The process for installing the Oracle Loader for Hadoop will depend on what hardware platform is running Hadoop. For customers who purchase Oracle Big Data Appliance, the installation is done with the Mammoth tool at the time that Oracle Big Data Appliance is installed and configured. For customers who have built their own clusters, they will need to install the software on their cluster.

There are a few software requirements to run Oracle Loader for Hadoop:

- Oracle Database Release 11g Release 2

- Cloudera Distribution including Apache Hadoop, or Apache Hadoop

- Hive if it will be used as a data source

After downloading the .ZIP file from the Oracle Web site, the following steps must be completed.

1. Uncompress the downloaded file into a directory on the Hadoop cluster. There are two distinct .ZIP files corresponding to the different versions of Hadoop. The appropriate file must be used for the version of Hadoop being used.

2. Create an environment variable called $OLH_HOME that references the directory where the files are installed.

3. Add $OLH_HOME/jlib/* to the HADOOP_CLASSPATH variable.

   Optionally, make the following variable addition if Oracle NoSQL database will be used as a data source:
   Add the kvstore*.jar file located in $KVHOME/lib to the HADOOP_CLASSPATH variable.

NOTE
Consult the Oracle Big Data Connectors User's Guide for the correct current versions of all the components and files mentioned.

Invoking Oracle Loader for Hadoop

Oracle Loader for Hadoop is invoked by running a Hadoop job called OraLoader from the command line, a script or from Oracle Data Integrator. OraLoader is a powerful tool with lots of flexibility to meet a wide range of input and output formats. These options are described in detail in the *Oracle Big Data Connectors User's Guide*, but the basics will be described in this section.

Before executing OraLoader, there are a few steps that must be completed:

1. Ensure that the target table exists in an Oracle database.

2. Ensure that an InputFormat class exists for the source data that will be loaded. Specifically, that InputFormat class needs to be in the HADOOP_ CLASSPATH. $OLH_HOME/jlib/* should be used to include the Oracle Big Data Connector–provided Input Classes.

3. Create an Oracle Loader for Hadoop configuration file that specifies all the properties of the job. Details on how to create configuration files are described later in this chapter.

4. Create a loader map file that describes the columns to be loaded.

When these steps are completed, Oracle Loader for Hadoop can be invoked with the following basic syntax:

```
hadoop jar $OLH_HOME/jlib/oraloader.jar oracle.hadoop.loader.OraLoader -conf
/home/oracle/gamesConfiguration.xml
```

NOTE
If the HADOOP_CLASSPATH does not contain the $OLH_HOME/jlib/ entry, the following code can be added at the end of the command:*

```
-libjars $OLH_HOME/jlib/oraloader-examples.jar
```

The flexibility of Oracle Loader for Hadoop arises from the options that exist for each of the previous steps, which will be examined in the following sections.

NOTE
For offline modes, make sure that the HDFS target directory does not already exist. Oracle Loader for Hadoop will create a new directory to place the output files and the job will fail if the directory already exists.

Oracle Loader for Hadoop requires that the target table that will be loaded already exists in the Oracle database. This is required so that Oracle Loader for Hadoop can read the table's metadata and optimize the load. The Oracle table must be partitioned if Oracle Loader for Hadoop is using OCI Direct Path output format. Oracle Loader for Hadoop will only load one table at a time and supports all partition strategies except reference partitioning and virtual column-based partitioning.

Input Formats

Oracle Loader for Hadoop is a MapReduce application that receives its input from a file or output from another MapReduce application. In order to process the input, Oracle Loader for Hadoop uses the org.apache.hadoop.mapreduce.RecordReader implementation and requires that it returns an Avro IndexedRecord input object from the getCurrentValue() method. Avro is a data serialization framework that can leverage remote procedure calls, which provides a straightforward way for Oracle Loader for Hadoop to interact with data. Oracle Loader for Hadoop uses the IndexedRecord object for two purposes. The first is to identify the names of the input fields so that they can be mapped to database column names. The second is to help with debugging in case of an error while reading a given record. The IndexedRecord object will provide information about the data file URI, information about the InputSplit, and the record offset of the file being processed.

Oracle provides four predefined input formats with Oracle Loader for Hadoop to address the most common file formats developers will encounter. Additionally, customers who are using the Oracle NoSQL database standalone or as part of the Oracle Big Data Appliance have access to an additional input format for accessing the Oracle NoSQL database. These InputFormat classes are described in Table 7-3.

The input class and other properties are specified in a configuration file as described later in this chapter. A portion of a configuration file that specifies that a delimited file will be used for the InputFormat class is shown here:

```
<property>
    <name>mapreduce.inputformat.class</name>
    <value>oracle.hadoop.loader.lib.input.DelimitedTextInputFormat</value>
</property>
```

Input Category	InputFormat Class	Description
Text File	oracle.hadoop.loader.lib.input.DelimitedTextInputFormat	Delimited text files
Text File	oracle.hadoop.loader.lib.input.RegexInputFormat	Text files that can be parsed by regular expressions
Hive	oracle.hadoop.loader.lib.input.HiveToAvroInputFormat	Hive table
Avro	oracle.hadoop.loader.lib.input.AvroInputFormat	Binary format Avro record files
Oracle NoSQL Database	oracle.kv.hadoop.KVAvroInputFormat	Oracle NoSQL Database: Leverages the value portion of the key/value pair

TABLE 7-3. *InputFormat Class Descriptions*

DelimitedTextInputFormat

The DelimitedTextInputFormat is used for text files that have a standard separator like commas or tabs. Each record must be terminated by a newline character and the field delimiter must be a single character. There are three optional properties that can be set for this format:

- **oracle.hadoop.loader.input.fieldTerminator**   This property sets the field delimiter, which has a default value of a comma (,). This property must be a single character.

- **oracle.hadoop.loader.input.initialFieldEncloser**   This property specifies an optional single character that encloses the front of a field. There is no default and the most common encloser is a double quote (").

- **oracle.hadoop.loader.input.trailingFieldEncloser**   This property specifies an optional single character that encloses the end of a field. The default is the value of the initialFieldEncloser and the most common encloser is a double quote (").

Each of the input formats generate Avro schema field names for each of the fields. By default, the values will have the form of F0,F1,...,F*n* where *n* represents the number of columns of the input. If the number of fields is not consistent throughout the file, then the number of columns (F*n*) will represent the maximum number of fields on any line. It is also possible to provide names for each field by specifying the oracle.hadoop.loader.input.fieldNames property in the configuration file. This property accepts a comma-separated list of column names. Assigning names to the columns will assist in creating the loader map file especially if a single input file will be used to load multiple Oracle tables that have different columns.

RegexInputFormat

The RegexInputFormat is similar to the DelimitedTextInputFormat in that it is designed to handle text files that are row-based in nature. The RegexInputFormat is useful for data that is not clearly text-delimited, but has patterns embedded in the record. Examples include log files that include URLs. The URL may need to be parsed to retrieve specific components like the protocol (http or https), the top-level domain, and any embedded parameters. The RegexInputFormat follows the same requirements around newline and column name properties, but does not require the field terminator or enclose properties. Instead, the RegexInputFormat requires the oracle.hadoop.loader.input.regexPattern property. This property is used to set the regular expression for the whole line. The regular expression must fully describe the complete input line using groups to identify fields. This will be mapped to the column names for the Avro schema field names. The regular expression must fully describe the whole line of each record and cannot ignore any text. It is important to ensure that there are the same number of groups as the number of fields in the file. This is required since the regex will not execute recursively. The regular expressions use java.util.regex as part of the Java Platform Standard Edition 6.

AvroInputFormat

The AvroInputFormat is used for files containing standard Avro files. No special properties are required and the column names are generated from the Avro schema.

HiveToAvroInputFormat

The HiveToAvroInputFormat is used to access data that is stored in Hive tables. This input format will convert the rows in the Hive table into Avro records and will convert Hive column names into field names. The HiveToAvroInputFormat will read the Hive metastore to get information about the location of files, column names, SerDe, and any other relevant information needed.

The HiveToAvroInputFormat requires two self-describing properties.

- oracle.hadoop.loader.input.hive.tableName
- oracle.hadoop.loader.input.hive.databaseName

Depending on the configuration of Hive, additional properties may be needed to locate the metastore. A full listing of Oracle Loader for Hadoop properties is located in the *Oracle Big Data Connectors User's Guide*.

NOTE
Oracle Loader for Hadoop will only load all partitions of a Hive partitioned table.

KVAvroInputFormat

The KVAvroInputFormat is an input format that is included with the Oracle NoSQL Database. This input format will only return the value portion of the key-value pairs stored in the Oracle NoSQL database. The keys can be accessed by implementing custom classes using the AvroFormatter.

Custom Input Formats

Custom formats can also be created if the data input does not meet the requirements of the formats provided by Oracle Loader for Hadoop. To implement a new InputFormat, a Java class will need to be written and then accessed via the Oracle Loader for Hadoop call. To access the .jar file containing the custom class, use the –libjars option of the OraLoader call.

Since the purpose of Oracle Loader for Hadoop is to load data into Oracle Tables, generally data will already have been processed into a form that is ready to be inserted into a table. So this option will only be used on data sources that already have data in a well-defined format like a NoSQL database such as Cassandra.

Oracle Loader for Hadoop Configuration Files

Oracle Loader for Hadoop requires several configuration properties when called. These properties describe the location of the Oracle database, the schema user and table to be loaded, the loader map file, and the input format. There are many other properties that can be used depending on the input and output formats. These properties can be called with the –D option on the command line, or via a configuration file with the –conf option. The configuration file is a simple XML file that stores the values of the properties via name and value tags and an optional description tag.

While there are many properties that can be specified, Table 7-4 lists the common properties that are used in most configuration files.

Property Name	Description
mapreduce .inputformat.class	Name of one of the provided input format classes or a custom input class.
	For example, oracle.hadoop.loader.lib.input .DelimitedTextInputFormat
mapred.input.dir	Comma-separated list of files or directories where data that will be read resides on HDFS. Wildcards can be used.
	For example, /user/oracle/data_files
mapreduce .outputformat.class	Name of one of the four provided output classes.
	For example, oracle.hadoop.loader.lib.output .OCIOutputFormat
mapred.output.dir	HDFS directory where output will be stored for either of the offline modes.
	For example, /user/oracle/olh_output
oracle.hadoop.loader .loaderMapFile	Name of XML file that contains the mapping of the Avro fields to the Oracle target table columns. This directory will reside on the Linux OS.
	For example, file:///home/oracle/signal_data/olh/ loadermap_signal.xml
oracle.hadoop.loader .connection.url	Specifies the Oracle database connection string.
	For example, jdbc:oracle:thin:@//localhost:1521/ orcl
oracle.hadoop.loader .connection.user	The name of the Oracle database user to be used to log in to the database. This will be used as the default schema if a table is not fully qualified.
	For example, SCOTT
oracle.hadoop.loader .defaultDateFormat	Specifies the default date format based on the java .text.SimpleDateFormat class for any date fields. This property will apply to all date field fields. This value can be overridden as part of the loader map file.
	For example, yyyy-MM-dd:HH:mm:ss
oracle.hadoop .loader.output .fieldTerminator	Used with DelimitedTextOutputFormat files and specifies a character or UTF-16 to be used to separate fields in the output file.
	For example, or \u0009 (0009 is the code for a tab)

TABLE 7-4. *Common Oracle Loader for Hadoop Properties*

Category	Output Mode	Value
Online	Oracle OCI Direct Path Output	oracle.hadoop.loader.lib.output .OCIOutputFormat
	JDBC Output	oracle.hadoop.loader.lib.output .JDBCOutputFormat
Offline	Oracle Data Pump Output	oracle.hadoop.loader.lib.output .DataPumpOutputFormat
	Delimited Text Output	oracle.hadoop.loader.lib.output .DelimitedTextOutputFormat

TABLE 7-5. *Output Format Classes*

The mapreduce.outputformat.class property will use one of the values listed in Table 7-5 depending on the Output Mode specified.

Here is an example of a configuration file that will load a comma-separated file that is stored on HDFS directly to an Oracle table via the OCI output format. This example uses Oracle Wallet to store the user credentials. For information on using Oracle Wallet, refer to the *Oracle Database Advanced Security Administrator's Guide*.

```xml
<?xml version="1.0" encoding="UTF-8" ?>
<configuration>
<!--                        Input settings                        -->
    <property>
        <name>mapreduce.inputformat.class</name>
        <value>oracle.hadoop.loader.lib.input.DelimitedTextInputFormat</value>
    </property>
    <property>
        <name>mapred.input.dir</name>
        <value>/user/oracle/games/games*.csv</value>
    </property>
    <property>
        <name>oracle.hadoop.loader.input.fieldTerminator</name>
        <value>,</value>
    </property>
<!--                        Output settings                        -->
    <property>
        <name>mapreduce.outputformat.class</name>
        <value>oracle.hadoop.loader.lib.output.OCIOutputFormat</value>
    </property>
    <property>
        <name>mapred.output.dir</name>
        <value>olh_output_dir</value>
    </property>
```

```
<!--                        Table information                    -->
    <property>
        <name>oracle.hadoop.loader.loaderMapFile</name>
        <value>file:///home/oracle/loaderMap_games.xml</value>
    </property>
<!--                      Connection information                 -->
    <property>
        <name>oracle.hadoop.loader.connection.url</name>
        <value>jdbc:oracle:thin:@localhost:1521/orcl</value>
    </property>
    <property>
        <name>oracle.hadoop.loader.connection.user</name>
        <value>SCOTT</value>
    </property>
    <property>
        <name>oracle.hadoop.connection.wallet_location</name>
        <value>/u01/wallets/oracle</value>
    </property>
    <property>
        <name>oracle.hadoop.connection.tns_admin</name>
        <value>/u01/app/oracle/product/11.2.0/dbhome_1/network/admin</value>
    </property>
</configuration>
```

NOTE
The connection.user property only specifies the login credentials and the default schema. The specific table and schema where data will be loaded are specified in the loader map file.

When using Oracle Wallet as an external password store, the following properties must be set in the configuration file:

■ oracle.hadoop.connection.wallet_location

■ oracle.hadoop.connection.url or oracle.hadoop.connection.tnsEntryName

■ oracle.hadoop.connection.tns_admin

Loader Maps

The loader map is used to map the Avro records that come from the output of the input format class to the target columns in the Oracle database. There are two different properties that can be set in the configuration file to specify the scope and names of the input fields to the target table columns.

- **oracle.hadoop.loader.targetTable** This property should be used for scenarios where the input file has the same number of fields as the target table and the input format specifies the exact same names as the database column names. This property specifies the schema name and table that will be loaded. This property can be used in conjunction with the oracle .hadoop.loader.input.fieldNames property. This method does not allow for any field-specific formatting.

- **oracle.hadoop.loader.loaderMapFile** Use this property when more control over the mapping of input fields to database columns is desired. This property specifies an XML file that will contain several pieces of information about the Oracle table. The file will specify

  - The Oracle database schema

  - The Oracle table name

  - The Avro field names mapped to Oracle column names

  This property will be used to cover any of the following scenarios:

  - The field names do not match the target table column names.

  - A subset of the fields will be loaded into an Oracle table.

  - A subset of columns in an Oracle table will be loaded.

  - Specific field formatting needs to be controlled.

In most cases, the oracle.hadoop.loader.loaderMapFile will be used as it provides the most flexibility for mapping field names to specific table columns. This is the loaderMap_games.xml loader map as specified in the previous configuration example.

```
<?xml version="1.0" encoding="UTF-8"?>
<LOADER_MAP>
<SCHEMA>SCOTT</SCHEMA>
<TABLE>SIGNALS</TABLE>
<COLUMN field="F0">HOME_TEAM</COLUMN>
<COLUMN field="F1">AWAY_TEAM</COLUMN>
<COLUMN field="F2">HOME_SCORE</COLUMN>
<COLUMN field="F3">AWAY_SCORE</COLUMN>
<COLUMN field="F4" format="MM-dd-yy">GAME_DATE</COLUMN>
</LOADER_MAP>
```

NOTE
The date format used leverages the java.text .SimpleDateFormat class.

Additional Optimizations

When running Oracle Loader for Hadoop jobs, it is possible that data errors may occur on individual rows. This may be due to an incorrect data type mapping or erroneous values for a given field such as a text value in a numeric field or null values inserted into a non-null field. While errors can be logged by setting the oracle.hadoop.loader.logBadRecords to true, if there are a significant number of errors, continuing processing may not be warranted. This is especially true with large files. If a job is allowed to continue running, significant time will be wasted while processing all the rows with few if any rows inserted into the database. Additionally, significant space will be used by the log files.

Row Reject Limit

In order to prevent this scenario, Oracle Loader for Hadoop has an optional property called oracle.hadoop.loader.rejectLimit that will stop the job when a specified number of rejected rows are encountered. If the property is not set or set to a negative number, the job will run until completion. A positive value should be specified based on the needs of the application. Setting it to "0" should be used only if the job should completely fail on any error. More commonly, a value should be set so that any rejected rows can easily be reprocessed after errors are fixed. If the Hadoop property for speculative execution is turned on, it is possible that the number of errors could become artificially inflated since rows are processed more than once. This scenario should be taken into account when setting this property.

Leveraging InfiniBand

In order to optimize performance over InfiniBand, Hadoop jobs need to leverage the Sockets Direct Protocol (SDP). The Sockets Direct Protocol (SDP) is a networking protocol developed to support stream connections over the InfiniBand fabric.[1] To take advantage of SDP in online modes, there are certain properties that need to be set when executing the load. The first is an option for the JVM to the Hadoop job command.

```
HADOOP_OPTS="-Doracle.net.SDP=true -Djava.net.preferIPv4Stack=true"
```

Additionally, the oracle.hadoop.loader.connection.url property needs to specify the SDP protocol. An example of this value is

```
<value>jdbc:oracle:thin:@(DESCRIPTION=(ADDRESS=(PROTOCOL=SDP)
(HOST=localhost) (PORT=1522))
(CONNECT_DATA=(SERVICE_NAME=orcl))) </value>
```

---

[1] http://docs.oracle.com/javase/tutorial/sdp/sockets/index.html

NOTE
Port 1522 is used here to point at an SDP-enabled listener. An Oracle DBA should be contacted to ensure that the listener is configured and which port should be used.

Comparison to Apache Sqoop

Apache Sqoop is a tool that is designed to move data between HDFS and relational databases. Sqoop has both export and import capabilities that leverage JDBC to move the data between the two platforms. Sqoop export addresses the same use case as Oracle Loader for Hadoop but without the same level of capabilities. Sqoop provides core capabilities but has no knowledge of the Oracle database and provides significantly less throughput than Oracle Loader for Hadoop.

Sqoop only supports the loading of delimited files from HDFS to an Oracle database, whereas Oracle Loader for Hadoop also supports the use of regular expressions, Hive tables, Avro files, and the Oracle NoSQL database. Oracle Loader for Hadoop also supports custom input formats through the use of custom code. Sqoop has no mechanism for gathering any metadata about the target. Sqoop cannot load from a Hive table and read the metastore to determine data types or column names. Sqoop cannot interrogate the Oracle data dictionary to determine what partitions exist on the target table to aid in loading of the database in parallel.

Sqoop handles data loading by creating `INSERT` statements. This requires additional Oracle processing that will slow down the load and increase the likelihood of row insert failures. The most common reason for failure would be data type conversions. While this can also occur with Oracle Loader for Hadoop, Sqoop cannot handle the failures gracefully. The Sqoop export process works as a series of transactions where some transactions can fail while others succeed. This can result in a partial load of the Oracle database with no easy way to roll back, track, or finish the load.

Oracle Loader provides greater flexibility, increased performance, and access to more input types than Sqoop. These features ultimately reduce developer cost and increase responsiveness to data process needs.

Oracle SQL Connector for HDFS

Oracle SQL Connector for HDFS provides SQL access to data stored in HDFS or Hive tables from the Oracle database as if the data were stored in Oracle. Using Oracle external tables, users can query data residing in Hadoop via Oracle SQL allowing for the full use of Oracle SQL constructs. This includes the ability, in a single query, to join data that resides in Hadoop with other data that resides in the Oracle database. This means that data stored in HDFS does not need to be physically stored in the Oracle database either temporarily or permanently in order to be queried. Users also have access to all the analytical capabilities that Oracle provides that do not exist in Hive. This includes analytical functions, statistical functions, and a robust security model as examples.

Oracle external tables are objects that allow data that resides outside of the database to be queried as if the data were stored in Oracle. The external object was first introduced into the Oracle database in 2001 as part of version 9*i* as a means to allow more efficient data loading of files into data warehouses. External tables consist of metadata that describe the columns, format of input data, and the location of data.[2] In Oracle 11g, a new preprocessor parameter was introduced to allow processing to occur on the incoming data. This preprocessor allows for functionality like decompression of files while the data is being queried. The preprocessor feature is what has enabled Oracle SQL Connector for HDFS to plug in to the existing external table object. External tables also have the ability to reference multiple files simultaneously, enabling parallel streaming to the Oracle database. This capability allows for a high degree of parallelization from Hadoop to the Oracle database when connecting an Oracle Big Data Appliance and an Exadata Database Machine. Parallelization is controlled by the access to multiple files stored in HDFS across parallel query threads. This is done automatically by Oracle SQL Connector for HDFS to gain maximum performance benefits. Oracle has shown that they can get 12T/hour throughput using Oracle SQL Connector for HDFS when using the Oracle Big Data Appliance in conjunction with the Oracle Exadata Database Machine.[3]

While external tables provide the ability to use all the advanced capabilities of Oracle SQL statements including PL/SQL and other options to the database, external tables also have some limitations. External tables will always read all of the data at query time, so this is similar conceptually to a full table scan. Because of the externalization of the data from the database, indexes are also not supported. External tables also do not support deletes, inserts, and updates. While this may be an annoyance for developers who are accustomed to working with databases, Hadoop users are familiar with these limitations while accessing HDFS. Since HDFS does not allow data files to be edited, the concept of row deletes, inserts, and edits does not exist.

---

[2] See http://docs.oracle.com/cd/E11882_01/server.112/e25494/tables013.htm#ADMIN12896 for more details on external tables.

[3] Reference: High Performance Connectors for Load and Access of Data from Hadoop to Oracle Database, www.oracle.com/technetwork/bdc/hadoop-loader/connectors-hdfs-wp-1674035.pdf

Oracle SQL Connector for HDFS provides access to data files from three sources:

■   Delimited text files on HDFS

■   Hive tables

■   Oracle Data Pump files stored in HDFS

External tables have a very robust syntax to handle a wide variety of files. However, for most delimited files, the syntax is very straightforward. The following external table definition highlights the main sections of an external table:

```
CREATE TABLE FOOTBALL_SCORES
                  (HOME_TEAM        VARCHAR2(20),
                   AWAY_TEAM        VARCHAR2(20),
                   HOME_SCORE        NUMBER(3),
                   AWAY_SCORE        NUMBER(3),
                   GAME_DATE        DATE
                  )
   ORGANIZATION EXTERNAL
   (
     TYPE ORACLE_LOADER
     DEFAULT DIRECTORY game_data_dir
     ACCESS PARAMETERS
     (
        records delimited by newline
        badfile game_data_dir:'scores.bad'
        logfile game_data_dir:'scores.log'
        fields terminated by ','
        missing field values are null
        ( HOME_TEAM, AWAY_TEAM, HOME_SCORE, AWAY_SCORE, GAME_DATE char
date_format date mask "dd-mon-yyyy"
        )
     )
     LOCATION ('scores_wk1.csv', 'scores_wk2.csv')
   )
   PARALLEL
   REJECT LIMIT UNLIMITED;
```

While there are many configuration options of external tables, there are two parameters that are specific to enabling Oracle SQL Connector for HDFS functionality. The PREPROCESSOR and the LOCATION arguments must be set. The PREPROCESSOR argument, which is not shown in the previous example, tells the external table the location and name of the Oracle SQL Connector for HDFS program to execute. The Oracle SQL Connector for HDFS program is called hdfs_stream and is located in a directory specified during the installation step. The LOCATION argument specifies a location file(s) that describes the location of data files as Universal Resource Identifiers or URIs on HDFS. This is a different way of accessing files compared to the default behavior of external tables. When files are located on the Oracle database server, the LOCATION argument simply specifies the file names as they appear on the operating system.

The location file is an XML file that has two sections. The header section contains information about when the file was created, what version of Oracle SQL Connector for HDFS is being used, and the file name itself. The <uri_list> section contains the URI information pointing to a single file or multiple files on HDFS. A location file may have multiple <uri_list_item> entries. A sample location file for access to a single file on HDFS is shown here:

```
<?xml version="1.0" encoding="UTF-8" standalone="yes"?>
<locationFile>
    <header>
        <version>1.0</version>
        <fileName>osch-20130209080405-5417-1</fileName>
        <createDate>2013-02-09T20:04:05</createDate>
        <publishDate>2013-02-09T08:04:05</publishDate>
        <productName>Oracle SQL Connector for HDFS  Release 2.0.1 -
Production</productName>
        <productVersion>2.0.1</productVersion>
    </header>
    <uri_list>
        <uri_list_item size="66" compressionCodec="">hdfs://localhost.localdomain:
8020/user/oracle/games.csv</uri_list_item>
    </uri_list>
</locationFile>
```

If a location file needs to access multiple files on HDFS, it will have multiple URIs. The <uri_list> section of the location file will look like the following example.

```
<uri_list>
        <uri_list_item size="66" compressionCodec="">hdfs://localhost.localdomain:
8020/user/oracle/games.csv</uri_list_item>
        <uri_list_item size="132" compressionCodec="">hdfs://localhost.localdomain:
8020/user/oracle/games2.csv</uri_list_item>
        <uri_list_item size="99" compressionCodec="">hdfs://localhost.localdomain:
8020/user/oracle/games3.csv</uri_list_item>
        <uri_list_item size="66" compressionCodec="">hdfs://localhost.localdomain:
8020/user/oracle/games4.csv</uri_list_item>
</uri_list>
```

The syntax of the <uri_list> is explained later in this chapter, within the "ExternalTable Tool for Delimited Text Files" section.

With the role of external tables described, let's take a look at how to start working with the Oracle SQL Connector for Hadoop. To get started there are just a few steps that need to be completed as described in Table 7-6.

Step	Frequency
Install Oracle SQL Connector for Hadoop	This is a one-time step.
Create External Table	This will be created once for each HDFS file or group of files.
Create Location Files	This file will also be created when the external table is created in the prior step. The location files will also be created every time HDFS files are added or deleted.
Query Data	As often as needed.

TABLE 7-6.   *Oracle SQL Connector for HDFS Configuration Steps*

Installation of Oracle SQL Connector for HDFS

Oracle SQL Connector for HDFS is installed on the Oracle database server. Additional installation is required on the Hadoop cluster if accessing Hive tables. Required configuration scenarios are described in Table 7-7.

There are a few software requirements that need to be considered before installation takes place.

- Install the same version of Hadoop on the Oracle database server that exists on the Hadoop cluster. This can be CDH3, CDH4, or Apache Hadoop.

- Make sure that the same Java Development Kit (JDK) is installed on both the Hadoop cluster and Oracle database server. The minimum supported version is 1.6_08.

- The Oracle database must be running on a Linux operating system. The Exadata Database Machine and Oracle Big Data Appliance already are running the same version of Oracle Enterprise Linux.

- The version of Oracle Database in use should be Oracle Database Release 11*g* Release 2 (11.2.0.2 or 11.2.0.3).

Sources of Data	Database Platform Install Required	Hadoop Cluster Install Required
HDFS Files	Y	N
Oracle Data Pump Files	Y	N
Hive Tables	Y	Y

TABLE 7-7.   *Installation Checklist*

For customers who will be using Hive as a data source, Oracle Big Data Connectors support the following versions of Hive:

Hive 0.7.0, 0.7.1, or 0.9.0

NOTE
Consult the Oracle Big Data Connectors User's Guide *for the latest supported versions.*

NOTE
Consult the Oracle Big Data Connectors User's Guide *for the correct current versions of all the components and files. Hadoop and the Oracle SQL Connector for HDFS software must be installed on all database servers when using Real Application Clusters or Oracle Exadata Database Machine.*

For customers who will be using Oracle Data Pump files as a source, an additional patch is needed for the Oracle Database. Patch 14557588 can be downloaded from Oracle.

Prior to the start of installation and configuration of Oracle SQL Connector for Hadoop, make sure that Hadoop is installed on the Oracle database server and that connectivity has been confirmed. This is most easily confirmed by using the following command.

```
hadoop fs -ls
```

If a directory listing is not returned, check to make sure the pathing is set correctly and the Hadoop install has been set up correctly and can be accessed by the oracle user on Linux.

Installing Oracle SQL Connector for HDFS is straightforward and requires a few simple steps:

1. Download the file Oracle SQL Connector for HDFS for Linux (for example, orahdfs-2.0.1.zip) to the Oracle database server.

2. Using the Oracle Database user on Linux, create a directory where Oracle SQL Connector for Hadoop will be installed; for example, /u01/connectors/orahdfs-2.0.1.

3. Unzip the file (for example orahdfs-2.0.1.zip) to this directory.

4. In the orahdfs-2.0.1/bin directory, edit the hdfs_stream file and modify the OSCH_HOME and PATH variables in the script.

    ■ OSCH_HOME=/u01/connectors/orahdfs-2.0.1

    ■ export PATH=/usr/lib/hadoop/bin:/usr/bin:/bin

This is required since the script will not inherit any environment variables. The script has detailed instructions.

The log directory can also be modified to another directory if specific log file directory requirements exist.

5. Ensure that the hdfs_stream script has the following permissions.

```
-rwxr-xr-x 1 oracle oinstall Dec 22 12:54 hdfs_stream
```

6. Confirm that the hdfs_stream is configured correctly by executing the following command.

```
$ ./hdfs_stream
```

The command will display the following text if successful.

```
Usage: hdfs_stream locationFile
```

7. Create a database directory object that points to the orahdfs-version/bin directory where hdfs_stream resides. Grant READ and EXECUTE privileges on this directory to anyone who will be using the Oracle SQL Connector for Hadoop. This directory is the same as specified in the first option in step 4:

```
SQL> CREATE OR REPLACE DIRECTORY osch_bin_path AS '/u01/
connectors/orahdfs-2.0.0/bin'
```

Now that the Oracle SQL Connector for HDFS has been installed on the Oracle database, users need to be given access to Oracle SQL Connector for Hadoop. This is accomplished by granting specific privileges to any user who will need access. Each user should be granted the following privileges:

- CREATE SESSION

- EXECUTE on the UTL_FILE PL/SQL package. The UTL_FILE is a package that gives PL/SQL programs the ability to interact with the underlying operating system.

- Users should not be granted write access to the OSCH_BIN_PATH directory to prevent accidental corruption of Oracle SQL Connector for HDFS files.

HIVE Installation

If Hive tables will be used as a data source for external tables, additional installation and configuration steps will be needed on the Hadoop cluster. This is not required if using Oracle Big Data Appliance as it will be configured when the appliance is installed. For custom Hadoop clusters, the following steps need to be taken:

1. Download the file Oracle SQL Connector for HDFS Release for Linux (for example, orahdfs-2.0.1.zip) to the Hadoop cluster (for example, /u01/ connectors/orahdfs-2.0.1).

2. Unzip the file (for example, orahdfs-2.0.1.zip) to a directory that can be accessed by Hadoop.

3. Add the files in the jlib subdirectory to the HADOOP_CLASSPATH environment variable (for example, /u01/connectors/orahdfs-2.0.1/jlib/*).

4. The following should be added to the HADOOP_CLASSPATH if not already included for the user running the tool.

   ■ $HIVE_HOME/lib/*

NOTE
With the 2.0.1 version of the connectors, this setting may cause conflicts with Pig if Jython is used on the cluster. In this situation, this setting should be added to a script that calls Oracle SQL Connector for HDFS and temporarily alters the HADOOP_CLASSPATH.

   ■ $HIVE_CONF_DIR or $HIVE_HOME/conf

NOTE
Consult the Oracle Big Data Connectors User's Guide *for the correct current versions of all the components and files.*

SQL Connector will not work if Oracle Audit Vault is installed on the Oracle database on which Oracle SQL Connector for Hadoop will be running. This is due to a restriction on the preprocessor feature of external tables. This is a security feature that prevents a back-door to get around the audit vault.

Creating External Tables Using Oracle SQL Connector for HDFS

After installing Oracle SQL Connector for Hadoop, the process to configuring external tables to access data on HDFS can be initiated. Creating external tables is a straightforward process and can be accomplished in one of two ways. The first involves writing DDL in the Oracle database based on the syntax of external tables. This process would be familiar to anyone already accustomed to creating external tables including DBAs, ETL developers, and many data modelers. However, this process will require an additional step related to how Oracle SQL Connector for HDFS uses location files. The second way to create an external table is by using a

Java-based Hadoop command-line tool that comes with Oracle SQL Connector for HDFS, which will create a ready-to-query external table. The command-line tool is called ExternalTable.

ExternalTable Configuration Tool

The ExternalTable tool can either create the external table in the Oracle database directly or use the tool to create the DDL, which can then be submitted to the database. The direct creation method makes certain assumptions about the definition of the external table, which may not be appropriate for all scenarios. By using the --noexecute parameter, the DDL can be generated and then modified for the specific needs of the data source. The default behavior of the ExternalTable tool will be different depending on the data source to be accessed. For example, the ExternalTable tool will use VARCHAR2 as a data type for all columns when accessing a delimited text file. This is because the tool does not interrogate the fields to determine what data type exists in each column. While this could be done by checking every value, in each column, on every line, it would take too much time when referencing large files. Sampling isn't an effective method either, since columns could have mixed text and numeric values. It is therefore possible that a field could have values of varied types since sampling would not check every record. A final possibility is that numeric columns may not always be treated as numbers. Sometimes they may be treated as characters. If the data source is a Hive table, then the column types are already defined in the hive table definition and Oracle SQL Connector for HDFS will use the appropriate data type.

The following is an example of how to execute the ExternalTable tool. Details on each of the parameters are described over the next several pages.

```
hadoop jar $OSCH_HOME/jlib/orahdfs.jar oracle.hadoop.exttab.ExternalTable
-D oracle.hadoop.exttab.tableName=GAMES
-D oracle.hadoop.exttab.dataPaths=hdfs:/user/oracle/games*.csv
-D oracle.hadoop.exttab.columnCount=5
-D oracle.hadoop.exttab.defaultDirectory=FOOTBALL_DIR
-D oracle.hadoop.connection.url=jdbc:oracle:thin:@localhost:1521:orcl
-D oracle.hadoop.connection.user=SCOTT
-createTable
```

Data Source Types

Oracle SQL Connector for HDFS can access data from three distinct data sources. While all of these data sources have different formats, they all have one thing in common. They all store data on HDFS. Oracle SQL Connector for HDFS will always stream files that are stored in HDFS to the external table at query time regardless of which source is used. No MapReduce code will be generated. The sources that are used are

- Delimited text files that reside on HDFS.

- Hive tables. Oracle SQL Connector for HDFS will read the metadata of the Hive tables so that it can access the files stored on HDFS. Oracle SQL Connector for HDFS will not generate HiveQL or MapReduce code to retrieve data at query time.

- Oracle Data Pump files that are stored on HDFS. Oracle SQL Connector for HDFS will read the file header of the data pump file to determine how to create the external table. Data Pump files must be generated by Oracle Loader for Hadoop.

Configuration Tool Syntax

The ExternalTable command provides several different functional capabilities via a single command-line tool. The functions are specified by several properties that can be set to affect the behavior of the tool in creating external tables. The following tasks can be executed via the ExternalTable tool:

- Create an external table directly in the Oracle database and create the location files that point to HDFS.

- Refresh (publish) the location files of an existing external table when new HDFS files need to be accessed by the external table.

- Show the contents of the location files.

- Show the DDL for an external table.

The syntax of the ExternalTable tool is as follows:[4]

```
hadoop jar $OSCH_HOME/jlib/orahdfs.jar \
oracle.hadoop.exttab.ExternalTable \
[-conf config_file]... \
[-D property=value]... \
-createTable [--noexecute]
| -publish [--noexecute]
| -listlocations [--details]
| -getDDL
```

There are many properties that control the format of the external table, and are described in detail in the *Oracle Big Data Connectors User's Guide*. However, there

---

[4] Source: Oracle Big Data Connectors User's Guide Release 2 (2.0) E36961-02.

are several properties that are required for all data sources and other commonly used optional properties that specifically apply to each data source.

Required Properties

There are several properties specified with the –D option that are required with every call of the ExternalTable tool. These properties are

- **oracle.hadoop.exttab.tableName**   This property specifies the name of the external table that will be created or modified in the Oracle database.

- **oracle.hadoop.exttab.defaultDirectory**   This property specifies the Oracle database server directory where the external file will store log files and the location file. This property is the default directory if not specified in any of the optional properties. This directory must be created in the Oracle database prior to executing the ExternalTable tool.

- **oracle.hadoop.connection.url**   This property specifies the JDBC URL that will allow the ExternalTable tool to connect to the Oracle database. Since the tool is called from a command line on the Hadoop cluster, it will need to connect and log in to the Oracle database.

- **oracle.hadoop.connection.user**   This property specifies the user and schema where the external table will be created. A prompt for this user's password will be issued when the command-line tool is run if the oracle.hadoop .connection.wallet_location is not specified. The oracle.hadoop.connection .wallet_location is a path where the connection credential is stored.

Additional properties are required for each data source. These properties either provide additional metadata or tell the ExternalTable tool where to gather the metadata. The required properties for each data source are as follows:

Delimited Text Files:

- **oracle.hadoop.exttab.dataPaths**   This property specifies the HDFS file directory and files to be accessed by the external file. This property can specify multiple files separated by a comma and can use wild cards. File names can use pattern-matching characters to match multiple files or directories.

- **oracle.hadoop.exttab.columnCount** or **oracle.hadoop.exttab .columnNames**   One of these properties must be specified to tell the external table how many columns there will be. The columnNames property should be a comma-separated list of column names. If the columnCount property is used, each column will be named C1..C*n*.

Hive Tables:

- **oracle.hadoop.exttab.sourceType**   This property should be set to the value hive. This property's default is text and thus is not required for Delimited Text Files.

- **oracle.hadoop.exttab.hive.tableName**   This property specifies the Hive table name that will be used to define the external table.

- **oracle.hadoop.exttab.hive.databaseName**   This property specifies the Hive database name where the Hive table resides.

Oracle Data Pump Format Files:

- **oracle.hadoop.exttab.sourceType**   This property should be set to the value datapump. This property's default is text and thus is not required for Delimited Text Files.

- **oracle.hadoop.exttab.dataPaths**   This property specifies the HDFS file directory or files to be accessed by the external file. File names can use pattern-matching characters to match multiple files or directories. All files specified must be uncompressed or use the same compression method.

Optional Properties

There are optional properties that can be used to customize the format of an external table. These optional file formats will most often be used when dealing with delimited text files as there can be many different file and field characteristics. Some of the more commonly used optional properties are

- **oracle.hadoop.exttab.dataCompressionCodec**   Defaults to none

- **oracle.hadoop.exttab.fieldTerminator**   Defaults to comma (,)

- **oracle.hadoop.exttab.recordDelimiter**   Defaults to \n

ExternalTable Tool for Delimited Text Files

Creating an external table to access files on HDFS is a simple process. Consider a directory on HDFS called /user/oracle/football that contains two comma-separated files. The files contain results of football games for a given week. The file names are games_2012wk1.csv, games_2012wk2.csv, and so on. A sample of one of the files is

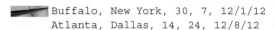
```
Buffalo, New York, 30, 7, 12/1/12
Atlanta, Dallas, 14, 24, 12/8/12
```

To create an external table called GAMES in the Oracle database in the SCOTT schema, we would issue the following command:

```
hadoop jar $OSCH_HOME/jlib/orahdfs.jar oracle.hadoop.exttab.ExternalTable
-D oracle.hadoop.exttab.tableName=GAMES
-D oracle.hadoop.exttab.dataPaths=hdfs:/user/oracle/games*.csv
-D oracle.hadoop.exttab.columnCount=5
-D oracle.hadoop.exttab.defaultDirectory=FOOTBALL_DIR
-D oracle.hadoop.connection.url=jdbc:oracle:thin:@localhost:1521:orcl
-D oracle.hadoop.connection.user=SCOTT
-createTable
```

Here we specified that there are five columns and that the location file and log files will be put in an Oracle directory called FOOTBALL_DIR. Also notice that we reference all files by using the games*.csv specification in the oracle.hadoop.exttab .dataPaths property. This command will create an external table that can be queried immediately. The external table definition is as follows:

```
CREATE TABLE "SCOTT"."GAMES"
 (
  "C1"                                  VARCHAR2(4000),
  "C2"                                  VARCHAR2(4000),
  "C3"                                  VARCHAR2(4000),
  "C4"                                  VARCHAR2(4000),
  "C5"                                  VARCHAR2(4000)
 )
ORGANIZATION EXTERNAL
 (
    TYPE ORACLE_LOADER
    DEFAULT DIRECTORY "FOOTBALL_DIR"
    ACCESS PARAMETERS
    (
      RECORDS DELIMITED BY 0X'0A'
      disable_directory_link_check
      CHARACTERSET AL32UTF8
      STRING SIZES ARE IN CHARACTERS
      PREPROCESSOR "OSCH_BIN_PATH":'hdfs_stream'
      FIELDS TERMINATED BY 0X'2C'
      MISSING FIELD VALUES ARE NULL
      (
        "C1" CHAR,
        "C2" CHAR,
        "C3" CHAR,
        "C4" CHAR,
        "C5" CHAR
      )
    )
```

```
LOCATION
(
   'osch-20130211102841-9684-1',
   'osch-20130211102841-9684-2'
)
) PARALLEL REJECT LIMIT UNLIMITED;
```

Most of the DDL created looks just like a typical external table definition for any file that would reside on the Oracle database server. The two primary differences are the PREPROCESSOR and LOCATION parameter settings. The PREPROCESSOR setting picks up the OSCH_BIN_PATH that was created during the installation steps and points to the known script hdfs_stream. This is done automatically for the developer.

The LOCATION parameter is not as obvious. LOCATION is not pointing at the files specified in the oracle.hadoop.exttab.dataPaths property. Rather, two new location files are created that contain the information about where to find the files on HDFS. These location files are stored in the FOOTBALL_DIR directory on the Oracle database server and use the osch-timestamp-number-*n* format. Where timestamp is of the format yyyyMMddhhmmss, *number* is a random number and *n* represents a sequence for specifying multiple location files.

The number of location files is controlled by the oracle.hadoop.exttab .locationFileCount. The default value is four, so in the previous example where there are only two data files on HDFS, only two location files are created. The oracle .hadoop.exttab.locationFileCount property controls the degree of parallelism for the external table, so this value should always be set lower than or equal to the number of files to be accessed. If there are more files on HDFS than the value of oracle .hadoop.exttab.locationFileCount, then each location file will have multiple URIs in each file. Since this parameter has a direct effect on the amount of resources consumed by the Oracle database, some thought should go into how many location files are created. If an HDFS directory has thousands of files and the oracle.hadoop .exttab.locationFileCount is set to a large value, significant resources will be used on the Oracle database. Oracle SQL Connector for HDFS starts up separate access processes for each file, which use large I/O buffers that take memory from the system global area (SGA). Under most scenarios, this should not cause a strain on the system. Considerations should be given to the expected workload when external tables will be queried, the number of concurrent users querying the external tables, and the number of different external tables that will be queried.

Location files are XML files that contain several tags and can be manually edited to add or remove HDFS file URIs. The uri_list_item tag contains three separate pieces of information:

- The size of the HDFS file in bytes. The ExternalTable tool will use the HDFS file sizes to balance the total size of all files in each location file. This will help ensure even parallel processing of queries of the external table. If one file is significantly larger than other files, it is possible that a single location file will contain a single HDFS file URI while others will contain several URIs. If the location files were not balanced, than one location file could process files that would take significantly more time to stream into the database, resulting in inefficient parallelization.

- The compressionCodec, if any, that will be used.

- The URI of the file on HDFS.

An example of an uri_list_item:

```
<uri_list_item size="66" compressionCodec="">hdfs://localhost.localdomain:
8020/user/oracle/games9.cs
v</uri_list_item>
```

Testing DDL with --noexecute

Before executing the ExternalTable tool with the –createTable option, it is recommended that the --noexecute option be used. This will display the DDL that will be created and the format of the location file and will catch any errors that may occur. This is a useful debugging tool that should be used before executing any command.

Adding a New HDFS File to the Location File

External table definitions are based on data files that are defined at creation time. Therefore, an external table location file will only know about the files on HDFS that exist when the external table is created. It is very common for additional data files to be created and added to an HDFS directory on a regular basis either by the Hadoop **fs** command or by tools like flume. As these files get added, the external table will not recognize the new files and thus queries may not be considered accurate. In order for the external table to include these files, the location files must be updated. This can be done by manually editing the files as described earlier, but this could be tedious and prone to errors.

The ExternalTable tool provides a way to refresh the location files. This is accomplished via the –publish option and works in the same manner, with the same properties as the –createTable option. In fact, the same exact options that were used to create the external table should be used to re-create the location files. The command to modify our GAMES table would be

```
hadoop jar $OSCH_HOME/jlib/orahdfs.jar oracle.hadoop.exttab.ExternalTable
-D oracle.hadoop.exttab.tableName=GAMES
-D oracle.hadoop.exttab.dataPaths=hdfs:/user/oracle/games*.csv
-D oracle.hadoop.exttab.columnCount=5
-D oracle.hadoop.exttab.defaultDirectory=FOOTBALL_DIR
```

```
-D oracle.hadoop.connection.url=jdbc:oracle:thin:@localhost:1521:orcl
-D oracle.hadoop.connection.user=SCOTT
-publish
```

This command could be added to a script that is executed on a regular basis, so that the external table always has an update view of all the data. The publish option will redefine the external table definition and re-create the location files, so as soon as the command is executed, new queries will access the new definition. Any existing queries will continue to run until the query is completed.

Manual External Table Configuration

There may be some file formats where the ExternalTable tool will not create an external table in the format that meets defined requirements. The most common reason is that the tool creates all fields as VARCHAR2 data types. Since the data is not physically stored in the database, this is generally not an issue from a storage perspective, but it may have issues at query time. A user can always do data type conversion in the query if the database doesn't handle it automatically, but this can be a hassle. So if you want to have different data types or include other external table definition capabilities that the tool does not support, manual creation of the external table and location files is necessary.

While any one can start typing the syntax of an external table, making sure to include the PREPROCESSOR and LOCATION properties, this method is prone to errors, as is anything when typed from scratch. A better way is to use the --noexecute option of the ExternalTable tool as described previously. By using the --noexecute option, the DDL can be viewed, copied, and edited in any manner needed. So if only one field needs to be changed, say to a date field, this would be a simple edit. After the edited DDL is pasted into the database, the –publish option of the ExternalTable tool will need to be run to populate the location files. This would be much easier than manually editing the location files.

When creating an external table in Oracle that uses non-VARCHAR2 data types, care must be used to handle data type conversions. There are two sections of an external table where data types are defined. The Oracle data type is defined at the top of the statement after the CREATE TABLE statement. This is the same as creating any Oracle table. The second location is the ACCESS PARAMETERS section. Here the data type of the file would be specified, and in the case of a date field, the date mask for the field. The external table definition of our GAMES table would look like the following if the C5 column were redefined as a date field:

```
CREATE TABLE "SCOTT"."GAMES"
  (
   "C1"                           VARCHAR2(4000),
   "C2"                           VARCHAR2(4000),
   "C3"                           VARCHAR2(4000),
```

```
  "C4"                                VARCHAR2(4000),
  "C5"                                date
)
ORGANIZATION EXTERNAL
(
   TYPE ORACLE_LOADER
   DEFAULT DIRECTORY "FOOTBALL_DIR"
   ACCESS PARAMETERS
   (
     RECORDS DELIMITED BY 0X'0A'
     disable_directory_link_check
     CHARACTERSET AL32UTF8
     STRING SIZES ARE IN CHARACTERS
     PREPROCESSOR "OSCH_BIN_PATH":'hdfs_stream'
     FIELDS TERMINATED BY 0X'2C'
     MISSING FIELD VALUES ARE NULL
     (
       "C1" CHAR,
       "C2" CHAR,
       "C3" CHAR,
       "C4" CHAR,
       "C5" CHAR  DATE_FORMAT DATE MASK "mm/dd/yy"
     )
   )
   LOCATION
   (
     'osch-20130211094408-1544-1',
     'osch-20130211094408-1544-2'
   )
) PARALLEL REJECT LIMIT UNLIMITED;
```

Hive Sources

Now that we have discussed the mechanisms of creating external tables using a delimited text file, let's consider using Hive as the data source. The process for creating external tables is the same, but the properties are different and there are other considerations that need to be thought through.

When using Hive as a data source, the first concept to understand is that Oracle SQL Connector for HDFS will not be generating HiveQL or any other MapReduce code. Oracle SQL Connector for HDFS will read the Hive metadata from the metastore to find where the data files are stored and determine the columns and data types of the table. Oracle SQL Connector for HDFS will read a table's metadata and support either Hive-managed tables or Hive external tables. The location of the data files will be read from the metastore and will be used to configure the location file for the Oracle external table. A key benefit of using Hive tables is that additional metadata about the columns are exposed that are not available with delimited text files. When using the ExternalTable tool for text files, a list of columns or the number of columns in the file must be specified. Additionally, all columns are created as VARCHAR2 columns. Any modifications would require manual redefinitions of the Oracle external table DDL. When using Hive tables, the metastore provides the column names as well as the data types, so the ExternalTable tool can use this information when defining the Oracle external table. At query time, there is no difference between using a Hive table as a data source or delimited text file. Oracle SQL Connector for HDFS will always stream the files directly from HDFS.

Hive provides robust capabilities to handle a wide range of data file formats by leveraging the capabilities of MapReduce. Since Oracle SQL Connector for HDFS does not generate MapReduce, some of these capabilities are not supported when using the Oracle SQL Connector for Hadoop. Oracle SQL Connector for HDFS only supports tables using ROW FORMAT DELIMITED or FILE FORMAT TEXTFILE clauses.

ExternalTable Example

The following listing is an example of the use of ExternalTable with a Hive table as the source.

```
hadoop jar $OSCH_HOME/jlib/orahdfs.jar oracle.hadoop.exttab.ExternalTable -D
oracle.hadoop.exttab.tableName=GAMES_HIVE -D
oracle.hadoop.exttab.sourceType=hive -D
oracle.hadoop.exttab.hive.tableName=GAMES_HIVE -D
oracle.hadoop.exttab.hive.databaseName=default -D
oracle.hadoop.exttab.defaultDirectory=FOOTBALL_DIR -D
oracle.hadoop.connection.url=jdbc:oracle:thin:@localhost:1521:orcl -D
oracle.hadoop.connection.user=SCOTT
-createTable
```

The external table created from this command looks like this:

```
CREATE TABLE "SCOTT"."GAMES_HIVE"
(
  "HOME_TEAM"                    VARCHAR2(4000),
  "AWAY_TEAM"                    VARCHAR2(4000),
  "HOME_SCORE"                   INTEGER,
  "AWAY_SCORE"                   INTEGER,
  "GAME_DATE"                    TIMESTAMP(9)
)
ORGANIZATION EXTERNAL
(
   TYPE ORACLE_LOADER
   DEFAULT DIRECTORY "FOOTBALL_DIR"
   ACCESS PARAMETERS
```

```
   (
     RECORDS DELIMITED BY 0X'0A'
     disable_directory_link_check
     CHARACTERSET AL32UTF8
     STRING SIZES ARE IN CHARACTERS
     PREPROCESSOR "OSCH_BIN_PATH":'hdfs_stream'
     FIELDS TERMINATED BY 0X'01'
     MISSING FIELD VALUES ARE NULL
     (
       "HOME_TEAM" CHAR NULLIF "HOME_TEAM"=0X'5C4E',
       "AWAY_TEAM" CHAR NULLIF "AWAY_TEAM"=0X'5C4E',
       "HOME_SCORE" CHAR NULLIF "HOME_SCORE"=0X'5C4E',
       "AWAY_SCORE" CHAR NULLIF "AWAY_SCORE"=0X'5C4E',
       "GAME_DATE" CHAR DATE_FORMAT TIMESTAMP MASK "YYYY-MM-DD
HH24:MI:SS.FF" NULLIF "GAME_DATE"=0X'5C4E'
     )
   )
   LOCATION
   (
     'osch-20130212061222-4492-1',
     'osch-20130212061222-4492-2',
     'osch-20130212061222-4492-3',
     'osch-20130212061222-4492-4'
   )
 ) PARALLEL REJECT LIMIT UNLIMITED;
```

NOTE
This external table has nongeneric column names and the data types are specified. The MISSING FIELDS section also has additional properties specified.

Oracle Data Pump Sources

Configuring an external table against an Oracle data pump file is similar to creating one against a delimited text file. The minimum configuration properties are the same with two differences. The first difference is obvious in that oracle.hadoop.exttab .sourceType must be set to datapump, whereas it is optional for delimited text files. The second difference is that the oracle.hadoop.exttab.columnCount or oracle .hadoop.exttab.columnNames property does not need to be set. Oracle Data Pump files created by Oracle Loader for Hadoop contain column names and other metadata embedded in the file, which the ExternalTable tool can read when creating the external table. This means that the ExternalTable tool will only work with Oracle Data Pump files created by Oracle Loader for Hadoop. A generic Oracle Data Pump file created by the Oracle EXPDP will not contain this metadata and cannot be used by the Oracle SQL connector for Hadoop Distributed File System. An example of creating an external table from an Oracle Data Pump file is as follows:

```
hadoop jar $OSCH_HOME/jlib/orahdfs.jar oracle.hadoop.exttab.ExternalTable
-D oracle.hadoop.exttab.tableName=GAMES_DP
-D oracle.hadoop.exttab.dataPaths=hdfs:/user/oracle/olh_datapump/oraloader*
-D oracle.hadoop.exttab.sourceType=datapump
-D oracle.hadoop.exttab.defaultDirectory=FOOTBALL_DIR
-D oracle.hadoop.connection.url=jdbc:oracle:thin:@localhost:1521:orcl
-D oracle.hadoop.connection.user=SCOTT
-createTable
```

This will create an external table that looks like this:

```
CREATE TABLE "SCOTT"."GAMES_DP"
(
    "HOME_TEAM"                         VARCHAR2(4000),
    "AWAY_TEAM"                         VARCHAR2(4000),
    "HOME_SCORE"                        VARCHAR2(4000),
    "AWAY_SCORE"                        VARCHAR2(4000),
    "GAME_DATE"                         VARCHAR2(4000)
)
ORGANIZATION EXTERNAL
(
    TYPE ORACLE_LOADER
    DEFAULT DIRECTORY "FOOTBALL_DIR"
    ACCESS PARAMETERS
    (
      external variable data
      disable_directory_link_check
      PREPROCESSOR "OSCH_BIN_PATH":'hdfs_stream'
    )
    LOCATION
    (
      'osch-20130224013020-887-1'
    )
) PARALLEL REJECT LIMIT UNLIMITED;
```

NOTE
This external table definition is much simpler in its structure as the ORACLE_LOADER can access metadata from the Oracle Data Pump file directly. This is achieved via the access parameter named EXTERNAL VARIABLE DATA.

Configuration Files

As previously described, the ExternalTable tool needs several required and optional configuration properties to be specified on the command line. While this provides the flexibility needed to address a wide range of data sources and source configurations, typing all the options and ensuring that the correct parameters and values are set can lead to errors. To help simplify the use of the ExternalTable tool, these properties can be included in a configuration file and then specified at the command line with the –conf option. This allows for a library of configuration files that can address a range of needs such as:

■ Storing the connection URL that will be used by many developers

■ Creating a template for each of the different sources' common properties

■ Specific delimiters for different types of files

■ An easy way to publish location files

Configuration files are simple XML files that specify the name and value for each property. The general format of the property tag is

```
<property>
    <name>property name</name>
    <value>value</value>
</property>
```

If we wanted to simplify the publish option of the ExternalTable tool, the following command line would be called:

```
hadoop jar $OSCH_HOME/jlib/orahdfs.jar oracle.hadoop.exttab.ExternalTable -conf
publish_games.xml -publish
```

The format of the configuration file called publish_games.xml would be

```
<?xml version="1.0"?>
<configuration>
    <property>
        <name>oracle.hadoop.exttab.tableName</name>
        <value>GAMES</value>
    </property>
    <property>
        <name>oracle.hadoop.exttab.dataPaths</name>
        <value>hdfs:/user/oracle/games*.csv</value>
    </property>
    <property>
        <name>oracle.hadoop.exttab.columnCount</name>
        <value>5</value>
```

```
        </property>
        <property>
            <name>oracle.hadoop.exttab.defaultDirectory</name>
            <value>FOOTBALL_DIR</value>
        </property>
        <property>
            <name>oracle.hadoop.connection.url</name>
            <value>jdbc:oracle:thin:@localhost:1521:orcl</value>
        </property>
        <property>
            <name>oracle.hadoop.connection.user</name>
            <value>SCOTT</value>
        </property>
</configuration>
```

Using configuration files does not prohibit the use of other properties via the –D option in the command line. This provides the flexibility to share configuration files for multiple uses.

The last two options for the ExternalTable tool are used for debugging or examining the definition of the external table created in the Oracle database. The –getDDL option will show the DDL as it is created in the database. This is the same DDL that can be viewed when using the –createTable option with the --noexecute parameter. However, not all the properties need to be specified with –getDLL. All that is needed is the oracle.hadoop.exttab.tableName property and the JDBC connection properties. This is an example to get the DDL for the GAMES table created in the SCOTT schema.

```
hadoop jar $OSCH_HOME/jlib/orahdfs.jar oracle.hadoop.exttab.ExternalTable
-D oracle.hadoop.exttab.tableName=GAMES
-D oracle.hadoop.connection.url=jdbc:oracle:thin:@localhost:1521:orcl
-D oracle.hadoop.connection.user=SCOTT -getDDL
```

NOTE
The –getDDL option leverages the DBMS_ METADATA PL/SQL package and thus applies the same security restrictions for accessing tables that a user would experience if they were logged in to the Oracle database.

The –listLocations option uses the same properties as the –getDDL option and is used to show details about the location file. The –listLocations option will show all the location file names and the HDFS files that are included in each file. If the –details option is included, then the command will return the location file details in XML format.

TIP
If a certain property is not needed for a particular option, it will be ignored. This allows reuse of configuration files for multiple scenarios.

```
hadoop jar $OSCH_HOME/jlib/orahdfs.jar oracle.hadoop.exttab.ExternalTable
-D oracle.hadoop.exttab.tableName=GAMES
-D oracle.hadoop.connection.url=jdbc:oracle:thin:@localhost:1521:orcl
-D oracle.hadoop.connection.user=SCOTT -listLocations
```

Querying with Oracle SQL Connector for HDFS

Querying data via an external table using Oracle SQL Connector for HDFS is completely transparent to the user. Any SQL that can be created against an Oracle table can now be used to query data that resides on Hadoop or more specifically HDFS. This capability gives Oracle users and applications real-time access to data on Hadoop.

For ETL tools and applications, this provides the ability to query data as if it were already in the Oracle database. As an example, an ETL tool can now use a CREATE TABLE AS SELECT statement to easily load a target table. Additionally, multiple files on Hadoop can be joined together, each with a parallel thread loading data into the database. Oracle will handle the join and filtering conditions to ensure accurate data. These are core database capabilities that Oracle has spent over 30 years implementing, improving, and hardening. Conceptually, this is no different than Oracle loading blocks of data off disks or storage arrays.

From a query perspective, Business Intelligence (BI) tools can now access data that resides on Hadoop without having to write specific drivers to generate MapReduce or HiveQL. HiveQL is a SQL-like language used by Hive that is most closely aligned with the SQL-92 standard. The version of the SQL standard supported is critical as many BI tools generate SQL based on more recent standards. BI tools will create complex queries, like subqueries, which Oracle supports and Hive offers only limited support.

Additionally, Oracle users who write queries can leverage all the capabilities and SQL structures that they are accustomed to. This eliminates the need to find an alternate way to do what they want. A simple example is how to join tables. Oracle developers are accustomed to joining tables with the following syntax:

```
select sum(b.population) / sum(a.complaints)
from service_requests a , population b
where (a.borough = b.borough)
group by a.borough
```

This will not work with HiveQL. Queries would need to be rewritten as

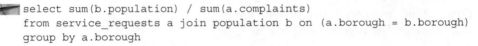

```
select sum(b.population) / sum(a.complaints)
from service_requests a join population b on (a.borough = b.borough)
group by a.borough
```

While this is a simple example, more complex examples arise when time-series analysis that requires windowing functions is needed. These functions are not SQL-92–compliant and thus not available in Hive. Queries can also join tables that come from different sources. A query can join a native Oracle table with a Hive table via Oracle SQL Connector for HDFS. A query can also join HDFS files with data stored in Oracle OLAP cubes. Anything that can be done in an Oracle database, can now be done against Hadoop data.

Oracle also provides a robust security model that is unmatched in any RDBMS. By comparison, Hive and newer tools like Impala only offer limited security capabilities. Using Oracle SQL Connector for HDFS, end users can be given access to data on Hadoop with row-level and column-level security. So a single table can now give secured access to multiple users without having to worry about them seeing each other's data. And without having to physically segregate the data.

Since Oracle SQL Connector for HDFS streams all data to the Oracle database and leverages the standard memory and caching structures of the database, some thought should go into what Hadoop data sources should be exposed to users. This is especially true when connecting Hadoop to an Oracle database that is not using the Exadata Database Machine. If a small two-node cluster that has 96GB of RAM is used and a 2TB data file is accessed via Oracle SQL Connector for HDFS, the machine will be overwhelmed. It is important to make sure there are available resources on the Oracle database to handle any additional load that users will put on it.

Oracle R Connector for Hadoop

In order to take further advantage of the instances of R installed on the Big Data Appliance, developers need a way to connect and interact with the cluster from their workstations. The Oracle Connector for Hadoop provides a collection of R packages that are installed on the R client just like any other R package. Oracle R Connector for Hadoop offers a wide range of functionality as described in Table 7-8.

For R users, Oracle R Connector for Hadoop provides the ability to copy data between R, HDFS, Hive, Oracle, and the user's local file system. Additionally, users can manipulate and transform data on any of these data sources and use R to write mappers and reducers to be executed as MapReduce code on the Hadoop cluster. These jobs can be scheduled and the results stored in any of the supported locations. The details on how to use the Oracle R Connector for Hadoop are covered in Chapter 10.

| Interfaces | Hive, Oracle Tables, Hadoop framework, Local R environment |
| Analytic Techniques | Linear regression, neural networks for prediction, matrix completion using low rank matrix factorization, clustering, and non-negative matrix factorization |

TABLE 7-8. *Oracle R Functionality Techniques*

Oracle Data Integrator Application Adapter for Hadoop

Oracle Data Integrator is Oracle's leading ELT tool for a wide range of data integration requirements. As an ELT technology, Oracle Data Integrator leverages either the source or target data platform to perform all data processing steps. The Oracle Data Integrator architecture provides tremendous performance benefits since it reduces the amount of data movement required compared to tools where a separate ETL server is required. Since Hadoop is designed to handle large volumes of data, it would be smart to leverage this platform for its data processing capabilities. Oracle Data Integrator uses knowledge modules, which are code templates that perform a specific task, as the basis for building data integration processes. In order to take advantage of the Hadoop platform, Oracle Data Integrator needs knowledge modules that can manipulate the data that resides on Hadoop.

Oracle Data Integrator Application Adapter for Hadoop provides the knowledge modules to provide the following basic data integration capabilities:

- Loading data into Hadoop

- Transforming and validating data that resides in Hadoop

- Loading data from Hadoop into an Oracle database, leveraging both Oracle Loader for Hadoop and Oracle SQL Connector for HDFS

Oracle Data Integrator knowledge modules were created to take advantage of Hive as the interface to create MapReduce jobs. Since there are various types of activities that a typical ETL process will require, Oracle created the knowledge modules to address the capabilities listed in Table 7-9.

Knowledge Module	Function	Source	Target
IKM File to Hive (Load Data)	Load data from HDFS or files system into a Hive table.	File System	Hive
IKM Hive Control Append	Uses SQL to transform or validate data that resides in Hive.	Hive	Hive
IKM Hive Transform	Used to transform unstructured data that resides in Hive by calling shell scripts, such as perl, awk, and so on.	Hive	Hive
IKM File-Hive to Oracle (Oracle Loader for Hadoop)	Used to load data into an Oracle database by leveraging Oracle Loader for Hadoop or Oracle SQL Connector for HDFS.	Hive or File System	Oracle
CKM Hive	Used to define constraints while loading data into a Hive table.	None	Hive
RKM Hive	Used to extract Hive metadata into ODI so that they can be used by any mapping.	Hive	None

TABLE 7-9. *Included Knowledge Modules*

ODI has several different categories of knowledge modules that address similar types of integration problems. The knowledge module categories included in the application adapter for Hadoop are

- **IKM** Integration Knowledge Modules
- **CKM** Check Knowledge Modules
- **RKM** Reverse-Engineering Knowledge Modules

These capabilities can be combined with other non-Hadoop–specific knowledge modules to provide a complete end-to-end ELT platform.

By using Oracle Data Integrator, Hadoop can be included as part of a complete integration strategy particularly for existing data warehouse and analytics platforms. The graphical interface allows for easy data workflows that span files, Hadoop, relational databases, and other sources and targets of information. The application adapters provide encapsulated knowledge so that developers do not need to know all the details of HDFS or Hive. They can simply access a particular knowledge module, fill in the relevant options, and the appropriate code will be generated. Since Oracle Data Integrator Application Adapter for Hadoop contains standard ODI knowledge modules, they can be combined with any other knowledge modules.

Oracle Data Integrator Application Adapter for Hadoop makes it easier to use the capabilities of Oracle Loader for Hadoop and Oracle SQL Connector for HDFS by generating the required configuration files for each of these objects. The IKM File-Hive to Oracle will generate the configuration and mapping files based on the options specified by the developer at design time using ODI Studio. ODI will then execute Oracle Loader for Hadoop when the ODI job is executed. This enhances the ability to include Hadoop data processing jobs to track lineage and provide additional metadata about the process. Jobs can also be scheduled and tracked just like any other ODI job.

The general types of processes of loading data into Hadoop that ODI enables are as follows:

- Bulk extract using DB Utilities to Hive/HDFS

- Load data files into Hive/HDFS

- Transform and validate data in Hive/HDFS

- Load processed data from Hive/HDFS into Oracle

CHAPTER
8

Oracle NoSQL Database

N oSQL database systems have become a growing part of the database technology landscape. Originally driven by Web-scale requirements, businesses are identifying additional opportunities for using these new data storage technologies. As mentioned in the earlier chapters, Oracle NoSQL Database is one of the storage technologies in the *data acquisition* part of Oracle's Big Data approach (represented as a canonical *acquire-organize-analyze-decide* data cycle). Oracle NoSQL Database serves as the data management platform for simple data and simple queries, for applications that require horizontally scalable data management (volume), and for low-latency queries (velocity) over both structured and unstructured data (variety) in the NoSQL repository.

Given the variety of NoSQL implementations, one of the challenges of NoSQL databases is to understand the implication and impact on application behavior of a given NoSQL database feature set. Additionally, NoSQL databases are not islands of data—they are an integral part of an overall Big Data solution. Data stored in a NoSQL database system often integrates and interacts with data in Hadoop (HDFS) as well as with the RDBMS databases within the corporation. Therefore, a second challenge with NoSQL database systems is to understand how the NoSQL database integrates with the rest of the solution architecture.

This chapter focuses on the primary features and capabilities of the Oracle NoSQL Database, how these affect application behavior, and how the Oracle NoSQL Database integrates into the Oracle Big Data Architecture. This chapter also includes a short section on how Oracle NoSQL Database compares to some of the other NoSQL databases available today.

What Is a NoSQL Database System?

The terms "NoSQL" or "Not-only-SQL" originated in 2009 to describe a collection of technical capabilities available in database systems that had evolved over the past decade as an alternative to general-purpose relational database systems (RDBMS). RDBMS systems, such as Oracle Database, are designed to provide general-purpose data management capabilities and standard APIs for a very wide variety of requirements and applications. NoSQL database systems, however, are designed with a specific type of application and a limited set of technical requirements in mind. Because the NoSQL database is designed to be used for specific kinds of applications, it is optimized for those use cases.

While the terms "NoSQL" or "Not-only-SQL" explain what NoSQL is not, they do little to explain what NoSQL is. It is perhaps most instructive to analyze NoSQL solutions relative to the relational database, the fundamental technology that has guided data management for the past 40 years. RDBMS systems include many features providing general-purpose functionality for a variety of application requirements. These features include standardized drivers, a query language (SQL), sophisticated query parsers/planners/executors, multiple storage and indexing options, server-side user-defined functions (stored procedures), security and authentication, and data lifecycle management, to name a few. Most importantly, RDBMS systems have been characterized by the transactional ACID properties: Atomicity, Consistency, Isolation, and Durability.

In contrast, NoSQL systems do not have an extensive set of standardized, general-purpose features. NoSQL databases are focused on providing low-latency data access for simple queries over large distributed data sets of simple structured and unstructured data, accessed via an application developer–centric interface. As such, NoSQL systems provide a focused set of features. Most importantly, NoSQL systems are often characterized by the BASE acronym:

- **Basically available**   Use replication to reduce the likelihood of data unavailability and use *sharding*, or partitioning the data among many different storage servers, to make any remaining failures partial. The result is a system that is always available, even if subsets of the data become unavailable for short periods of time.

- **Soft state**   While ACID transactional systems assume that data consistency is a hard requirement, NoSQL systems allow data to be inconsistent and relegate designing around such inconsistencies to application developers.

- **Eventually consistent**   Although applications may need to deal with instantaneous consistency, NoSQL systems ensure that at some future point in time the data assumes a consistent state. In contrast to ACID systems, which enforce consistency at transaction commit, NoSQL guarantees consistency only at some future time.

Companies such as Google, Amazon, Facebook, LinkedIn, Yahoo, and Twitter, as well as several open source projects, pioneered the implementation of these database systems. NoSQL database systems evolved as special purpose-built databases, designed to provide high throughput and fault-tolerant horizontally scalable simple data storage and retrieval with a bare minimum of additional functionality. They were designed for an emerging set of Web-scale applications that need to manage unprecedented data and operation volumes under tight latency constraints, but without the tight ACID transaction requirements of a traditional RDBMS. These applications typically required only simple primary key–based read/ write operations.

NoSQL systems provide horizontal scaling across a large number of servers (tens, hundreds, or even thousands of servers) by using a technique that has been deployed for many years in conventional RDBMS databases, called sharding. Sharding requires that a separate database run on each server and the data be physically partitioned so that each database has its own subset of the data stored on its own local disks. NoSQL systems maximize throughput and minimize latency by limiting how the sharded data is managed and accessed. Many early NoSQL systems typically did not provide support for operations that require accessing multiple shards of data—this includes joins, distributed transactions, and coordinated/synchronized schema changes—because of the I/O overhead and coordination required. Specifically, NoSQL systems were created to provide:

- Horizontally distributed data management of simple structured and unstructured data across a large cluster of commodity storage systems

- Highly fault-tolerant data management and the ability to continue operating even after multiple hardware and system failures

- High throughput with low latency for simple read/write operations, with limited BASE-style storage semantics

- Schema-less or flexible schema definitions allowing highly variable data and record structures

- Application and application developer–centric special purpose, low-overhead data models and APIs

- Developer-friendly simple system administration and deployment

As of February 2013, there are over 100 systems that call themselves NoSQL database systems.[1] Due to the variability of NoSQL system implementations mentioned earlier, one of the challenges in selecting a NoSQL database system is understanding how the capabilities of that database will correspond to technical application requirements, how it will facilitate application development, and how it will ultimately be deployed in production. Each NoSQL database system has different feature sets, development APIs, performance, scalability, and operational characteristics. It is crucial to understand these factors when choosing a NoSQL database system.

NoSQL Applications

Although many applications need a database to ensure efficient, reliable data access, not all applications require the full set of RDBMS functionality. If the application doesn't require all of the functionality in a typical RDBMS, it doesn't make sense that a developer would use or that a customer would pay for a large, complex system with hundreds of features that they don't need. In this case it makes

---

[1] "NoSQL." *Wikipedia: The Free Encyclopedia*. Wikimedia Foundation, Inc. http://en.wikipedia.org/wiki/. Accessed 24 Feb 2013.
"NoSQL." http://nosql-databases.org/. Accessed 24 Feb 2013.

much more sense to use a NoSQL database because it's the best tool for the application requirements.

NoSQL applications typically have the following requirements: simple data structures, simple queries, large volumes of data (terabytes to petabytes), minimal latency, and relaxable transaction semantics. For lack of a better term, we'll call these "Web-scale" or "last-mile-to-the-customer" applications. They are Web-scale in the sense that they manage massive amounts of data, with requirements for both high concurrency and low latency. They complete that "last mile" in the sense that they provide the highly scalable, low-latency data management platform at the edge of the data center for applications that bridge the gap between the corporate RDBMS systems and a large community of end customers or mobile devices over the Web.

Applications such as analyzing clickstream data from high-volume Web sites, high-throughput event processing, and social networking communications represent domains that produce extraordinary volumes of simple keyed data. Monitoring online retail behavior, accessing customer profiles, pulling up appropriate customer ads, and storing and forwarding real-time communication are examples of domains requiring low-latency access. Highly distributed applications such as real-time sensor aggregation and scalable authentication also represent domains that require the combination of high concurrency and low latency and are therefore well-suited to NoSQL database systems.

Oracle NoSQL Database

Oracle NoSQL Database is an enterprise-class, horizontally scalable key-value NoSQL database system. It provides highly reliable, highly available transactional storage for simple data and simple queries. It is designed to provide low-latency data access for Web-scale applications. Application development is simplified by its simple, developer-friendly Java and C APIs, configurable transactions, large object support, and automatic data and query distribution. This allows application developers to focus more on their value-add features and get their solutions into production sooner. Its operations-friendly reliability, manageability, and configurability features simplify application and database deployment and management.

The Oracle NoSQL Database is offered as either a software-only product or integrated with Oracle Big Data Appliance. Oracle NoSQL Database Community Edition is available under an open-source AGPL license, while Oracle NoSQL Database Enterprise Edition is available under an Oracle software license. Both the Community and Enterprise Editions can be downloaded directly from the Oracle Technology Network Web site (see links at the end of this chapter). The Oracle NoSQL Database can be used standalone or in conjunction with Oracle Database and Hadoop. It includes integration with the Oracle technology stack as well as with open source Apache Hadoop. The combination of its technical features, operational manageability, and integration in a comprehensive Big Data technology stack from Oracle make Oracle NoSQL Database a best-of-breed NoSQL database system from the leading provider of hardware and software solutions engineered to work together.

The Oracle NoSQL Database manages data across a configurable set of systems that function as storage nodes. Data is stored as records composed of key-value pairs, where the key is a string that contains both a Major and Minor key component and the value is a simple byte array. Records are written to a particular shard, based on the hashed value of the Major key. Shards are stored on storage nodes, which can be configured for replication to ensure high availability, rapid failover, and optimal query load balancing. The Oracle NoSQL Database driver links with the client application, transparently providing direct access to the shard for the requested key. Oracle NoSQL Database provides standard BASE-style storage semantics, as well as configurable ACID transactions for multirecord operations within a Major key. It provides both a Web-based console as well as a command-line interface for easy administration of the Oracle NoSQL Database storage and administration cluster. Oracle NoSQL Database provides integration interfaces with other Oracle products within the Big Data solution stack.

A Sample Use Case

Let's look at a specific example of an application that leverages the capabilities of Oracle NoSQL Database—customer profile management. In the past, customer profiles were typically limited to financial transaction–oriented data structures/repositories. Today, a customer profile includes a much richer data set that includes information from a wide variety of customer interaction points that include both structured and unstructured data. The data in a modern customer profile might include images, recordings, files, preferred products, preferred locations, Web browsing history, related customer links (friends and family), customer care history, retail activities, loyalty program information, and so on. Capturing and managing this new class of data is crucial to the enterprise, in order to more effectively obtain a 360-degree view of a customer and to optimize customer interactions. This information enables a broad category of Line-of-Business applications from marketing, advertising, customer service, risk analysis, fraud detection, personalized content, promotional campaigns, loyalty programs, inventory management, and so on. These Line-of-Business applications leverage the richer user-profile data in order to provide:

- More personalized customer experiences via targeted product offerings, special promotions, loyalty rewards, more informed/context sensitive interactions, and so on

- Better operational insight into how customers interact with them, how they perceive the company and its products and services, with a longer and more complete historical perspective

- Better competitive insight into how customers perceive their competition

- Better operational decision-making, based on a more detailed understanding of their customers

Modern customer profile management applications benefit directly from the capabilities of Oracle NoSQL Database because they provide:

- A horizontally scalable, distributed data management system to manage the large volume of data that is part of rich customer profiles. These profiles grow incrementally over time as additional detailed information is captured and as the customer base expands.

- A highly fault-tolerant system, ensuring that the customer profile data is always available.

- A flexible-schema or no-schema data store, which facilitates a wide variety of data record formats to be stored in a given customer profile and for those record formats to evolve over time.

- Specialized, high-throughput, low-latency application-specific read and write access to the portions of the customer profile.

The functionality that is required is very simple—the application needs to read and write a few records based on the primary key—the customer ID. These records combine structured and unstructured data, stored in a way (often denormalized) that allows the application to operate on the subset of data that it needs for that specific type of transaction. For example, a customer care application doesn't need the entire customer profile, only those aspects that are required for that functionality—perhaps customer care history, recent Web browsing history, and contact information. Customer profile management applications typically have to perform an extremely high number of these simple lookup operations based on a customer ID with minimal latency. The high concurrency and low latency requirements are critical to the business because these applications often implement the "last mile" interface with the customer, who in turn interacts directly with the content managed in the Oracle NoSQL Database. Real-world studies have shown that any increase in latency can be linked directly to reduced revenue and loss of business.[2] It is also the case that a subset of the customer profile data is integrated with and accessed by the corporate data warehouse running

---

[2] Amazon.com conducted an extensive study that demonstrated a direct relationship between increased latency and loss of revenue. For every 100ms (that's 1/10th of a second) of increased latency on their Web site, they observed a decrease of 1 percent in revenue. In other words, an almost imperceptible increase in latency translated directly into lost business because customers stopped browsing or using the site.

on the Oracle Database, as well as with Hadoop/MapReduce functionality that may be a part of the overall application architecture. The integration of data in the Oracle NoSQL Database with Oracle Database is critically important because it provides the platform that allows the execution of complex queries and offers analytical functions that provide insights and additional business value to the NoSQL data.

The example of these "last-mile" kinds of applications can be extended to sensor data (machine profiles, rather than customer profiles), advertising programs, financial data, product data, and so on. The bottom line is that for these kinds of operations—simple queries over simple data, with low latency and high concurrency requirements—Oracle NoSQL Database is the right tool for the job.

Architecture

The Oracle NoSQL Database client/server architecture consists of two major components: a client driver and a collection of storage nodes (see Figure 8-1). The client driver implements the hash partition map (mapping keys to shards) and the Shard

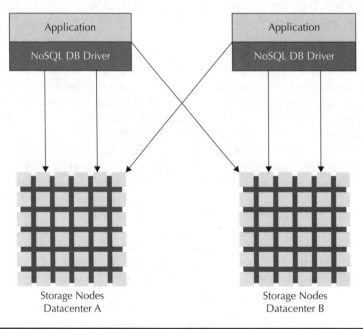

FIGURE 8-1. *Architectural components of Oracle NoSQL Database*

State Table (SST) (tracking the state and location of each data shard). The storage nodes manage the sharded data and implement the replication processing for each shard. Oracle NoSQL Database uses Oracle Berkeley DB Java Edition High Availability on the storage nodes to provide highly available, low-latency key-value storage. Berkeley DB Java Edition is an enterprise-grade key-value storage library that is used to power large-scale production Web sites and products including Amazon.com, LinkedIn, Yammer, Juniper Networks, and many others. In this section, we'll take a closer look at each of these architectural components.

Client Driver

The client driver is a Java .jar file that exports the API to applications. In addition, the client driver maintains a copy of the topology recorded in the Shard State Table (SST). The topology efficiently maps keys to shards. Each shard is stored on one or more storage nodes—one if the shard is unreplicated and more than one for a replicated shard. For each shard, the SST contains the host names and service name of all storage nodes that hold a copy of the shard and the data center in which each storage node resides. The client driver then uses the SST for two primary purposes: identifying the master node of a shard (where it sends write operations) and load-balancing read operations across all the nodes in a shard. Since the SST is a critical data structure, each client driver and storage node maintains its own copy, thus avoiding any single point of failure. Both the client drivers and replication nodes run a RequestDispatcher thread that uses the SST to (re)direct write requests to the master and read requests to the appropriate member of a shard.

The Oracle NoSQL Database Topology (a logical representation of the physical system configuration) is loaded during client driver or replication node initialization and is subsequently updated automatically by the administrator process if there are topology changes, such as adding more storage nodes. The SST is dynamic, automatically updating itself as topology and storage node state changes arrive. Each replication node runs a background thread, called the Replication Node State Update thread, that is responsible for ongoing maintenance of the SST. The update thread, as well as the RequestDispatcher, opportunistically collects information on remote replication nodes including the current state of the node in its shard, an indication of how up to date the node is, the time of the last successful interaction with the node, the node's trailing average response time, and the current length of its outstanding request queue. In addition, the update thread maintains network connections and re-establishes broken ones. This maintenance is done outside the RequestDispatcher's request/response cycle to minimize the impact of broken connections on latency.

Key-Value Pairs

In its simplest form, Oracle NoSQL Database implements a map from user-defined keys (strings) to data items. It records an internal version number for each key-value pair and only the latest version is retained in the store (see Table 8-1). Applications never need to worry about reconciling incompatible versions because Oracle NoSQL Database uses single-master replication; the master node always has the most up-to-date value for a given key, while read-only replicas might have slightly older versions. Applications can use version numbers to ensure consistency for Read-Modify-Write (RMW) operations.

A key is a string consisting of the concatenation of a Major Key Path and a Minor Key Path, both of which are specified by the application. Oracle NoSQL Database hashes the Major Key Path to provide good distribution across the database shards. Applications can take advantage of Minor Key Path capabilities to achieve data locality. All of the records sharing a Major Key Path are co-located on the same shard, thus achieving data locality (see Figure 8-2). Within a co-located collection of Major Key Paths, the full key, consisting of both the Major and Minor Key Paths, provides fast, indexed lookups (see Table 8-2). For example, an application storing

Major Key (UserID)	Minor Key (Type)	JSON Object
AA345	ACT	{ "fname" : "John" , "lname" : "Smith" , "addr" : "17 Happy St, Whoville, MT"...}
AA345	Likes	{ [{ "userid" : "FX123" } , { "userid" : "ZF987" } , ...] }
AA345	P201304	{ [{ "itemid" : "I3456"} , { "itemid" : "IA001" } , ...] }
AA345	P201303	{ [{ "itemid" : "7541"}] }
FX123	ACT	{ "fname" : "Sandy" , "lname" : "Clark" , "addr" : "2331 Main, Oakland, CT" ...}
FX123	Likes	{ [{ "userid" : "UU223" } , { "userid" : "AA345" } , ...] }
FX123	P201212	{ [{ "itemid" : "IOO667"} , { "itemid" : "ITR412"} , { "itemid" : "RTR8712" } ...] }
HB001	ACT	{ "fname" : "Juan" , "lname" : "Sanchez" , "addr" : "23 First St, Los Gatos, NM"...}

TABLE 8-1. *Example Key-Value Pairs*

Major Key (UserID)	Minor Key (Type)	JSON Object	Shard
AA345	ACT	John Smith …	Shard01
AA345	Likes	FX123 …	Shard01
AA345	P201304	I3456 …	Shard01
AA345	P201303	7541 …	Shard01
FX123	ACT	Sandy Clark …	Shard02
FX123	Likes	UU223 …	Shard02
FX123	P201212	IO0667 …	Shard02
HB001	ACT	Juan Sanchez …	Shard03

TABLE 8-2. *Keys and Shards*

customer profiles might use the user-name as a Major Key Path and then have
several Minor Key Paths for different records within that profile such as contact
information, browsing history, related customer links, and so on. Because
applications have complete control over the composition and interpretation of keys,
different Major Key Paths can have entirely different Minor Key Path structures.
Continuing our previous example, one might store customer profiles and product
profiles in the same database and maintain different Minor Key Paths for each. Prefix
key compression makes storage of key groups efficient.

A value, in its most basic form, is a simple opaque byte array, serialized and
deserialized by the application. Oracle NoSQL Database also allows the application

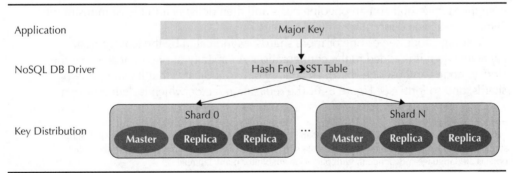

FIGURE 8-2. *NoSQL database driver and shards*

developer to express a value as a JSON[3] object, which is a de facto standard structure used in Big Data and NoSQL products today. Oracle NoSQL Database uses Avro[4] to serialize and deserialize the JSON objects. In addition to JSON objects, the Avro API also supports Object, Specific, and Raw data binding options. The Avro API supports schema evolution as well as dynamic runtime schema resolution.

The combination of highly efficient key-value storage, flexible Major plus Minor Key Path definitions, unstructured as well as structured value definitions, and serialization provides the application developer with a powerful and extremely flexible set of tools. These features can be leveraged to optimize how the application manages data in the Oracle NoSQL Database, simplify application development, and reduce time to market.[5]

Storage Nodes

A storage node (SN) is typically a physical machine with its own local persistent storage, either disk or solid state, a CPU with one or more cores, memory, and an IP address. Storage nodes may be added to the system and used to increase the number of shards or replicas in order to improve capacity and throughput, decrease latency, and increase availability. Oracle NoSQL Database configurations with more storage nodes will provide greater aggregate throughput and storage capacity than one with fewer nodes. Configurations with a greater number of shards will provide greater write throughput and lower latency than one with fewer shards. Configurations with a greater degree of replication will provide increased availability in the event of storage node failure, and decreased read latency over one with smaller degrees of replication.

A Storage Node Agent (SNA) runs on each storage node, monitoring that node's behavior. The SNA (a) receives configuration information from, and (b) reports monitoring information to, the Administration Service, which interfaces to the Oracle NoSQL Database monitoring dashboard. The SNA collects operational data from the storage node on an ongoing basis and then delivers it to the Administration Service when asked for it.

A storage node serves one or more shards, as indicated by the storage node *capacity* when it is added to the configuration. A capacity of one indicates that the storage node can host one shard; a capacity of two indicates that it can host two shards, and so forth (see Figure 8-3). The *replication factor,* which is defined when

---

[3] JavaScript Object Notation (JSON), is an open standard data interchange derived from the JavaScript scripting language for representing simple data structures and associative arrays, called objects. JSON objects are language-independent, with parsers available for many languages.

[4] Avro is a serialization framework developed as part of Apache Hadoop. It uses JSON for defining data types and serializes data into a very efficient compact binary format.

[5] See the Passoker Use Case that talks about a 75 percent time savings on application development and implementation using Oracle NoSQL Database. www.oracle.com/us/corporate/customers/customersearch/passoker-1-nosql-ss-1863507.html

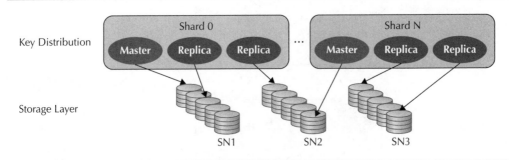

FIGURE 8-3. *Shards and storage nodes*

configuring the Oracle NoSQL Database installation, indicates how many copies will be maintained for each shard. One copy must be designated as the master, which is the copy that processes write operations; any additional copies of the shard are read-only replicas, but may assume the role of master if the master node fails. A typical configuration uses a replication factor of three to ensure that the system can survive at least two simultaneous faults and still continue to service read operations. Applications requiring greater or lesser reliability can adjust this parameter accordingly.

Replication

Oracle NoSQL Database uses replication to a) ensure data availability in the case of storage node failure, and b) provide read scalability across multiple copies of the data. Its single-master architecture requires that writes are applied at the master node and then propagated to the replicas. In the case of failure of the master node, the remaining storage nodes in a shard automatically hold a reliable election (using the Paxos protocol), electing one of the remaining nodes to be the master. The new master then assumes write responsibility. In the case of failure of a storage node that contains a read-only replica, the system continues to operate, servicing reads from the remaining replicas for that shard. Replicas rejoining the system are automatically brought back in sync with the current state of the data in the shard via background, throttled processes to minimize the impact on the overall system throughput.

Replication is implemented using the Oracle Berkeley DB Java Edition transaction and high-availability functionality on each of the storage nodes (see Figure 8-4). The Oracle NoSQL Database driver sends write operations directly to the storage node that contains the master node for the shard that maps to the Major Key Path being written. The Oracle Berkeley DB Java Edition database contained in the storage node will propagate the write operations to proper associated replicas. The Oracle Berkeley DB Java Edition storage engine is used in several NoSQL databases, including Oracle NoSQL Database, as well as in Enterprise deployments such as Yammer, Verizon Wireless, and many others.

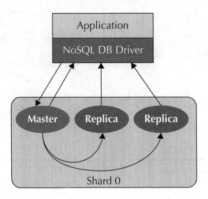

FIGURE 8-4. *Replication (per shard)*

Smart Topology

Oracle NoSQL Database employs a set of built-in rules that automate and simplify the task of assigning shards to the available storage nodes. As mentioned earlier, a storage node can manage one or more shards (based on *capacity*) and a shard can have one or more copies (based on *replication factor*, a master and *N* replicas). These rules generate an optimal allocation of resources, based on the available storage nodes and the requested configuration. These rules ensure that:

- A storage node with a capacity greater than one will only have one master. This limits the impact on the system of a failure of a given storage node.

- A storage node with a capacity greater than one is guaranteed to have all of its replicas come from different shards. This balances I/O throughput given that a "busy shard" will distribute its load over multiple storage nodes.

Online Elasticity

You can change the topology of an Oracle NoSQL Database system in several ways: a) modify the *replication factor* to increase read scalability; b) add storage nodes in order to create more shards, which will increase write scalability; and c) rebalance the storage node/shard allocation after a series of physical topology changes to improve load balancing and data distribution across storage nodes. Because a topology change can include multiple operations (for example: starting up a new set of replicas, moving data into a new shard, transferring shards between storage nodes), a topology change is represented by a *plan*. Plans can be created, viewed, validated, and deployed. Before deploying a plan, the Oracle NoSQL Database will validate it using its smart topology rules. When deploying a plan, it will spawn a series of background, low-impact threads to implement the necessary functions required by the plan. Each thread will execute a series of smaller unit subtasks for each stage of the operation. During the time that it takes to deploy a plan, the Oracle NoSQL Database system continues to be completely available. While the plan is being deployed, you can query the state of the plan, interrupt it, retry it (in case of interruption or failure), or even cancel it. While deploying a plan, Oracle NoSQL Database will ensure that the new resources are available to the system as soon as a given subtask is completed.

No Single Point of Failure

Through the combination of a) distributed, self-updating SST tables (both the client drivers and the storage nodes maintain local copies), b) built-in, field-tested replication, c) Smart Topology and automated resource allocation, and d) online elasticity, Oracle NoSQL Database provides an architecture with no single point of failure and optimized throughput.

Data Management

In the previous sections, we've discussed the Oracle NoSQL Database architecture and how the data is actually stored. In this section we'll discuss how an application manages and operates on the data that is stored in Oracle NoSQL Database. The data management capabilities of Oracle NoSQL Database were designed with the application developer in mind—they are designed to be simple to understand, easy to use, and highly flexible in order to adapt easily to varying application requirements and design patterns.

APIs

Oracle NoSQL Database offers both a C and a Java API. Applications can call the APIs from one or more client processes. Leveraging the SST, the client application processes transparently communicate directly with the appropriate Oracle NoSQL Database server process. This facilitates a flexible client/server architecture that also allows installation and use of Oracle NoSQL Database on a single system, facilitating initial application development and testing.

Incorporating Oracle NoSQL Database into applications is straightforward. APIs for basic create, read, update, and delete (CRUD) operations and a collection of iterators are distributed in a single jar file, which simplifies client application installation and management.

CRUD Operations

Data create and update operations are provided by several put methods. The putIfAbsent method implements creation while the putIfPresent method implements update. The put method does both by adding a new key-value pair if the key doesn't exist in the database or by updating the value if the key already exists. Updating a key-value pair generates a new version of the pair, so the API also includes a conditional putIfVersion method that allows applications to implement consistent Read-Modify-Write semantics.

The delete and deleteIfVersion methods unconditionally and conditionally remove key-value pairs from the database, respectively. Just as putIfVersion ensures Read-Modify-Write semantics, deleteIfVersion provides deletion of a specific version.

The get method provides keyed retrieval.

Support for conditional operator methods like putIfAbsent, putIfPresent, and deleteIfVersion allows the application to execute conditional operations within a single client/server round trip, thus optimizing client/server communication and reducing latency.

Multiple Update Operations

In addition to providing single-record operations, Oracle NoSQL Database supports the ability to bundle a collection of operations together using the execute method. This method provides transactional semantics across multiple update operations on records that have the same Major Key Path. For example, let's assume that we have the Major Key Path of "AB12345" as the Customer ID from the customer profile example, with several different Minor Key Paths for different records that contain profile information for "John Doe," such as contact and credit card information. Imagine that we discover that we have an incorrect phone number and credit card expiration date currently in the database. The application can package up the put operations together (one for each record or Minor Key Path) and execute them as a single ACID transaction.

Lookup Operations

In addition to basic CRUD operations, Oracle NoSQL Database supports two types of iteration: unordered iteration over records and ordered iteration within a Major Key set.

In the case of unordered iteration over the entire store, the result is not transactional; the iteration runs at an isolation level of read-committed, which means that the result set will contain only key-value pairs that have been persistently written to the database, but there are no guarantees of semantic consistency across key-value pairs.

The API supports both individual key-value returns using several `storeIterator` methods and bulk key-value returns within a Major Key Path via the various `multiGetIterator` methods. Although the iterator returns only a single key-value pair at a time, the `storeIterator` method takes a second parameter of *batchSize*, indicating how many key-value pairs to fetch per network round trip. This allows applications to simultaneously use network bandwidth efficiently, while maintaining the simplicity of key-at-a-time access in the API.

Transactions

While many NoSQL databases state that they provide eventual transaction consistency, Oracle NoSQL Database provides several different transaction consistency policies. These policies are defined by the application via read *Consistency* and write *Durability* policy objects. These objects can be defined globally for the entire application and overridden on a per-operation basis, depending on the application requirements.

The read Consistency policy tells the system what degree of read consistency is required for an operation. At one end of the spectrum, an application can specify a read Consistency of ABSOLUTE, which guarantees that all reads return the most recently written value for a designated key, which requires a read from the master node for that shard. At the other end of the spectrum, an application capable of tolerating inconsistent data can specify a Consistency of NONE, allowing the database to use query load balancing to efficiently return a value from any of the replication nodes for that shard. In between these two extremes, an application can specify time-based Consistency to constrain how old a record can be returned or version-based Consistency to support both atomicity for Read-Modify-Write operations and reads that are at least as recent as the specified version. The time-based and version-based read Consistency policies cause the client driver to choose any of the qualifying replication nodes, based on the Shard State Table, for that shard. The default read Consistency policy for Oracle NoSQL Database is NONE.

Figure 8-5 shows how the range of flexible consistency policies enables developers to easily create business solutions that provide the required data consistency guarantees while meeting application latency and scalability requirements.

Oracle NoSQL Database also provides a range of write Durability policies. The write Durability policy tells the system how to persist the data and how many

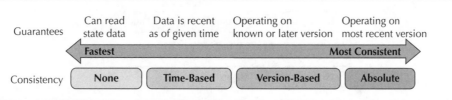

FIGURE 8-5.   *Read Consistency policies*

replicas must acknowledge the write operation before it is considered to be committed. All write operations are executed on the master node for that shard. At one extreme, applications can specify a Durability policy (DISK, ALL) that requires write requests to block until the record has been written to stable storage on all of the replicas and all of the replicas have returned an acknowledgment to the master (synchronous replication). This has obvious performance and latency implications, but ensures that if the application successfully writes data, that data will persist and can be recovered even if all the copies become temporarily unavailable due to multiple simultaneous failures. At the other extreme, applications can specify a Durability policy of MEMORY,NONE that allows write operations to return as soon as the system has recorded the existence of the write to local memory on the master without waiting for any of the replicas to return an acknowledgement, even if the data is not persistent anywhere. Such a policy provides the best write performance, but provides no durability guarantees. The default write Durability policy for Oracle NoSQL Database is that writes are persisted to local memory and that a majority of replicas have to acknowledge the write (durability via replication). This policy is called MEMORY,MAJORITY. By specifying where to persist the data and what fraction of the replicas must acknowledge processing the write operation (none, all, or a simple majority), applications can enforce a wide range of durability policies.

Figure 8-6 shows how the range of flexible write Durability policies enables developers to easily create applications that balance the requirements for write durability guarantees while meeting application latency and scalability requirements.

Predictable Performance

Oracle NoSQL Database focuses on not simply providing excellent throughput and performance, but also implementing functionality designed to provide *predictable* performance. Oracle NoSQL Database achieves this via a combination of configuration options and product architecture. Oracle NoSQL Database provides out-of-box optimized configuration settings for the JVM (Java Virtual Machine) environment as well as optimized database caching and object management designed to minimize the impact of Java Garbage Collection processing. From an architectural perspective, Oracle NoSQL Database operates multiple background threads on the storage nodes

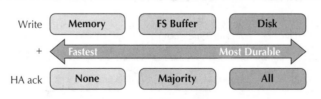

FIGURE 8-6. *Write Durability policies*

to perform routine data management tasks. These tasks are implemented such that they perform smaller, more frequent units of work and therefore have less impact on the throughput of a large production system. Other NoSQL databases often suffer significant performance and throughput degradation when Java Garbage Collection or other routine data management tasks are automatically executed.

Integration

Oracle NoSQL Database is integrated with other related products such as Oracle Database, Oracle Big Data Connectors, Oracle Event Processing, Oracle RDF Graph, Oracle Coherence, and Hadoop/MapReduce. As mentioned earlier, integration with the rest of the enterprise technology stack is crucial because most Big Data projects require integrating multiple, complementary data management technologies. Other NoSQL database systems often require that the developer figure out how to implement integration with their other IT assets. Oracle is the only vendor that has a comprehensive offering of integrated technologies.

Oracle NoSQL Database integrates with Oracle Database via External Tables. The application developer defines a formatter class and an external table properties XML file using sample code and sample templates from the Oracle NoSQL Database distribution. The formatter class accesses the NoSQL database repository, converting the data into a format that can be read by the External Table reader, for example, CSV. The XML property file links the table name with the formatter class and parameters needed to access the Oracle NoSQL Database. The Oracle DBA then defines an External Table via SQL in Oracle Database. Once these simple steps are completed, NoSQL data can be accessed directly via SQL from Oracle Database. Having made the NoSQL database data available via External Tables, it can now participate in any SQL query that uses Oracle Database, including Oracle Advanced Analytics, Oracle Fusion Middleware applications, and Oracle OBI EE.

Oracle NoSQL Database integrates with Hadoop by providing a KVInputFormat method API that generates data in a format that is expected as the input format by MapReduce jobs in Hadoop. This allows Oracle NoSQL Database to appear like any other MapReduce data source, thus allowing NoSQL database data to participate in MapReduce processes.

Oracle NoSQL Database integrates with the Oracle Loader for Hadoop (OLH), which is part of the Oracle Big Data Connectors, using the same KVInputFormat method API. This allows NoSQL database data to participate in the high-performance data-loading capabilities of the Oracle Loader for Hadoop, described earlier in this book.

Oracle NoSQL Database integrates with Oracle Event Processing via a NoSQL Database Cartridge (provided by OEP) that allows the OEP rules engine to read data from the Oracle NoSQL Database, thus allowing the Event Processing rules and logic to incorporate data from the NoSQL repository.

Oracle NoSQL Database integrates with Oracle RDF Graph via an adapter (provided by Oracle NoSQL Database) that loads RDF data into the NoSQL database and supports SPARQL queries over that data. This allows applications to store and query graph data as part of the data set that is managed on Oracle NoSQL Database, thus adding to the rich data set being captured in NoSQL and enabling applications to combine key-value– and graph-based queries within a single database.

Oracle NoSQL Database integrates with Oracle Coherence via a transparent caching mechanism whereby Coherence persists changes to cached objects to NoSQL and faults objects into the Coherence cache from NoSQL when required. Applications can choose to implement either a shared access strategy where both Coherence and independent applications can access the data in NoSQL, or they can choose a Coherence-only access, where applications only read and write data through the Coherence cache.

Through these and other Oracle integration interfaces, Oracle NoSQL Database is truly a part of an integrated technology ecosystem. This allows developers and customers to leverage their existing IT assets and facilitates building solutions that use the right storage technology for the right job without having to sacrifice integration or take on additional integration tasks (and risk).

Installation and Administration

By their very nature, NoSQL databases are distributed storage systems. They typically span tens or hundreds of servers, and can even encompass thousands of servers. In this kind of environment simple installation and administration are key requirements to overall system manageability. Oracle NoSQL Database has been designed to provide a simple, recoverable, scriptable management interface.

Simple Installation

Oracle NoSQL Database is simple to install, whether on a single system for development and testing purposes or on a large cluster of systems for benchmarking or production purposes. The developer or administrator installs and starts the NoSQL database software package on each storage node in the configuration. Once installed and started, the system is configured and deployed using the Administration CLI via a series of scriptable commands. Once configured and deployed, applications can start accessing the Oracle NoSQL Database by connecting to any one of the storage nodes in the system.

Administration

Oracle NoSQL Database comes with an Administration Service, accessible from both a Command Line Interface (CLI) and a Web console. Using the CLI, administrators can configure a database instance, start it, stop it, and monitor system performance.

The administrator can also expand database storage, by specifying additional storage nodes, changing the replication factor, or rebalancing the data in the existing storage nodes. When rebalancing data in the system, by adding new shards or by simply rebalancing the existing set of shards, Oracle NoSQL Database will automatically redistribute the data to the new storage nodes without interrupting service. The data distribution will be handled by background, throttled processes, which minimize the throughput impact to the running system.

The Administration Service is itself a highly available service. Consistent with the Oracle NoSQL Database "No Single Point of Failure" philosophy, it is also replicated and is maintained independently of normal system operation. Therefore, normal data read/write operations are not dependent upon the availability of the Administration Service. Thus, both the database and the Administration Service remain available during configuration changes.

In addition to facilitating configuration changes, the Administration Service also collects and maintains performance statistics and logs important system events, providing online monitoring and input to performance tuning. Oracle NoSQL Database also provides a JMX and SNMP interface to allow external monitoring packages to query and display state and performance information for the NoSQL database.

How Oracle NoSQL Database Stacks Up

Generally speaking, when comparing any of the other NoSQL databases with Oracle NoSQL Database, you will find the following key differentiators:

- Oracle NoSQL Database is developed and supported by Oracle, the leading database technology provider in the world.

- Oracle NoSQL Database is tightly integrated with a comprehensive technology ecosystem, including Oracle Database, Oracle Event Processing, Oracle RDF, Oracle Coherence, Oracle Big Data Connectors, and Oracle Communications Manager (Elastic Charging Engine). Most NoSQL database companies only have one product, and none of the other NoSQL database systems have as comprehensive of an integrated technology ecosystem. This facilitates leveraging existing IT assets and infrastructure in building a comprehensive Big Data solution.

- Oracle NoSQL Database provides both BASE-style storage semantics and shard-level configurable ACID transactions. Very few NoSQL databases offer this level of flexibility. This makes application development much simpler because applications can rely on the transaction semantics that are built into the database rather than having to implement application code to have to deal with its absence.

■ Oracle NoSQL Database is simple to deploy and manage. Many other NoSQL database systems work well in small configurations, but large configurations are unwieldy and difficult to manage. Oracle NoSQL Database is designed to be easy to deploy and manage for both developers and system administrators, regardless of the size of your cluster.

■ Oracle NoSQL Database is highly tuned to deliver predictable response times. Most other NoSQL databases have problems with file system cleanup, data compaction, data rebalancing, and Java Garbage Collection with significant impact on their overall throughput predictability. It's not about how fast you can run right now; it's about how predictable performance is over the long haul. The Oracle NoSQL Database team understands the high concurrency and low latency requirements of today's challenging Web-scale applications and has implemented a system driven toward predictable and consistent performance.

■ Oracle NoSQL Database has been benchmarked extensively, ranging from tens to hundreds of storage nodes in a configuration with billions of records. It has consistently demonstrated near-linear scalability and high reliability throughout the range of configurations used. Most other NoSQL database systems have tested configurations of tens of storage nodes and millions of records. This allows customers to deploy solutions using Oracle NoSQL Database, with the confidence that when they need the scalability of storage, processing and data, it will be there.

Useful Links

■ **Landing pages**
Product page: www.oracle.com/us/products/database/nosql/overview/index.html
OTN: www.oracle.com/technetwork/products/nosqldb/overview/index.html

■ **Documentation**   http://docs.oracle.com/cd/NOSQL/html/index.html

■ **Downloads**   www.oracle.com/technetwork/products/nosqldb/downloads/index.html

■ **Benchmarks**   www.oracle.com/technetwork/products/nosqldb/overview/benchmark-result-1575736.html

■ **OTN Technical Discussion Forum**   https://forums.oracle.com/forums/forum.jspa?forumID=1388

PART
III

Analyzing Information and Making Decisions

CHAPTER
9

In-Database Analytics:
Delivering Faster
Time to Value

T he key section of Oracle's Big Data workflow is the "Analyze" section because it is at this point in the workflow that the data captured during the "Stream" and "Acquire" phases is transformed into real insight and business value. This workflow is shown in Figure 9-1.

Big Data is built on a broad range of data streams that contain low-level detailed data points. It is not possible to simply take this raw data and present it in a BI report because the number of data points would be overwhelming. The best approach is to look for patterns and hidden nuggets within these data streams. The role of Big Data analytics is to help data scientists, business users, and developers to make these discoveries in a timely manner.

The aim of this chapter is to provide a high-level overview of the various key analytical features that are part of the Oracle Database that support the "Analyze" section of Oracle's Big Data workflow.

Introduction

To get the value from these Big Data streams, developers, data scientists, and business users need access to a wide variety of analytical features with the ability to mix and match these features as required. To get maximum value from these Big Data streams, integration with other key data sources, such as operational data sources, data marts, and/or data warehouses, is a key requirement.

The Oracle Big Data workflow is designed to support this requirement and allows users to analyze all their data because it provides access to a broad range of analytical features. Big data projects need access to a broad range of analytical features such as:

- Data mining

- Predictive analytics

- Text mining

FIGURE 9-1. *Oracle's Big Data workflow*

- Spatial analytics

- Semantic analytics

- Multidimensional analytics

- Statistics

In the past, many businesses deployed standalone specialized analytic engines and client tools to help develop, test, and refine their analysis. This typically involved working with small amounts of data shipped from a centralized data store (typically a data warehouse) and loaded into a specialized processing engine. Once the correct result set had been created, the results were either viewed in-place or shipped back to the data warehouse so that other users could access the results. This approach is often referred to as "taking the data to the analytics."

The problem with this approach of using of multiple, isolated analytical engines is that it creates too many other problems including fragmented analysis, increased data movement, reduced data security, and lack of code reusability. This is important because if producing the analysis takes too long, then any opportunity uncovered could well be lost, which might mean that fraudulent activities are missed, sales are lost, or customers are lost to competitors. If the data is not correctly secured, a company's reputation can be quickly damaged and large fines can be imposed by government agencies.

As Big Data projects evolve, it is becoming clear that analyzing each Big Data stream in isolation is not enough. Business users are looking to broaden the scope of their analysis, and they expect to be able to mix and match the analytic toolsets they use while using one single common language and a single common query tool. From an overall system management perspective, DBAs need to be able to enforce a single security model to ensure that sensitive data is correctly protected and have a single workload management environment to control scheduling and access to system resources.

There are important security aspects that need to be addressed when considering how business users analyze these new data sources. As the nature of the data being captured has become more "personalized," governments have enforced strict data governance rules. The requirement to analyze data in-place without moving it has grown. Continually moving data around and trying to replicate a consistent security model across multiple isolated engines is not a viable solution.

Workload management is becoming a key feature of Big Data and data warehouse environments as business users demand access to more data. Service level agreements for operational discovery workflows mean that DBAs need to have full control over the amount of resources allocated and the priority attached to each query and/or process. Many data "discoveries" have to be incorporated into existing ETL workflows or embedded within applications for lights-out processing: identifying fraudulent activity during an online transaction, flagging a customer to the call center staff as likely to "churn" so the correct incentives can be offered, and creating customer lists for campaign management teams during data refresh cycles. Reliable and consistent performance is a key consideration in production systems. When Big Data workflows are integrated into operational applications or data warehouse processing, they must not impact overall system performance.

Oracle was one of the first database vendors to recognize this need and has been investing in bringing the "analytics to the data." The Oracle Database includes all the features listed so far, and it also allows developers and business users to add their own functions and procedures using a wide variety of different programming languages. As we move into the realms of Big Data and the need to merge Big Data with operational data, the role of in-database analytics has become a key factor in determining the success of many Big Data projects. Oracle's single integrated analytic platform offers many advantages such as:

- **Reduced latency**   Data can be analyzed in-place.

- **Reduced risk**   A single set of data security policies can be applied across all types of analysis.

- **Increased reusability**   All data types are accessible via SQL making it very easy to reuse analysis and analytical workflows across many tools: ETL, business intelligence reports, and dashboards and operational applications.

- **Lower total cost of ownership**   Reuse existing SQL skills and consolidate analytical processing onto a single database platform.

By making all the data available from inside the data warehouse and moving the analytics to the data, Oracle is able to provide a wide range of analytical functions and features and ensure that data governance and security is enforced at every stage of the analytic process, while at the same time providing timely delivery of analytical results.

Oracle's In-Database Analytics

Oracle has long been a pioneer in the area of in-database analytics. The Oracle Database started with a rich set of built-in SQL analytic features that allowed developers to process data directly inside the database using standard SQL syntax rather than having to move data to a separate platform, process it using a proprietary language, and then return the results to the database. With each release of the Database, the types of data supported by the in-database analytics and the types of SQL analytics available to process that data continue to expand. The latest release of the Oracle Database covers a wide variety of data types and structures, including: numerical, text, images, videos, voice, XML, network, spatial, semantic, and multidimensional.

Over time, access to this rich set of analytical features and functions has broadened to include data scientists and business users as well as application

FIGURE 9-2. *Oracle's in-database analytics ecosystem*

developers, ETL developers, and DBAs. Each release of the Oracle Database broadens the democratization of analytics across even more types of users, as shown in the diagram in Figure 9-2.

The analysis of Big Data opens up the ability to explore a new range of opportunities, but to maximize the returns on the investment in this new technology, these new sources cannot be analyzed in isolation. As with every other analytical process, the same requirements apply: timely access to data, access to a broad range of analytical features and functions, data security, and rapid time to value.

To help explain some of these new business opportunities, Oracle has created a demo application: Oracle MoviePlex Store. The home page for this screen is shown in Figure 9-3 with pointers to some of the user information that is captured by the application.

This is an application built to demonstrate how to acquire a Big Data stream in the form of clicks a user makes while on our movie Web site. It then demonstrates how to analyze that information to create actionable business insight. The storefront for our application, shown in Figure 9-3, indicates that our user, Frankie, has started watching a new movie but has not completed it. Based on previous sessions and viewing habits of similar customers, we have made a number of recommendations of movies that we think Frankie will enjoy.

We can extend the application to include information about the most popular genres, locations, actors, and directors by showing word count maps, or tag clouds (as shown in Figure 9-4) and integrating this information into the application's search feature.

We can take this same visualization and provide it to the business users to give them additional insight into the organization of data within our application. By capturing search information, we can help explain how customers are using the site.

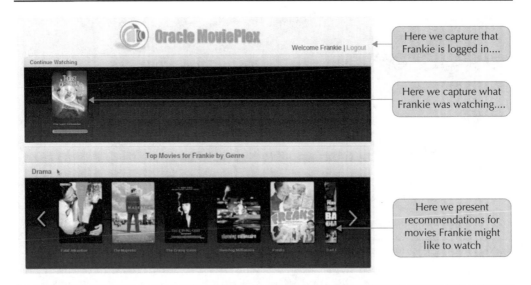

FIGURE 9-3. *Front screen of the Oracle MoviePlex Store application*

In this example we are using Big Data in a number of different ways. We are using the captured information to send recommendations back to the customer, in real time. Secondly, our business users are going to want to use this new data source (clickstream) to ask a completely new set of questions:

- Do our customers typically watch a movie from start to finish or do they watch over a number of sittings?

- Which movies can we recommend to our users in real time?

- What are the viewing habits of our customers split by key demographics?

FIGURE 9-4. *Word count visualization*

- How can we optimize our marketing spend; which customers should we target with promotional offers?

- How can we optimize our bandwidth usage based on customer usage patterns?

- How can we predict customer demand for a movie before it is released?

- Which movies are "sleepers" that would benefit from additional marketing campaigns?

- Which are the most active users on our site in terms of recommendations?

- Which users are most likely to follow these recommendations?

These are just some of the questions that our business users might want to ask. There are many more. How can Oracle's in-database analytics help answer these types of questions?

Why Running In-Database Is So Important

Many of the questions listed in the preceding section require mixing different types of analytics. In turn, when users start analyzing this data, they are likely to expand their exploration and incorporate multiple layers of analytical processing: drilling from a data mining process to a spatial analysis to further refine a result set. By keeping processing inside the database, Oracle has created a powerful, scalable analytics platform that can support this layering process and that is accessible via SQL.

Oracle allows specialized teams, such as data scientists, to use the tools they are most familiar with, which means they do not have to learn a completely new language—with the additional delay and cost impact this can have on a project. Sharing the results of analysis becomes much easier as well. Using in-database analytics, all result sets and insights remain inside the database and are accessible via SQL. Standard business intelligence tools can directly access any results and even merge those results with other datasets.

Introduction to Oracle Data Mining and Statistical Analysis

Data mining goes beyond simple analysis, and it is usually one of the key parts in any Big Data and data warehouse project. When trying to find answers to complex questions using business intelligence tools, the standard "drill-pivot-slice-and-dice" model is not sufficient. A different approach is needed to analyze the large data sets that are now commonplace in many organizations. The objective is to discover patterns and trends within a data stream using sophisticated mathematical algorithms to evaluate, segment, and predict—this is sometimes referred to as *knowledge discovery*. Table 9-1 provides a list of common problems that rely on the use of data mining and statistical techniques.

Sample Problem	Type of Problem	Algorithm	Applicability
Predict customer response to a marketing campaign	Classification	Logistic Regression (GLM) Decision Trees Naïve Bayes Support Vector Machine	Classical statistical technique Embedded within an application Wide/narrow data/text
Predict the likely profitability of a new customer	Regression	Multiple Regression (GLM) Support Vector Machine	Classical statistical technique Wide/narrow data/text
Given customer response to a marketing campaign program, find the most significant predictors	Attribute Importance	Minimum Description Length (MDL)	Attribute reduction Identify useful data Reduce data noise
Identify customer purchasing behavior that is significantly different from the norm	Anomaly Detection	One Class SVM	Quality control
Find the items that tend to be purchased together and specify their relationship— market basket analysis	Association Rules	A priori	Product grouping
Segment data into clusters and rank the probability that an individual will belong to a given cluster	Clustering	Hierarchical K-Means Hierarchical O-Means	Product grouping Text mining Gene analysis
Combining attributes into a new reduced set of features	Feature Extraction	Non-negative Matrix Factorization (NMF)	Text analysis Feature reduction

TABLE 9-1. *Common Problems That Rely on the Use of Data Mining and Statistical Techniques*

In our MoviePlex application, there are three data mining techniques we use to enrich our application and the data flowing to our data warehouse:

- **Association rules** To recommend movies to people as they browse the list of movies on our site

- **Clustering** To identify customer groupings that can be used to better target marketing campaigns

- **Anomaly detection** To identify possible fraudulent activities

Oracle's In-Database Advanced Analytics

Oracle's data mining and statistical features are managed from within the Oracle Database. This eliminates data movement and duplication and maintains data security by keeping data under the control of the database. This in turn minimizes latency in translating raw data into valuable information. All the data and results remain within a single, secure, scalable platform and are accessed using the power of SQL. Oracle provides four approaches to access its in-database data mining features:

Target Audience	Product
For data scientists, PL/SQL developers, SQL developers, and DBAs	Oracle Data Mining and the data mining extension for SQL Developer
For application developers	Oracle Data Mining PL/SQL API and Data Mining SQL scoring functions
Excel users	Excel Spreadsheet Add-In for Predictive Analytics
For data scientists familiar with the R statistical programming language and environment, and database developers needing to invoke R scripts from SQL and integrate results in SQL-based tools and applications	Oracle R Enterprise

Oracle Data Mining

Oracle Data Mining (ODM) provides powerful in-database data mining functionality as native SQL functions. This allows a wide range of users with experience of SQL to uncover patterns and relationships and insights hidden within their existing datasets using their normal tools such as SQL Developer. The results are also accessible using SQL, which means that business users can access the predictions, recommendations, and discoveries using their existing business intelligence tools.

Oracle Data Mining provides a collection of in-database data mining algorithms that solve a wide range of business problems. Both technical and business users can work with Oracle Data Mining via a series of different interfaces:

- SQL-aware data scientists, data warehouse developers, and DBAs will typically use SQL Developer.

- SQL-aware application developers will use the PL/SQL and SQL APIs.

- Business users will benefit from using the Excel plug-in and SQL access with their BI tool.

Using Oracle's in-database data mining features, developers and business users can build and apply predictive models to help them target their best customers, develop detailed customer profiles, and find and prevent fraud. A typical methodology for using data mining would contain the following steps.

Step 1: Problem Definition   The first part of any data mining project is to understand the key objectives and requirements. This will determine the business problem and whether an answer is actually possible. In some cases data may not be available to support the analysis. At this point it is also important to develop an implementation plan for the resulting model.

Step 2: Data Gathering and Preparation   Having established that the required data is available, the next phase is to determine its suitability. Certain data points may need reformatting to make them useful and usable, and other data points might need to be discarded. At this point it is also advisable to ensure the quality of the source data. The work done during this phase will have a significant impact on the overall results generated by the data mining process.

Step 3: Building the Model   This phase involves selecting the most appropriate modeling technique and fine-tuning the various model parameters to optimize the results. It is likely that the phase will highlight issues with the source data and it will be necessary to go back to Step 2 to fine-tune the data.

Step 4: Evaluating the Model   It is vital to evaluate how well the model created in Step 3 meets the objectives defined at Step 1. It may be necessary to return to Step 2 or even Step 1 and work through the process again incorporating new data items or even fewer data items. Typically, this will be an iterative process and it may take a number of loops before moving to Step 5.

Step 5: Knowledge Deployment   Once the model has been validated, it can be deployed within the target application, ETL workflow, or warehouse environment. It is at this point that business users can start to gain business insight and derive actionable information from the results.

Step 6: Re-evaluating the Model   It is important to constantly review a model after it has been deployed. As the model impacts behavior, the original nature and patterns in the source data will evolve over time, and this change needs to be incorporated into the model. Regular review points should be built into project plans to re-evaluate and if necessary rebuild the model to ensure its effectiveness.

Oracle Data Mining Extension for SQL Developer

Oracle SQL Developer enables data scientists, Oracle developers, and DBAs to build, evaluate, and deploy data models directly against data sets stored in the Oracle Database. Built-in advanced visualizations and statistical analysis provide the ability to explore the data graphically while evaluating multiple data mining models. The Oracle Data Miner workflow captures and documents the complete methodology listed in the preceding section. A screenshot of the SQL Developer interface for a data mining workflow is shown in Figure 9-5.

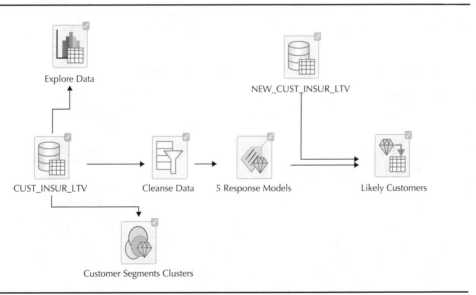

FIGURE 9-5.   *Data mining extension for SQL Developer*

The SQL Developer extension is designed to support this multistep workflow. Once the business problem has been defined, Oracle Data Mining has data exploration tools and an automatic data preparation mode, and this can significantly speed up the time it takes to access the source data and transform it. The SQL Developer Workflow Editor can profile the source data. This allows the developer to visualize, validate, and inspect the data for patterns.

Data Miner analyzes the source data and computes a wide variety of information about each attribute including histograms; number of distinct values; average, minimum, and maximum values; and so on.

The Workflow Editor of the Component Palette lists a series of the most common data transformation steps to help format the data in the most effective way to support the requirements of each model. Figure 9-6 shows some of the prebuilt transformations that are part of the SQL Developer extension.

The transformation instructions are embedded in the model itself and reused whenever the model is applied. Where business- or industry-specific transformations are required, it is possible to add these as custom transformations using SQL and PL/SQL. These custom transformations are then embedded within the model and executed whenever the model is applied.

The process of building a data mining model may require more than one data set—this is one of the reasons why in-database data mining is more efficient than using an external proprietary engine. One data set may be required for the build (or training) stage of the model; another data set may be required for the scoring step. To help create these data sets, such as the build (or training) data set, Oracle Data Mining provides a sampling feature that allows the data scientist to input a

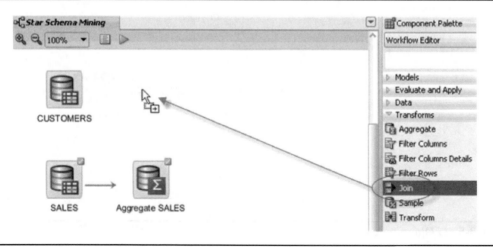

FIGURE 9-6. *SQL Developer Data Mining Transformation Library*

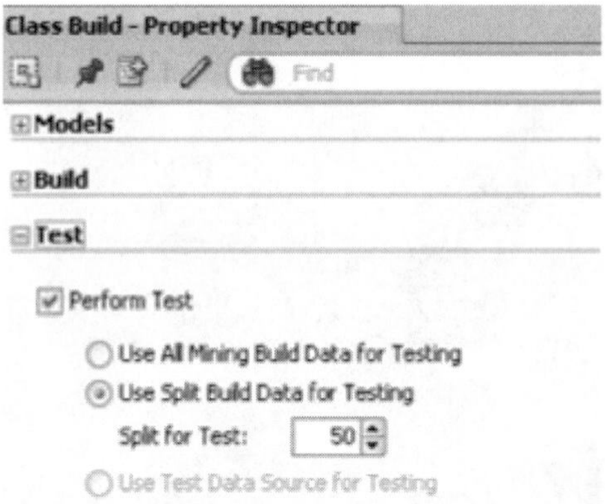

FIGURE 9-7. *SQL Developer Data Mining data sampling*

sample size for the training or test part of the model-building process. This feature is shown in Figure 9-7.

This automates and simplifies the process of managing multiple data sets, leaving the data scientist to concentrate on optimizing the model.

SQL Developer provides specific visualizations for evaluating the results of a model. These can also be used to compare results from multiple models. As data mining and model development is typically an iterative approach, it is important to compare and contrast the results from each run. Figure 9-8 shows the "Compare Test Results" feature for different runs of various models.

This particular view provides five tabs: Performance, Performance Matrix, ROC, Lift, and Profit. The Performance tab provides numeric and graphical information for each model on predictive confidence, average accuracy, and overall accuracy. The Lift tab provides a graphical presentation showing lift for each model.

Deploying a model is a relatively easy task. Oracle Data Miner workflows can be exported and imported across instances using normal Oracle Database procedures:

■ Oracle Data Pump

■ EXPORT_MODEL and IMPORT_MODEL

■ Importing from Predictive Model Markup Language (PMML)

The DBA can use any of these techniques to deploy a data model in other environments for further testing, QA review, or directly into production.

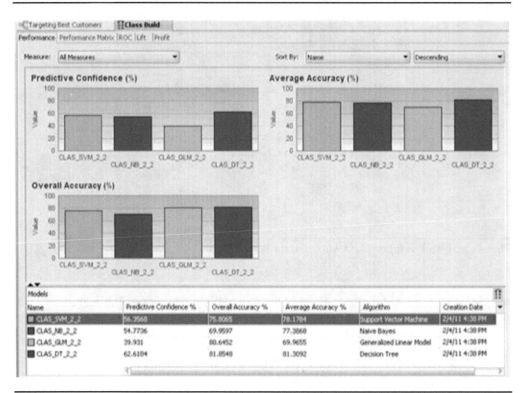

FIGURE 9-8. *SQL Developer Data Mining model results view*

Because Oracle Data Mining builds and applies data mining models inside the Oracle Database, the results are immediately available. BI reporting tools and dashboards can easily display the results of data mining. Additionally, Oracle Data Mining supports scoring in real time: Data can be mined and the results returned within a single database transaction. For example, a sales representative could run a model that predicts the likelihood of fraud within the context of an online sales transaction.

All results (predictions and insights) can be saved and shared with others to automate other advanced analytical processes. The results are accessed using SQL and can be incorporated into BI dashboards and reports.

If necessary, at this stage the results can be linked to our other forms of analysis such as spatial analytics and/or multidimensional structures to gain greater and broader business insight and derive even more actionable information.

Oracle Data Mining APIs

There are three PL/SQL packages to support Oracle's in-database data mining operations:

- **DBMS_DATA_MINING**   Provides routines for building, testing, and applying data mining models.

- **DBMS_DATA_MINING_TRANSFORM**   Provides data transformation. These can be used in conjunction with any other SQL-based transformations.

- **DBMS_PREDICTIVE_ANALYTICS**   Provides automated data mining routines for PREDICT, EXPLAIN, and PROFILE operations.

The DBMS_DATA_MINING package provides support for a wide variety of operations such as creating, dropping, and renaming a model, scoring a model, describing a model, computing tests, and exporting and importing models.

The DBMS_PREDICTIVE_ANALYTICS package provides all the power of predictive data mining while masking nearly all of the underlying complexity. This package automates the whole end-to-end process of predictive data mining from data preparation to model building to scoring. It can also explain the relative influence of specific attributes on the prediction using the EXPLAIN routine.

Application developers can use these packages to automate and embed the results of data mining models within their applications, and data warehouse developers can use these APIs to incorporate data mining operations into their data-loading processes and workflows.

Oracle Spreadsheet Add-in for Predictive Analytics

Oracle has brought the power of in-database data mining to Excel with its Spreadsheet Add-in for Predictive Analytics. This provides a simple wizard-based interface in Microsoft Excel that allows business users to apply predictive analytics to their Oracle and/or Excel data. Excel users can use this add-in to harness the power of Oracle Data Mining without the need to have a deep understanding of Oracle Database or data mining processes.

Three simple wizards, shown in the upcoming Figures 9-9 through 9-11, expose the following features: Explain, Profile, and Predict. They make it easy for business users to uncover hidden patterns within their data using these advanced forms of analysis. Each wizard is based on a set of simple steps: connect to an Oracle database, select a source table, view or point to data in an open Excel spreadsheet, add any additional information required by the model such as a target variable, and finally click OK. The results from each model are returned as a new worksheet.

One of the challenges of analyzing Big Data streams is not only the volume in terms of the number of rows but also the number of attributes. When we're working on a specific business problem, some columns may be more important than others, and this can help us narrow down the data set that needs to be used in our analysis. The Explain feature helps identify the most important attributes within a dataset by sifting through the data searching for attributes that have the greatest influence on a predetermined target attribute. The Explain feature is shown in Figure 9-9.

The output from this process is a ranked list of attributes as shown in Figure 9-9 in the first column. In our MoviePlex application, we could use the Explain feature to identify the most important attributes associated with customer churn or customers who are most likely to respond to a marketing campaign.

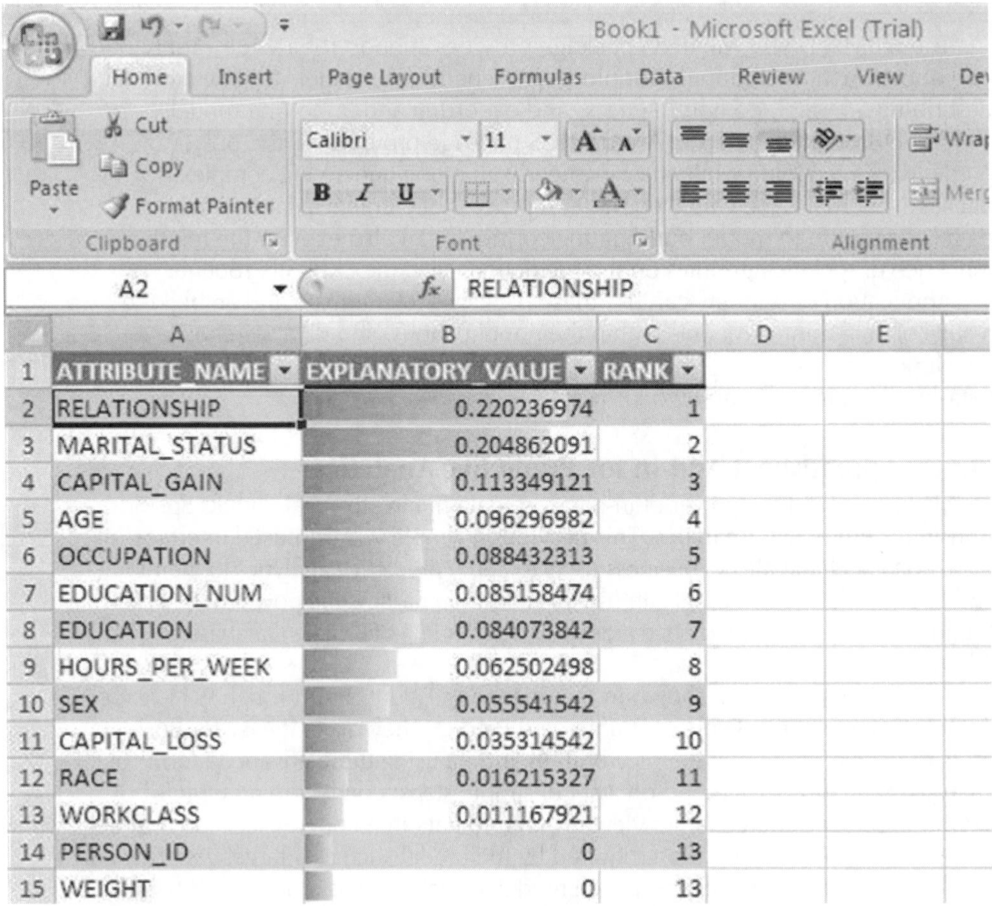

ATTRIBUTE_NAME	EXPLANATORY_VALUE	RANK
RELATIONSHIP	0.220236974	1
MARITAL_STATUS	0.204862091	2
CAPITAL_GAIN	0.113349121	3
AGE	0.096296982	4
OCCUPATION	0.088432313	5
EDUCATION_NUM	0.085158474	6
EDUCATION	0.084073842	7
HOURS_PER_WEEK	0.062502498	8
SEX	0.055541542	9
CAPITAL_LOSS	0.035314542	10
RACE	0.016215327	11
WORKCLASS	0.011167921	12
PERSON_ID	0	13
WEIGHT	0	13

FIGURE 9-9. *Excel worksheets with results from the Explain feature in the Oracle Data Mining Spreadsheet Add-in*

The Profile feature, shown in Figure 9-10, allows us to find customer segments and their profiles based on a target attribute. The output is a list of multiple profiles for each target value, and this information can be used to gain a deeper insight into the relationships within the dataset. In our MoviePlex application, this feature could be used to identify the profile of our most profitable customers and the profile of customers most likely to stop using our service and sign up with a rival service (customer churn).

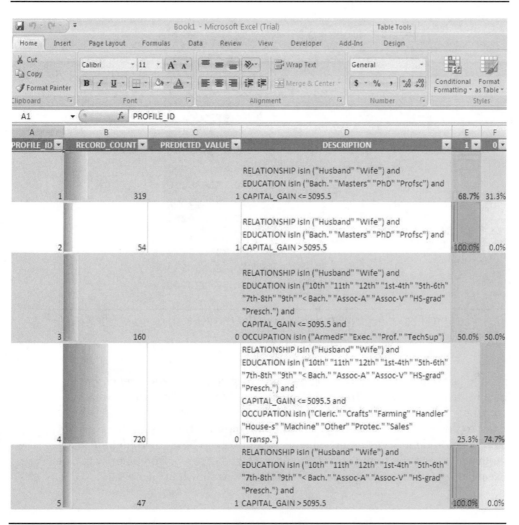

FIGURE 9-10. *Excel worksheets with results from the Profile feature within the Oracle Data Mining Spreadsheet Add-in*

	A	B	C	D	E	F
1	Overall predictive confidence = 0.65					
2	PERSON_ID	CLASS	PREDICTION	PROBABILITY		
3	2	0	0	0.818733703		
4	7	0	1	0.202838757		
5	8	0	0	0.897031067		
6	9	0	0	0.972000428		
7	10	0	0	0.987589587		
8	11	0	0	0.983983943		
9	12	0	1	0.864771065		
10	15	0	0	0.981935298		
11	16	0	0	0.995889683		
12	17	0	0	0.994326201		
13	18	0	0	0.995533379		
14	22	0	0	0.823855673		
15	24	0	0	0.988153933		
16	25	0	1	0.674070765		

FIGURE 9-11. *Excel worksheets with results from the Predict feature within the Oracle Data Mining Spreadsheet Add-in*

The last step in this natural progression of digging deeper and deeper into the data is the Predict feature. This makes predictions about specific scenarios along with a confidence probability for each prediction. This is shown in Figure 9-11.

We can use Predict to identify the customers most likely to respond to a marketing campaign or identify customers who are most likely to be a "high lifetime value customer." The results from Explain, Profile, and Predict can be combined with other Excel data points to produce reports or dashboards as shown in Figure 9-12.

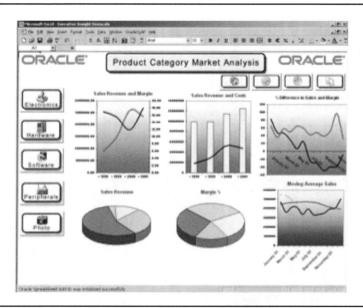

FIGURE 9-12. *Sample Excel dashboard*

Introduction to R

R is a statistical programming language and environment. It is an open source project for statistical computing and graphics, which is well suited to data analysis. It provides a framework for analyzing and mining data sets and includes support for a variety of data types, a large library of built-in tools to manage data, a comprehensive set of statistical models, and it provides advanced data visualizations that can be customized. Many large data-driven companies such as LinkedIn, Google, and Facebook are adopting it.

R's statistical and analysis capabilities are based on the concept of packages. It is extensible, and additional packages can be downloaded from a public library known as the Comprehensive R Archive Network (CRAN). The CRAN library provides access to a wide variety of packages containing specialized and industry-specific statistical methods that have been developed by data scientists.

When visualizing large and complex datasets, the basic pie, area, line, and bar charts are simply not good enough to present the patterns, relationships, and anomalies that R can help uncover and highlight. To help present result sets, R contains a number of visualizations, such as multipanel charts and 3-D surfaces, that can be used to extend certain BI tools as shown in Figure 9-13.

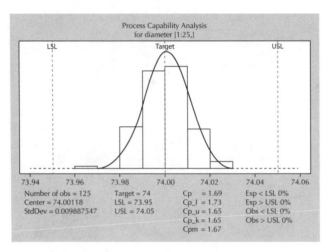

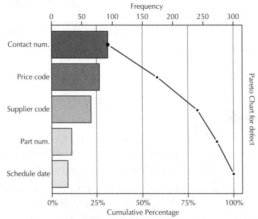

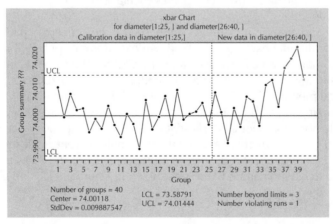

FIGURE 9-13. *Examples of R data visualizations*

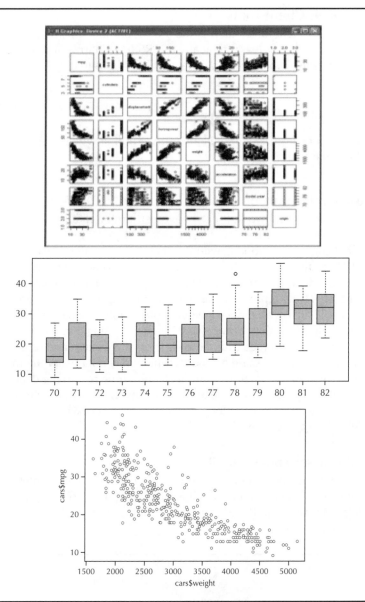

FIGURE 9-13.   *Examples of R data visualizations (continued)*

Working with R: R Client Tools

There are a number of client tools that provide a development environment for working with R. At Oracle our teams typically use RStudio (http://rstudio.org), but there are many others available. One advantage of RStudio is that it has two modes of operation:

- RStudio Desktop runs locally on a PC.

- RStudio Server runs on a remote Linux server and provides access to RStudio via a Web interface.

What Are the Limitations of R?

While R is an excellent framework, it does have certain limitations that Big Data projects can very quickly expose.

The main challenge when working with R is that it is constrained by available memory. The data scientist is typically forced to extract a subset of the data that will fit into the available memory. This means they have to spend time carefully creating a smaller dataset that is truly representative of the complete dataset. This poses the question: if you could access all the data, would you be able to create a better model?

Another key challenge is that R processing is generally single-threaded and does not exploit the available resources without using special packages and programming. This means that processing times are extended, which may not be a problem when developing a new model, but when trying to make real-time recommendations, as used in the MoviePlex application, the extended processing times could result in lost revenue and adversely impact the performance of the Web site, which could drive customers to switch to a competitor's site.

Oracle R Enterprise: Enhancing R

Oracle has extended the open source version of R to create Oracle R Enterprise. This integrates open source R with Oracle Database, allowing users to transparently manipulate database data from R and execute R scripts at the database server, as shown in Figure 9-14.

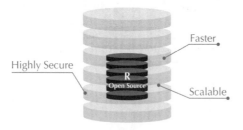

FIGURE 9-14. *Oracle R Enterprise—embeds R inside the Oracle Database*

Oracle R Enterprise removes the two key limitations of open source R: memory constraints and single-threaded processing.

Data scientists and R users can run their existing R commands and scripts against data stored in Oracle Database. They can develop, refine, and deploy R scripts that leverage the parallelism and scalability of the Oracle Database without having to learn SQL.

Oracle R Enterprise also extends the standard database governance and security framework to R by ensuring that the relevant data security layers are correctly enforced. This ensures that data scientists cannot access sensitive information and then share that information as part of their results.

So how can we leverage R to help us enhance our movie store application? Using R we can create a model to recommend movies based on the browsing patterns of both the current user and also users who share similar tastes or who have a similar demographic profile.

Figure 9-15 highlights the key advantage of R—the data scientist keeps their existing client and is not forced to learn SQL but can still access data stored in the Oracle database and interact with that data, returning results to the R console window. Using Oracle's Big Data technology, R users can access the clickstream data stored on Hadoop and join it with demographic data stored in the Oracle database. This is the key advantage of Oracle's Acquire-Organize-Analyze-Decide workflow in that we can use Big Data streams to enrich operational data and use operational data to enrich Big Data.

Having accessed the movie log table, we now need to parse that data to determine which movies to recommend as the user clicks through the movie catalog. To do this, we need to use an a priori algorithm, which will create association rules. These rules are written to a table in the Oracle database where they can be accessed by the movie application framework. Our application developer can use standard Oracle connection, metadata, and query objects to access the recommendations and incorporate them into the application interface.

FIGURE 9-15. *Connecting to the Oracle Database from RStudio and accessing the movie demo schema*

Connecting R to Data Sources

Oracle has extended the library of R objects to allow data scientists to source data from tables inside Oracle Database and from Hadoop and return the results to the R console, as shown in Figure 9-16. The most important new data management metadata objects are

- **ore.frame** Maps to a database table, which is an extension of the R data.frame object

- **ore.matrix** Maps to a database table, storing the data in a matrix object, and is an extension of the R matrix object

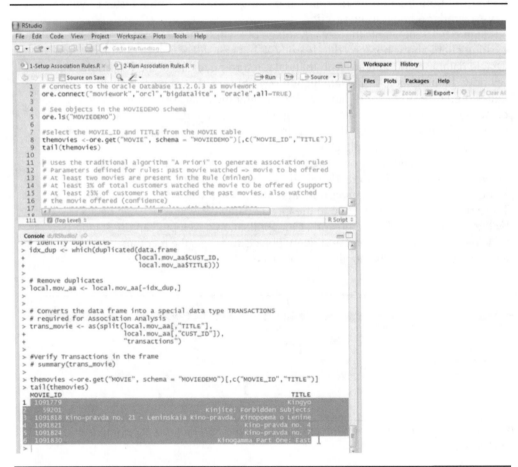

FIGURE 9-16. *Returning results from Oracle table to R Studio console*

Additional functions have been added to help manage data retrieval from Oracle tables and pushing results from R into the Oracle Database. The two most important functions are

- **ore.pull**   Pulls the contents of an Oracle database table or view into an in-memory R data frame

- **ore.push**   Stores an R object in the Oracle database as a temporary object

This Transparency Layer is a good example of leveraging database-processing power as R users can take advantage of the inherent parallelism of Oracle Database during query execution without having to specifically write parallel-aware scripts. Data scientists can use the standard parallelized functions and let the Oracle Database control and manage how many parallel R engines are used. The Embedded R Execution capability allows R users to execute R scripts within the database server R engines, where more memory and CPU resources are likely to be available. Using the in-database R engine, data scientists can execute scripts and let the database manage the process. This simplifies the process of optimizing the parallel processing of R jobs and ensures that these jobs remain under the overall control of the database resource and workload manager.

To access data on a Hadoop cluster, data scientists can use the Oracle R Connector for Hadoop. This provides an interface between the local R environment and Hadoop and allows data scientists to copy data between R-memory, the local file system, and the Hadoop file system—HDFS. R programs can interact directly with Hadoop's MapReduce programming framework to collate and prepare data for use in an R model. The three main sets of functions are

- **orch.***   Provides an interface between the local R environment and Hadoop. Enables the copying of data between R memory, the local file system, and HDFS.

- **hadoop.***   Provides an interface to Hadoop MapReduce.

- **hdfs.***   Provides an interface to the Hadoop file system.

By integrating data stored on Hadoop and data stored in the Oracle Database, a data scientist can create a much richer source data set and perform highly scalable data analysis and predictive modeling.

In our MoviePlex application, we use R to create a list of recommended movies grouped by genre and based on each customer's individual browsing habits and the browsing habits of similar customers. Figure 9-17 shows the application home page

FIGURE 9-17. *Using advanced analytics to drive recommendations*

with the latest set of recommendations for our application user. The recommendation script is executed on demand as the customer interacts with the site.

The in-database R engine can also execute R scripts embedded inside SQL statements or PL/SQL programs, so it is easy to incorporate the advanced analytical capabilities of R into existing SQL BI tools, ETL/ELT workflows, and applications.

We could extend our use of R by leveraging its "real-time" capabilities and scalability to track fraudulent and/or malicious activity on our site. As we are capturing click information, we can search through this data stream looking for bot and spider traffic that could be degrading the performance of our Web site. This information could help us to better manage the provisioning of our whole infrastructure layer to ensure that pages on our Web site load in a timely and consistent manner.

Making BI Tools Smarter

As we stated earlier, many of the traditional BI visualizations are just not up to the job of presenting results derived from sophisticated analysis. This is why Oracle has extended its business intelligence tools by adding support for both R processing and R's advanced visualizations. Both Oracle Business Intelligence EE and BI Publisher can now invoke R calculations via standard SQL and present the results from those calculations using specialized visualizations.

It is possible to create dashboards and prompt-driven reports that present data derived from R models using standard BI visualizations and using the advanced data visualizations provided by R, as shown in Figures 9-18 and 9-19.

This means that R operations and results can be quickly and easily shared with other business users directly inside their existing Oracle BI tools. For business users there is no need to learn a new interface or language. Everything is controlled using

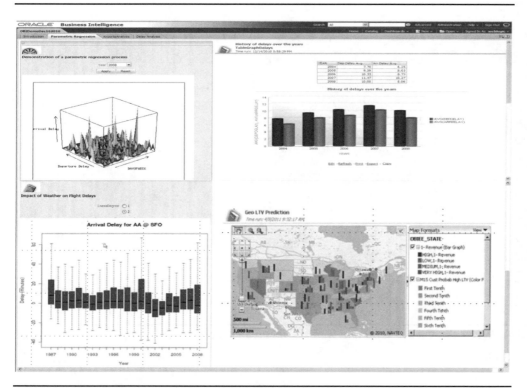

FIGURE 9-18. *Advanced visualizations for big data in Oracle Business Intelligence*

the familiar language of SQL and the familiar interfaces of Oracle Business
Intelligence and Oracle BI Publisher.

Text Mining

Text mining is conventional data mining using "text features." Text features are
usually keywords, frequencies of words, or other document-derived features. Once
the text features have been identified, textual data can be mined in exactly the same
way as any other data.

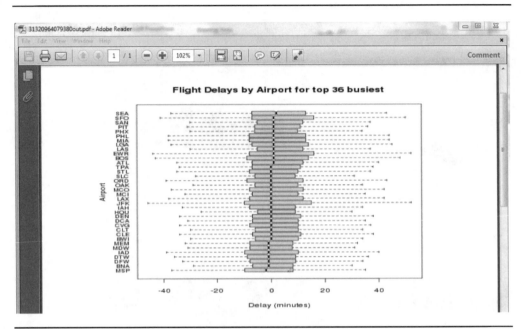

FIGURE 9-19. *Interactive reporting with advanced analytics and BI Publisher*

Many Big Data use cases are based on the analysis of textual information such as sentiment analysis, e-discovery, and word/tag clouds. With the use of in-database analytics, it is possible to take existing discoveries to new levels by combining this type of analysis with other nontextual data sets to add additional layers of richness. Some of the use cases for text mining include

- Create and manage taxonomies
- Classify documents
- Capture the use of aliases
- Classify and cluster documents returned from a search
- Extract features to prepare data for subsequent mining processes

Examples using some or all of the text mining operations in the preceding list include

■ Customer account data may include text fields that describe support calls and other interactions with the customer. Analysis of this textual data may help resolve future calls and/or provide feedback on whether customers' issues are being resolved in an efficient manner.

■ Insurance claim data may include a claim status description, supporting documents, e-mail correspondence, and other information. Analysis may uncover patterns of activities that are likely to be fraudulent or break internal/external compliance rules.

■ Patient data may include comments by doctors and nurses, and analysis of these comments may help determine which combinations of treatments provide the best outcome and provide an ordered list of results.

■ Conversion of reviews, articles, and so on into a sentiment analysis.

We could apply text mining in a number of different ways within our MoviePlex application. For example, when users search our Web site, the ability to apply simple clustering techniques would allow the application to score and group the hits returned by the search process to provide a more meaningful user experience.

Oracle Data Mining Support for Text Mining

Oracle Data Miner uses the facilities of Oracle Text to preprocess text columns. In general text has to be transformed to extract meaning from the text. Once the data has been properly transformed, it can be used for building, testing, or scoring data mining models. Examples of the types of models that can be created are listed in Table 9-2.

Model Type	Typical Functions
Rule-based classification	Efficiently classify a stream of documents according to a set of queries. For example, each time an e-mail arrives at a call center, send it to all interested agents. Or each time a news item arrives, post it to the relevant Web sites or pages.
Supervised training	Use a training set of documents to define a classifier for large data sets. Decision trees and support vector machines (SVMs) are examples of such techniques.
Clustering	Group similar documents together according to their content. The package supports flat and hierarchical clustering.

TABLE 9-2. *Oracle Text Mining Models*

The Data Mining extension for SQL Developer provides text nodes to help speed up the process of transforming text data. One of the built-in text transformation methods is to convert a string of text into either a token or a theme. For example, a text-based data source such as a series of comments could be transformed into a series of tokens with counts for the number of times a token appears. Figure 9-20 shows the Oracle Data Mining text transformation feature in SQL Developer. This information can then be used as a filter on data flowing on through the model, or it can be used in more sophisticated ways to drive other processes within the model.

The main issue with text mining is that it can generate a huge number of attributes, many of which provide little significant information for use by other data algorithms. Oracle Data Mining supports the Non-Negative Matrix Factorization (NMF) algorithm for feature extraction. This allows an NMF model to consolidate text attributes and generate a reduced set of more meaningful attributes. The results can be far more effective for use in classification, clustering, or other types of data mining models. Figure 9-21 shows the SQL Developer results window with the output from text transformation.

Text extraction could be applied to the data coming from our external movie database service to generate (potentially many thousands) of "text features." These features could then be used as attributes by other data mining algorithms—these text

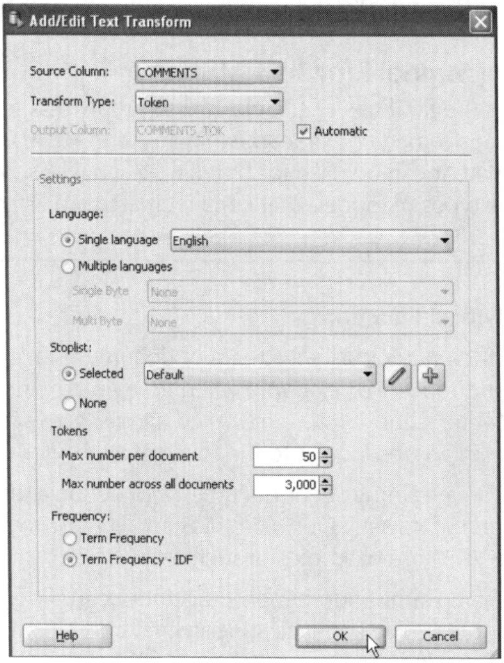

FIGURE 9-20. *Oracle Data Mining text transformation feature in SQL Developer*

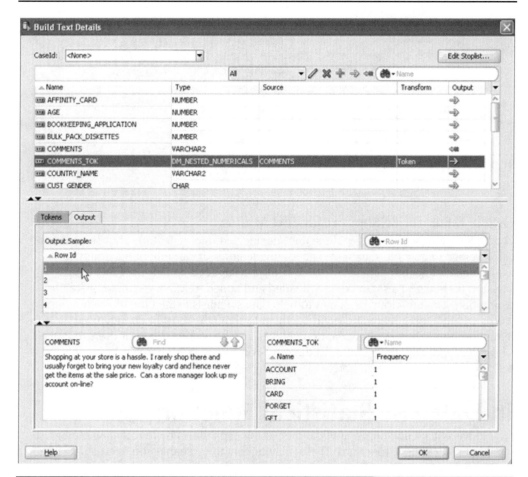

FIGURE 9-21. *SQL Developer results window showing output from text transformation*

features or attributes could be used to predict the potential success of a movie and help
with planning future demand, bandwidth, and storage requirements. Alternatively, they
could be used to automatically assign a movie to a specific category or subcategory to
reduce the amount of manual maintenance needed for our application.

We could extend the MoviePlex application to include movie-based news feeds
with articles arriving, as they are posted online. Users of our MoviePlex application
could register their interests in specific movie-related topics. As the news articles
arrive, the database can apply the sets of registered interests against each article.
When a user signs into their MoviePlex account, the application could display an
up-to-date list of relevant movie news items linked to their specific areas of interest.

FIGURE 9-22. *Word count visualization*

Oracle R Enterprise Support for Text Mining

Oracle R Enterprise does not include any specific text mining features, but since it can leverage Oracle's in-database data mining features, it can inherit the ability to analyze textual data. R can be extended using packages posted on the CRAN Web site, and these packages can be downloaded and added to R. For example, there are word count or word cloud packages to help data scientists extract the most common words within a text stream and organize them to show the most frequently used terms. Figure 9-22 shows how the derived data can be presented to our users. In our MoviePlex application we could list the most commonly used search terms within specific groupings as shown here.

In-Database Statistical Functions

Oracle has enhanced SQL's analytical processing capabilities by introducing a new family of analytic SQL functions. These analytic functions enable you to calculate:

- Correlations
- Cross-tabulations
- Descriptive statistics
- Distribution fitting
- First/last analysis
- Hypothesis testing
- Lag/lead analysis
- Linear regression statistics

■   Moving window calculations

■   Rankings and percentiles

■   Statistical aggregates

Ranking functions include cumulative distributions, percent rank, and N-tiles. Moving window calculations allow you to find moving and cumulative aggregations, such as sums and averages. Lag/lead analysis enables direct inter-row references so you can calculate period-to-period changes. First/last analysis enables you to find the first or last value in an ordered group.

Other enhancements to SQL include the CASE expression and partitioned outer join. CASE expressions provide if-then logic useful in many situations. Partitioned outer join is an extension to ANSI outer join syntax that allows users to selectively densify certain dimensions while keeping others sparse. This allows reporting tools to selectively densify dimensions, for example, the ones that appear in their cross-tabular reports while keeping others sparse.

Making BI Tools Smarter

These functions form the foundation of many of the in-database analytical features, such as Oracle Data Mining and Oracle R Enterprise, and access to them has been integrated into many of the more advanced business intelligence tools. Oracle Business Intelligence includes a feature called "Embedded Database Function," which allows the SQL generation engine to access all the unique capabilities of the Oracle Database—pushing the analytics to the data. The key benefits of this approach are to:

■   Maximize the investment made in the database platform by pushing as much processing as possible down to the database layer

■   Deliver better business decisions by providing business users with access to a wide range of analytical features that can easily be mixed and matched to gain better insight

■   Reduce total cost of ownership by using a single integrated analytics platform based on a single common query language (SQL) that can be accessed by any SQL-based BI tool

Data scientists and application developers can use these functions to create their own specialized functions to segment and predict data based on internally developed algorithms and embed them into their applications and/or existing workflows.

Many advanced business intelligence tools make use of Oracle's in-database statistical functions by providing business users with simplified analytical templates or wizards that translate these functions into business terms. Table 9-3 provides some typical examples of business questions and the functions that can be used to answer them.

Type of Query	Function
List the brands that make up 20% of sales	Banding
Which region's sales growth for 2012 as compared to 2011 was greater than 20%?	Lag/Lead
List the top ten and bottom ten salespeople per region	Ranking
What are each product's sales as a percentage of sales for its product group?	Reporting Aggregate
What is the 13-week moving average for sales?	Windowing

TABLE 9-3. *Typical Examples of Business Questions and the Functions That Can Be Used to Answer Them*

To enhance performance, analytic functions can be parallelized: multiple processes can simultaneously execute all of these statements. These capabilities make calculations easier and more efficient, thereby enhancing database performance, scalability, and simplicity.

Spatial Analytics

Location-based analytics is fast becoming a must-have feature for working with Big Data since it can add yet another layer of enrichment to the analytical and visualization processes. In many cases location is the key to unraveling hidden patterns within massive datasets. To quote from Tobler's first law of geography:

> Everything is related to everything else, but nearby things are more related than distant things.

This clearly highlights the importance of location and the influence of the "neighborhood." Many Big Data streams contain geolocation information, and where the information is not directly encoded in the data, it can be inferred using a data point within the data stream.

Oracle's in-database geospatial features allow data scientists and business users to analyze, estimate, and predict the influence of the "neighborhood," and this information can be used to further enrich existing data sets that are subsequently used in data mining processes.

Every Oracle database includes a built-in feature called Locator that enables any business application to directly incorporate location information and realize competitive advantages based on geospatial analytics. This provides storage, analysis, and indexing of location data, making spatial data accessible through

SQL and standard programming languages. Many developers use these features to support complex geographic information systems (GIS) applications, enterprise applications, and location-based services applications.

Geocoding is the process of associating geographic references, such as addresses and postal codes, with location coordinates (longitude and latitude). With Oracle Spatial, a fully functional geocoding engine is provided. It delivers a wide range of features including: support for international address standardization, Point-of-Interest matching by querying geocoded data stored in Oracle Database, reverse geocoding, and batch geocoding along with many other geocoding subprograms. Its unique unparsed address support adds great flexibility and convenience to geospatial-based applications and analytical processing.

Understanding the Spatial Data Model

The data model used to store and analyze spatial data requires the use of some special terminology. A spatial data model is based on a hierarchical structure consisting of three core components: elements, geometries, and layers. Each layer in the model is composed of a number of "geometries" where each "geometry" is based on a number of "elements."

The *element* within this data model is the basic building block, and Oracle Spatial supports a wide range of element types including: points, line strings, and polygons. Each coordinate in an element is stored as an X, Y pair and the number of coordinate pairs needed to describe the element varies according to the shape.

A *geometry* is the actual visual presentation of a spatial feature and can be based on a single element or a collection of elements. The geometries for each layer are stored in the Oracle database in standard relational tables.

Finally, a *layer* is a collection of geometries, and these are typically used to add features to a spatial image. For example, on a map a layer could be used to describe specific topographical features, while another layer could describe associated demographic data.

Querying the Spatial Data Model

When querying spatial data, Oracle uses two distinct operations to optimize performance. The combined output of these two operations yields the desired result set. These two operations are known as "primary" and "secondary" filter operations. The primary filter reduces the complexity of the overall operation by filtering the data based on geometry. The output from this step is a superset of the exact result set and it is then passed to the secondary filter for final processing. This second step then applies the "exact" calculations to produce the final answer to the spatial query. This secondary filter operation can sometimes be very expensive in terms of processing, but Oracle's in-database optimizations constrain the overall impact because the operation only acts on the result set returned from primary filters rather than the entire data set. All of this happens transparently within the database once the query has been submitted.

Many spatial queries are based on the desire to determine spatial relationships within a dataset, and Oracle Spatial provides three specific methods to support this requirement: SDO_RELATE, SDO_WITHIN_DISTANCE, and SDO_NN.

The SDO_RELATE filter determines the intersections for a given geometry. The SDO_WITHIN_DISTANCE filter can be used to determine if two data points are within a specific distance, and the SDO_NN filter identifies the nearest neighbor to a specific geometry. Each of these filters accepts a number of different parameters that allow for fine-grained control over the filtering process.

Using Spatial Analytics

In the case of the MoviePlex demo, we can capture the IP address of the customer's device as part of our clickstream data feed and then convert that to a geospatial location (longitude and latitude). At this point we need to consider not only how the data will be visualized, essentially on some sort of map, but also what other forms of analysis we can derive from that data. For example, we might want to add additional data points that indicate how close a customer or group of customers is to the nearest public library since libraries often provide a DVD loan service that might impact our business model. Alternatively, we might want to link the GPS coordinates to a specific location to help identify the usage model—home, airport, shopping mall, and so on.

Oracle Spatial provides the framework for doing this. It can capture and store the geospatial coordinates in their native format and then use that information to calculate distance to another object, or match a given location to a library of major locations such as airports.

In the MoviePlex application, the raw data coming from an external movie database service includes details of the locations used in a film. Therefore, movie search results could be layered on a map showing the locations used in the making of each film. Layering additional data is a simple process with Oracle Spatial; for example, the map could show the total budget and revenue by location. From a business perspective it would be possible to determine if the locations influence viewing figures—if a movie is filmed in Chicago, will customers in Chicago be more likely or less likely to watch it? Or we could target customers in a city or county by sending them information about films and documentaries that feature their local area.

Spatial data can be materialized for inclusion in other analytical processes such as multidimensional models (OLAP) and data mining applications. Data at a specific location is often influenced by data in the neighborhood. It is possible to use data mining techniques and spatial information to "bin" data into regions. The analysis features in Oracle Spatial let users exploit such spatial correlations in a wide variety of ways:

- **Materializing spatial correlation (neighborhood influence)**   In assessing the value of a house, examine the values of similar houses in a neighborhood

- **Spatial clustering**   Determine regions where crime rates are high, to decide where to deploy additional police resources

- **Location prospecting**   Identify the best locations for opening new hospitals based on the demographics of surrounding neighborhoods and patient data

Using co-location mining it could be possible to uncover areas where there are significant competitive threats to our MoviePlex business model. If there is a pizza restaurant franchise with a video store located close by, then customers might be more likely to collect a video from their local rental store while getting pizza instead of using our online streaming service.

Integrating spatial analytics with OLAP is an obvious "next step" for many business users. Oracle Spatial can be used to enrich the multidimensional model by creating new dimensional attributes and/or measures. These attributes can be used to apply advanced filtering to a dimension to create a more advanced approach to guided data exploration. As OLAP models typically contain a time dimension, we could track the number of video stores within a set of predefined radii (one mile, two miles, five miles) over time. If the number of stores within a specific neighborhood was declining over time, this might be a good candidate area for a localized marketing campaign.

We could use the spatial analytics to create additional attributes for our customer depending on how and where they are using our service: at home, on the move (local), on the move (regional), on the move (national), and on the move (international). This type of segmentation would provide an additional layer of filtering for our customer dimension.

Making BI Tools Smarter

Oracle has extended its business intelligence tools to include support for spatial analytics. This allows users to visualize their analytical datasets using maps, bringing the intuitiveness of spatial visualizations to the world of business intelligence.

Each map can contain any number of layers, and Oracle BI allows the user to very quickly add or remove layers to uncover new data patterns and identify possible new business opportunities. Figure 9-23 shows the BI report based on a spatial map with related analytics.

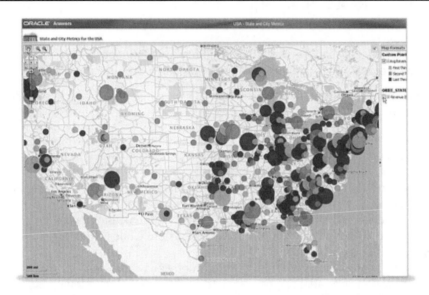

FIGURE 9-23. *Results from spatial analytics displayed in Oracle Business Intelligence*

Graph-Based Analytics

A graph database, which is sometimes referred to as a Resource Description
Framework (RDF) store, uses structures such as nodes, properties, and relationships
to store data rather than the tabular structures used in relational databases. RDF
stores are typically used within the context of the semantic web. Graph databases
can be used to store RDF (semantic) data, but they also support other storage and
query models. These types of databases are typically used for storing and processing
data sets that contain very complex relationships, and typical use cases include
social network analysis, network optimization, content management, bioinformatics,
and decision and process management.

The Oracle Database provides in-database native support for managing and
processing semantic data based on the W3C open standards using XML, RDF, OWL,
SPARQL, and SQL. The integration of this storage model inside the database provides
semantic developers with a scalable and secure platform to support a broad spectrum
of semantic applications.

Graph Data Model

Nodes in relational terms represent entities, and in our MoviePlex application,
nodes would include things such as movie genre, director, location, and customer.
Each node has a title, which identifies it from other nodes, and it has one or more

properties that describe it. Relationships act as links between nodes and they can provide a wide range of information about how nodes are joined, including the importance or weight of the relationship. These relationships can be based on data sourced from both structured and unstructured sources. One of the main advantages of the graph storage model is that it allows the data schemas to continuously evolve over time, which makes them tremendously flexible.

Querying Graph Data

Once we have defined our graph data model, it becomes possible to navigate and infer relationships using a linked standard terminology. When querying and exploring these relationships, a special query language is typically used, which in many cases is typically SPARQL. This language is similar to SQL and uses the same basic constructs. A SPARQL query consists of a SELECT statement to select the required data as a subset, and a WHERE clause containing the types of filter patterns to apply to the data. Here is an example of a SPARQL query:

```
PREFIX abc: <http://oracle.com/MoviePlexOntology#>
SELECT ?genre ?movie
WHERE {
  ?x abc:genre ?genre ;
     abc:isOscarWinner ?y .
  ?y abc:location ?city ;
     abc:isInCountry abc:USA
}
```

In this statement the variables are indicated by a "?" or "$" prefix and only the bindings for "?genre" and the "?movie" will be returned by the query where the movie is based in the United States and has been an Oscar winner.

Where Oracle differs from other graph technologies is in its support for both SQL and SPARQL query languages when querying semantic data. Business users, developers, and DBAs can use the language that best suits their particular skillset and/or the needs of the application. Oracle has extended the capabilities of SQL to provide support for SPARQL-like graph patterns, which means that developers can write queries that bring together data from both relational and RDF data sources. Using SQL as the common language avoids "moving" data from the SQL engine to the RDF engine, making the whole query visible to the RDBMS optimizer as a single SQL query (maximizing the possibility of getting the best execution plan chosen by the optimizer).

SQL developers can embed semantic features into their applications without having to learn a new language and seamlessly incorporate semantic-based data into other analytical queries. Using the other in-database analytic features, it is possible to incorporate semantic-based data into data mining processes or multidimensional models, which greatly increases the opportunity to enrich business intelligence reports and dashboards.

Oracle also provides a Java interface to its RDF data store. The Jena Adapter for Oracle Database provides a Java-based interface for managing named graph data. This adapter provides network analytical functions on top of semantic data through integrating with the Oracle Spatial network data model.

One of the challenges with our MoviePlex business model is managing the type of content and type of download offered when a customer wants to view a movie. For example, when presenting a list of movies, it might be necessary to remove violent and/or adult films either because the customer has opted to block them or because the customer might not meet the age requirements to view them. We could use a graph model to create a richer content filter based not just on the standard movie rating but also incorporating other elements of the movie's characteristics.

Once a movie has been selected, the type of file to download needs to be determined, which could be based on a wide range of criteria:

- **Type of device**   TV or mobile device (phone, tablet, computer)

- **Screen format**   16:9 or 4:3 or 2.35:1

- **Resolution**   3D, HD, 4K UHDTV, 8K UHDTV

- **Network connection**   3G or 4G for mobile devices vs. domestic cable broadband or ADSL broadband

As network technology is changing rapidly and new types of devices are always arriving in the market, it would make sense to model these requirements in the most flexible way possible to ensure that each download request is serviced using the most appropriate file. Using Oracle's semantic technologies, we can define an RDF model for our movies that encapsulates these additional pieces of information. This can then be loaded into the Oracle database and used as an additional filtering process in the MoviePlex application to provide a mechanism for determining which type of file should be made available for download based on network connection and type of device.

It is possible to extend this "flexibility" even further. We can create a simple movie taxonomy using the textual information, which is part of each movie entry coming from our external movie database service. This could be based on a set of core topics such as actor, writers, location, producers, director, studio, and so on. Each topic could be used to drive word, or tag, clouds using the features outlined earlier that are provided by Oracle Advanced Analytics. This taxonomy can be used to drive the MoviePlex Web site by automating the process of adding and cataloging new movies within our application based on the textual information provided for each movie. As with similar textual information, we can use graph analytics to provide word count type visualizations as shown earlier in Figure 9-22.

Multidimensional Analytics

Oracle OLAP is a multidimensional analytic engine that is part of the Oracle Database. Data structures within Oracle OLAP are based on high-level objects such as dimensions, attributes, relations, and cubes. While dimensions, attributes, and cubes are common concepts within relational data warehousing, multidimensional schemas provide an additional layer of sophistication.

Dimensions are lists of unique values that identify and categorize data. They form the edges of cubes. Dimensions have structure that helps in the navigation around the cube and the definition of calculations. A typical dimension includes levels, hierarchies, and attributes. Most dimensions will have at least one hierarchy, but Oracle OLAP also supports completely flat dimensions where no hierarchy exists.

Attributes contain descriptive information about dimension members that are used for data selection and identification. They are used for labeling cross-tabular and graphical data displays, selecting data, organizing dimension members, and so on.

Cubes are containers of measures (facts) and calculations. They simply provide a convenient way of collecting up measures with the same dimensions; therefore, all measures in a cube are candidates for being processed together at all stages: data loading, aggregation, and storage. Figure 9-24 provides an overview of how data sources are organized into a cube and then presented to business users via BI reports and dashboards.

Cubes can contain both data and sophisticated calculations. One of the powerful features of the Oracle OLAP technology is the ability to easily create sophisticated business calculations. Oracle OLAP contains a powerful calculation engine that

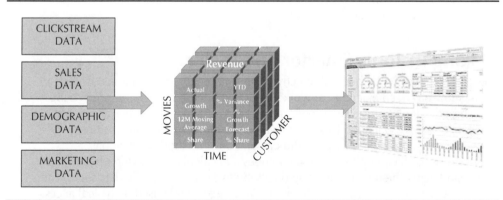

FIGURE 9-24. *Integrating Big Data into a multidimensional model and displaying results in Business Intelligence dashboard*

allows you to extend cubes by including business calculations as calculated measures. There are four categories of calculations:

- Basic
- Advanced
- Prior/Future comparison
- Timeframe

Each category contains a series of predefined calculation templates that can be applied to any measure. These formulae can help business users answer questions such as:

- Based on total revenue, which movie categories generate 80 percent of revenue and which movie categories fall into the 20 percent bucket?

- What is the percentage contribution of each movie category and the movies within each category, and how has this changed over time (percentage change)?

- What is the percentage contribution of each customer grouping and how has this changed over time (percentage change)?

- What is the percentage contribution of the "most-valued" customers compared to other customers and how has this changed over time (percentage change)?

- What is the forecasted revenue over the next three to five years by customer grouping and movie category?

Making BI Tools Smarter and Faster

The OLAP cubes can be queried directly using simple SQL, and Oracle Business Intelligence has been extended to work directly with these multidimensional cubes, cube-based calculations, dimensions, and attributes. By making cubes accessible via SQL, Oracle Application Express developers can incorporate dimensions, attributes, measures, and very powerful calculations into their applications.

Business users can interact with their cubes and calculated measures by drilling within and across hierarchies, filtering on attributes to create specific data slices. The data points within the cube are typically partially aggregated based on typical access paths as part of the process of building the cube. This allows the DBA to balance the competing requirements of cube build times vs. storage space vs. query performance. As the data is queried, any data points that have not been precomputed are efficiently aggregated at run time.

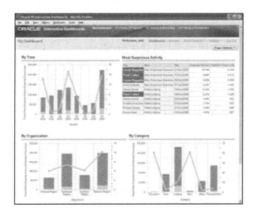

FIGURE 9-25.   *Multidimensional analysis using Oracle Business Intelligence and Oracle OLAP Option*

This outstanding query performance can also be leveraged transparently. By deploying a cube as a materialized view, the Oracle Database optimizer can transparently redirect SQL queries to levels within the cubes. As a cube can contain multiple levels, a single cube can replace multiple single-level materialized views. This simplifies the overall administration process for the DBA and provides increased performance for the business users, especially where business users are accessing pages within a dashboard that contain multiple reports as shown in Figure 9-25.

In-Database Analytics: Bringing It All Together

Many technical and high-level benefits can be derived from having a database with a large portfolio of analytical features, and these have been outlined in previous sections.

One of the main advantages for business users and data warehouse developers of having a single integrated analytical platform is the ability to combine different analytical functions within a single query and the ability to use one type of analysis to drive another.

Integrating Analytics into Extract-Load-Transform Processing

Many Big Data streams are pushed to data warehouse platforms for deeper analysis. The "push" process is usually incorporated into existing ELT workflows. Oracle has always recommended using "E-L-T" rather than "E-T-L" as the optimal way to manage data flowing into a data warehouse because it creates the opportunity to leverage a wide variety of in-database features, including in-database analytics.

The key to adding value in a data warehouse is to do as much as possible, as close to the data as possible, as early in the process as possible. Oracle Database is able to integrate analytical processing as part of an E-L-T workflow because interaction with all the in-database analytical features is done using SQL. This means that data warehouse developers can use their existing skills and tools to broaden the scope of their E-L-T processing.

With in-database analytics, it is possible to expand the basic E-L-T processing to include other high-value processing features. It is possible to add significant value to the data warehouse environment by expanding this processing to include a new, and critically important, stage—"P," for predict. By incorporating a *predict* stage as part of the upstream processing, all business users can benefit from the results, no matter which reporting tool they are using.

By using in-database data mining features within ELT procedures, it is possible to predict new values for missing data points or derive new columns of data. This approach can help reduce the amount of revenue allocated to the ever-popular "Unknown Value" bucket, which is a common factor in many data warehouse hierarchies. This elevates the ETL process to a whole new level and adds real business value.

Delivering Guided Exploration

There are many advantages to creating analytical mash-ups. For example, an OLAP schema contains data sets (or cubes) that are high-quality, organized, cleaned, and precisely formatted. One of the complaints of accessing OLAP cubes is that the complexity and volume of data can make it difficult to uncover meaningful patterns via ad-hoc exploration.

Developers and business analysts can use Oracle's in-database analytics to help guide users in discovering new correlations that lead directly to actionable insight. For example, cubes derived from the analysis of Big Data are often built on large numbers of dimensions. As the number of dimensions increases, business users find it more and more difficult to position dimensions in their report layout to create meaningful analysis. Data mining can be used to quantify the importance of each dimension, and developers can then refine their cubes to include only the top five most important dimensions.

Using data mining anomaly detection, it is possible to highlight underperforming products, customers, or operations based on a wide variety of attributes. These underperforming items can be flagged or grouped within specific hierarchies to prompt users to explore the related data to get a better understanding of the reasons behind the lack of success.

Delivering Analytical Mash-ups

Many police forces and governments around the world have experimented with combining both data mining and spatial analytics to create maps showing criminal activity. This information can be used to help determine how, where, and when to allocate police resources. As many government agencies are keen to push their data into the public domain, many people are now using this data to help them decide where to purchase their next house.

By using predictive analytics, it is possible to automate the discovery of patterns using functions that can sweep through tables and identify previously hidden patterns. An example of pattern discovery is the analysis of retail sales data to identify seemingly unrelated products that are often purchased together. This information can be used to drive the creation of data-driven hierarchies that allow business users to directly monitor key buying patterns over time. Other pattern discovery problems include detecting clusters in a column that can then be used to drive completely new hierarchies and drill-paths.

Crime reports typically contain a lot of textual information from witness statements, forensic information, and individual observations of police officers. By applying general data mining, text mining, and spatial analytics to this textual information, it is possible to identify specific "danger patterns" associated with each type of crime. Overlaying that information with information about the time of each incident and the surrounding geospatial features (for example, the proximity of points of interest, such as a nightclub), it is possible to use both information sets to produce predictive and proactive analysis of criminal activity.

Conclusion

Big Data is built on a broad range of data streams that contain low-level detailed data points. It is not possible to simply take this raw data and present it in a BI report because the number of data points would be overwhelming. The best approach is to look for patterns and hidden nuggets within these data streams. The role of Big Data analytics is to help data scientists, business users, and developers to make these discoveries in a timely manner.

This chapter has outlined the key analytical features that are part of the Oracle Database that support the "Analyze" section of Oracle's Big Data workflow. To get maximum value from these Big Data streams, integration with other key data sources, such as operational data sources, data marts, and/or data warehouses, is a key requirement. The Oracle Big Data workflow is designed to support this requirement and allows users to analyze all their data using the in-database analytical features that are an integral part of the Oracle Database.

CHAPTER
10

Analyzing Data with R

I n this chapter, the focus is on analyzing data with R while making it scalable
using Oracle's R technologies. Initial sections provide an introduction to open
source R and issues with traditional R and database interaction. Subsequent
sections cover Oracle's strategic R offerings: Oracle R Enterprise[1] 1.3, Oracle R
Distribution, ROracle, and Oracle R Connector for Hadoop[2] 2.0.

Introduction to Open Source R

R is an open-source language and environment for statistical computing and
data visualization, supporting data manipulation and transformations, as well as
conventional and more sophisticated graphics. With millions of users worldwide,
R is widely taught in universities, and increasingly used by data analysts and data
scientists in enterprise environments.

R is a statistics language similar to SAS or SPSS. It is powerful in that users can
accomplish much computation with minimal specification. It is extensible in that
users can write their own functions and packages, leveraging object-oriented and
functional programming language constructs. An R *package* is a collection of
typically related functions, data, and compiled code, organized using a well-defined
format. R itself is organized as a set of packages.

User-defined packages enable automating analysis and can be used by the
individual, shared within the organization, or published to the Comprehensive R
Archive Network (CRAN) for sharing with the R community. R has a wide range of
statistics and data visualization capabilities. While the default arguments are often
sufficient to get started, there are plenty of *knobs* to customize or fine-tune results.

Perhaps one aspect that has also helped R's adoption is that it is easy to install
and use, and it is free—downloadable from the R project Web site. Consider
downloading and installing R from the CRAN Web site today.

CRAN, Packages, and Task Views

R package growth has been exponential, with thousands of contributors, and that
trend continues. Today, there are over four thousand packages in the R ecosystem.
Each package provides specialized functionality, in areas such as bioinformatics,
financial market analysis, and numerous others. Table 10-1 shows CRAN Task
Views, which are areas of concentration for sets of related R packages. Each Task
View Web page provides a description of the packages supporting that area.

---

[1] As introduced in Chapter 9, Oracle R Enterprise and Oracle Data Mining are the two components of the
Oracle Advanced Analytics option to Oracle Database Enterprise Edition.

[2] Oracle R Connector for Hadoop is a component of the Oracle Big Data Connectors software suite,
which also includes Oracle Loader for Hadoop, Oracle Data Integrator Application Adapter for Hadoop,
and Oracle Direct Connector for HDFS.

Task View	Description
Bayesian	Bayesian Inference
ChemPhys	Chemometrics and Computational Physics
ClinicalTrials	Clinical Trial Design, Monitoring, and Analysis
Cluster	Cluster Analysis and Finite Mixture Models
DifferentialEquations	Differential Equations
Distributions	Probability Distributions
Econometrics	Computational Econometrics
Environmetrics	Analysis of Ecological and Environmental Data
ExperimentalDesign	Design of Experiments (DoE) and Analysis of Experimental Data
Finance	Empirical Finance
Genetics	Statistical Genetics
Graphics	Graphic Displays and Dynamic Graphics and Graphic Devices and Visualization
HighPerformanceComputing	High-Performance and Parallel Computing with R
MachineLearning	Machine Learning and Statistical Learning
MedicalImaging	Medical Image Analysis
Multivariate	Multivariate Statistics
NaturalLanguageProcessing	Natural Language Processing
OfficialStatistics	Official Statistics and Survey Methodology
Optimization	Optimization and Mathematical Programming
Pharmacokinetics	Analysis of Pharmacokinetic Data
Phylogenetics	Phylogenetics, Especially Comparative Methods
Psychometrics	Psychometric Models and Methods
ReproducibleResearch	Reproducible Research
Robust	Robust Statistical Methods
SocialSciences	Statistics for the Social Sciences
Spatial	Analysis of Spatial Data
SpatioTemporal	Handling and Analyzing Spatio-Temporal Data
Survival	Survival Analysis
TimeSeries	Time Series Analysis
gR	gRaphical Models in R

TABLE 10-1. *CRAN Task Views*

Algorithm Class	Packages
Neural Networks	**nnet** Single-hidden-layer neural network **RSNNS** Stuttgart Neural Network Simulator
Recursive Partitioning	**rpart** Regression, classification, and survival analysis for CART-like trees **RWeka** Partitioning algorithms available in Weka, for example, C4.5 and M5 **Cubist** Rule-based models with linear regression models in terminal leaves **C50** C5.0 classification trees, rule-based models, and boosted versions
Random Forests	**randomForest** Reference implementation of the random forest algorithm **ipred** Bagging for regression, classification, and survival analysis as well as bundling **randomSurvivalForest** Random forest algorithm for censored data **quantregForest** Quantile regression forests
Boosting	**gbm** Various forms of gradient boosting **bst** Hinge-loss optimized by boosting implementation **GAMBoost** Fit-generalized additive models by a boosting algorithm
Support Vector Machines and Kernel Methods	**e1071** Svm() interface to the LIBSVM library **kernlab** Implements a flexible framework for kernel learning **klaR** SVMlight implementation for one-against-all classification
Bayesian Methods	**BayesTree** Bayesian Additive Regression Trees **tgp** Bayesian nonstationary, semiparametric nonlinear regression
Optimization Using Genetic Algorithms	**rgp** Optimization routines **rgenoud** Optimization routines
Association Rules	**arules** A priori algorithm with efficient data structures for sparse data **Eclat** Mining frequent itemsets, maximal frequent itemsets, closed frequent itemsets, association rules

TABLE 10-2.   *Machine Learning and Statistical Learning Task View*

Table 10-2 depicts a sampling of content available in the Machine Learning and Statistical Learning task view. While Oracle Database and the Oracle Advanced Analytics options provide a rich set of in-database data mining algorithms and statistical functions, there are others that may be required by a project for which open source R adds value.

GUIs and IDEs

Although R comes with a default integrated development environment (IDE), there are many other IDEs to choose from. For example, one is a third-party, open source IDE called RStudio, which has a more finished look to it as well as some convenient features. Note, however, that Oracle has no affiliation with RStudio and does not provide support for RStudio.

As shown in Figure 10-1, users can view and edit R scripts in the upper left-hand frame, and then select a portion of an R script to execute by clicking Run. In the figure, the R script loads the `igraph` package and then accesses online documentation for `igraph`. Documentation appears in the Help tab (not shown).

One can switch between plots, packages, help, and even navigate to previously accessed help and generated plots. In the example, a *Barabasi game*, or small-world graph generated by the Barabasi algorithm, has been initialized. Here, the Barabasi

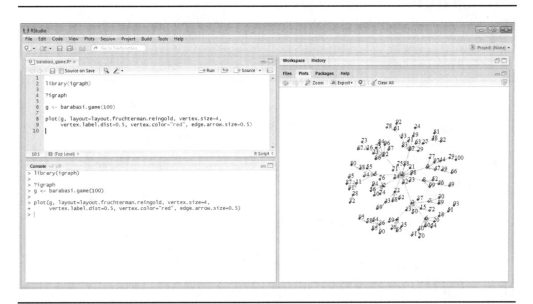

FIGURE 10-1.   *RStudio IDE*

algorithm produces a preferential attachment model with 100 nodes, which is then plotted with a `fruchterman.reingold` layout.

While RStudio is the top-ranked interface after the built-in R console, according to a 2011 KDNuggets survey, there are many others, such as R Commander and `rattle`. The package `Rcmdr`, which supports R Commander, is one of the oldest GUIs for R based on the `tcltk` package. R Commander takes, for example, the most commonly used statistical functions and exposes them through a drop-down menu interface with dialogs that prompt the user for needed arguments. This enables users who are not familiar with programming but know what they want to accomplish to use R. The underlying code that is generated by R Commander can be exposed for further editing by the user.

The `rattle` (R Analytic Tool to Learn Easily) GUI provides a Gnome-based interface to data mining functionality in R—all without needing to know details of R programming. The `rattle` interface presents the user with the standard sequence of steps, or workflow, that an analyst would commonly go through to solve a data mining problem.

Both R Commander and `rattle` can be used within the standard R interface, or within RStudio.

Traditional R and Database Interaction vs. Oracle R Enterprise

Most enterprise data is stored in relational databases. As illustrated in Figure 10-2, a common way for data analysts to access data is through flat files. A request is made

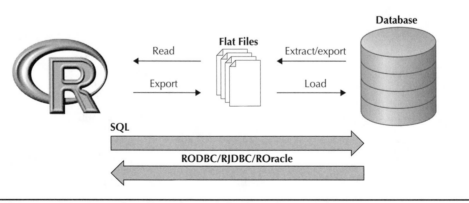

FIGURE 10-2.   *Aspects of traditional R and database interaction*

to a DBA who produces an extract and makes it available to the analyst. When completed, results consisting of predictive models, data scores, or other analytical results are exported to flat files for import back to the database. From there, results can be accessed by enterprise applications.

As is commonly experienced, this approach introduces significant latency for data access, especially if the correct data was not provided the first time or the analyst determined that different or additional data was required. This can result in multiple iterations before the analyst gets the needed set of tables or columns, adding hours, days, or weeks to a project. In addition, when using data extracts, which are often stored on local user hard drives, enterprises need to address data backup, recovery, and security.

For those users familiar with SQL, there are R packages for direct database access, for example, RODBC, RJDBC, and ROracle. While this type of access is an improvement over flat file exchange, it requires a paradigm shift between R and SQL. Users must think in terms of SQL queries, not R objects, and have the package map data from tables into data.frames, and vice versa, which may or may not have the semantics required by the user.

When it comes time to deploy an analytics-based solution involving R, application developers may resort to a carefully scripted cron job to operationalize the process of extracting data, running the R script, and returning results. However, this can produce a complex architecture and more moving parts that must be tracked and managed. Moreover, the R scripts and any reusable R objects written out to files must be managed at the file system level as part of production deployment. To avoid some of these issues, an application architect may require the results of analysis, such as R models, to be translated into SQL, C, or Java, for inclusion in applications. This translation process is tedious and error-prone and can result in significant delay between model creation and production deployment.

Another concern for enterprise data is that R is a client and interpreter bundled together as a single executable. As a single-user tool, despite recent improvements, much of its functionality is not multithreaded or parallel. Moreover, it cannot generally leverage CPU capacity on a user's desktop without the use of special packages and coding.

R also normally requires the data it operates on to be loaded into memory. There are CRAN packages that support out-of-memory data, such as those related to the bigmemory package, but these may still require data extracts and as such would not alleviate enterprise concerns over backup, recovery, security, and overall application complexity. In general, analyzing enterprise-sized data sets may not be possible if the data cannot be loaded into memory. Even if loading some larger data sets is possible, R's call-by-value semantics means that as data flows into functions, for each function invocation, a copy of the data may be made. As a result, memory can quickly be exhausted when trying to analyze data.

To address the needs of enterprises for advanced analytics, Oracle R Enterprise enhances open source R in several ways. First, it allows R users to analyze and manipulate data in Oracle Database through R, transparently. For base R functionality, users write code as though working with `data.frames`, but the R functions are overloaded to execute in the database on database data—transparently translated to SQL. This leverages the database as a high-performance and scalable compute engine. With this *Transparency Layer*, users experience reduced latency, reduced application complexity, and increased performance and security, while operating on bigger data (not limited by the memory constraint of R). In all, SQL knowledge is no longer required to manipulate database data.

Oracle R Enterprise also enables users to take advantage of data-parallel and task-parallel execution through Oracle Database. This *Embedded R Execution* enables "lights out" execution of R scripts. The R scripts developed to support database applications can be stored and managed in the database R script repository. Embedded R Execution can be accessed by both R and SQL interfaces. The SQL interface enables working seamlessly with database applications and facilitates integration with OBIEE RPDs and dashboards and Oracle BI Publisher documents. Open source CRAN packages can be installed at the database server R engine and used in embedded R scripts.

Oracle R Enterprise exposes in-database predictive analytics algorithms seamlessly through R. These include algorithms from the Oracle Advanced Analytics' Oracle Data Mining component, and those new to the Oracle R Enterprise component, including stepwise linear regression and artificial neural networks. To enhance predictive model performance, native R models can be used to score data in-database, effectively translating the native R model into SQL. Executing the corresponding SQL leverages Oracle Database as a powerful compute engine.

One of the features unique to Oracle R Enterprise is how R scripts are dynamically integrated into the SQL language. As discussed in the section "Embedded R Execution," users can define R scripts, store them in Oracle Database, and invoke them by name within SQL statements.

Lastly, when it comes to operationalizing analytics results, often seen as the killer of applications projects, Oracle R Enterprise integrates R into the IT software stack, without requiring additional components, like `Rserve`. By making R functions accessible from SQL, database and enterprise application developers can readily leverage the results of the analytics side of the house without complex plumbing, recoding, or mapping of results to database tables.

Oracle's Strategic R Offerings

A key goal for Oracle is to deliver enterprise-level advanced analytics based on the R environment. To enable this, Oracle provides Oracle R Enterprise, Oracle R Distribution, an enhanced open source `ROracle` package for database connectivity and, in terms of Big Data on Hadoop, Oracle R Connector for Hadoop.

Oracle R Enterprise

Oracle R Enterprise (ORE) is a component of the Oracle Advanced Analytics option to Oracle Database Enterprise Edition. ORE eliminates R's memory constraints by working on data directly in the database. By leveraging in-database analytics, ORE augments R with both scalability and high performance. Moreover, ORE provides a comprehensive, database-centric environment covering the full range of analytical processes in R where R users can rapidly develop and deploy R scripts that work on database data. Being integrated with Oracle Database, ORE can execute R scripts through the database—leveraging Oracle Database as a high-performance computing (HPC) environment.

The integration with the SQL language enables invoking R scripts from SQL to support enterprise applications. This also enables Oracle BI Publisher documents and OBIEE dashboards to access analytics results produced by R, including graphs and images. R users can also leverage the latest R algorithms and contributed packages.

From a high-level architectural perspective, Figure 10-3 depicts the R workspace console (IDE) where users interactively execute R scripts. ORE overloads R functions that normally operate on `data.frames` and pushes down their execution to Oracle Database, where transformations and statistical computations are performed on database tables. ORE introduces `ore.frame` objects that serve as proxies for database tables and views.

In Oracle Database, the statistics engine consists of native database functionality, such as standard SQL, SQL data mining functions, and various DBMS packages, as well as enhancements specific to ORE. As noted earlier, results from ORE can be exposed through OBIEE dashboards and Web Services-based applications.

Three key points are: ORE requires little or no change to the R user experience, the database provides the ability to scale to large data sets, and analytics results can be embedded in operational or production systems—supporting areas of interactive development, production deployment, and end-user consumption.

Figure 10-4 depicts an OBIEE dashboard where the graph is produced by invoking a parameterized R script for execution through the database. As shown in the figure,

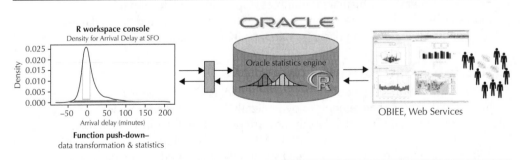

FIGURE 10-3.   *High-level architectural perspective of Oracle R Enterprise*

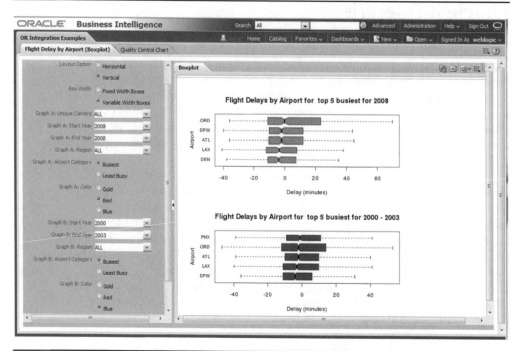

FIGURE 10-4. *ORE integrated with OBIEE dashboard for dynamic, parameterized graph generation*

one can select data subsets and customize graph characteristics, such as orientation, color, and box plot width. When the user clicks Apply (hidden in the figure), the request is sent to the database for execution by a database server R engine. The graph is returned for display in the dashboard and can be represented as a base 64 encoding of the PNG image as part of an XML string, or as a PNG BLOB table column. R scripts can compute structured results for display in dashboard tables, as well as to generate sophisticated graphics. Open source CRAN packages that perform statistical calculations and generate graphs can be installed at the database server R engine for generating dashboard graphs in a similar manner.

Oracle R Distribution

Oracle R Distribution, a free download from Oracle, is Oracle's redistribution of open source R, with enhancements to dynamically load high-performance math libraries from Intel, AMD, and Solaris if they are present on the machine. (Note, however, that these libraries, such as Intel's MKL, are not included with Oracle R Distribution and may need to be licensed separately.) High-performance libraries include core math functions such as sparse solvers, fast Fourier transforms, vector math, and others that transparently increase the performance of R functions relying on them.

Oracle provides support for Oracle R Distribution for customers of Oracle R Enterprise, Big Data Appliance, or Oracle Linux—so Oracle stands behind the R software. The lack of a major corporate sponsor has made some companies leery of fully adopting R. With Oracle R Distribution, enterprise customers have greater confidence in adopting R enterprise-wide. Oracle R Distribution is available and supported on Oracle Enterprise Linux, AIX, and Solaris.

ROracle

The database interface driver `ROracle` is an open source R package now maintained by Oracle, providing high-performance connectivity between R and Oracle Database. Oracle R Enterprise uses `ROracle` for connectivity between R and Oracle Database. `ROracle` has been re-engineered using the Oracle Call Interface (OCI) with optimizations and bug fixes made available to the open source community. `ROracle` implements the database interface (DBI) package definitions.

Oracle R Connector for Hadoop

Oracle R Connector for Hadoop—one of the components of the Oracle Big Data Connectors—provides an R interface to a Hadoop cluster, allowing R users to access and manipulate data in Hadoop Distributed File System (HDFS), Oracle Database, and the file system. R users can write MapReduce functions using R and execute Hadoop jobs using a natural R interface. In addition, Oracle R Connector for Hadoop provides several native Hadoop-based analytics techniques as part of the package. Data stored in Hive can be accessed and manipulated through a transparency layer similar to that of ORE.

Oracle R Enterprise: Next-Level View

From the perspective of a collaborative execution model, Oracle R Enterprise (ORE) leverages three layers of computational engines, as depicted in Figure 10-5. The first layer is the R engine on a user's desktop, where users work interactively on database data and perform local post-processing of results provided by the database. The Transparency Layer allows R users to access database tables and views via proxy objects. These proxy objects of type `ore.frame` are a subclass of `data.frame`. Through function overloading, invoking functions on `ore.frame` objects results in generated SQL that is executed in the database.

The second compute engine is Oracle Database itself. Through the Transparency Layer, the SQL generated through R function invocation is executed in the database—taking advantage of query optimization, database parallelism, and

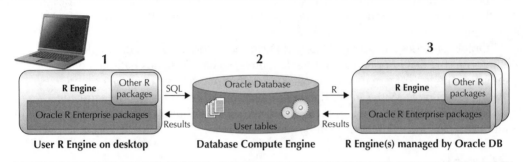

FIGURE 10-5. *Computational engines supporting Oracle R Enterprise*

scalability. In vanilla R, a series of function invocations is executed sequentially, producing a result from each function. With ORE, the SQL generated through a series of functions can be stacked and not executed until an intermediate result is needed for subsequent computation, or the user requests the result. This allows the database query optimizer to optimize the stacked SQL prior to execution. When configured for parallelism, Oracle Database will automatically take advantage of multiple processors to execute SQL queries, which also applies to the SQL generated through the Transparency Layer. Scalability is achieved since data is not loaded into the client R engine prior to function invocation.

The third compute engine is composed of R engines spawned to execute on the database server machine, under the control of Oracle Database. By executing at the database server, data can be loaded to the R engine and written to the database more efficiently than between the R client and the database.

Embedded R Execution enables

- Data and task parallelism

- The return of rich XML or PNG image output

- SQL access to R

- Running parallel simulations

- Use of third-party (CRAN) and custom packages at the database server

Oracle R Enterprise enables a simplified architecture, while eliminating the constraints of the client R engine, as shown in Figure 10-6. This architecture enables enterprises and data analysts to get even greater value from Oracle Database for advanced analytics by leveraging R with database scalability and performance. When combined with Oracle Exadata, these benefits are further amplified.

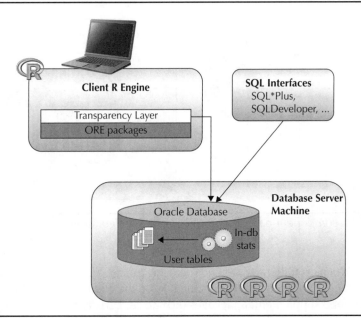

FIGURE 10-6.   *Oracle R Enterprise architecture*

Once analysts complete their work, solution deployment is immediate. Traditionally, an analyst's results, such as predictive models, would be manually translated into SQL for in-database scoring against large data sets. With Oracle R Enterprise, the R scripts can be stored in the database R script repository and invoked by name, directly within SQL statements. In addition, R objects both intermediate and final can be store in a database R *datastore*, which is discussed in a later section.

Oracle R Enterprise Installation and Configuration

From a prerequisites standpoint, Oracle R Enterprise is supported on 64-bit Linux x86-64, Microsoft Windows, Solaris on both SPARC and x86, IBM AIX, as well as Oracle Exadata and SPARC SuperCluster. Check the Oracle R Enterprise documentation for the latest version of R supported. Oracle Database 11.2.0.3 or above is suggested, although earlier 11.2 releases are supported with a patch, as indicated in the ORE installation guide.

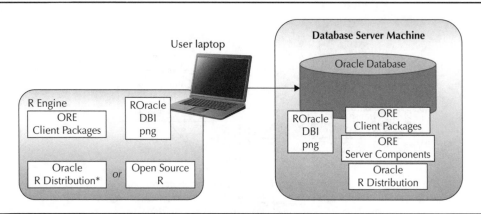

FIGURE 10-7. *ORE component packages and R engine configuration*

Figure 10-7 depicts ORE package and R engine configuration. Users first install R, either the Oracle R Distribution or open source R, on the client and server machines. ORE packages and supplemental packages (ROracle, DBI, and png) are then installed into R, both at the client and server. At the database server, ORE libraries (.so) are linked with Oracle Database.

When installing on Exadata, ORE packages and R must be installed on each Exadata node. The ORE package installation consists of the client packages shown in Table 10-3, along with the supplemental packages noted previously. See the *Oracle R Enterprise Installation and Administration Guide* for complete installation requirements and instructions.

ORE Package	Description
OREbase	Corresponds to R's base package
OREstats	Corresponds to R's stat package
OREgraphics	Corresponds to R's graphics package
OREeda	Exploratory data analysis package
OREdm	Exposes Oracle Data Mining algorithms
OREpredict	Enables scoring data in Oracle DB using R models
ORExml	Supports XML translation between R and Oracle Database

TABLE 10-3. *ORE Packages*

Using Oracle R Enterprise

This section provides detailed examples using the ORE Transparency Layer, Embedded R Execution, and predictive analytics.

Transparency Layer

The Transparency Layer supports in-database data exploration, data preparation, and data analysis often en route to the application of predictive analytics, where users have access to a mix of in-database and open source R techniques.

Transparency means that for base R functionality, R users can write code as though working with R `data.frames` and then transparently have that code operate on database data, leveraging the database as a high-performance and scalable compute engine. R users do not need to learn a different programming paradigm or environment such as SQL to access and manipulate database data. They can operate on database data as though they were native R objects using R syntax. While `ore.frame` objects have been explicitly mentioned, ORE maps a range of primitive object types, for example, `ore.vector` and `ore.numeric`, to database data.

Transparency also means that for R scripts that leverage base R functionality, minimal change is required to work with database data. Internally, transparency means that R functions are transparently translated to SQL for in-database execution, gaining performance and scalability.

A major benefit of the Transparency Layer is that as R functions are translated to SQL, much of this SQL is *stacked*—not immediately executed, but accumulated. When a result is finally needed, either for a computation or for viewing by the user, the stacked SQL is executed. This allows the database to perform query optimization on that SQL. This is not possible in native R or even interactive one-off invocations of SQL where intermediate results are pulled back to the client.

Connecting to Oracle Database

To get started with the Transparency Layer, users first connect to an Oracle database that has ORE installed. As shown in Example 1, users check if already connected to a database using the function `is.ore.connected`. In this example, arguments to `ore.connect` specify the `"rquser"` schema with SID `"orcl"` on the local host. The password is specified in this example, but there are other options to avoid clear-text passwords.

Example 1:

```
if (!is.ore.connected())
   ore.connect("rquser", "orcl", "localhost", "password", all=TRUE)
ore.ls()
ore.disconnect()
ore.connect("rquser", "orcl", "localhost", "password")
ore.sync(table="MYDATA")
ore.attach()
```

The argument all, if set to TRUE, loads metadata about all the tables from the schema into ore.frame objects, making them available for use as R objects with the same name as the table—implicitly invoking the ore.sync and ore.attach functions. Invoking ore.ls lists the tables and views available as ore.frame objects in the attached schema. The function ore.disconnect will end an ORE session and free any temporary database objects. Connecting to the database without the all argument, the arguments to ore.sync in the example specify to load one table, "MYDATA". If the schema contains a large number of tables that will not be used during the R session, this limits the number of ore.frame objects created (space) and the amount of time required to retrieve the corresponding table metadata. If a schema has thousands of tables, but only one or a few are needed, this savings can be significant. To make the objects available in the search path, the script invokes ore.attach. From here, users can do some interesting transformations and analysis on database data from R.

Data Manipulation

Example 2 illustrates two common database data manipulation operations: column and row selection. Projecting columns from a database table using an ore.frame object can be specified in a few ways:

- Specify the columns by name in a vector

- Provide a vector of column numbers

- Specify which columns to remove by using a minus sign

Example 2:

```
# Column selection
df <- ONTIME_S[,c("YEAR","DEST","ARRDELAY")]
class(df)
head(df)
head(ONTIME_S[,c(1,4,23)])
head(ONTIME_S[,-(1:22)])

#Row selection
df1 <- df[df$DEST=="SFO",]
```

```
class(df1)
df2 <- df[df$DEST=="SFO",c(1,3)]
df3 <- df[df$DEST=="SFO" | df$DEST=="BOS",1:3]
head(df1)
head(df2)
head(df3)
```

In the column selection R script, the first line selects YEAR, DEST, and ARRDELAY by column name. The next line selects three columns by column index, specified as a numeric vector. The following line removes columns 1 through 22 by putting a minus sign in front of the vector 1 through 22.

How does one remove a single column from a database table using SQL? Think about it. There are one thousand columns and the goal is to eliminate one column using a view. This will be discussed later.

To select rows from an ore.frame, specify a logical expression that is evaluated on each row. If the expression evaluates to true, that row is included in the result set. Notice that the column name is specified with the ore.frame object, as in df$DEST. If only DEST were specified, it would be an undefined variable at best, or refer to some other value or vector, likely producing an error when used in this scenario.

As in R, an arbitrarily complex logical expression can be specified with parentheses and logical operators for row selection. Row and column filtering can also be specified in the same statement. The first row selection example retrieves only rows where the destination contains "SFO." The second example includes the same rows, but retrieves only columns 1 and 3. The following example filters flights with a destination of "SFO" or "BOS," and takes columns 1, 2, and 3.

The results from the row selection code are shown in Listing 10-1. The first six rows of each result are shown using the overloaded head function. The function head works on ore.frame objects and retrieves table data from the database.

Listing 10-1 *Column and row selection results*

```
R> # Column selection
R> df <- ONTIME_S[,c("YEAR","DEST","ARRDELAY")]
R> class(df)
[1] "ore.frame"
attr(,"package")
[1] "OREbase"
R> head(df)
  YEAR DEST ARRDELAY
1 1987  MSP       4
2 1987  SJC       6
3 1987  OAK       7
4 1987  PHX       9
5 1987  CLT       0
6 1987  CVG       4
```

```
R> head(ONTIME_S[,c(1,4,23)])
   YEAR DAYOFMONTH TAXIOUT
1 1987          1       NA
2 1987          1       NA
3 1987          1       NA
4 1987          1       NA
5 1987          1       NA
6 1987          1       NA
R> head(ONTIME_S[,-(1:22)])
   TAXIOUT CANCELLED CANCELLATIONCODE DIVERTED
1       NA         0             <NA>        0
2       NA         0             <NA>        0
3       NA         0             <NA>        0
4       NA         0             <NA>        0
5       NA         0             <NA>        0
6       NA         0             <NA>        0R> #Row selection
R> df1 <- df[df$DEST=="SFO",]
R> class(df1)
[1] "ore.frame"
attr(,"package")
[1] "OREbase"
R> df2 <- df[df$DEST=="SFO",c(1,3)]
R> df3 <- df[df$DEST=="SFO" | df$DEST=="BOS",1:3]
R> head(df1)
   YEAR DEST ARRDELAY
1 1987  SFO       24
2 1987  SFO       68
3 1987  SFO       -3
4 1987  SFO        5
5 1987  SFO       37
6 1987  SFO       11
R> head(df2)
   YEAR ARRDELAY
1 1987       24
2 1987       68
3 1987       -3
4 1987        5
5 1987       37
6 1987       11
R> head(df3)
   YEAR DEST ARRDELAY
1 1987  SFO       24
2 1987  SFO       68
3 1987  SFO       -3
4 1987  SFO        5
5 1987  SFO       37
6 1987  BOS       NA
```

For joining data, R provides the function `merge`. In ORE, `merge` is overridden to work on `ore.frame` objects. In Example 3, two data frames are created and then merged. Taking the same data, database tables are created using `ore.create` to enable repeating the invocation using `ore.frame` objects representing database tables. The results are the same between the two `merge` invocations, as shown in Listing 10-2.

Example 3:

```
df1 <- data.frame(x1=1:5, y1=letters[1:5])
df2 <- data.frame(x2=5:1, y2=letters[11:15])
merge (df1, df2, by.x="x1", by.y="x2")


ore.drop(table="TEST_DF1")
ore.drop(table="TEST_DF2")


ore.create(df1, table="TEST_DF1")
ore.create(df2, table="TEST_DF2")
merge (TEST_DF1, TEST_DF2,
       by.x="x1", by.y="x2")
```

Listing 10-2   *Merge results*

```
R> df1 <- data.frame(x1=1:5, y1=letters[1:5])
R> df2 <- data.frame(x2=5:1, y2=letters[11:15])
R> merge (df1, df2, by.x="x1", by.y="x2")
  x1 y1 y2
1  1  a  o
2  2  b  n
3  3  c  m
4  4  d  l
5  5  e  k
R>
R> ore.drop(table="TEST_DF1")
R> ore.drop(table="TEST_DF2")
R>
R> ore.create(df1, table="TEST_DF1")
R> ore.create(df2, table="TEST_DF2")
R> merge (TEST_DF1, TEST_DF2,
+         by.x="x1", by.y="x2")
  x1 y1 y2
1  5  e  k
2  4  d  l
3  3  c  m
4  2  b  n
5  1  a  o
```

The R documentation for `merge` notes an `all` argument that if set to FALSE gives a natural join—a special case of inner join. Another argument, `all.x = TRUE`, gives a left (outer) join, `all.y = TRUE` produces a right (outer) join, and `all=TRUE` produces a (full) outer join. The same arguments apply in ORE.

The function `merge` can take an argument `incomparables` that identifies values that cannot be matched. Often, this is set to NA for the missing value. RDBMSs do not match NULLs when doing comparison, which would be the equivalent of specifying `incomparables = NA` in R. Such functionality requires special handling, for example, to convert the missing values to some other value first.

To transform data, for example, recoding, Example 4 depicts using the `transform` function. Each transformation is listed as an argument to the `transform` function, with an `ore.frame` object as the first argument. The `ifelse` function performs the recoding and assigns the result to the named columns.

Example 4:

```
ONTIME_S <- transform(ONTIME_S,
      DIVERTED = ifelse(DIVERTED == 0, 'Not Diverted',
                 ifelse(DIVERTED == 1, 'Diverted', '')),
      CANCELLATIONCODE =
                 ifelse(CANCELLATIONCODE == 'A', 'A CODE',
                 ifelse(CANCELLATIONCODE == 'B', 'B CODE',
                 ifelse(CANCELLATIONCODE == 'C', 'C CODE',
                 ifelse(CANCELLATIONCODE == 'D', 'D CODE', 'NOT CANCELLED')))),
      ARRDELAY = ifelse(ARRDELAY > 200, 'LARGE',
                 ifelse(ARRDELAY >= 30, 'MEDIUM', 'SMALL')),
      DEPDELAY = ifelse(DEPDELAY > 200, 'LARGE',
                 ifelse(DEPDELAY >= 30, 'MEDIUM', 'SMALL')),
      DISTANCE_ZSCORE =
                 (DISTANCE - mean(DISTANCE, na.rm=TRUE))/sd(DISTANCE, na.rm=TRUE))
```

Persisting R and ORE Objects

The designers of R incorporated the ability to save and load R objects to and from disk. The whole R workspace of objects can be saved to a file, which can be reloaded in a new R session. This allows users to come back to their previous R environment after quitting the R engine. Using this capability, predictive models can be built in one session and saved for scoring in another, or multiple, possibly parallel, R sessions in the future. This is accomplished through the R `save` and `load` functions, where one or more objects are serialized and unserialized, respectively. Consider Example 5 where two R objects, a linear model and `data.frame`, are saved to a file, and then reloaded. When objects are restored, they have the same names as when they were saved.

Example 5:

```
# R Session 1
x1 <- lm(...)
x2 <- data.frame(...)
save(x1,x2,file="myRObjects.RData")

# R Session 2
load("myRObjects.RData")
ls()
"x1"    "x2"
```

One concern for enterprise deployments using this approach is the need to manage such files through the OS file system. File system location information, along with backup, recovery, and security issues, must be factored into the deployed solution. A more database-centric solution is preferred.

In addition, serializing ORE objects, such as ore.frames, and saving them using R save and load does not work across sessions, since any referenced temporary tables or views are not saved across R sessions. If these proxy object references are not saved properly, restoring such objects makes them incomplete and inoperative.

To address this need for saving R and ORE objects in a database-centric manner, ORE provides object persistence in Oracle Database through an *R datastore*. This capability also facilitates passing sets of potentially complex objects to Embedded R Execution functions, either as a named datastore provided as an embedded R function argument, or a statically named datastore within the function. Objects created in one R session can be saved in a single datastore entry in the database. The name of this datastore can be passed to embedded R functions as an argument for loading within that function. Datastore facilitates passing one or multiple objects.

Example 6 is similar to Example 5. The main difference is the use of ore.save and ore.load, and providing the name of the datastore by which to retrieve ORE objects from the database.

Example 6:

```
# R Session 1
x1 <- ore.lm(...)
x2 <- ore.frame(...)
ore.save(x1,x2,name="ds1")

# R Session 2
ore.load(name="ds1")
ls()
"x1"    "x2"
```

In Example 7, a temporary `ore.frame`, DAT1, is created using `ore.push` on the R data set `iris`. An `ore.lm` model is then built that uses DAT1, a standard R `lm` model using the `mtcars` data set, followed by an Oracle Data Mining (ODM) Naïve Bayes model using `ONTIME_S`. Invoking `ore.save` on the three models with the datastore name "`myModels`" stores these objects in the database. Any referenced tables, views, or ODM models remain persistent in the database. When an ORE session ends, ORE objects are treated as temporary database objects and dropped unless explicitly saved in a datastore.

Example 7:

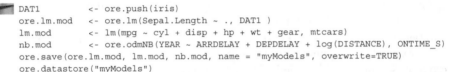

```
DAT1            <- ore.push(iris)
ore.lm.mod      <- ore.lm(Sepal.Length ~ ., DAT1 )
lm.mod          <- lm(mpg ~ cyl + disp + hp + wt + gear, mtcars)
nb.mod          <- ore.odmNB(YEAR ~ ARRDELAY + DEPDELAY + log(DISTANCE), ONTIME_S)
ore.save(ore.lm.mod, lm.mod, nb.mod, name = "myModels", overwrite=TRUE)
ore.datastore("myModels")
```

The function `ore.save` has several optional arguments, for example, users may provide the names of specific objects, or provide a list of objects. Users can also specify a particular environment to search for the objects to save. The argument `overwrite`, if set to TRUE, will overwrite an existing named datastore. If `append` is set to TRUE, objects can be added to an existing datastore. Users may also provide descriptive text for the datastore that appears in a summary listing. To view the contents of a datastore, the function `ore.datastoreSummary`, which takes the datastore name as argument, lists each object's name, class, size, and length. If the object is a `data.frame` or `ore.frame`, the number of rows and columns are also provided.

The `ore.load` function restores the saved R objects to the `.GlobalEnv` environment by default. Consider the case where a new R engine is started and connected to the database schema just used to save these objects. After invoking `ore.load` with the name "`myModels`," the saved objects can be referenced by their original names. Function `ore.load` has the flexibility to load all objects from the datastore, or a list of named objects within the datastore. Users can also specify the environment into which these objects should be loaded if different from `.GlobalEnv`.

In the section "Embedded R Execution," the use of datastores is revisited with the SQL API.

Data Preparation for Time Series

Time series data exists in many domains. Stock and trading data and retail and employment data are just a few examples. The ability to filter, order, and transform time series data often is a prerequisite for understanding trends and seasonal effects.

R has a rich set of time series analysis packages that can take advantage of data preprocessing using ORE filtering, aggregation, and moving window functions on large time series data. See the *CRAN Task View for Time Series Analysis* for a complete list. While ORE leverages R time series functions to perform, for example, forecasting using an ARIMA model, until that final step, the data preparation can be pushed to the database for execution.

ORE provides support for analyzing time series data through date and time transparency, by mapping Oracle date-related data types, such as DATE and TIMESTAMP, to R data types. Through the Transparency Layer, R users can perform date arithmetic, aggregations and percentiles, as well as moving window calculations, such as rolling max and rolling mean, among others.

In Oracle Database, the representations for date and time are unified—there is a single concept to capture this. However, R uses several classes and representations for date and time data, for example, Date, POSIXct, POSIXlt, and difftime. Including date and time processing in ORE enables providing a consistent mapping between data types for transparent database data access.

Table 10-4 lists the mapping of SQL data types to ORE data types for date and time. Notice that ORE introduces ore.datetime and ore.difftime as new data types. For INTERVAL YEAR TO MONTH, ore.character is a primitive type, so SQL INTERVAL YEAR TO MONTH columns are converted to character strings. While users can work with tables containing these columns, such columns will be treated as simple strings.

As part of the Transparency Layer, users can perform a wide range of operations on date and time data, ranging from binary operations, row functions, vector operations, aggregates, set operations, group by analysis, and moving window aggregation. The function ore.sort can be used with date and time columns, as well as ore.groupApply's INDEX argument in Embedded R Execution.

Example 8 illustrates some of the statistical aggregate functions. For data, a sequence of 500 dates spread evenly throughout 2001 is generated along with a random difftime and a vector of random normal values. This data.frame is pushed to Oracle Database using ore.push, which creates an ore.frame corresponding to a temporary database table.

Oracle SQL Data Type	ORE Data Type
DATE	ore.datetime
TIMESTAMP	ore.datetime
TIMESTAMP WITH TIME ZONE	ore.datetime
TIMESTAMP WITH LOCAL TIME ZONE	ore.datetime
INTERVAL YEAR TO MONTH	ore.character
INTERVAL DAY TO SECOND	ore.difftime

TABLE 10-4. *Oracle SQL Date-Related Data Types Mapping to ORE Data Types*

Example 8:

```
N <- 500
mydata <- data.frame(datetime =
              seq(as.POSIXct("2001/01/01"), as.POSIXct("2001/12/31"),
                  length.out = N),
              difftime = as.difftime(runif(N), units = "mins"),
              x = rnorm(N))
MYDATA <- ore.push(mydata)
class(MYDATA)
class(MYDATA$datetime)
head(MYDATA,3)
## statistic aggregates
min(MYDATA$datetime)
max(MYDATA$datetime)
range(MYDATA$datetime)
median(MYDATA$datetime)
quantile(MYDATA$datetime, probs = c(0, 0.05, 0.10))
```

The statistical aggregates of min, max, range, median, and quantile produce results on the ore.frame and are computed in the database. Notice that MYDATA is an ore.frame and the datetime column is of class ore.datetime, as shown in Listing 10-3. For example, the minimum date value is January 1, 2001. Using the quantile function, produce results for the 0, 5 percent, and 10 percent quantiles. Consider computing this on a table with millions or billions of entries. To perform this in R would require loading the full data set to the client, if that were even possible due to memory constraints. With ORE, this is done transparently in the database.

Listing 10-3 *Results for statistical aggregates involving dates*

```
R> class(MYDATA)
[1] "ore.frame"
attr(,"package")
[1] "OREbase"
R> class(MYDATA$datetime)
[1] "ore.datetime"
attr(,"package")
[1] "OREbase"
R> head(MYDATA,3)
            datetime        difftime          x
1 2001-01-01 00:00:00 54.459730 secs 1.5160605
2 2001-01-01 17:30:25 25.298211 secs 1.0586786
3 2001-01-02 11:00:50  1.654283 secs 0.9161595
R> ## statistic aggregates
R> min(MYDATA$datetime)
[1] "2001-01-01 EST"
R> max(MYDATA$datetime)
```

```
[1] "2001-12-31 EST"
R> range(MYDATA$datetime)
[1] "2001-01-01 EST" "2001-12-31 EST"
R> median(MYDATA$datetime)
[1] "2001-07-02 01:00:00 EDT"
R> quantile(MYDATA$datetime, probs = c(0, 0.05, 0.10))
                          0%                        5%                       10%
"2001-01-01 00:00:00 EST" "2001-01-19 04:48:00 EST" "2001-02-06 09:36:00 EST"
```

Sampling

Sampling is an important capability for statistical analytics. To perform sampling in R, users must either load the data fully into memory or, if the data is too large to load into R at once, load subsets of the data and construct a sample from each subset. With ORE, instead of pulling the data and then sampling, users can sample directly in the database and either pull only those records that are part of the sample into R, or leave the sample as an ore.frame in the database for further processing.

ORE enables a wide range of sampling techniques, for example:

- Simple random sampling

- Split data sampling

- Systematic sampling

- Stratified sampling

- Cluster sampling

- Quota sampling

- Accidental/convenience sampling

    - Via row order access

    - Via hashing

Consider Example 9 for simple random sampling, which involves selecting rows at random. A small demo data.frame is created and pushed to the database, creating an ore.frame. Out of 20 rows, sample 5 rows using the R sample function to produce a random set of indices. This allows getting a sample from MYDATA, which is an ore.frame, as shown in Listing 10-4.

Example 9:

```
set.seed(1)
N <- 20
myData <- data.frame(a=1:N,b=letters[1:N])
MYDATA <- ore.push(myData)
```

```
head(MYDATA)
sampleSize <- 5
simpleRandomSample <- MYDATA[sample(nrow(MYDATA), sampleSize), , drop=FALSE]
class(simpleRandomSample)
simpleRandomSample
```

Listing 10-4 *Simple random sampling results*

```
R> set.seed(1)
R> N <- 20
R> myData <- data.frame(a=1:N,b=letters[1:N])
R> MYDATA <- ore.push(myData)
R> head(MYDATA)
  a b
1 1 a
2 2 b
3 3 c
4 4 d
5 5 e
6 6 f
R> sampleSize <- 5
R> simpleRandomSample <- MYDATA[sample(nrow(MYDATA), sampleSize), , drop=FALSE]
R> class(simpleRandomSample)
[1] "ore.frame"
attr(,"package")
[1] "OREbase"
R> simpleRandomSample
    a b
4   4 d
6   6 f
8   8 h
11 11 k
16 16 p
```

Embedded R Execution

Embedded R Execution refers to the ability to execute R code on the database server, where one or more R engines are dynamically started, controlled, and managed by Oracle Database. By having the R engine on the database server machine, the need to pull data into the user's client R engine is eliminated. Moreover, data transfer is more efficient between the database-side R engine and Oracle Database. Embedded R Execution also enables data-parallel and task-parallel execution of R functions.

While ORE provides an R interface to enable interactive execution of embedded R functions, the SQL interface enables database applications to invoke R scripts seamlessly as part of SQL statements, supporting database-based applications. In addition, results from R functions can be returned as standard database tables for structured data or rich XML with both structured data and complex R objects.

Embedded R Execution also enables returning PNG images produced by R graphics functions. These can be returned in a table with a BLOB column containing the PNG image representation, or as an XML string containing the base 64 encoding of the PNG image. Since R provides a rich environment for producing high-quality and sophisticated graphics, applications can generate such images at the database server and feed these to OBIEE dashboards, reports with BI Publisher, or similar tools.

Embedded R Execution allows users to work with CRAN packages on the database server. Desired packages are installed in the database server R engine and loaded in the R function being executed (via `library(<package>)`), just as they would if executed at the client. It should be noted that ORE does not modify CRAN packages to take advantage of the Transparency Layer's in-database execution, nor does it automate parallel or scalable execution of CRAN packages. The original package behavior and characteristics for scalability or performance remain.

Embedded R Execution provides in-database storage and management for the R functions. This *R script repository* can greatly simplify application deployment. R functions can be stored and removed from the R script repository using either the R or SQL API. Viewing R scripts is achieved by accessing the database table `sys.rq_scripts`. An added benefit of the Embedded R Execution SQL API is the ability to schedule R scripts for execution as part of DBMS_SCHEDULER jobs.

It is important to facilitate the use of R script results by applications both during interactive development and testing by data scientists and application developers, and during deployment to streamline inclusion with dashboards and reporting frameworks. As suggested a moment ago, Embedded R Execution yields improved performance and throughput. Since the database server, such as Exadata, is more powerful than a desktop machine, R functions can benefit from significantly greater compute and memory resources.

R Interface

The R interface of Embedded R Execution consists of the functions: `ore.doEval`, `ore.tableApply`, `ore.rowApply`, `ore.groupApply`, and `ore.indexApply`, as shown in Table 10-5. Each takes an R function, or closure, as one of its arguments, which is the function to invoke at the database server and referred to as *f* in the text that follows. Alternatively, the name of a function stored in the R script repository can be specified. The Embedded R Execution functions provide capabilities intended for different situations.

- ■ `ore.doEval` invokes *f* in the database. There is no automatic loading of `ore.frame` data to *f*, but *f* can be invoked with arguments. `ore.doEval` can return an `ore.frame` object or a serialized R object.

- ■ `ore.tableApply` takes an `ore.frame` as input that is provided all at once to *f*. Like `ore.doEval`, it can return an `ore.frame` object or serialized R objects. Note that care should be taken to ensure the database server R engine can realistically handle the volume of data contained in the table corresponding to the `ore.frame`.

R Interface Function	Purpose and Signature
`ore.doEval()`	Invoke standalone R script supplying function FUN or function name FUN.NAME `ore.doEval(FUN, ..., FUN.VALUE = NULL, FUN.NAME = NULL)`
`ore.tableApply()`	Invoke R script with `ore.frame` as input X `ore.tableApply(X, FUN, ..., FUN.VALUE = NULL, FUN.NAME = NULL, parallel = FALSE)`
`ore.rowApply()`	Invoke R script on one row at a time, or multiple rows in chunks from `ore.frame` X `ore.rowApply(X, FUN, ..., FUN.VALUE = NULL, FUN.NAME = NULL, rows = 1, parallel = FALSE)`
`ore.groupApply()`	Invoke R script on data partitioned by grouping column INDEX of an `ore.frame` X `ore.groupApply(X, INDEX, FUN, ..., FUN.VALUE = NULL, FUN.NAME = NULL, parallel = FALSE)`
`ore.indexApply()`	Invoke R script N times `ore.indexApply(times, FUN, ..., FUN.VALUE = NULL, FUN.NAME = NULL, parallel = FALSE)`
`ore.scriptCreate()`	Create an R script in the database `ore.scriptCreate(name)`
`ore.scriptDrop()`	Drop an R script in the database `ore.scriptDrop(name, FUN)`

TABLE 10-5. *ORE Embedded R Execution R Interface Functions*

- `ore.rowApply` allows specifying the number of rows each invocation of *f* should receive. The function *f* is invoked multiple times, potentially in parallel, until all input data is processed. The return value is a list with the return value from each invocation of *f*.

- `ore.groupApply` partitions the input data according to a specified column's values, and invokes *f* on each partition. The return value from `ore.groupApply` is a list containing the return value from each invocation of *f*.

- ■ `ore.indexApply` invokes *f* N times. The return value is a list with the return value from each invocation of *f*.

- ■ `ore.scriptCreate` creates an entry in the R script repository for the function *f* with the provided name. Such functions can be referenced by Embedded R Execution functions.

- ■ `ore.scriptDrop` removes the named function from the R script repository.

For security, since the ability to define R scripts in the database is a powerful capability, only users who are granted the RQADMIN role are allowed to execute the `ore.scriptCreate` and `ore.scriptDrop` functions.

The functions `ore.tableApply`, `ore.rowApply`, and `ore.groupApply` each take an `ore.frame` as input. Functions `ore.doEval` and `ore.indexApply` can obtain data differently: They can take no input data, generate their data within the R function, load data from a file, explicitly pull it from the database, or leverage the Transparency Layer. Functions `ore.tableApply`, `ore.rowApply`, and `ore.groupApply` can access data similarly to supplement the data passed as a function argument.

The return value of the R function, specified using `FUN.VALUE`, can either be null, which results in an `ore.object` being returned, or a `data.frame` signature, which results in an `ore.frame` being returned from the function.

Embedded R Execution functions can take a variable number of arguments, corresponding to those of the function *f*. Arguments are passed to the function on invocation using the same name as specified in the defined R function. There are special *control arguments* with reserved names that affect the behavior of Embedded R Execution. For example, `ore.connect` set to TRUE enables auto-connection. This and other control arguments are discussed in more detail later.

Row apply allows specifying the number of rows to process as one chunk. This is valuable to perform batch scoring in parallel since multiple R engines can be leveraged. Group apply allows specifying the column on which to partition data, which also enables parallel execution.

Each Embedded R Execution function requires the specification of the R function to execute, either as a string that contains the R function (using the `FUN` argument), or the name of an R script that has already been created in the R script repository (using the `FUN.NAME` argument).

To illustrate using Embedded R Execution, consider the simple R script shown in Example 10 and illustrated in Figure 10-8. It illustrates getting a structured result back from the R function, such as a `data.frame`. Since data is generated within the function, this script uses `ore.doEval`. The function argument scales the first n integers by the argument `scale`. Notice that argument values num=10 and `scale` =100 are provided as defaults to the R function.

Example 10:

```
res <-
    ore.doEval(function (num = 10, scale = 100) {
            ID <- seq(num)
            data.frame(ID = ID, RES = ID / scale)
            })
class(res)
res
local_res <- ore.pull(res)
class(local_res)
local_res
```

The R script is passed through the client R engine to the database. The database spawns an R engine on the database server to execute the embedded R function. The result is passed back to the database, and then to the client R engine. The result res is returned as a serialized ore.object. When printed, this object is deserialized as an R data.frame. If the result is pulled to the client using ore.pull, it is materialized as a data.frame.

Note how seamlessly these embedded R functions blend with the rest of the R code. User-defined R functions can be passed any R object as input created in the R session, and the output can be pulled to the client, if desired. The results are shown in Listing 10-5.

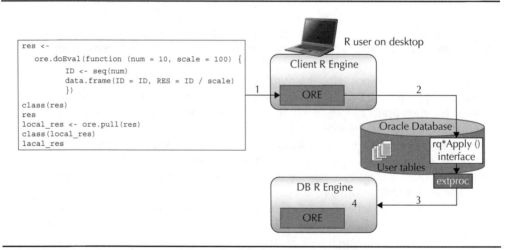

FIGURE 10-8. *Example using ORE Embedded R Execution with* ore.doEval

Listing 10-5   *Results for ORE Embedded R Execution Example 10*

```
R> res <-
+    ore.doEval(function (num = 10, scale = 100) {
+            ID <- seq(num)
+            data.frame(ID = ID, RES = ID / scale)
+            })
R> class(res)
[1] "ore.object"
attr(,"package")
[1] "OREbase"
R> res
   ID  RES
1   1 0.01
2   2 0.02
3   3 0.03
4   4 0.04
5   5 0.05
6   6 0.06
7   7 0.07
8   8 0.08
9   9 0.09
10 10 0.10
R> local_res <- ore.pull(res)
R> class(local_res)
[1] "data.frame"
R> local_res
   ID  RES
1   1 0.01
2   2 0.02
3   3 0.03
4   4 0.04
5   5 0.05
6   6 0.06
7   7 0.07
8   8 0.08
9   9 0.09
10 10 0.10
```

In Example 11, the arguments for `num` and `scale` are passed to the function. These appear as additional arguments to the `ore.doEval` function. Recall that in the `ore.doEval` function signature, these are represented as "`...`". The names of these arguments are the same as those in the R function definition.

Example 11:

```
res <-
    ore.doEval(function (num = 10, scale = 100) {
              ID <- seq(num)
              data.frame(ID = ID, RES = ID / scale)
              },
          num = 20, scale = 1000)
class(res)
res
```

In Example 12, a named script "SimpleScript1" is created in the R script repository and invoked using ore.doEval with the argument FUN.NAME, which is the function name in the repository. The ability to store R scripts in the database and reference them by name is a major convenience when writing database applications that use results from R.

Example 12:

```
ore.scriptDrop("SimpleScript1")
ore.scriptCreate("SimpleScript1",
          function (num = 10, scale = 100) {
            ID <- seq(num)
            data.frame(ID = ID, RES = ID / scale)
            })
res <- ore.doEval(FUN.NAME="SimpleScript1",
                  num = 20, scale = 1000)
```

Example 13 illustrates data parallel execution through the database using the function ore.groupApply. The user-defined R function specifies to build a linear model predicting airline flight arrival delay. However, the goal is to build one model per destination airport. This is specified using the INDEX argument in ore.groupApply. When ore.groupApply is finished executing, an ore.list proxy object is returned. The actual result remains in the database. The ore.list object can be involved in subsequent operations or retrieved to the client R engine for local operations.

Example 13:

```
modList <- ore.groupApply(
    X=ONTIME_S,
    INDEX=ONTIME_S$DEST,
```

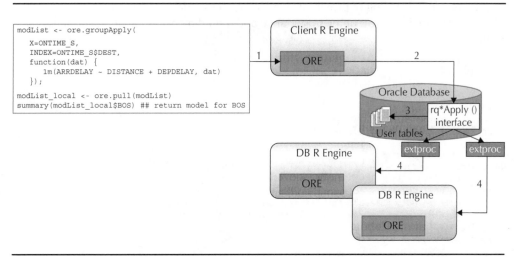

FIGURE 10-9. *Example using ORE Embedded R Execution with* `ore.groupApply`

```
function(dat) {
    lm(ARRDELAY ~ DISTANCE + DEPDELAY, dat)
});
modList_local <- ore.pull(modList)
summary(modList_local$BOS) ## return model for BOS
```

So what is happening behind the scenes? Through `ore.groupApply`, the embedded R function (the one that builds the model using `lm`) is sent to the database, as depicted in Figure 10-9. The data is partitioned by the `INDEX` column, `DEST`. Next, the database server `rq*Apply` interface starts external process R engines—one per data partition—and loads the data efficiently into the `dat` argument of the function. The resulting models are returned as a single `ore.list` object to the R client, with one model per destination airport. As with `ore.rowApply`, potentially many database server-side R engines can be spawned (or reused) to get *painless* data parallelism, managed by the database. The number of R engines spawned is determined by database *degree of parallelism* settings.

Using the R interface of Embedded R Execution, functions can return not only structured data, but images as well. Example 14a depicts using the Random Forest algorithm to build a model to predict `Species` from the `iris` data set. The defined function produces a `randomForest` model, the model importance, and multidimensional scaling of proximity. It also produces a pairs plot of the predictors. The return value is a `list` of the importance and multidimensional scaling goodness of fit, or GOF.

Example 14a:

```
ore.doEval(function () {
  library(randomForest)
  set.seed(71)
  iris.rf <- randomForest(Species ~ ., data=iris,
                          importance=TRUE, proximity=TRUE)
  imp <- round(importance(iris.rf), 2)
  iris.mds <- cmdscale(1 - iris.rf$proximity, eig=TRUE)
  op <- par(pty="s")
  pairs(cbind(iris[,1:4], iris.mds$points), cex=0.6, gap=0,
        col=c("red", "black", "gray")[as.numeric(iris$Species)],
        main="Iris Data: Predictors and MDS of Proximity Based on RandomForest")
  par(op)
  list(importance = imp, GOF = iris.mds$GOF)
})
```

Listing 10-6 shows the results of this function. The code shows the structured result, and the illustration that follows shows the pairs plot returned to the user's desktop R client. Both the structured results and the image were generated by an R engine at the database server.

Listing 10-6 *Results for ORE Embedded R Execution Example 14a*

```
R> library(randomForest)
R> ore.doEval(function () {
+    library(randomForest)
+    set.seed(71)
+    iris.rf <- randomForest(Species ~ ., data=iris,
+                            importance=TRUE, proximity=TRUE)
+    imp <- round(importance(iris.rf), 2)
+    iris.mds <- cmdscale(1 - iris.rf$proximity, eig=TRUE)
+    op <- par(pty="s")
+    pairs(cbind(iris[,1:4], iris.mds$points), cex=0.6, gap=0,
+          col=c("red", "black", "gray")[as.numeric(iris$Species)],
+          main="Iris Data: Predictors and MDS of Proximity Based on RandomForest")
+    par(op)
+    list(importance = imp, GOF = iris.mds$GOF)
+ })
$importance
              setosa versicolor virginica MeanDecreaseAccuracy MeanDecreaseGini
Sepal.Length    6.04       7.85      7.93                11.51             8.77
Sepal.Width     4.40       1.03      5.44                 5.40             2.19
Petal.Length   21.76      31.33     29.64                32.94            42.54
Petal.Width    22.84      32.67     31.68                34.50            45.77

$GOF
[1] 0.7282700 0.7903363
```

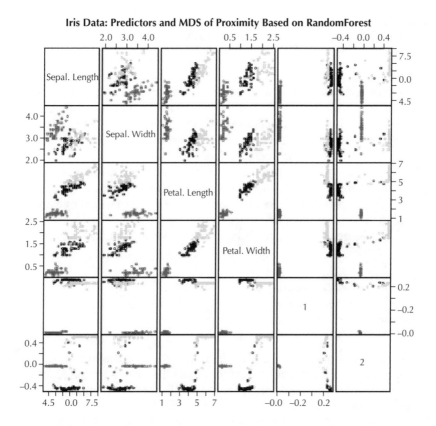

Iris Data: Predictors and MDS of Proximity Based on RandomForest

When dealing with PNG images, additional control arguments are available that affect image settings. For example, as shown in Example 14b, including arguments `ore.graphics=TRUE` along with `ore.png.height=700` and `ore.png.width=500`, users can change the aspect ratio of the image. Any arguments allowed by the PNG graphics device driver can be supplied using `ore.png.` as a prefix to arguments of the `png` function.

Example 14b:

```
ore.doEval(function () {
    ...
}, ore.graphics=TRUE, ore.png.height=700, ore.png.width=500)
```

Control arguments in general have the `ore.` prefix. Such arguments are not passed to the user-defined R function, but they control what happens either before or after execution of the R function. Arguments for `ore.connect`, `ore.graphics`, and `ore.png` have been covered already. The argument `ore.drop` controls the input data. If TRUE, a one-column input data.frame will be converted to a vector. This input remains as a data.frame if set to FALSE.

SQL Interface

The SQL interface consists principally of the functions rqEval, rqTableEval, rqRowEval, and "rqGroupEval." (There is not an actual function named rqGroupEval, since it needs to be constructed differently in SQL.) In addition, there are two functions, sys.rqScriptCreate and sys.rqScriptDrop, for managing R scripts—just in the R interface. (See Table 10-6.)

Recall that one motivation for providing the SQL interface is to allow using ORE within a SQL-based application. Each of these rq*Eval functions provides capabilities intended for different situations. There are similarities to the corresponding R interface functions, but there are important differences too.

Syntactically, the general form consists of a few basic arguments:

```
rq*Eval(
   cursor(select * from <table-1>),
   cursor(select * from <table-2>),
   <output type> or 'select <column list> from <table-3 or dual>',
   <grouping col-name from table-1> or <num rows>,
   '<R-script-name>')
```

The first argument is the input cursor, which specifies the data to be provided to the R function's first argument. This is used for all but the rqEval table function. How the data is prepared depends on the type of rq*Eval table function being invoked, just as in the R interface.

As already noted, rqEval takes no input data; it just executes the R function, possibly with arguments. rqTableEval supplies the entire table at once to the R

SQL Interface Function	Purpose
rqEval()	Invoke standalone R script
rqTableEval()	Invoke R script with full table as input
rqRowEval()	Invoke R script on one row at a time, or multiple rows in chunks
"rqGroupEval()"	Invoke R script on data partitioned by grouping column
sys.rqScriptCreate	Create named R script
sys.rqScriptDrop	Drop named R script

TABLE 10-6. *ORE SQL Interface Functions*

function. `rqGroupEval` provides one partition of the data to the R function at a time. And, `rqRowEval` supplies up to N rows to the R function.

Arguments can optionally be passed to the R function through a cursor as the second argument. This can include reading values from a table, or from `dual`, but they must be scalar values, and only a single row may be supplied. If there are no arguments, `NULL` should be specified. As discussed later, the *control arguments* discussed in the R interface are also allowed in the SQL interface. To provide control arguments in the SQL syntax, include a "column" as, for example, `cursor(select 1 ore.connect from dual)`, which indicates that the column `ore.connect` is assigned the value 1 (interpreted as TRUE).

The output type can be specified as `NULL`, a SQL select statement, `'XML'`, or `'PNG'`. If NULL, the result is returned as a serialized BLOB. The SQL select statement describes the table definition representing the form of the data returned in the `data.frame` output from the invoked R function. The XML and PNG options are discussed next.

When using the rqGroupEval-style functionality, the next argument would be the column on which to partition the data. All rows with the same value of the specified column are provided to the R function. When using `rqRowEval`, this argument reflects the number of rows to provide to the R function at one time.

The last argument specifies the name of the R function to execute as stored in the R script repository using `sys.rqScriptCreate`. The input arguments to the R function include data from the input cursor (if applicable), and arguments from the arguments cursor.

Example 15 shows how arguments can be passed to the R function `"Example15"`, which takes three arguments: the input `data.frame`, an argument `levels`, and the argument `filename`. Notice that `"ore.connect"` is also provided as a control argument and, as for the R interface, this is not passed to the R function.

Example 15:

```
begin
  sys.rqScriptDrop('Example15');
  sys.rqScriptCreate("Example15",
 'function(dat,levels, filename) {
    ...
  }');
end;
/

select count(*)
from table(rqTableEval(
  cursor ( select x as "x", y as "y", argument_value as "z"
           from geological_model_grid),
```

```
cursor( select 30 as "levels", '/oracle/image.png' as "filename",
        1 "ore.connect" from dual),
NULL,
'Example15'));
```

Passing arguments using this approach allows only scalar numeric and scalar string arguments. To pass nonscalar R objects, such as models or lists, and so on, users can pass the name of a datastore (a scalar) that can be used to load the objects using ore.load within the R function.

In Example 16, a user-defined R function named 'Example16' that builds a linear model and saves the model in a datastore is defined. This function is invoked through the subsequent SQL query. Using the table function rqTableEval, the input data is passed in the first SQL cursor. This data is passed to the first argument dat of the R function. The R function's remaining input arguments are passed in the second cursor, namely ore.connect and the name of the datastore in which to save the model. The result is specified to be returned as an XML string. The last argument is the name of the function to execute, 'Example16'.

Example 16:

```
begin
   sys.rqScriptDrop('Example16');
   sys.rqScriptCreate('Example16',
   'function(dat,datastore_name) {
     mod <- lm(ARRDELAY ~ DISTANCE + DEPDELAY, dat)
     ore.save(mod,name=datastore_name, overwrite=TRUE)
   }');
end;
/
select *
   from table(rqTableEval(
       cursor(select ARRDELAY, DISTANCE, DEPDELAY from   ontime_s),
       cursor(select 1 as "ore.connect", 'myDatastore' as "datastore_name"
              from dual),
       'XML',
       'Example16' ));

-- Part 2
begin
 sys.rqScriptDrop('Example16s');
 sys.rqScriptCreate('Example16s',
 'function(dat, datastore_name) {
     ore.load(datastore_name)
     prd <- predict(mod, newdata=dat)
     prd[as.integer(rownames(prd))] <- prd
     res <- cbind(dat, PRED = prd)
     res}');
end;
/
```

```
select *
from table(rqTableEval(
    cursor(select ARRDELAY, DISTANCE, DEPDELAY from   ontime_s
            where  year = 2003 and month = 5 and dayofmonth = 2),
    cursor(select 1 as "ore.connect",
                'myDatastore' as "datastore_name" from dual),
    'select ARRDELAY, DISTANCE, DEPDELAY, 1 PRED from ontime_s',
    'Example16s'))
order by 1, 2, 3;
```

In the second part of Example 16, data is scored using the model. The function named 'Example16s', also stored in the R script repository, first loads the model from the datastore before computing the predictions. In the SQL query, rqTableEval's first argument specifies the data to score. R function arguments are again provided in the second argument. The name of the datastore indicates which R model to load. The return value is specified as a table with four named columns. The results of the execution are provided in Listing 10-7.

Listing 10-7   *ORE Embedded R Execution using* rqTableEval *results for Example 16*

```
SQL> begin
  sys.rqScriptDrop('Example16');
  sys.rqScriptCreate('Example16',
 'function(dat,datastore_name) {
   mod <- lm(ARRDELAY ~ DISTANCE + DEPDELAY, dat)
   ore.save(mod,name=datastore_name, overwrite=TRUE)
  }');
end;
/
select *
  from table(rqTableEval(
     cursor(select ARRDELAY, DISTANCE, DEPDELAY from   ontime_s),
     cursor(select 1 as "ore.connect", 'myDatastore' as "datastore_name"
            from dual),
     'XML',
     'Example16' ));
  2    3    4    5    6    7    8    9
PL/SQL procedure successfully completed.

SQL>   2    3    4    5    6    7

NAME
--------------------------
VALUE
--------------------------

<root><ANY_obj><ROW-ANY_obj><value></value></ROW-ANY_obj></ANY_obj></root>

SQL> -- Part 2
begin
 sys.rqScriptDrop('Example16s');
 sys.rqScriptCreate('Example16s',
```

```
 'function(dat, datastore_name) {
    ore.load(datastore_name)
    prd <- predict(mod, newdata=dat)
    prd[as.integer(rownames(prd))] <- prd
    res <- cbind(dat, PRED = prd)
    res}');
end;
/
select *
from table(rqTableEval(
    cursor(select ARRDELAY, DISTANCE, DEPDELAY from   ontime_s
            where  year = 2003 and month = 5 and dayofmonth = 2),
    cursor(select 1 as "ore.connect",
                  'myDatastore' as "datastore_name" from dual),
    'select ARRDELAY, DISTANCE, DEPDELAY, 1 PRED from ontime_s',
    'Example16s'))
order by 1, 2, 3;
SQL>    2    3    4    5    6    7    8    9   10   11
PL/SQL procedure successfully completed.

SQL>    2    3    4    5    6    7    8    9

  ARRDELAY   DISTANCE  DEPDELAY        PRED
---------- ---------- ---------- ----------
       -24       1190         -2 -3.1485154
       -20        185         -9 -8.6626137
       -16        697         -9 -9.2859791
       -15        859         -8 -8.5206878
       -15       2300         -4 -6.4250082
       -10        358          0 -.21049053
       -10        719         -8 -8.3502363
        -8        307         -2 -2.0734536
        -4       1050         -5 -5.8656481
        -3        150          5 4.85539194
        -2        140         -5 -4.7577135
...
```

For the output of rq*Eval functions, recall that data can be returned in XML or PNG formats. This is useful in several contexts. Since R script output often does not conform to a predefined table structure and can have heterogeneous data results, rich XML output allows applications embedding ORE to work with complex statistical results, new data, and graphs.

Oracle BI Publisher uses XML to populate documents. This XML can be dynamically generated using the Embedded R Execution SQL interface and fed to BI Publisher, or any other tool or application that can consume XML. By wrapping R objects through this generic and powerful XML framework, operational XML-based applications can readily integrate R executed via SQL.

The PNG output type indicates that PNG image streams should be returned. PNG image streams enable database-based applications to consume images directly from tables. R scripts can produce multiple images. As with XML output, PNG output allows for multiple images, which are returned as multiple rows in a table, with the images stored in a column of type BLOB, for *binary large object*. This feature facilitates direct integration with OBIEE 11.1.1.7 and above through the RPD.

Example 17 is our "Hello World!" example for ORE XML. The R function takes no arguments and returns the string "Hello World!". Its invocation using `rqEval` specifies XML as the output. The results are depicted in Listing 10-8. Notice the structure of the XML, which includes the value "Hello World!". This technique is what allows loading graphs generated in R into BI Publisher documents, as shown in the next example.

Example 17:

```
set long 20000
set pages 1000
begin
  sys.rqScriptCreate('Example17',
 'function() {"Hello World!"}');
end;
/
select name, value
from table(rqEval(NULL,'XML','Example17'));
```

Listing 10-8   *ORE Embedded R Execution XML output "Hello World!" results*

```
SQL> set long 20000
set pages 1000
begin
  sys.rqScriptCreate('Example17',
 'function() {"Hello World!"}');
end;
/
select name, value
from table(rqEval(NULL,'XML','Example17'));
SQL> SQL>   2    3    4    5
PL/SQL procedure successfully completed.

SQL>    2
NAME
--------------------------------------------------------------------------------
VALUE
--------------------------------------------------------------------------------

<root><vector_obj><ROW-vector_obj><value>Hello World!</value></ROW-vector_obj></
vector_obj></root>
```

Example 18 illustrates that ORE has the ability to generate an XML string from a graph produced on the database server, along with structured content. This R script with `rqEval` produces a scatter plot of 100 random normal values. The values 1 to 10 are returned in the variable `res`. Executing this using `rqEval` as before, the XML generated is shown in Listing 10-9. The resulting graph is captured in Figure 10-10.

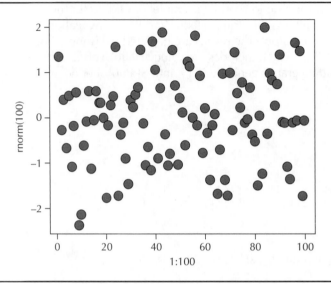

FIGURE 10-10. *Scatterplot produced in R function of Example 18*

Example 18:

```
set long 20000
set pages 1000
begin
  sys.rqScriptCreate('Example18',
  'function(){
          res <- 1:10
          plot( 1:100, rnorm(100), pch = 21,
              bg = "red", cex = 2 )
          res
          }');
end;
/
select    value
from      table(rqEval( NULL,'XML','Example18'));
```

Listing 10-9 *ORE Embedded R Execution XML output with image string results*

```
SQL> set long 20000
set pages 1000
begin
  sys.rqScriptCreate('Example18',
  'function(){
```

```
              res <- 1:10
              plot( 1:100, rnorm(100), pch = 21,
                  bg = "red", cex = 2 )
              res
              }');
end;
/
select    value
from      table(rqEval( NULL,'XML','Example18'));
SQL> SQL>   2    3    4    5    6    7    8    9    10
PL/SQL procedure successfully completed.

SQL>   2
VALUE
--------------------------------------------------------------------------------
```

```
<root><R-data><vector_obj><ROW-vector_obj><value>1</value></ROW-vector_obj><ROW-
vector_obj><value>2</value></ROW-vector_obj><ROW-vector_obj><value>3</value></RO
W-vector_obj><ROW-vector_obj><value>4</value></ROW-vector_obj><ROW-vector_obj><v
alue>5</value></ROW-vector_obj><ROW-vector_obj><value>6</value></ROW-vector_obj>
<ROW-vector_obj><value>7</value></ROW-vector_obj><ROW-vector_obj><value>8</value
></ROW-vector_obj><ROW-vector_obj><value>9</value></ROW-vector_obj><ROW-vector_o
bj><value>10</value></ROW-vector_obj></vector_obj></R-data><images><image><img s
rc="data:image/pngbase64"><![CDATA[iVBORw0KGgoAAAANSUhEUgAAAeAAAAHgCAIAAADytinCA
AAgAElEQVR4nOzddVxU2f8/8NfQCAaiqKwd2K66u0qJMHQoSCm2a6LY+kFFF+07Y2VdR
VwbWQXBAEGRjpnfH//zgOzBzR2IKfD8/qH33Oe0bmzZ1zT7T7C4XC4IAIIUQwStCEECkjK
EETQoiMogRCEyihI0YBAaoyhE0OKIJQghgyMoSNGEyhK0IQRCoQhAyMsK0
TKKEjQhhMgoStCEoQiMogRNCCoiIMogRBAoyhE0OIITKoQhAyMsSOChKO
IQQIqMoRNCCoiMogRNCCoiIMogRMYihI0IYhBAyMsTEChIO
YTIKErQhBAyMooyBEKJIjMSTMRjSAB
AIoyTEKJIjMogRNCCoiIyiBEOIITTKKEjQhhMgoStCEoyhI0I...
```

Predictive Analytics

The ORE analytics packages consist of OREeda (for exploratory data analysis), OREdm (for data mining), and OREpredict. OREeda contains ORE's database-enabled linear and stepwise regression, and neural network algorithms. OREeda also has Base SAS equivalent functions. OREdm exposes Oracle Data Mining algorithms through an R interface with support for attribute importance, classification, regression, anomaly detection, and clustering. OREpredict provides the function ore.predict, which allows scoring select R models such as rpart and lm in the database—translating the R models to SQL transparently to operate on database data.

OREeda

This subsection provides discussion and examples involving ore.lm, ore.stepwise, and ore.neural.

Functions ore.lm and ore.stepwise   The function ore.lm mimics the R lm least squares regression function, but it performs the calculations on ore.frames, leveraging Oracle Database as the compute engine. It produces the same results as R, but no data is moved from the database to the client to build the model.

The function `ore.stepwise` performs the stepwise least squares regression. With stepwise regression, the choice of predictive variables is performed automatically, by adding terms or removing terms, or both. One objective with stepwise regression is to produce a model with fewer (ideally fewest) terms required for a quality model.

Why provide in-database versions of these popular R algorithms? One motivation is the need to handle data with complex patterns (for example, collinearity) where R does not address the need. The function `ore.stepwise` also provides variable selection criteria used by SAS PROC REG, namely being p-value–based instead of information criteria–based, as is R's `step` function. A side benefit of this is that ORE produces dramatic performance gains. Keeping the data in the database allows building models faster on more data, since the memory limitations of R are avoided.

Table 10-7 highlights performance results on `ore.stepwise` from the Oracle Micro-Processor Tools environment. On a bilinear model, `ore.stepwise` was 66 times faster than R's step function. On a quadratic model, it was 180 times faster.

	Method	R^2	Number of Regressors	mean(rel_error)	Elapsed Time (seconds)
Bilinear model	step	0.9658	86	3.52e–02	2110.0
	ore.stepwise	0.9966	124	3.50e–02	32.1
	Performance difference				ore.stepwise is approximately 65x faster than step at similar R^2 and relative error as stepwise.
Quadratic model	step	0.9962	154	1.05e–02	12600.0
	ore.stepwise	0.9963	210	1.04e–02	69.5
	Performance difference				ore.stepwise is approximately 180x faster than step at similar R^2 relative error.

TABLE 10-7. *Performance Results from Oracle Micro-Processor Tools Use of ORE*

The models produced by R's `step` and `ore.stepwise` have a different number of regressors because both the selection mechanisms and interaction terms are handled differently. Function `ore.stepwise` does not differentiate between main terms and interactions, but detects strict linear dependencies and eliminates from the start regressors involved in multicollinear relations. Better performance is a side effect. With `ore.stepwise`, ORE enables the Oracle Micro-Processor Tools environment to significantly expand the data analysis capabilities through R combined with in-database high-performance algorithms, opening the door to new applications.

Let's compare `ore.lm` with R's `lm` function using the `longley` data set. This small macroeconomic data set provides a well-known example for a highly collinear regression and consists of seven economic variables observed yearly over 16 years. The goal is to predict the number of people employed using six predictors such GNP.deflator, GNP, unemployed, and so on. In Listing 10-10a, the residuals distribution and variable coefficients, among other results, are depicted from the model summary.

Listing 10-10a   *lm results*

```
R> fit1 <- lm(Employed ~ ., data = longley)
R> summary(fit1)

Call:
lm(formula = Employed ~ ., data = longley)

Residuals:
    Min       1Q    Median       3Q      Max
-0.41011 -0.15767 -0.02816  0.10155  0.45539

Coefficients:
                Estimate Std. Error t value Pr(>|t|)
(Intercept)   -3.482e+03  8.904e+02  -3.911 0.003560 **
GNP.deflator   1.506e-02  8.492e-02   0.177 0.863141
GNP           -3.582e-02  3.349e-02  -1.070 0.312681
Unemployed    -2.020e-02  4.884e-03  -4.136 0.002535 **
Armed.Forces  -1.033e-02  2.143e-03  -4.822 0.000944 ***
Population    -5.110e-02  2.261e-01  -0.226 0.826212
Year           1.829e+00  4.555e-01   4.016 0.003037 **
---
Signif. codes:  0 '***' 0.001 '**' 0.01 '*' 0.05 '.' 0.1 ' ' 1

Residual standard error: 0.3049 on 9 degrees of freedom
Multiple R-squared: 0.9955,    Adjusted R-squared: 0.9925
F-statistic: 330.3 on 6 and 9 DF,  p-value: 4.984e-10
```

To use `ore.lm`, the function name is changed and an `ore.frame` is provided. The input `ore.frame` is created by pushing the `longley data.frame` to the database using `ore.push`. Listing 10-10b depicts that the results are identical.

Listing 10-10b *ore.lm results*

```
R> LONGLEY <- ore.push(longley)
R> oreFit1 <- ore.lm(Employed ~ ., data = longley)
R> summary(oreFit1)

Call:
ore.lm(formula = Employed ~ ., data = longley)

Residuals:
    Min      1Q   Median      3Q      Max
-0.41011 -0.15980 -0.02816  0.15681  0.45539

Coefficients:
               Estimate Std. Error t value Pr(>|t|)
(Intercept)  -3.482e+03  8.904e+02  -3.911 0.003560 **
GNP.deflator  1.506e-02  8.492e-02   0.177 0.863141
GNP          -3.582e-02  3.349e-02  -1.070 0.312681
Unemployed   -2.020e-02  4.884e-03  -4.136 0.002535 **
Armed.Forces -1.033e-02  2.143e-03  -4.822 0.000944 ***
Population   -5.110e-02  2.261e-01  -0.226 0.826212
Year          1.829e+00  4.555e-01   4.016 0.003037 **
---
Signif. codes:  0 '***' 0.001 '**' 0.01 '*' 0.05 '.' 0.1 ' ' 1

Residual standard error: 0.3049 on 9 degrees of freedom
Multiple R-squared: 0.9955,      Adjusted R-squared: 0.9925
F-statistic: 330.3 on 6 and 9 DF,  p-value: 4.984e-10
```

Example 19 begins with `ore.stepwise`, which specifies a formula to consider pairs of variables. Argument `add.p` as 0.1 is specified, which is the F-test p-value threshold for adding a term to the model. Argument `drop.p` as 0.1 is also specified, which sets the threshold for removing a term from the model. The `ore.stepwise` `add.p` and `drop.p` arguments behave like SAS PROC REG's SLE and SLS selection criteria, respectively. As shown in Listing 10-11, the execution results include the summary of steps taken by the algorithm, adding terms with their corresponding residual sum of squares after each model. Notice that because pairs of variables are considered, the variable `GNP.deflator` is paired with `Unemployed` in Step 1. The coefficients produced for the selected variables are also provided.

Example 19:

```
LONGLEY <- ore.push(longley)
    # Two stepwise alternatives
oreStep1 <- ore.stepwise(Employed ~ .^2, data = LONGLEY,
                         add.p = 0.1, drop.p = 0.1)
oreStep1
oreStep2 <- step(ore.lm(Employed ~ 1, data = LONGLEY),
                 scope = terms(Employed ~ .^2, data = LONGLEY))
oreStep2
```

Listing 10-11 *Results of executing ore.stepwise*

```
R> oreStep1 <- ore.stepwise(Employed ~ .^2, data = LONGLEY,
+                           add.p = 0.1, drop.p = 0.1)
R> oreStep1

Aliased:
[1] "Unemployed:Armed.Forces" "Unemployed:Population"
"Unemployed:Year"
"Armed.Forces:Population"
[5] "Armed.Forces:Year"       "Population:Year"

Steps:
                        Add Drop     RSS Rank
1 GNP.deflator:Unemployed <NA> 384.426    2
2                GNP:Year <NA> 218.957    3
3        GNP.deflator:GNP <NA> 130.525    4
4 GNP.deflator:Population <NA>  81.211    5
5        GNP:Armed.Forces <NA>  18.244    6
6                    Year <NA>  14.492    7

Call:
ore.stepwise(formula = Employed ~ .^2, data = LONGLEY, add.p = 0.1,
    drop.p = 0.1)

Coefficients:
    (Intercept)         Year     GNP.deflator:GNP  GNP.
deflator:Unemployed
GNP.deflator:Population
     -3.539e-01    3.589e-05         -2.978e-03
2.326e-04
        2.303e-05
GNP:Armed.Forces     GNP:Year
       6.875e-06    2.007e-04
```

The second part of Example 19 illustrates building a model using ore.lm, which produces a model that is a subclass of lm. The R step function uses the ore.lm model with the specified scope to iteratively add and drop terms before settling on the "best" model. Here, the scope argument uses terms generated from the provided formula and data. The execution results are shown in Listing 10-12. Notice how the results of each step are presented. It starts with all the predictors and the effect of dropping each one from the model. It then drops GNP, since that has the lowest AIC value, and continues the process until the model shows no further improvement, that is, the lowest AIC is not better than the AIC shown for the step.

Listing 10-12   *Results of executing R step with ore.lm*

```
R> oreStep2 <- step(ore.lm(Employed ~ 1, data = LONGLEY),
+                    scope = terms(Employed ~ .^2, data = LONGLEY))
Start:  AIC=41.17
Employed ~ 1

                Df Sum of Sq      RSS      AIC
+ GNP           1    178.973    6.036  -11.597
+ Year          1    174.552   10.457   -2.806
+ GNP.deflator  1    174.397   10.611   -2.571
+ Population    1    170.643   14.366    2.276
+ Unemployed    1     46.716  138.293   38.509
+ Armed.Forces  1     38.691  146.318   39.411
<none>                         185.009   41.165

Step:  AIC=-11.6
Employed ~ GNP

                Df Sum of Sq      RSS      AIC
+ Unemployed    1      2.457    3.579  -17.960
+ Population    1      2.162    3.874  -16.691
+ Year          1      1.125    4.911  -12.898
<none>                          6.036  -11.597
+ GNP.deflator  1      0.212    5.824  -10.169
+ Armed.Forces  1      0.077    5.959   -9.802
- GNP           1    178.973  185.009   41.165

Step:  AIC=-17.96
Employed ~ GNP + Unemployed

                Df Sum of Sq      RSS      AIC
+ Armed.Forces  1      0.822    2.757  -20.137
<none>                          3.579  -17.960
+ Year          1      0.340    3.239  -17.556
+ GNP:Unemployed 1     0.182    3.397  -16.795
```

```
+ Population            1     0.097   3.482 -16.399
+ GNP.deflator          1     0.019   3.560 -16.044
- Unemployed            1     2.457   6.036 -11.597
- GNP                   1   134.714 138.293  38.509

Step:  AIC=-20.14
Employed ~ GNP + Unemployed + Armed.Forces
                         Df Sum of Sq    RSS     AIC
+ Year                    1     1.898  0.859 -36.799
+ GNP:Unemployed          1     0.614  2.143 -22.168
+ Population              1     0.390  2.367 -20.578
<none>                                  2.757 -20.137
+ Unemployed:Armed.Forces 1     0.083  2.673 -18.629
+ GNP.deflator            1     0.073  2.684 -18.566
+ GNP:Armed.Forces        1     0.060  2.697 -18.489
- Armed.Forces            1     0.822  3.579 -17.960
- Unemployed              1     3.203  5.959  -9.802
- GNP                     1    78.494 81.250  31.999

Step:  AIC=-36.8
Employed ~ GNP + Unemployed + Armed.Forces + Year

                         Df Sum of Sq    RSS     AIC
<none>                                 0.8587 -36.799
+ Unemployed:Year         1    0.0749 0.7838 -36.259
+ GNP:Unemployed          1    0.0678 0.7909 -36.115
+ Unemployed:Armed.Forces 1    0.0515 0.8072 -35.788
+ GNP:Armed.Forces        1    0.0367 0.8220 -35.498
+ Population              1    0.0193 0.8393 -35.163
+ GNP.deflator            1    0.0175 0.8412 -35.129
+ Armed.Forces:Year       1    0.0136 0.8451 -35.054
+ GNP:Year                1    0.0084 0.8502 -34.957
- GNP                     1    0.4647 1.3234 -31.879
- Year                    1    1.8980 2.7567 -20.137
- Armed.Forces            1    2.3806 3.2393 -17.556
- Unemployed              1    4.0491 4.9077 -10.908
R> oreStep2

Call:
ore.lm(formula = Employed ~ GNP + Unemployed + Armed.Forces +
    Year, data = LONGLEY)

Coefficients:
 (Intercept)           GNP    Unemployed  Armed.Forces        Year
  -3.599e+03    -4.019e-02    -2.088e-02    -1.015e-02   1.887e+00
```

Function `ore.neural`   The function `ore.neural` implements a neural network algorithm. Neural networks in some sense mimic the function of neurons in the brain. They are very good at nonlinear statistical modeling, able to learn complex nonlinear relationships between input and output variables. Neural networks have been used to find patterns in data, including those associated with function approximation, classification, data processing, and robotics.

The function `ore.neural` supports a single-layer feed-forward neural network for regression. It supports one hidden layer with a specifiable number of nodes and uses the bipolar sigmoid activation function. The output uses the linear activation function. The algorithm benefits from a state-of-the-art numerical optimization engine that provides robustness, accuracy, and a small number of data reads for improved performance. `ore.neural` achieves performance by reading one hundred thousand rows of data in a block, performing computations on that data, and then discarding the block before proceeding to the next block. In contrast, R's `nnet` requires the entire data set to fit in memory. Note that although the number of rows is unconstrained, the number of columns is currently limited to one thousand, which is the number of columns permitted in a database table.

Consider Example 20, which uses the p53 Mutants data set. The goal is to model mutant p53 transcriptional activity (active vs. inactive) based on data extracted from biophysical simulations. `ore.neural` was able to complete the computation on the full data, whereas R's `nnet` did not due to memory constraints. To obtain a comparison of error rates, a subset of nine columns from K9 is used to allow `nnet` to complete. Column V1 is the target against the remaining eight variables. Specifying a neural network with 20 hidden nodes, the `nnet` script specifies to generate predictions using the input data and to compute the sum of the error squared, which is done in R memory. Essentially the same specification occurs for `ore.neural`. However, the data is first pushed to the database, the model built, and predictions generated in the database. Notice, however, that the error is also computed using the Transparency Layer, in the database.

Example 20:

```
# nnet example
d <- read.csv('./K9-9.data', header=TRUE)
fit <-nnet(V1 ~., data = d, size=20, linout=TRUE)
p <-predict(fit, newdata=d)
z <- p - d$V1
sum(z^2)

# ore.neural example
d <-read.csv('./K9-9.data', header=TRUE)
dd <- ore.push(d)
fit <- ore.neural(V1 ~., data = dd, hiddenSize=20)
pp <- predict(fit, newdata=dd)
z <- pp - dd$V1
sum(z^2)
```

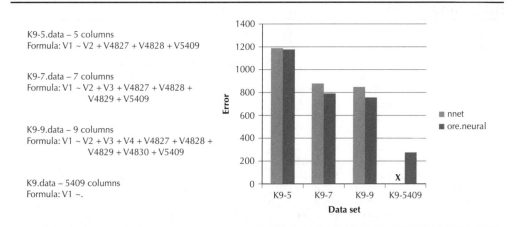

K9-5.data – 5 columns
Formula: V1 ~ V2 + V4827 + V4828 + V5409

K9-7.data – 7 columns
Formula: V1 ~ V2 + V3 + V4827 + V4828 +
            V4829 + V5409

K9-9.data – 9 columns
Formula: V1 ~ V2 + V3 + V4 + V4827 + V4828 +
            V4829 + V4830 + V5409

K9.data – 5409 columns
Formula: V1 ~.

FIGURE 10-11.   *Error rate comparison between* nnet *and* ore.neural

Figure 10-11 highlights three things: First, the error rate improves as more predictors are added. Second, ore.neural produced lower error rates than nnet, consistently. And third, on the full data set, nnet did not complete, while ore.neural did.

Using the K9 data set, Example 21 builds a neural network model using ore.neural with two targets, V1 and V2. A subset of five columns from K9 is pushed to the database, and the model fitted. Notice the use of cbind to specify the multiple targets. After scoring the data, the variable pred contains a two-column ore.frame, one column for each target, or response variable. cbind combines the prediction with the original data as depicted in Listing 10-13. Using head, the first two columns contain the predicted values followed by the original target columns and predictors.

Example 21:

```
dd   <- read.csv('~/K9-5.data', header=TRUE)
od   <- ore.push(dd)
fit  <- ore.neural(cbind(V1, V2) ~ V4827 + V4828 + V5409,
                   data = od, hiddenSize=10)
pred <- predict(fit, newdata=od)
res  <- cbind(pred,od)
head(res)
```

Listing 10-13 *Results of Example 21 using* `ore.neural` *with two targets*

```
R> dd    <- read.csv('~/K9-5.data', header=TRUE)
R> od    <- ore.push(dd)
R> fit   <- ore.neural(cbind(V1, V2) ~ V4827 + V4828 + V5409,
+                     data = od, hiddenSize=10)
R> pred <- predict(fit, newdata=od)
R> res  <- cbind(pred,od)
R> head(res)
          o1            o2       V1       V2 V4827   V4828 V5409
1 -0.18541160 -0.019421025 -0.161 -0.014 0.023 -0.001    -1
2 -0.11777635 -0.002044806 -0.158 -0.002 0.010  0.003    -1
3 -0.15176917 -0.013006371 -0.169 -0.025 0.016  0.003    -1
4 -0.11975969 -0.006174594 -0.183 -0.051 0.010  0.010    -1
5 -0.12313956 -0.002837944 -0.154  0.005 0.011  0.001    -1
6 -0.08733031  0.008628771 -0.150  0.016 0.005  0.003    -1
```

OREdm

Oracle R Enterprise is part of the Oracle Advanced Analytics (OAA) option to Oracle Database Enterprise Edition. OAA consists of both Oracle R Enterprise and Oracle Data Mining, providing complementary functionality. As a result, the predictive analytics capabilities of the OAA option provide the broadest analytical toolset for the enterprise. The choice of tool within OAA should be based on various factors: the technique required, interface preference, data volume, and skill set.

Oracle Data Mining provides a convenient workflow-based GUI as well as a well-integrated SQL API for model building and scoring. ORE provides a programming interface based both on R and SQL, with the ability to invoke R scripts from SQL. In general, in-database techniques should be used to avoid data access latency and achieve high performance and scalability. ORE exposes several Oracle Data Mining algorithms through R functions. These allow R users to benefit from these powerful in-database data mining algorithms.

ORE appeals to traditional statisticians and quantitative analysts who are comfortable writing R code but need to leverage the database as a computational engine. The ability to execute R scripts through SQL means that R scripts developed by analysts can be more immediately operationalized in production SQL-based applications.

The `OREdm` package works transparently on database data from R using Oracle Data Mining algorithms. The function signature for building models uses an R `formula` object to specify *target* and *predictors,* or the *response* and *terms* as referred to in R. Objects of type `ore.frame` are used to provide input data for model building and data scoring. Data scoring is performed using the overloaded `predict` function.

The names of most model-building arguments have been matched to corresponding R function arguments. Argument default values are explicitly specified as part of the

Algorithm	Main R Function	Mining Type/Function
Minimum Description Length	`ore.odmAI`	Attribute Importance for Classification or Regression
Decision Tree	`ore.odmDT`	Classification
Generalized Linear Models	`ore.odmGLM`	Classification Regression
KMeans	`ore.odmKMeans`	Clustering
Naïve Bayes	`ore.odmNB`	Classification
Support Vector Machine	`ore.odmSVM`	Classification Regression Anomaly Detection

TABLE 10-8.   *OREdm-Supported Algorithms*

function signature. The result of model building is an R object that references the Oracle Data Mining model in the database.

As for objects in R, models are treated as transient objects. When the session ends, objects are automatically cleaned up. OREdm models are treated similarly with the side effect that the corresponding Oracle Data Mining model is also automatically deleted at the end of an ORE session. If a model needs to persist across R sessions, OREdm model objects can be explicitly saved using the datastore function `ore.save`.

Table 10-8 lists the set of Oracle Data Mining algorithms supported in ORE, their corresponding R function for building the model, and the mining type or function they support. These in-database algorithms enable attribute importance, classification, regression, anomaly detection, and clustering.

As an example, the function signature for the OREdm Naïve Bayes classification algorithm for building models and scoring is provided here. The function `ore.odmNB` supports Oracle Data Mining's auto-data preparation option and the ability to specify class priors. Users can also specify how to treat rows that contain missing values.

```
ore.odmNB(
  formula,                    # formula specifying attributes for model build
  data,                       # ore.frame of the training data set
  auto.data.prep = TRUE,      # Setting to perform automatic data preparation
  class.priors = NULL,        # data.frame containing target class priors
  na.action = na.pass)        # Allows missing values (na.pass), or removes rows
                              #    with missing values (na.omit)
  predict(
```

```
object,                    # Object of type "ore.naiveBayes"
newdata,                   # Data used for scoring
supplemental.cols = NULL,  # Columns to retain in output
type = c("class","raw"),   # "raw" - cond. a-posterior probs for each class
                           # "class" - class with max prob
na.action = na.pass)
```

The `predict` function, which takes an object of type `ore.odmNB`, allows the specification of supplemental columns, that is, those from `newdata` that should be output with the predictions. Users can also specify whether the single predicted class and probability should be returned, the probability associated with each class, or both.

In the annotated example in Listing 10-14, the `ORE` package is loaded and a connection to the database made. The data set is the `titanic3` data set from the `PASWR` package, which provides data on survival of passengers aboard the Titanic. This data is pushed to the database and prepared by changing the values of column `survived` from 1 and 0, to Yes and No, respectively. This and subsequent transformations are done using the ORE Transparency Layer. The data is sampled into train and test sets for model building and assessing model quality. Priors can also be set when building a Naïve Bayes model by creating a `data.frame` with prior values per class. The model is built using the function `ore.odmNB` with arguments for the formula specifying the target and predictors, the `ore.frame` data, and the class priors `data.frame`.

Listing 10-14 *Annotated example using* ore.odmNB

```
library(ORE) ◄——— Login to database for transparent access via ORE
ore.connect("rquser","orcl","localhost","rquser",all=TRUE)

data(titanic3,package="PASWR")
t3 <- ore.push(titanic3) ◄——— Push data to db for transparent access
                                         Recode column from 0/1
t3$survived <- ifelse(t3$survived == 1, "Yes", "No") ◄— to No/Yes keeping data in
n.rows <- nrow(t3)                                       database

set.seed(seed=6218945)
random.sample <- sample(1:n.rows, ceiling(n.rows/2))
t3.train <- t3[random.sample,]
t3.test  <- t3[setdiff(1:n.rows,random.sample),] ◄———Sample keeping data in database

priors <- data.frame( ◄———Create priors for model building
    TARGET_VALUE = c("Yes", "No"),
    PRIOR_PROBABILITY = c(0.1, 0.9))

nb  <- ore.odmNB(survived ~ pclass+sex+age+fare+embarked,
            t3.train, class.priors=priors) ◄——— Build model using R formula
                                                 using Transparency Layer data
nb.res  <- predict (nb, t3.test,"survived") ◄——— Score data using ore.frame
head(nb.res,10) ◄——— Display first ten rows     with OREdm model object
                     of data frame using
                     Transparency Layer
```

```
with(nb.res, table(survived,PREDICTION, dnn = c("Actual","Predicted")))
library(verification)                    Retrieve result from database         Compute confusion matrix
res <- ore.pull(nb.res)                 for using verification package        using Transparency Layer
perf.auc <- roc.area(ifelse(res$survived == "Yes", 1, 0), res$'Yes')
auc.roc <- signif(perf.auc$A, digits=3)
auc.roc.p <- signif(perf.auc$p.value, digits=3)
roc.plot(ifelse(res$survived == "Yes", 1, 0), res$'Yes', binormal=T, plot="both",
         xlab="False Positive Rate",
         ylab="True Postive Rate", main= "Titanic survival ODM NB model ROC
Curve")
text(0.7, 0.4, labels= paste("AUC ROC:", signif(perf.auc$A, digits=3)))
text(0.7, 0.3, labels= paste("p-value:", signif(perf.auc$p.value, digits=3)))
nb
summary(nb)          View model object summary
ore.disconnect()     Disconnect from database
                     Model, train, and test objects are
                     automatically removed when session ends
                     or R objects are removed
```

Continuing in Listing 10-14, the data is scored using the `predict` function passing the Naïve Bayes model just created. The supplemental column `survived` is included. After looking at the first few rows of scores, a confusion matrix is computed using the Transparency Layer function `table`. To illustrate using in-database results with open source packages, the `verification` package is loaded and the data pulled to the client R engine. The final steps involve computing and plotting the ROC metric, viewing the model summary, and disconnecting from the database. Upon exiting the R session, or removing the Naïve Bayes object stored in the variable nb, the Oracle Data Mining model in the database is automatically deleted. No further cleanup is required.

Listing 10-15 shows the model summary, followed by the ROC Curve. ROC provides a metric for assessing model quality, and for comparing models. The further the curve is to the upper left, the better the model. A typical additional metric is the AUC, or *area under the curve*, which gives a single value for comparison.

Listing 10-15 *Results from annotated `ore.odmNB` example*

```
R> summary(nb)

Call:
ore.odmNB(formula = survived ~ pclass + sex + age + fare + embarked,
    data = t3.train, class.priors = priors)

Settings:
         value
prep.auto    on
```

```
Apriori:
 No Yes
0.9 0.1

Tables:
$embarked
     'Cherbourg' 'Queenstown', 'Southampton'
No    0.1569620              0.8430380
Yes   0.3178295              0.6821705

$fare
     ( ; 51.931249600000001), [51.931249600000001; 51.931249600000001]
(51.931249600000001;   )
No                                                         0.91370558
0.08629442
Yes                                                        0.67307692
0.32692308

$pclass
     '1st', '2nd'     '3rd'
No     0.3417722 0.6582278
Yes    0.6346154 0.3653846

$sex
        female      male
No   0.1670886 0.8329114
Yes  0.6769231 0.3230769


Levels:
[1] "No"   "Yes"
```

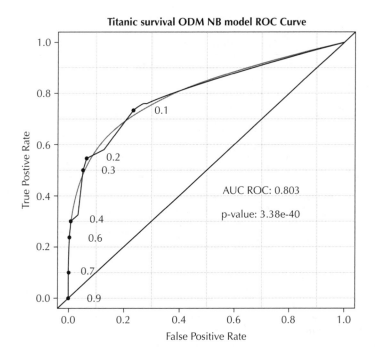

OREpredict

The `OREpredict` package provides a commercial-grade scoring engine for R-generated models. This means high-performance, scalable, in-database scoring on `ore.frames`, but using models built via popular R functions. `OREpredict` also simplifies application workflow, since data need not be pulled to an R engine for scoring. The `OREpredict` functions generate SQL using the R model details. The main function is `ore.predict`, which is an S4 generic function, where a specific method exists for each R model type that ORE supports.

Table 10-9 lists the R models supported in `OREpredict`.

Example 22 illustrates using the `iris` data set to first build a linear model using the R `lm` function to predict `Sepal.Length` and then predict using `OREpredict`. The `iris` data set is pushed to the database and `ore.predict` is invoked using the `irisModel` created in R. Note that the `ore.frame` `IRIS` (in capitals) is provided as the data to be scored.

Class	Package	Description
glm	stats	Generalized Linear Model
negbin	MASS	Negative binomial Generalized Linear Model
hclust	stats	Hierarchical Clustering
kmeans	stats	K-Means Clustering
lm	stats	Linear Model
multinom	nnet	Multinomial Log-Linear Model
nnet	nnet	Neural Network
rpart	rpart	Recursive Partitioning and Regression Tree

TABLE 10-9. *OREpredict-supported R models*

Example 22:

```
irisModel <- lm(Sepal.Length ~ ., data = iris)
IRIS       <- ore.push(iris)
IRISpred   <- ore.predict(irisModel, IRIS, se.fit = TRUE,
                          interval = "prediction")
IRIS <- cbind(IRIS, IRISpred)
head(IRIS)
```

Binding the prediction column to the rest of the data set allows comparison of the prediction with the original sepal length. The results are shown in Listing 10-16.

Listing 10-16 *OREpredict results using lm model*

```
R> irisModel <- lm(Sepal.Length ~ ., data = iris)
R> IRIS       <- ore.push(iris)
R> IRISpred   <- ore.predict(irisModel, IRIS, se.fit = TRUE,
+                          interval = "prediction")
R> IRIS <- cbind(IRIS, IRISpred)
R> head(IRIS)
  Sepal.Length Sepal.Width Petal.Length Petal.Width Species     PRED    SE.PRED
LOWER.PRED UPPER.PRED
1          5.1         3.5          1.4         0.2  setosa 5.004788 0.04479188
4.391895    5.617681
2          4.9         3.0          1.4         0.2  setosa 4.756844 0.05514933
4.140660    5.373027
3          4.7         3.2          1.3         0.2  setosa 4.773097 0.04690495
4.159587    5.386607
4          4.6         3.1          1.5         0.2  setosa 4.889357 0.05135928
4.274454    5.504259
5          5.0         3.6          1.4         0.2  setosa 5.054377 0.04736842
```

```
4.440727   5.668026
6          5.4       3.9        1.7        0.4   setosa 5.388886 0.05592364
4.772430   6.005342
```

Summing up predictive analytics, ORE provides a rich set of predictive analytics capabilities that includes in-database algorithms from Oracle Data Mining, ORE-provided algorithms, as well as the ability to supplement existing techniques with those from CRAN. Using select R algorithms, data can be scored directly in the database. In-database model building and scoring yields both performance gains and scalability.

Oracle R Connector for Hadoop

Oracle R Connector for Hadoop (ORCH) provides native R access to a Hadoop cluster, which for Oracle is the Oracle Big Data Appliance. ORCH users can access and manipulate data in HDFS, Oracle Database, and the file system. Further, users can write MapReduce programs exclusively in the R language and invoke MapReduce jobs through a natural R interface. ORCH facilitates transitioning work from the lab to production without requiring knowledge of Hadoop interfaces, the Hadoop call-level interface, or IT infrastructure. This is depicted in Figure 10-12.

Just as in ORE, where users can leverage CRAN packages at the database server, CRAN packages can also be used to work on HDFS-resident data within mapper and reducer functions. To enable this, such packages must be installed on each task node on the Hadoop cluster.

To introduce programming with ORCH, consider a text analysis example as depicted in Figure 10-13. The goal is to count the number of times each word occurs in a set of documents, referred to as a *corpus*. In HDFS, these documents are

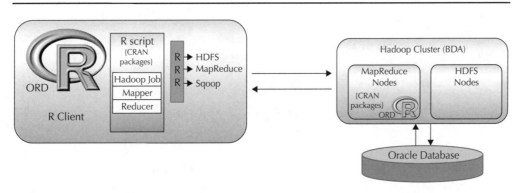

FIGURE 10-12.   *Oracle R Connector for Hadoop Architecture*

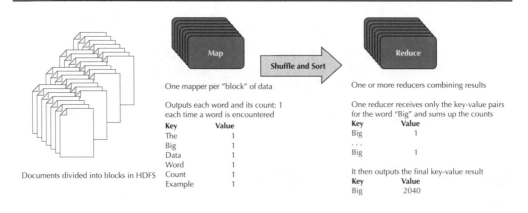

FIGURE 10-13. *Text analysis involving word counts using Hadoop*

divided into blocks and each block is processed by a mapper task. The mapper function parses the text and outputs each word it encounters with the value 1. The text "The Big Data word count example" is output as *key* and *value* pairs, where the key is the word (which may show up multiple times) and the corresponding value is 1. The middle phase, *shuffle and sort*, puts all the values of the same key together and provides them to a reducer. The reducer then sums the values to produce the word count for that particular word.

The corresponding ORCH R code that implements this is provided in Example 23. Data is first loaded from a file and *put* in HDFS using hdfs.put. This provides a handle to the HDFS data. The Hadoop job is executed using hadoop.exec with this handle, the mapper, reducer, and configuration settings.

Example 23:

```
corpus  <- scan("corpus.dat", what=" ",quiet= TRUE, sep="\n")
corpus  <- gsub("([/\\\":,#.@-])", " ", corpus)
input   <- hdfs.put(corpus)
res     <- hadoop.exec(dfs.id = input,
                mapper = function(k,v) {
                        x <- strsplit(v[[1]], " ")[[1]]
                        x <- x[x!='']
                        out <- NULL
                        for(i in 1:length(x))
                          out <- c(out, orch.keyval(x[i],1))
                        out
                },
                reducer = function(k,vv) {
```

```
        orch.keyval(k, sum(unlist(vv)))
      },
      config = new("mapred.config",
        job.name      = "wordcount",
        map.output    = data.frame(key='', val=0),
        reduce.output = data.frame(key='', val=0) )
  )
res
hdfs.get(res)
```

The mapper splits the words and outputs each word with the count of 1. This is done using the function `orch.keyval`. The reducer sums the list of values it receives, which is a vector of 1s. The configuration specification allows users to control details of the Hadoop job, for example, a job name to allow identifying a job easily through standard Hadoop tools. More importantly, the format of the mapper and reducer output can be specified. In this example, both the mapper and reducer output specify that the key is a character string and the value is numeric. Lastly, the result is retrieved from HDFS using the function `hdfs.get`.

Invoking MapReduce Jobs

ORCH provides `hadoop.exec` and `hadoop.run` for invoking MapReduce jobs. The function `hadoop.exec` requires input data to reside in HDFS already, whereas `hadoop.run` will attempt to load data such as an `ore.frame` or `data.frame` to HDFS for the user. After the input data, there are four principal sections: *mapper, reducer, variable export*, and *job configuration*. Each mapper receives a set of rows, referred to as a *block*, from HDFS as key-value pairs. The optional *key* has the same data type as that of the input, but the *value* can be either a `list` or `data.frame`. The mapper outputs results to be passed to the reducer using the `orch.keyval` function, which takes two arguments: a key and a value. The value can be any R object if packed with the `orch.pack` function.

Testing ORCH R Scripts Without the Hadoop Cluster

Once a MapReduce job is specified, it is often a good idea to test it locally before unleashing it on the Hadoop cluster, which is likely a shared and valuable resource. To do this, ORCH provides a *dry run* mode where the MapReduce job, and corresponding R code, runs locally, for example, on a laptop or desktop system. This enables testing R code on a sample of the data. To enable a dry run, no change to the MapReduce code is required—simply invoke `orch.dryrun` with the argument value TRUE. Data is obtained from HDFS and streamed into the mapper and reducer functions, which are executed serially on the local machine. As a result, the data likely must be changed to be small enough to fit in memory. Upon job success, the resulting data is placed in HDFS, as it would be if run on the Hadoop cluster.

Example 24 contains a MapReduce job that computes the average arrival delay for all flights to San Francisco. Notice that `orch.dryrun` is set to TRUE. The mapper checks if the key is "SFO" and then outputs the results. The reducer sums up the arrival delay and takes the average, outputting the key, which is "SFO," and the value, which is the average arrival delay. Finally, the result is output by getting the HDFS file, with the handle stored in `res`.

Example 24:

```
orch.dryrun(T)
dfs <- hdfs.attach('ontime_R')
res <- NULL
res <- hadoop.run(
    dfs,
    mapper = function(key, ontime) {
        if (key == 'SFO') {
            keyval(key, ontime)
        }
    },
    reducer = function(key, vals) {
        sumAD <- 0
        count <- 0
        for (x in vals) {
            if (!is.na(x$ARRDELAY)) {
                sumAD <- sumAD + x$ARRDELAY
                count <- count + 1
            }
        }
        res <- sumAD / count
        keyval(key, res)
    }
)
res
hdfs.get(res)
```

To have the MapReduce job run on the cluster, simply make one change: set `orch.dryrun` to FALSE.

```
orch.dryrun(F)
```

The MapReduce code is exactly the same, except perhaps for changing the data from a sample HDFS file to the full data desired.

ORCH also allows the export of any R variable to the mapper and reducer functions. This supports passing data from the client R environment to mapper and reducer functions. The job configuration options allow users to fine-tune how Hadoop operates on the data or interacts with the environment. This is discussed further later.

Interacting with HDFS from R

When working with ORCH, there are a variety of places from which to get data: HDFS, the database, and the file system. For HDFS, as shown in Example 25, ORCH provides functions to obtain the present working directory, list the files in HDFS, make directories, and change directories. On an HDFS file (or more correctly stated, directory), users can ask for its size, the number of component file parts, and get a sample of the data. This sample, however, is not necessarily a random sample. From the database, users can list database tables and perform basic ORE functionality. From R, all the standard functions for interacting with the file system are available.

Example 25:

```
hdfs.pwd()
hdfs.ls()
hdfs.mkdir("xq")
hdfs.cd("xq")
hdfs.ls()
hdfs.size("ontime_s")
hdfs.parts("ontime_s")
hdfs.sample("ontime_s",lines=3)
```

Figure 10-14 highlights a few examples for getting data into HDFS. Notice that in each case, users can remove an HDFS file using `hdfs.rm`. The first example

Data from File
Use hdfs.upload
Key if first column: YEAR
	`hdfs.rm('ontime_File')`
	`ontime.dfs_File <- hdfs.upload('ontime_s2000.dat',`
	`                          dfs.name='ontime_File')`
	`hdfs.exists('ontime_File')`

Data from Database Table
Use hdfs.push
Key column: DEST
	`hdfs.rm('ontime_DB')`
	`ontime.dfs_D <- hdfs.push(ontime_s2000,`
	`                          key='DEST',`
	`                          dfs.name='ontime_DB')`
	`hdfs.exists('ontime_DB')`

Data from R data.frame
Use hdfs.put
Key column: DEST
	`hdfs.rm('ontime_R')`
	`ontime <- ore.pull(ontime_s2000)`
	`ontime.dfs_R <- hdfs.put(ontime,`
	`                          key='DEST',`
	`                          dfs.name='ontime_R')`
	`hdfs.exists('ontime_R')`

FIGURE 10-14. *Loading data into HDFS using ORCH*

shows uploading data from the file system to HDFS. The function `hdfs.upload` accepts arguments for the data file and HDFS file name. The first column of the data file is expected to be the key column for the HDFS file. ORCH supports comma-separated-value (CSV) file data.

The second example uses `hdfs.push`, which takes an `ore.frame` as input. The `ore.frame` corresponds to a table in Oracle Database. Data from the database can be pushed to HDFS in a single function call. In addition, the key column can be explicitly specified. In the third example, `hdfs.put` supports loading a `data.frame` into HDFS, also specifying a key column.

Corresponding functions are available to take data from HDFS: `hdfs.get` returns an R in-memory object of the HDFS data, `hdfs.pull` moves data from HDFS to Oracle Database using the underlying Sqoop facility of Hadoop, and `hdfs.download` copies data from HDFS to the local file system.

HDFS Metadata Discovery

ORCH uses metadata about data files stored in a particular HDFS directory to know how to interpret it. ORCH `hdfs.*` functions take HDFS directories as input, not individual files. The filenames within directories can be any valid filename. ORCH requires a valid data directory to include an `__ORCHMETA__` file, which minimally contains the metadata described in Table 10-10. ORCH allows metadata to be discovered dynamically from CSV files using `hdfs.attach`. However, if files are large, it will be faster to create the ORCHMETA file that describes the HDFS content manually, since data is scanned to determine correct data types.

`__ORCHMETA__` Field	Description or Value
`orch.kvs`	TRUE (the data is key-value type)
`orch.names`	Column names, for example, "speed," "dist"
`orch.class`	data.frame
`orch.types`	Column types, for example, "numeric," "numeric"
`orch.dim`	Data dimensions (optional), for example, 50,2
`orch.keyi`	Index of column treated as key 0 means key is null ("\t" character at start of row) –1 means key not available (no tab at start of row)
`orch.rownamei`	Index of column used for rownames 0 means no rownames

TABLE 10-10.   *__ORCHMETA__ File Structure*

In Figure 10-15, the upper portion lists the component files in an HDFS directory followed by the content of the metadata file __ORCHMETA__. While the upper portion used the Hadoop command line, the lower portion shows that the same can be done from R using ORCH. The function `hdfs.id` returns a handle to the HDFS file and then `hdfs.describe` allows viewing the metadata content. The metadata describe a `data.frame` with two numeric columns: MOVIE_ID and GENRE_ID, with no key specified. Without a metadata file, users should invoke `hdfs.attach` to auto-discover this metadata.

```
[oracle@bigdatalite 2.13]$ hadoop fs -ls /user/oracle/moviework/advancedanalytics/data/movie_genre_subset
Found 7 items
-rw-r--r--   3 oracle hadoop          0 2012-10-15 12:52 /user/oracle/moviework/advancedanalytics/data/movie_genre_subset/_SUCCESS
-rw-r--r--   3 oracle hadoop        337 2012-10-15 12:52 /user/oracle/moviework/advancedanalytics/data/movie_genre_subset/__ORCHMETA__
drwxr-xr-x   - oracle hadoop          0 2012-10-15 12:51 /user/oracle/moviework/advancedanalytics/data/movie_genre_subset/_logs
-rw-r--r--   3 oracle hadoop      49413 2012-10-15 12:51 /user/oracle/moviework/advancedanalytics/data/movie_genre_subset/part-m-00000
-rw-r--r--   3 oracle hadoop      18038 2012-10-15 12:51 /user/oracle/moviework/advancedanalytics/data/movie_genre_subset/part-m-00001
-rw-r--r--   3 oracle hadoop        671 2012-10-15 12:51 /user/oracle/moviework/advancedanalytics/data/movie_genre_subset/part-m-00002
-rw-r--r--   3 oracle hadoop       4743 2012-10-15 12:52 /user/oracle/moviework/advancedanalytics/data/movie_genre_subset/part-m-00003
[oracle@bigdatalite 2.13]$ hadoop fs -cat /user/oracle/moviework/advancedanalytics/data/movie_genre_subset/__ORCHMETA__
orch.kvs           TRUE
orch.names         "MOVIE_ID","GENRE_ID"
orch.rownamei      0
orch.class         "data.frame"
orch.types         "numeric","numeric"
orch.key1          -1
orch.desc.name     "MOVIE_ID","GENRE_ID"
orch.desc.Sclass          "numeric","numeric"
orch.desc.type     "NUMBER","NUMBER"
orch.desc.len      22,22
orch.desc.precision      0,0
orch.desc.scale -127,-127
orch.desc.nullOK          FALSE,FALSE
```

```
R> mg.dfs <- hdfs.id("/user/oracle/moviework/advancedanalytics/data/movie_genre_subset")
R> mg.dfs
[1] "/user/oracle/moviework/advancedanalytics/data/movie_genre_subset"
attr(,"dfs.id")
[1] TRUE
R> hdfs.describe(mg.dfs)
          name                                                          values
1         path /user/oracle/moviework/advancedanalytics/data/movie_genre_subset
2       origin                                                         unknown
3        class                                                      data.frame
4        types                                                numeric, numeric
5          dim
6        names                                               MOVIE_ID, GENRE_ID
7      has.key                                                           FALSE
8   key.column                                                           -1:NA
9     null.key                                                           FALSE
10 has.rownames                                                          FALSE
11        size                                                           72865
12       parts                                                               4
R> y <- hdfs.attach("/user/oracle/moviework/advancedanalytics/data/movie_genre_subset")
R> y
[1] "/user/oracle/moviework/advancedanalytics/data/movie_genre_subset"
attr(,"dfs.id")
[1] TRUE
```

FIGURE 10-15. *ORCH metadata file content*

Working with Hadoop Using the ORCH Framework

Using, or not using, a mapper or reducer function in a Hadoop job can produce some useful behaviors. For example, consider a simple MapReduce job to run a piece of R code in parallel on different chunks of HDFS data. In Oracle R Enterprise Embedded R Execution, this corresponds to `ore.rowApply`. In ORCH, users accomplish this by providing a mapper, but using a default reducer that passes the results through. The function `orch.keyvals` (notice the "s") unlists the reducer input and writes it as multiple key values.

```
hadoop.exec(file, mapper={...}, reducer={orch.keyvals(k,vv)})
```

Alternatively, to run R code in parallel on partitions of the data, that is, by HDFS key column, specify only the reducer and use the mapper specified next, which partitions the data. This functionality corresponds to the `ore.groupApply` function.

```
hadoop.exec(file, mapper={orch.keyval(k,v)}, reducer={...})
```

Of course, the full MapReduce functionality is provided for both a mapper and reducer, or further configuring a job with the `config` argument.

```
hadoop.exec(file, mapper={...}, reducer={...})
hadoop.exec(file, mapper={...}, reducer={...}, config={...})
```

MapReduce jobs can be configured using a wide range of fields. A job configuration object is of type `mapred.config` and contains the fields shown in Listing 10-17 with their default values. Any of these can be overridden as needed. For example, users may want to provide a name for jobs that will show up in standard Hadoop monitoring interfaces. Users may also need to characterize the mapper and reducer output if it is different from the input.

Listing 10-17   *ORCH MapReduce job configuration*

```
R> jobconfig = new("mapred.config")
R> class(jobconfig)
[1] "mapred.config"
attr(,"package")
[1] ".GlobalEnv"
R> jobconfig
Object of class "mapred.config"
data frame with 0 columns and 0 rows
Slot "job.name":    ◄──────────── User-defined job name
[1] ""
Slot "map.tasks":   ◄──────────── Desired #mappers
[1] -1
```

```
Slot "reduce.tasks":  ◄─────────── Desired #reducers
[1] -1
Slot "min.split.size":  ◄─────────── Desired minimum # rows sent to mapper
[1] -1
Slot "map.output":  ◄─────────── Schema of mapper output
data frame with 0 columns and 0 rows
Slot "reduce.output":  ◄─────────── Schema of reducer output
data frame with 0 columns and 0 rows
Slot "map.valkey":  ◄─────────── Should key be included in mapper value?
[1] FALSE
Slot "reduce.valkey":  ◄─────────── Should key be included in reducer value?
[1] FALSE
Slot "map.input":  ◄─────────── Data type of val that is input to mapper: data.frame or list
[1] "vector"
Slot "map.split":
[1] 1  ◄─────────── Max chunk size desired by mapper
Slot "reduce.input":
[1] "list"  ◄─────────── Data type of val that is input to reducer: data.frame or list
Slot "reduce.split":
[1] 0  ◄─────────── Max chunk size desired by the reducer - zero indicates no limit
Slot "verbose":
[1] FALSE  ◄─────────── Should diagnostic info be generated?
```

ORCH Predictive Analytics on Hadoop

While MapReduce is a powerful programming paradigm and Hadoop a powerful computing environment, not everyone wants to or can write MapReduce programs to harness that power. To make Hadoop-based analytics more accessible, ORCH contains a set of built-in algorithms with a convenient R interface. The underlying algorithms are built on the ORCH framework using MapReduce for scalable, high-performance execution. These R interfaces are generally consistent with typical R predictive analytics functions.

Functions include linear models, low-rank matrix factorization, neural networks, and non-negative matrix factorization, as listed in Table 10-11.

For an example, consider orch.lm. The function orch.lm is a scalable lm implementation on top of Hadoop, able to process well over a thousand columns of data, with no effective restriction on the number of rows. The result is of class orch.lm and a subclass of lm with corresponding functions print and summary. The orch.lm interface allows a formula specification, as in the lm and ore.lm functions.

In Example 26, the iris data set is used to predict Petal.Width given the cube of the Sepal.Length and the combination of Sepal.Width and Petal.Length. After fitting the model, the fit is printed to display the coefficients for each term. Invoking summary provides output similar to a standard lm model with the min and

Function	Description
orch.lm	Fits a linear model using tall-and-skinny QR (TSQR) factorization and parallel distribution. The function computes the same statistical arguments as the Oracle R Enterprise ore.lm function.
orch.lmf	Fits a low-rank matrix factorization model using either the Jellyfish algorithm or the Mahout alternating least squares with weighted regularization (ALS-WR) algorithm.
orch.neural	Produces a neural network to model complex, nonlinear relationships between inputs and outputs to find patterns in the data.
orch.nmf	Provides the main entry point to create a non-negative matrix factorization model using the Jellyfish algorithm. This function can work on much larger data sets than the R NMF package, because the input does not need to fit into memory.

TABLE 10-11. *ORCH Analytic Functions*

max of the residuals, and coefficients with standard error, t value, and significance, among other statistics. This is depicted in Listing 10-18.

Example 26:

```
formula <- 'Petal.Width ~ I(Sepal.Length^3) + (Sepal.Width + Petal.Length)^2'
dfs.dat <- hdfs.put(iris)
fit = orch.lm(formula, dfs.dat)
print(fit)
```

Listing 10-18 *Results of orch.lm for Example 26*

```
R> print(fit)
Call:
orch.lm(formula = formula, dfs.dat = dfs.dat)
Coefficients:
    (Intercept)    I(Sepal.Length^3)    Sepal.Width    Petal.Length
Sepal.Width:Petal.Length
    -0.558951258       -0.001808531    0.076544835     0.374865543
0.044639138

R> summary(fit)
Call:
```

```
orch.lm(formula = formula, dfs.dat = dfs.dat)
Residuals:
      Min        Max
-0.5787561  0.5982218
Coefficients:
                       Estimate   Std. Error    t value     Pr(>|t|)
(Intercept)         -0.558951258 0.3114271138 -1.7948060 7.476772e-02
I(Sepal.Length^3)   -0.001808531 0.0003719886 -4.8617906 2.990386e-06
Sepal.Width          0.076544835 0.0936509172  0.8173421 4.150739e-01
Petal.Length         0.374865543 0.0813489249  4.6081192 8.829319e-06
Sepal.Width:Petal.Length  0.044639138 0.0244578742  1.8251438 7.003728e-02
Multiple R-squared: 0.9408,    Adjusted R-squared: 0.9392
F-statistic: 576.6 on 4 and 145 DF
```

ORCHhive

Hive is a SQL-like abstraction on top of Hadoop that is becoming a de facto standard for SQL-based apps on Hadoop. It effectively converts SQL queries to MapReduce jobs that are run on the Hadoop cluster. This allows users to write HiveQL, which is based on SQL, to manipulate data without knowledge of MapReduce programming.

So while Hive provides an abstraction layer using SQL syntax on top of MapReduce, ORCHhive provides an R abstraction on top of HiveQL, just as ORE provides an R abstraction on top of SQL. This allows Big Data scalability and performance for R users on Hadoop, but doing so easily and transparently from R. A key motivation for ORCHhive is to allow users to prepare Big Data for further analytic techniques using the ORCH MapReduce framework.

ORCHhive supports a wide range of R functions for transparent interaction with Hive tables. Table 10-12 includes a list of supported functions from storage methods to methods on primitive types like logical, numeric, and character vectors, as well as ore.frames and aggregation functions.

ORCH provides the same ORE functions to work with Hive. Although this is an ORE-like interface, it is a feature available only with ORCH. Consider the ORCHhive R script in Example 27. Users connect to Hive using ore.connect, specifying type="HIVE". There are no login credentials since Hadoop does not have authentication. Users simply indicate they are connecting to the local Hive environment. Next, attach the current environment into the R search path using ore.attach. The tables in Hive are now available to ORCH. Create a Hive table in HDFS using ore.push, using the iris data set. The Transparency Layer is highlighted by binning the data using standard R syntax. These operations are performed on Hadoop using Hive tables. As with other ore.frames, users can ask for the column names. Lastly, the overloaded aggregate function is used to compute summary statistics over each petal length bin created earlier. In the output shown in Listing 10-19, Large petals have a minimum value of 6 and a maximum value of 6.9.

Storage methods	ore.create, ore.drop, ore.push, ore.pull, ore.get
Methods	is.ore.frame, is.ore.vector, is.ore.logical, is.ore.integer, is.ore.numeric, is.ore.character, is.ore, as.ore.frame, as.ore.vector, as.ore.logical, as.ore.integer, as.ore.numeric, as.ore.character, as.ore
ore.vector methods	show, length, c, is.vector, as.vector, as.character, as.numeric, as.integer, as.logical, "[", "[<-", I, Compare, ore.recode, is.na, "%in%", unique, sort, table, paste, tapply, by, head, tail
ore.logical methods	<, >, ==, <=, >=, !, xor, ifelse, and, or
ore.number methods	+, -, *, ^, %%, %/%, /, is.finite, is.infinite, is.nan, abs, sign, sqrt, ceiling, floor, trunc, log, log10, log2, log1p, logb, acos, asin atan, exp, expm1, cos, sin, tan, zapsmall, round, Summary, summary, mean
ore.character methods	nchar, tolower, toupper, casefold, gsub, substr, substring
ore.frame methods	show, attach, [, $, $<-, [[, [[<-, head, tail, length, nrow, ncol, NROW, NCOL, dim, names, names<-, colnames, colnames<-, as.list, unlist, summary, rbind, cbind, data.frame, as.data.frame, as.env, eval, +, -, *, ^, %%, %/%, /, Compare, Logic, !, xor, is.na, is.finite, is.infinite, is.nan, abs, sign, sqrt, ceiling, floor, trunc, log, log10, log2, log1p, logb, acos, asin, atan, exp, expm1, cos, sin, tan, round, Summary, rowSums, colSums, rowMeans, colMeans, unique, by, merge
Aggregate functions	OREStats: fivenum, aggregate, quantile, sd, var (only for vectors), median, IQR

TABLE 10-12.   *ORCHhive-Supported Functionality*

Example 27:

```
# Connect to Hive
ore.connect(type="HIVE")
# Attach the current environment into search path of R
ore.attach()
# create a Hive table by pushing the numeric columns of the iris data set
IRIS_TABLE <- ore.push(iris[1:4])
# Create bins based on Petal Length
IRIS_TABLE$PetalBins = ifelse(IRIS_TABLE$Petal.Length < 2.0, "SMALL PETALS",
                       ifelse(IRIS_TABLE$Petal.Length < 4.0, "MEDIUM PETALS",
```

```
              ifelse(IRIS_TABLE$Petal.Length < 6.0,
                    "MEDIUM LARGE PETALS", "LARGE PETALS")))
#PetalBins is now a derived column of the HIVE object
names(IRIS_TABLE)
# Based on the bins, generate summary statistics for each group
aggregate(IRIS_TABLE$Petal.Length, by = list(PetalBins = IRIS_TABLE$PetalBins),
        FUN = summary)
```

Listing 10-19   *Results of executing ORCHhive Example 27*

```
ore.connect(type="HIVE")
ore.attach()
# create a Hive table by pushing the numeric
# columns of the iris data set
IRIS_TABLE <- ore.push(iris[1:4])
# Create bins based on Petal Length
 IRIS_TABLE$PetalBins =
    ifelse(IRIS_TABLE$Petal.Length < 2.0, "SMALL PETALS",
+   ifelse(IRIS_TABLE$Petal.Length < 4.0, "MEDIUM PETALS",
+   ifelse(IRIS_TABLE$Petal.Length < 6.0,
+   "MEDIUM LARGE PETALS", "LARGE PETALS")))
ore.connect(type="HIVE")
ore.attach()
# create a Hive table by pushing the numeric
# columns of the iris data set
IRIS_TABLE <- ore.push(iris[1:4])
# Create bins based on Petal Length
 IRIS_TABLE$PetalBins =
    ifelse(IRIS_TABLE$Petal.Length < 2.0, "SMALL PETALS",
+   ifelse(IRIS_TABLE$Petal.Length < 4.0, "MEDIUM PETALS",
+   ifelse(IRIS_TABLE$Petal.Length < 6.0,
+   "MEDIUM LARGE PETALS", "LARGE PETALS")))

#PetalBins is now a derived column of the HIVE object
> names(IRIS_TABLE)
[1] "Sepal.Length" "Sepal.Width"  "Petal.Length"
[4] "Petal.Width"  "PetalBins"

# Based on the bins, generate summary statistics for each group
aggregate(IRIS_TABLE$Petal.Length,
        by = list(PetalBins = IRIS_TABLE$PetalBins),
+          FUN = summary)
1          LARGE PETALS   6 6.025000 6.200000 6.354545 6.612500  6.9 0
2 MEDIUM LARGE PETALS   4 4.418750 4.820000 4.888462 5.275000  5.9 0
3        MEDIUM PETALS   3 3.262500 3.550000 3.581818 3.808333  3.9 0
4         SMALL PETALS   1 1.311538 1.407692 1.462000 1.507143  1.9 0
Warning message:
ORE object has no unique key - using random order
```

Oracle R Connector for Hadoop and Oracle R Enterprise Interaction

ORCH and ORE can be combined in a variety of ways to solve interesting problems. If ORE and ORCH are installed on a user's client machine, not only can data be moved between HDFS and the database, but also preprocessed database data can be provided to MapReduce jobs. Similarly, results from MapReduce jobs can be post-processed in the database once data is moved there.

For example, a CUSTOMER table may reside in Oracle Database and require cleaning or aggregation prior to use by a MapReduce job that makes a wide range of recommendations for those customers. These recommendations could be produced by scoring hundreds or thousands of models per customer, where the models were generated using ORE and stored in an ORE datastore, only to be retrieved and passed into ORCH as exported variables.

In another configuration, ORE can be installed on Big Data Appliance (BDA) task nodes such that mapper and reducer functions can make call-outs to one or more databases for ORE-based processing, using the Transparency Layer or Embedded R Execution.

Conversely, ORCH can be installed on the Oracle Database server such that Embedded R Execution can invoke ORCH functionality. One immediate use is the scheduling of database jobs for recurring execution. Here, the database can control when and how often ORCH MapReduce jobs get executed as part of a database application.

Summary

The Oracle R Enterprise component of the Oracle Advanced Analytics option provides a comprehensive, database-centric environment for end-to-end analytical processes in R. Both the results of R script execution and the R scripts themselves can be immediately deployed to production environments. Oracle R Enterprise improves user efficiency by allowing the use of R directly against database data, leveraging in-database analytical techniques, and native SQL Oracle Data Mining functions. Using Oracle Database as a computational engine provides scalability and performance through in-database execution, query optimization, parallelism, and elimination of data movement. The rich set of open source R packages can be used in combination with database-managed data-parallel and task-parallel execution of R scripts—leveraging Oracle Database as a high-performance computing (HPC) environment. As a result, ORE provides a framework for sophisticated model building and data scoring. By integrating R into the SQL language, operationalization of analyst-generated R scripts enables more immediate integration with the IT software stack.

Oracle R Connector for Hadoop allows R users to leverage the powerful Hadoop environment from R. Both mapper and reducer functions are written using the R language and environment. The ORCH HDFS interface facilitates access to database data, file-based data, and R `data.frames`. Using the dry run capability, R-based MapReduce jobs can be tested and debugged in the local system prior to unleashing a newly written program on the full Hadoop cluster. ORCH provides a number of advanced analytics algorithms that make it easy for users to gain Hadoop scalability for commonly used techniques. In addition, users can manipulate HIVE data transparently from R using familiar R syntax and semantics.

Oracle customers have the added benefit of using Oracle R Distribution, which provides, among other benefits, Oracle support, making R a viable option for world-class enterprises.

CHAPTER
11

Endeca Information
Discovery

E ndeca was founded in 1999 and headquartered in Cambridge, Massachusetts. The name Endeca derives from the German word *entdecken*, meaning "to discover."

Endeca's original products included eCommerce search, customer experience management, enterprise search, and business intelligence applications. On October 18, 2011, Oracle Corporation announced its acquisition of Endeca.

Why Did Oracle Select Endeca?

Endeca offers leading unstructured data management, Web commerce, and business intelligence solutions. Endeca's products help enterprises analyze unstructured data, deliver better business intelligence, and provide a superior customer experience. More than 600 global enterprises rely on Endeca's solutions to increase the value of their online customer interactions and business knowledge through Endeca's advanced business intelligence and guided navigation solutions.

Oracle and Endeca have many of the same customers, across many industries—and the products are complementary. Endeca is recognized as a leader for its unique approach in hybrid search/analytical technology that enables consistent search, navigation, and analytics on diverse and changing information.

Endeca's products complement Oracle's solutions in a number of ways. First and foremost, Oracle offers best-in-class structured data management and analytics; Endeca offers an unstructured data management and analytics engine, which was formerly called MDEX.

In addition, Oracle offers leading eCommerce and merchandising solutions; Endeca offers a leading catalog search, navigation, and customer experience management solution. Last but not least, Oracle offers leading BI solutions for structured data analytics; Endeca offers leading unstructured data analytics solutions.

In summary, the Endeca acquisition yet again demonstrated Oracle's ability in selecting a product that is not only a leader and innovator in its space but also in alignment with Oracle's strategic product direction, and at the same time complements Oracle's existing product portfolio.

Product Suites Overview

The Endeca acquisition by Oracle was relatively recent. As a result, there are a mixture of references to its legacy product terms and new product names. It's important to first look at the legacy terms and their mapping to the new product names.

Product Mapping

Here is a mapping of legacy Endeca products to their new Oracle names.

Legacy Endeca Name	New Oracle Name
Endeca Latitude	Oracle Endeca Information Discovery
Endeca MDEX Engine	Oracle Endeca Server
Endeca Content Management System Connectors	Oracle Endeca Content Management System Connectors
Endeca Text Enrichment	Oracle Endeca Text Enrichment
Endeca Text Enrichment with Sentiment Analysis	Oracle Endeca Text Enrichment with Sentiment Analysis

New Product Suite

Following are the descriptions of the new branded components of the Endeca product suite. They are categorized into two product groups, the eCommerce Products and the Business Intelligence Products.

eCommerce Products

- **Oracle Endeca Commerce**   Oracle Endeca Commerce enables companies to deliver a personalized, consistent customer buying experience across all channels—online, in-store, mobile, or social. Whenever and wherever customers engage with your business, Oracle Endeca Commerce delivers, analyzes, and targets just the right content to just the right customer to encourage clicks and drive business results.

- **Oracle Endeca Experience Manager**   Oracle Endeca Experience Manager provides a single, flexible platform to create, deliver, and manage content-rich, cross-channel customer experiences.

- **Oracle Endeca Guided Search**   Oracle Endeca Guided Search is the most effective way for customers to dynamically explore your storefront and find relevant and desired items quickly.

- **Oracle Endeca for Mobile**   Oracle Endeca for Mobile powers full-featured customer experiences for the mobile Web, and iPhone and iPad apps.

- **Oracle Endeca for Social**   Oracle Endeca for Social allows businesses to integrate with Facebook to enhance the customer experience across channels and capture additional sales with a transactional Facebook storefront.

- **Oracle Endeca Commerce Business Intelligence**   Oracle Endeca Commerce Business Intelligence brings advanced business intelligence to the commerce world, giving teams fast insight into all the data they need to make accurate in-the-moment decisions.

Business Intelligence Product   Oracle Endeca Information Discovery (EID) employs a key-value store back end that stores diverse and unstructured data, and enables business analysts to draw new insights, come to meaningful conclusions, and make more informed decisions faster.

The remainder of this chapter will focus on the Endeca Information Discovery platform.

Endeca Information Discovery Platform

Endeca Information Discovery helps organizations quickly explore samples of all relevant data. It combines structured and unstructured data from disparate systems. In addition, it automatically organizes information for search, discovery, and analysis. Last but not least, it enables IT and business to rapidly assemble easy-to-use analysis applications.

Major Functional Areas

Endeca Information Discovery includes three main functional areas, namely Advanced Search, Faceted Navigation, and Visuals Analysis:

- Advanced Search allows a user to perform functions that include search look-ahead, spell-correction, and data-driven filtering.

- Faceted Navigation is a feature of Endeca Information Discovery that enables users to select attributes after they enter the search term, to drill up and down as well as left and right, based on the combinations of criteria, similar to a commerce Web site.

- Visual Analysis features include charting and cross-tabs, geographic visualization, and tag clouds.

Key Features

The key features of Endeca Information Discovery are

- Faceted data model

- Integration capabilities

- Enrichment

- Ease of development

- Language support and geographies

The following sections explain each of these features.

Faceted Data Model

A faceted data model is a marquee feature of Endeca Information Discovery.

It is mainly a form of key-value store, and its model consists of records and attributes. Each record is a collection of attribute and value pairs. There is no segmentation into tables and no overarching schema.

It enables easier loading and update of data from any data sources. It accommodates distinctive structure in that each record is self-describing, representing its own, and possibly unique, schema. It supports multivalued fields and unstructured fields.

What's behind this solid foundation is the modeling capability.

It's not a relational model, but a faceted data model that makes it easy to load data from a variety of data sources. They could be feeds from XML sources, structured records from a database, or unstructured documents from a content management system. All of these sources can be represented in the key-value structure in an integrated manner. Although no up-front modeling of the schema is needed, some preparation work needs to be done to understand different data sources and the relationship and mapping of these sources.

Over time, users can also update the record with new attributes. As a result, it's not only fast to establish an initial configuration, but also flexible to update and to keep pace with the ever-changing data landscape.

Integration Capabilities

Another key feature of Endeca Information Discovery is its integration capabilities: integration with structured data, semistructured data, and unstructured data.

Structured data can be directly loaded into a faceted model using standard ETL tools. Each row becomes a record and each column becomes an attribute. An example of such data is a sales transaction. Each transaction row becomes a record and every element of the transaction record becomes an attribute.

Semistructured data from enterprise applications, various feeds, and XML sources can also be loaded as attribute and value pairs. This is a common cause of heterogeneous record structure. For the sales transaction record, now we want to extend this record with more information about the specific products. The set of attributes that go with each product could be very different depending on the product. For example, a road bike has different components than a mountain bike. With Endeca Information Discovery, they become attribute and value pairs, and we start to get jagged records that look dissimilar to each other (that is, data sets that don't have the same data model, but with some commonality between them). With relational database technologies, this is difficult to implement. Key-value pair data structure makes it possible to implement and extend.

Unstructured data can be linked to records by any available key. In addition, unstructured elements can be also stored as their own records for side-by-side analysis. Some examples could include documents, RSS feeds, Twitter, Facebook, and data feeds from discussion forums. To continue with the sales transaction data we were talking about, we could now get into the record the customer reviews online and the customers' Facebook or Twitter comments on the product and transaction.

The way to accomplish it through Endeca Information Discovery is to take the textual fields into the records as a new attribute. We could put them in the same record with the sales transactions, product attributes, and customer review information.

Here's a summary of the data sources in the examples we mentioned.

Data Source Name	Data Source Type	Data Source Storage
Sales	Relational	Oracle Database
Product Details	Semistructured	XML
Employee Information	Relational	Oracle Database
Online Reviews	Unstructured	Text Files

Endeca allows the mapping of sales transactional records with product details and employee information through Product ID and Sales Rep ID. The online reviews can also be mapped to the transaction records through Transaction IDs captured. In addition, users can create a Whitelist Text Tagger to tag the employee first name or last name mentioned in the review text to an employee by full name.

Now unstructured, semistructured, and structured data are aligned, loaded, and could be analyzed side-by-side.

Enrichment

Enrichment is another key function of Endeca Information Discovery that extends the data model to include new data. An unstructured attribute can be enriched using text analytics to expand the structure of its containing record. Some of the common techniques include automatic tagging, named entity extraction, sentiment analysis, term extraction, and geospatial matching. The real power comes from text analytics that can pull out more structured data elements.

What Oracle Endeca uses behind the scene is Lexalytics Salience, a multilingual text-analysis and opinion-mining sentiment engine that allows an application to analyze social media sentiment.

Ease of Development

Ease of development is another key feature of Endeca Information Discovery. It supports quick and iterative creation of discovery applications. It is purely Web-based, with a drag-and-drop interactive design environment. It is extensible with live data support, meaning that you see what you build as you build it. Furthermore, it comes with a rich library of components. Here are some of the sample components:

- Chart
- Cross-tab
- Results table
- Metrics bar
- Performance metrics
- Range filters
- Record details
- Search box
- Find similar
- Bookmarks
- Guided navigation
- Breadcrumbs
- Sliders
- Data sources

Language Support and Geographies

Language Support and Geographies are worth mentioning as well. Endeca Server provides full search support for the following languages: English, French, Italian, German, Spanish, Dutch, and Portuguese.

Endeca Information Discovery and Business Intelligence

At this point, you might wonder how Endeca Information Discovery differs from a traditional Business Intelligence (BI) suite such as OBIEE and how it fits into the existing BI ecosystem. Let's take a closer look to compare and contrast these two solutions.

Difference in Roles and Functions

An important concept to remember here is that Business Intelligence and Information Discovery are peers. They solve different problems and create different types of value. Business Intelligence provides proven answers to known questions. Information Discovery provides fast answers to new questions. The key performance indicators (KPIs), reports, and dashboards produced by the Business Intelligence tools drive the need for exploration and discovery using Information Discovery Platform.

For example, when the report says that warranty claims on the top-selling product went up 15 percent last month, the new questions that surface could include "What has changed?", "What's the root cause of this change?", and "What are customers saying about this product recently?" That exploration happens in Endeca as a discovery application.

The relationship can go the other direction also. Information Discovery creates new KPIs for the Business Intelligence tools to deliver. For example, a consumer packaged goods (CPG) company learned through Information Discovery that preference for seemingly unrelated brands was highly correlated with certain customer segments. This came from a social media discovery application and established new KPIs that the company should track on an ongoing basis. These new KPIs will then be incorporated into standard reports and dashboards within the Business Intelligence applications.

Figure 11-1 provides a good illustration of the different but complementary roles of Business Intelligence and Information Discovery applications.

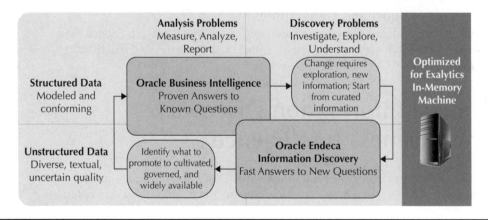

FIGURE 11-1. *Complementary roles of Business Intelligence and Information Discovery applications*

BI Development Process vs. Information Discovery Approach

The development processes of Information Discovery versus Business Intelligence applications could vary as well. Figure 11-2 depicts the differences in development process between traditional Business Intelligence and Information Discovery.

With traditional BI, the users know the answer they are looking for. They define requirements and build to the objective. It starts with requirement documentation, data model definition, and then implementation and development of a data model, metadata definition, data integration, and finally reports and dashboards development. When new requirements surface, a new iteration of this process is triggered.

With an Information Discovery application, the users may have an idea or interest, but they don't know what to anticipate. The answer for the initial question will lead to the next set of questions. As a result, the development process is more fluid. It requires that the data analysts explore the data as they develop and refine their hypothesis.

Here's a sample process users typically go through with Information Discovery.

They start with a hypothesis or a set of questions. They define and collect data sources including structured data from your existing data warehouse and unstructured data from weblogs, clickstreams, social media channels, and internal text logs and documents.

FIGURE 11-2. *Development processes for Business Intelligence and Information Discovery applications*

They use tools to explore results and reduce ambiguity. They might also apply analytical models to eliminate outliers, find concentrations, and make correlations. They then interpret the outcome and continuously refine their queries and models and establish an improved hypothesis.

In the end, this analysis might lead to a creation of new theories and predictions based on the data. Again, the process is very fluid in nature and is different from traditional Software Development Life Cycle (SDLC) and BI development.

Complementary But Not Exclusive

With that said, the traditional Business Intelligence and Information Discovery are not mutually exclusive. Instead, they are complementary in nature and provide the user community with a more powerful decision support foundation when combined, as Figure 11-3 illustrates.

Here's a comparison chart to further define the two areas of decision support capabilities.

	Oracle BI Foundation Suite	**Endeca Information Discovery**
Key Concept	**Proven answers to known questions**	**Fast answers to new questions**
How is that achieved?	Semantic model relates data sources and provides strong governance, confidence, and reuse	Ingest sources as needed for discovery. Model derived from incoming data
Data sources?	Data warehouse plus federated sources, mostly structured, and able to model the relationships	Multiple sources that may be difficult to relate and may change over time. Structured, semistructured and unstructured
Who uses?	Broad array of enterprise consumers via reports, dashboards, mobile, embedded in business processes, …	Nontechnical users doing exploration and discovery
Timing?	Company has months to complete	Company has weeks to complete

In short, understanding the differences and the complementary nature of Business Intelligence and Information Discovery will help you choose the right tool for the right requirement based on the business context.

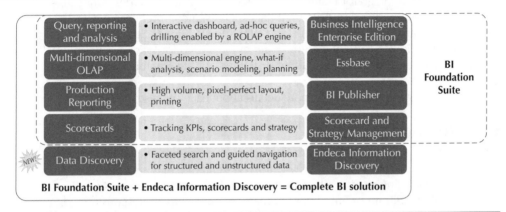

FIGURE 11-3. *Business Intelligence and Information Discovery are not exclusive*

Architecture

Business Intelligence and analytical solutions are key to gaining competitive advantages for an enterprise. Such solutions need to extend into unstructured sources. In order to make information actionable, the businesses need to be able to look across diverse sources, correlate them back to the structured data that they are already using to measure and drive the business, and enable decision makers to interact directly with that data to generate insights and improve business outcomes.

Oracle Endeca Information Discovery does just that. It extends data discovery capabilities across structured and unstructured sources. It unites the worlds of structured and unstructured data to provide business users with complete visibility into their business processes. It allows users to discover possible new patterns and insights as well as enabling better business decisions.

Oracle Endeca Server accomplishes this through empowered search, guided navigation, and analytics capabilities. This hybrid search and analytical database provides flexibility in combining diverse and changing data as well as extreme performance in analyzing that data. Oracle Endeca Server has the performance characteristics of in-memory architecture; however, it is not memory bound.

Oracle Endeca Studio is a tool to support self-service composition and configuration of applications, as well as constructing views and dashboards by business analysts. Oracle Endeca Studio is a discovery application composition environment for the Oracle Endeca Server. It provides drag-and-drop authoring to create highly interactive and enterprise-class information discovery applications with rich visualization.

Oracle Endeca Integrator features an ETL solution, which includes connectors for standard structured and unstructured data sources, a comprehensive data enrichment library, and direct connectors to the Oracle Endeca Server. Oracle Endeca Information Discovery includes a set of tools used for loading and optionally enriching diverse information, including structured and unstructured content into Oracle Endeca Server.

The following sections provide more details about each of these three components.

Oracle Endeca Server

Oracle Endeca Server is the core data management engine of Oracle Endeca Information Discovery. It supports navigation, search, and analysis of any kind of information including structured, semistructured, and unstructured content. It is highly scalable, column-oriented, and in-memory but not memory-constrained.

Oracle Endeca Server shares many of the characteristics of a state-of-the-art database such as clustering capabilities, query language, and performance management capabilities. Yet it is designed to incorporate unstructured, structured, and semistructured data. The basic design component of Endeca Server is a vertical record store designed to operate at high speed while handling large data volume. Information is stored in columnar form to achieve maximum compression.

Oracle Endeca Server is highly memory efficient and stores each column of information on a combination of disk and memory in two sort orders, by value and by a universal record key identifier. Each of the Oracle Endeca Server columns contains a tree-structured index cached in memory to improve the speed of finding and delivering data in Oracle Endeca Server.

An Endeca Server installation requires the WebLogic Server, ADF Runtime, and Java Development Kit (JDK) products.

Data Model

Oracle Endeca Server supports a flexible data model that reduces the need for up-front data modeling. This enables the integration of diverse and ever-changing data, and supports the iterative exploration and analysis needs of business users.

Oracle Endeca Server's data model is based on the concept of "records." Similar to facts in dimensional data modeling, each of these "records" consists of an arbitrary collection of attributes made up of key-value pairs. These attributes can have a single value, multiple values, or a hierarchy of values based on an external taxonomy definition. Values could be numeric, text of any length, date and time, geospatial, or Boolean.

Oracle Endeca Server does not employ a standard schema definition for the overall data structure. Instead, every record has its own schema. This enables the rapid integration of any type of data, structured or unstructured, from internal data sources or external, such as an enterprise data warehouse, without the constraints associated with traditional relational or dimensional data modeling.

The process of loading data into Oracle Endeca Server is straightforward. The developers submit a set of rows to a set of Web Services designed for data ingestion. The data rows need to be in alignment with the definition of the data store input. Data transformation can be done prior to the load or performed through a transformation layer. These Web Services include both incremental and bulk load. They can either create new records or append new attributes and values to existing records. By providing a flexible data load method, Oracle Endeca Server enables an iterative "model-as-you-go" approach to design discovery applications. IT developers can quickly load new data via standard ETL tools, observe the results in Endeca Studio, and decide whether to keep, enrich, and organize what has been loaded, or otherwise discard it. As soon as data is loaded, Oracle Endeca Server automatically derives common attributes from the available metadata and instantly exposes them for high-performance refinement and analysis through Endeca Studio.

Search
Oracle Endeca Server provides search features that are designed to incorporate structured, semistructured, and unstructured content. Advanced search features include type-ahead, automatic alphanumeric spell correction, positional search, Boolean and wildcard search, natural language processing, category search, and query clarification dialogs. Search is a critically important element that enables users to explore diverse data sets contained in Oracle Endeca Server.

The search capabilities in Oracle Endeca Server differ from the search feature available through standard BI products. Oracle Endeca Server supports exploratory search through "data dialoging and clarification" with refinements and summaries. Oracle Endeca Server stratifies results by a primary relevance strategy and then breaks ties within a stratum by ordering them with a secondary strategy, and so on.

There are two types of search: Value Search, which finds values and attributes, and Record Search, which finds records. Value Search will appear as "type-ahead" suggestions. Here's an example of Value Search. If the user types in the word "helmet," "type-ahead" suggestions will appear for products, resellers, categories, and surveys where "helmet" appears in the value. This helps the user clarify their search. The user might intend to search the product category of helmet to begin with, but this search will suggest and extend into different data subject areas that are relevant. So the analyst can discover something new about the data.

Application managers are able to explicitly compose these strategies based on their knowledge of their own domain. This approach gives both users and managers a deterministic way to set and understand relevance that goes far beyond the "black-box" search relevancy results from standard BI tools.

Queries and Filters
Business users need to express a wide range of queries apart from search. Oracle Endeca Server addresses this need by including interactive navigation, advanced

visualizations, analytics, range filters, geospatial filters, and other query types more commonly associated with BI tools. Unlike other technologies, these queries operate across structured, semistructured, and unstructured content stored in Oracle Endeca Server. In addition, the data set is extensible with ease.

Oracle Endeca Server query result sets are also summarized, providing users with guidance on how to refine and explore further. Summaries include navigation, maps, charts, graphs, tag clouds, concept clusters, and clarification dialogs. Users do not need to explicitly ask for or define these summaries. Oracle Endeca Information Discovery applications automatically generate them based on configurable controls and rules. For example, the discovery application might guide a procurement agent filtering for in-stock parts by visualizing the results on a map and calculating their average fulfillment time.

Furthermore, the user can interact with summaries and filters without resorting to writing complex SQL queries. The filter additions are accomplished through clicking a mouse.

Within Oracle Endeca Information Discovery, all parts of the summaries are clickable and searchable, which makes the exploratory experience intuitive and easy to use.

Query Response

To support an interactive user experience, the data store must be able to process and respond to interactive queries within subseconds. It also needs to accommodate new data and changes to existing data with minimal rework or remodeling. Oracle Endeca Server is able to accomplish these requirements through multicore query parallelism, in-memory caching of frequently accessed working column segments and query results, per-attribute column storage, and a multitude of compression techniques.

Analytics Language

Endeca Query Language (EQL) is a powerful integrated analytics language built within the Oracle Endeca Server. EQL enables power users to define and create new metrics to compose their own discovery applications. Built on the core capabilities of Oracle Endeca Server, EQL extends the capabilities of Oracle Endeca Server with a rich analytic language that allows users to explore aggregated and pivoted views of large volumes of data. EQL also supports a variety of data types, including numerical, geospatial, and date/time values that enable applications to work with temporal data, performing time-based sorting, filtering, and analysis. IT professionals have full access to the language for the purpose of building special formulas, metrics, and more that can be made available in discovery applications.

Some of the most important EQL features include tight integration with search and navigation, rich analytical functionality, and processing efficiency, as well as familiar development experience.

Here's an example of a simple EQL statement:

```
RETURN Sales AS SELECT
AVG(FactSales_Amount) AS AverageSalesVolume,
SUM(FactSales_Amount) AS TotalSaleVolume,
GROUP BY DimDate_CalendarYear
```

An EQL statement starts with either DEFINE or RETURN. DEFINE doesn't return the result set. Rather, it creates the dataset as a temp table. A DEFINE statement is typically followed by a RETURN statement that consumes the result set. Endeca uses the DEFINE statement to create Views that could then be used to generate charts and other advanced visualization.

The statement then needs to have one or many SELECT elements, separated by comma. The SELECT clause is composed of an expression followed by an alias. Expressions are usually one or more attributes, operators, or functions such as summation or average, as you see in the previous example.

The GROUP BY clause specifies the method of aggregation. Other EQL capabilities include joining, sorting, paging, and filtering. There's an extensive reference library for EQL under Endeca Information Discovery Documentation that allows developers and users to learn more about EQL's capabilities.

Oracle Endeca Studio

Powered by Oracle Endeca Server, Oracle Endeca Studio is a highly interactive, component-based environment for building enterprise-class analytic applications. Endeca Studio is built on robust Web-based infrastructure technologies that enable the construction of analytical applications delivered through standard Web browsers.

Oracle Endeca Studio has adopted a component-based approach to build highly interactive analytical solutions. Through this framework, IT professionals can quickly prototype functionalities, expose them to business users, and then refine them to meet core business requirements and to achieve better alignment with business needs. This iterative approach provides the increased agility to rapidly deliver analytic applications. Through this approach, business users are able to access to all the information they need in a powerful yet easy-to-use analytical application. It also gives them the capability to explore the information in an intuitive manner through interactive search and advanced visualizations. As a result, business users obtain unprecedented visibility, analytic power, and business insight.

In the next section, we'll describe in more detail Oracle Endeca Information Discovery's analytic capabilities.

Exploration and Discovery

With Oracle Endeca Information Discovery, users can explore related data in an impromptu manner without having to predefine hierarchies. It enables organizations to uncover the root cause of a problem through intuitive navigation to uncover answers to unanticipated questions. Some of the noteworthy features for exploration and discovery include side-to-side BI, high-dimensional analysis, and text analytics.

Side-to-Side BI Drilling up and down in reports and dashboards are important features of standard Business Intelligence. However, with Oracle Endeca Information Discovery, users can drill "sideways" across data sources to discover how different parts of the business or industry correlate with each other. It adds a whole new dimension that enables users to discover connections and associations that they have never been able to establish before.

An Endeca application can have as many dimensions as needed, and each record in the data set can be tagged with zero, one, or more dimension values within each dimension.

Here's an example of how this works. A bike can be tagged with the "Mountain Bike" dimension value in the Product Category dimension, and with the "Italy" dimension value in the Country dimension. By using multiple dimensions to classify the Endeca records, the users can introduce the possibility for complex navigation queries across multiple dimensions.

High-Dimensional Analysis Oracle Endeca Information Discovery provides insight by allowing organizations to unify diverse data from inside and outside the enterprise including highly dimensioned data that was once considered incompatible, which would have been too costly to combine with traditional methods.

Dimension hierarchies allow developers to exercise a higher level of control over the number of follow-on queries that are presented to users as they navigate. A large flat dimension with many dimension values is too unwieldy to navigate. The user would be presented with too many potential follow-on queries.

The actual tagging of records with dimension values occurs when developers process source data into a set of Endeca Server Engine indices. Alternatively, a developer can set up the Endeca application to derive dimensions automatically from the source data's properties. This shortens the development time because it is not necessary to manually tag each of the components. However, the automatically derived dimensions are always flat. Hierarchical dimensions must be created manually in Developer Studio.

Text Analytics In order to gain insight into customer sentiment, competitive trends, current news trends, and other critical business information, Oracle Endeca Information Discovery explores and analyzes structured data with unstructured content. Unstructured content is free-form text that can come in a variety of forms from disparate data sources including tweets, Facebook updates, and other social media channels, product reviews from the Web, business documents in content

management systems, and text fields in traditional data warehouses. Oracle Endeca
Information Discovery leverages text analytics and natural language processing to
extract new facts and entities like people, location, and sentiment from text that can
be used as part of the analytic experience.

The Text Enrichment component requires the Lexalytics Salience Engine and a
properties file, in addition to the input source text to process. The Salience Engine
must be installed on the same machine as Integrator. For version requirements,
please check Oracle's documentation and installation guide. When installing the
Salience Engine, the developer needs to write down the path to the Salience Engine
data directory and the Salience Engine license file. The developer must specify these
paths when configuring the Text Enrichment component. The source input is the text
to be processed by the Salience Engine. Supported input sources include files,
database columns, and Integrator Acquisition System (IAS) record store data. Input
text must end sentences appropriately with appropriate punctuation. It is usually a
period, but question marks or exclamation points are also accepted. In addition, the
input file must be separated by spaces. If sentences do not end correctly and are not
spaced correctly, themes will not be extracted correctly.

Component Library

Oracle Endeca Studio provides a wide array of reusable analytical and visualization
components so that developers do not need to program and code analytical
applications from scratch. These components can be assembled and configured by
BI developers and analysts. Major component library capabilities include

- Ability to filter components such as navigation, search box, and range filters,
  which allow users to explore and refine the data in view

- Data visualization components to assist in analyzing complex information
  including charts, tables, cross-tabs, metrics bars, tag clouds, and maps

- Personalization components such as bookmarks that allow view
  customization and collaboration

- Layout and style components, including tabbed containers, a default
  application skin, and multiple page layout options

The standard components are fully extensible. Java developers can use the
Studio SDK to create custom components to meet additional business requirements.

The modular nature of the Endeca Studio implies that these analytic applications
are simple to manage, adapt, and extend. Granular layout and configuration control
enable users to manage and personalize their experiences with greater ease and
efficiency.

Administrative Control Panel

Another key component of Endeca Studio is the Administrative Control Panel. It enables administrators to manage and monitor the operational aspects of the application through an intuitive control panel. They can use this user interface to modify data source connections, monitor component and Oracle Endeca Server query performance, configure state and security settings, and control how data attributes are grouped and displayed throughout the application.

Endeca Studio supports role-based authorization and integrates with LDAP/ Active directory, NTLM, OpenSSO, and SiteMinder.

Last but not least, administrators can choose to set up multiple user communities that are customizable with different views. They can also allow users to create their own personalized pages.

Oracle Endeca Integration Suite

Oracle Endeca Integration Suite is a powerful solution for loading diverse information including unstructured and semistructured content into Oracle Endeca Server. Supporting a variety of data integration products, system connectors, and content enrichment libraries, this Integration Suite makes it possible for users to efficiently combine information from any source into a single integrated view. In addition, it also enables enrichment of the content using natural language processing and regular expression techniques that can be used to drive the navigation experience.

The Oracle Endeca Integration Suite includes the following components: Integrator, Text Enrichment and Sentiment Analysis, Integrator Acquisition System, and Open Interfaces and Connectors. The next sections provide more details on each of the components.

Integrator

Integrator is an ETL platform used for integrating and enriching enterprise data and content.

Integrator is used for data extraction, transformation, and loading when an enterprise ETL solution is not already in place or is not desired. It allows business professionals to create data integration processes that connect to a wide variety of source systems, including relational databases, file systems, and more. In addition, Integrator supports the ability to implement business rules that extract information from source systems and transform it into business knowledge in the Oracle Endeca Server in an easy-to-use environment.

If you've used tools such as Oracle Data Integrator (ODI) or Oracle Warehouse Builder (OWB), you are familiar with the concept of a graphical ETL tool. Endeca Integrator uses a version of the open-source CloverETL tool through OEM for this task. Using the Integrator, the users either import or create references to the source data, define metadata for it such as the column structure, then create mappings or "edges" between the source data and either transformation operators, or operators that load data into the Endeca Server.

There are a number of key benefits of Integrator. It reduces manual workload and time. It enables communication among incompatible systems and provides an optimized process for data interpretation. Moreover, it establishes a single and consistent process for business-critical data with increased development efficiency.

Text Enrichment and Sentiment Analysis

The text enrichment and sentiment analysis component extracts concepts, entities, and meanings from unstructured text fields in databases or other content systems for entirely new types of analysis.

It provides information extraction and summarization capabilities. Extracted information includes entities such as people, places, organizations, quotations, and themes. It also utilizes the Salience Engine from Lexalytics. Depending on the version of the Salience Engine purchased, the engine also provides the ability to extract sentiment at the document, entity, and theme levels.

The supported text enrichment features include Sentiment Analysis, Named Entities, Themes, Quotations, and Document Summary.

Integrator Acquisition System (IAS)

The integrator acquisition system is a collection of connectors used for extracting, enriching, and integrating unstructured content from network file systems, Web sites, and content management system repositories. The currently supported systems are EMC Documentum, EMC Documentum eRoom, FileNet P8, FileNet Document and Image Services, Interwoven TeamSite, Lotus Notes/Domino, Microsoft SharePoint, and OpenText LiveLink.

Integrator Acquisition System provides file system and Web crawling capabilities along with a set of connectors that enable crawling of content management systems.

Open Interfaces and Connectors

The open interfaces and connectors use the Oracle Endeca Server's open Web services API to enable direct data integration from industry-standard ETL tools, such as Informatica PowerCenter, Apache Hadoop distributions such as the Cloudera Distribution of Hadoop supported by Oracle on the Big Data Appliance, and SOA-based data integration services. This Web Services interface can be used by commercial ETL tools or from custom code to load data and to query the engine.

Endeca on Exalytics

Exalytics is the best solution for high-performance Business Intelligence on structured data. It is also the optimal solution for unstructured analytics. Endeca has been designed from the ground up to take advantage of this class of hardware, including features like multicore parallel query processing and in-memory storage and analytics. Exalytics is an optimal way for customers to obtain Endeca's capabilities in-house with all the standard benefits of an Oracle engineered system.

Here is a brief summary of the software components and hardware descriptions of Endeca on Exalytics.

Endeca software breakthroughs:

- Multicore parallel query evaluation

- In-memory columnar storage and dynamic cache

- Adaptive in-memory data mapping

- Embedded search indices

- Free-form search, exploration, and analysis

Exalytics-optimized hardware:

- Processor: 4 Intel Xeon E7-4870, 40 cores total

- Memory: 1 Terabyte DRAM

- Hard Disk: 3.6 Terabytes

The best-in-class software features of Oracle Endeca Information Discovery are greatly enhanced through the optimized hardware innovation from Oracle Exalytics. This combination gives Oracle customers unprecedented experience of an integrated solution with quick time-to-value.

Scalability and Load Balancing

It is important to design and architect the information discovery application for scalability and high availability. In order to do that, we need to look at server clustering design.

Important Cluster Concepts

In this section, we'll drill into a few key concepts with regard to an Endeca cluster. We'll introduce Cluster, the Leader Node, Follower Nodes, and the Cluster Coordinator.

A *cluster* is composed of a set of Oracle Endeca Servers, each of which is hosting a cluster node. All servers can serve query requests.

In a clustered environment, it is important to ensure adequate performance and ease of cluster configuration. As a result, it is recommended to configure a cluster with each Oracle Endeca Server running a single Dgraph process for the same data store as the Dgraph process hosted on each other's Oracle Endeca Server.

The *leader node* is a single Dgraph process in the cluster responsible for processing queries and for receiving updates to the data files and to the configuration.

This node is responsible for obtaining information about the latest versions of the data files and propagating this information to the follower nodes through the Cluster Coordinator.

When establishing a new cluster, the leader node is started first and then the follower nodes are added. The leader node has the following characteristics:

- Each cluster must have one and only one leader node.

- The leader node must have write access to the same shared file system on which the data files are stored and to which all follower nodes also have access.

- The Cluster Coordinator service must be running on the leader node.

- The entities outside the cluster (such as connectors in Endeca Integrator and components of Endeca Studio) must be able to access the Oracle Endeca Server that is hosting the Dgraph process for the leader node.

The leader node periodically receives full or incremental data file updates from Endeca Integrator. It also receives administration or configuration updates. It is the only node in the cluster that has access with write permissions to the on-disk representation of the index.

Once the leader node acquires access to the new version of the data files, it updates the data files, adds new information, and deletes information that has become obsolete. The Cluster Coordinator notifies all follower nodes, alerting them to start using the updated version of the data files. The follower nodes acquire read-only access to an updated version of the data files.

A *follower node* is a node in the cluster responsible for processing queries. The follower node does not update the data files and it has read-only access to their latest copy.

A follower node can be started after the leader node and the cluster coordinator have been started. The follower node has the following characteristics:

- Each cluster can have more than one follower node.

- Each follower node must have a unique name across the cluster. The name also must be a valid directory name. For example, characters such as slashes (/) are not allowed.

- All follower nodes must reference the host name and port of the cluster coordinator service.

- All follower nodes must have read-only access to the same shared file system on which the data files are stored. The leader node must have write access to the file system, as mentioned earlier.

During the process of acquiring access to the recently updated data files, both the follower and the leader nodes continue to serve queries. Each query is processed against a specific version of the data files that is available to a cluster node at any given time. Query processing performance may degrade as the follower nodes acquire read-only access to the updated data files.

Cluster coordinator is an entity that provides a mechanism for the nodes to communicate with each other. The cluster coordinator provides communication between the nodes in the cluster. The cluster coordinator is also used to notify the follower nodes about data updates and updates to the configuration.

Oracle Endeca Server Cluster Architecture

This section discusses Endeca cluster architecture in the development and production environments.

A simple single-node cluster configuration is a common starting point for development environment and it can be expanded by adding more nodes.

A Single-Node Cluster in the Development Environment In a development environment, the simplest version of a cluster may consist of just one server hosting a Dgraph process for a data store, thus representing a single node. This node is by definition the leader node. In a single-node cluster, the only node is considered the leader node by default.

When running a single Oracle Endeca Server, you are not required to have a cluster. Without the cluster services, having a single running Oracle Endeca Server is a valid configuration for starting in the development environment.

Figure 11-4 represents a single-node cluster in a development environment. The Oracle Endeca Server is installed and is hosting a single data store with the Dgraph process running. The Oracle Endeca Server is receiving query requests from Endeca Studio or any other front-end application that is powered by the Oracle Endeca Server. The Oracle Endeca Server's host and port are included in the configuration for connectors from Endeca Integrator, which can send various types of data and updates to the Oracle Endeca Server.

The Dgraph process designated as the leader node must have write access to a shared file system on which the data for the specific data store is maintained. All other follower nodes added later must have read access to this file system.

Finally, the cluster is managed by the cluster coordinator. In a single-node cluster, the cluster coordinator service runs on the same server on which the Dgraph process is running.

A Multiple-Node Cluster in the Development Environment In the development environment, many cluster configurations are possible. It depends on the requirements

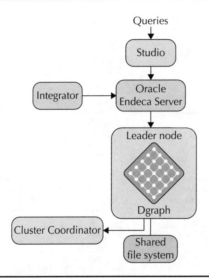

FIGURE 11-4. *Endeca single-node cluster in a development environment*

for the specific application. For example, while a single leader node is always required, the number of additional follower nodes may vary.

Figure 11-5 represents a possible multiple-node cluster in a development environment. The data flow in a multinode set up is as follows.

First, the queries are sent to the load balancer that is configured in front of several servers hosting Endeca Studio instances. The Studio instances point to a second load balancer between Endeca Studio and the Endeca Server cluster.

Endeca Integrator is configured to communicate with the host and port of the Oracle Endeca Server hosting the leader node to ensure a point of communication for sending data and updates.

All nodes in the cluster (Dgraph processes) communicate with each other through the cluster coordinator. The cluster coordinator service must be running on the leader node.

All nodes in the cluster have access to a shared file system on which data files for the data store are stored.

A Multiple-Node Cluster in the Production Environment   When you move to a production environment, you can duplicate a multinode development cluster as described in the preceding section and Figure 11-5.

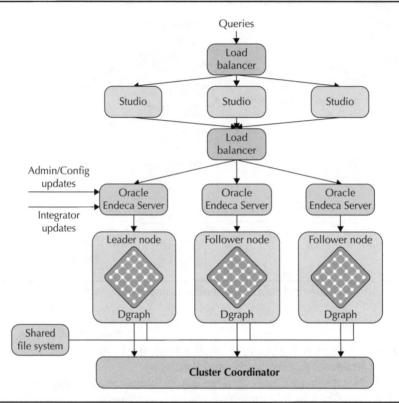

FIGURE 11-5. *Endeca multiple-node cluster in a development environment*

Unifying Diverse Content Sets

Business and IT professionals are in a perpetual dilemma of how to define business requirements for the BI applications.

The business can never be certain which questions will matter. There are too many variables to work out all the combinations, and the business environment is prone to changes that cannot be anticipated fully.

IT professionals are not able to effectively define a data model because the diversity of the source schemas makes conforming the data to a single model difficult and time-consuming especially when the sources include unstructured data. With the rapid change of requirements, the schemas change frequently. It requires costly and time-consuming rework. In short, it is difficult to answer unanticipated questions through predefined reports and models since answers often lead to new questions.

Oracle Endeca Information Discovery solves this constant struggle.

Endeca Differentiator

To begin with, Oracle Endeca Information Discovery takes a facet-based approach to represent the information. It stores each record or document as a set of facets. This leads users to accept the fact that records and documents have different numbers of fields, tags, and extracted terms, where some are shared but not all. It also enables the maintaining of the relationships in the source systems, whether native or created at index time. Taking a faceted approach to the information enables the integration of disparate data sources and structures, or the lack thereof.

In addition, Endeca establishes dimensions across very different data assets on the basis of the facets. The metarelational architecture enables users to establish all of the dimensional relationships that exist on the basis of the facets.

Moreover, every view of the information is generated on this basis. It includes an analysis of the facet relationships in the records and documents, and the dimensional relationships across them. However, every view is also calculated dynamically to take into account the unique set of dimensions the user selected in a unique order in addition to any business constraints such as security for that user or recommendations for that user and view.

Furthermore, the adaptive capability embraces the dimensionality in real-world data and content. That means no more siloed applications; no more "I am feeling lucky" searches; and no more waiting for IT to build the new view of the information the business users want. This adaptive capability closes the information access gap, providing every view to support every step in every user scenario.

Industry Use Cases

In this section, we'll examine a few case studies of how companies from different industries are leveraging Oracle Endeca Information Discovery to gain unique business insights.

Use Case 1: Product Quality Discovery and Analysis

This first use case is about how a discrete manufacturer uses Oracle Endeca Information Discovery to conduct product quality discovery and analysis.

Before Endeca, this company was experiencing a number of pain points. To begin with, product failure data couldn't be incorporated into improvement processes because it was in unstructured (text) format. There were significant difficulties in prioritizing manufacturing fixes due to the inability to quickly measure the risk of potential warranty exposures. Moreover, they faced inadequate information and traceability to reclaim warranty-related costs from suppliers.

So they looked to Endeca for earlier detection of warranty or quality concerns. They leveraged Endeca to conduct unlimited exploration across all dimensions of the source data systems. It helps them with increased supplier recovery as well as reduced detection-to-correction time and warranty-related costs. As a result, product launch risks are also reduced significantly.

Endeca allows this company to correlate structured product and supplier data with unstructured warranty claim information. This effectively reduces the issue discovery effort and time to correction.

Use Case 2: Insurance Claims Discovery and Analysis
The second use case is with a leading insurance provider.

In the past, their claims management system notes couldn't be incorporated into analysis because they were in unstructured (text) format. As a result, it was difficult to identify fraudulent claims without the ability to correlate information between different sources. Their existing BI tools were not designed properly to be used by front-line claims analysts with domain expertise.

They laid out a number of objectives while embarking on a product selection and comparison process, including Oracle Endeca Information Discovery. To begin with, they were looking for earlier and more accurate detection of fraudulent insurance claims. In addition, the new system also required unlimited exploration across all dimensions of the source data systems. It also needed to have a user-friendly and search-oriented interface. All of these features were aimed at reducing overall claims cost and increasing customer satisfaction.

They selected Oracle Endeca Information Discovery because it meets all of the desired requirements and objectives. With Endeca, notes in their claims management system are finally available alongside their structured data sources, supporting fraud detection efforts and improving call-handling quality.

Use Case 3: Criminal Intelligence Discovery and Analysis
The third use case pertains to law enforcement agencies and intelligence agencies, as well as city, state, and national government.

For law enforcement, time is of the essence to prevent and disperse crimes as they unfold. Information can be useless by the time it is cleaned, processed, and loaded into a data warehouse. In addition, reduction in operating budget and operations staff while activity levels are increasing limits their ability to quickly perform crime analysis. Moreover, activity history is spread across several different solutions, agencies, and data formats. They face significant challenges to manage increases in activities for major public events.

What they need is a solution that will allow them to enable advance detection and crime prevention, to reduce operating costs and increase intelligence visibility, as well as the ability of efficient deployment within first-line operations.

Endeca improves the existing intelligence research capability. As a result, it delivers a better service to the intelligence community. The contextual navigation offers law enforcement analysts visibility into critical information that was unattainable until now, enabling greater discovery for better intelligence decision making.

Use Case 4: Social Media and Sentiment Discovery and Analysis

The last use case is about social media and sentiment analysis that pertains to companies selling products or services directly to consumers as well as organizations and agencies that take their message directly to people.

The influence of social media has an increasing impact to either help a brand and reputations or create tremendous damage that has significant financial ramifications within a short period of time.

However, companies need to justify and refine budgets for social media campaigns and activity. It has also been traditionally difficult to figure out the best ways to capture, integrate, and analyze this growing amount of unstructured social data. Furthermore, most analytic tools are too generic to address key social media analytic requirements.

In order to defend brand and reputation in a cost-effective manner, companies need to gain deeper insight into overall social media impact and campaigns, to gauge social media sentiment on new products released, and to correlate consumer behavior with various new product and service offerings.

Endeca allows companies to measure the effectiveness of their campaigns, both online and offline, while improving and protecting their brands.

Hands-On with Endeca

This section provides an overview of how to set up Endeca Information Discovery and how to develop and deploy applications with the Endeca Information Discovery platform.

Installation and Configuration

Here are the basic instructions on how to install the platform including the installation order and how to install Endeca Information Discovery Quick Start.

Installation Order

Following the recommended order of installation helps to minimize component dependencies. Endeca recommends that components should be installed in this order:

1. **Oracle Endeca Server**   The last step in this installation lets you start the Oracle Endeca Server. Note that you can start the Oracle Endeca Server without creating an Endeca data store.

2. **Oracle Endeca Integrator**   After installing, open Integrator to verify that it was installed correctly.

3. **Oracle Endeca Studio**   After installing, log in to Studio to verify the installation. Use a created Endeca data store to provide the data source.

4. **Oracle Endeca Integrator Server (optional)**   After installing, use a browser to access the Integrator Server home page and log in.

Installing Endeca Information Discovery Quick Start

For the Quick Start, you run a combined installer that installs all of the Oracle Endeca Information Discovery modules. You can download the Oracle Endeca Information Discovery Quick Start files from the Oracle Software Cloud. Once you have downloaded the Oracle Endeca Information Discovery All-in-One Installer, you can begin installing the Oracle Endeca Information Discovery modules. The installer adds an Oracle Endeca Information Discovery entry to the Start menu with these subentries:

- **Integrator**   Starts Integrator

- **Start Studio Server**   Starts Studio

- **Stop Studio Server**   Stops Studio

- **Studio**   Opens the Studio home page in your browser (if Studio is running)

- **Uninstall Oracle Endeca Information Discovery**   Uninstalls Oracle Endeca Information Discovery

The installer also adds an Oracle Endeca Server entry to the Start menu with these subentries:

- **Start Endeca Server**   Starts Endeca Server

- **Stop Endeca Server**   Stops Endeca Server

Besides these entries, the installer adds a link to Integrator in the Start menu's Jump List of programs.

You load the Quick Start application data using Integrator.

The Quick Start application demonstrates Studio in action, using sales and product data from a fictitious bicycle manufacturer.

You can iteratively deploy applications similar to the Quick Start application, incorporating data from multiple disparate sources into easily consumable, interactive, online experiences.

Featuring familiar visualizations, such as charts, tag clouds, and tables, in addition to its patented search and Guided Navigation technology, Studio provides visibility and better decision-making capabilities to a broad range of business users.

To experience Studio, use the Quick Start application to analyze the performance of resellers and products across a wide variety of dimensional attributes.

Developing an Endeca Application

Developing an Endeca implementation can be broken down into four major tasks. The four tasks are the following:

1. Making initial implementation decisions

2. Setting up the environment

3. Building and testing the data back end

4. Building and testing a front-end Web application

Making Initial Implementation Decisions

There are two decisions you should make up front before you begin any development on your Endeca implementation. These two decisions are: deciding where you will get your source data and choosing a Web application server.

Getting Source Data   The first step in any Endeca project is to locate your source data and answer a series of questions. The questions you should answer are

■ Where does my raw source data come from?

■ Do I have multiple data sources?
   If so, and the joins between the sources are simple, you can have the Endeca do them. If the joins are complex, you should do them in your database management system before importing the data into Endeca. A join combines records from two or more tables in a relational database.

■ What data constitutes a record in my Endeca application?
   For example, an Endeca record could be a movie (encompassing all media formats), or it could be a movie in a particular format such as DVD, videotape, or laser disc.

■ Which source properties do I need to maintain for display and search in my Endeca implementation?

■ Which source properties should be excluded?

■ What dimensions do I want to use for my navigation controls?
   In general, you should have a column (or field) in your source data for each dimension that you want to include in your Endeca implementation, although you can also add dimensions to your records as they are processed.

■ What transformations must be done to standardize the properties and property values in your source data records for consistency?

In the previous example, we looked at data sources including sales transactions from the enterprise data warehouse, product information in a product master data hub with supplemental product description in XML format, employee information in an HCM application data store, and online reviews from the eCommerce site in the flat file output. Understanding the format, structure, and mapping of each of the data sources will help determine the data store and design the data integrator flows. The good news is that a developer does not have to have all the information at hand to start this process. Endeca supports an iterative development process that allows developers to incorporate new data sources and refresh the Studio applications after the addition.

Endeca supports limited data cleansing. If you have an existing data cleansing infrastructure, it may be more advantageous to use those facilities instead.

After evaluating your source data, you can choose a mechanism for controlling your environment.

Choosing a Web Application Server   The Web application server you choose determines the versions of the Presentation API you can use to communicate with the Endeca Server Engine.

As a result, you should decide which application server you want to use before you begin implementing your front-end Web application.

The simplest choice to make is to use the same Web application server you used during the basic Endeca installation because you know that server is already set up and functioning properly.

Setting Up the Environment

After making the initial implementation decisions, you can begin preparing the environment. Environment preparation includes

■ Preparing your source data

■ Creating a supporting directory structure

■ Setting up your Web application server

A production environment may also include such things as load-balancing switches, redundant machines, and firewalls. These are advanced topics that are not covered in this chapter.

Preparing Source Data   The source data should be prepared as much as possible before being processed by Endeca. To prepare the source data, follow these steps:

   1.   Perform any standardization required in your database management system.

2. Implement any joins required in your database management system.

3. Output your source data in a format that is compatible with the Endeca Information Transformation Layer.

Some examples of data preparation might include

■ Defining a primary key for each record

■ Concatenating fields to transform into a new attribute or field

■ Creating derived attributes from one or many existing attributes

The format of source data with which it is easiest to work is a two-dimensional and delimited format where each row corresponds to a record and each column corresponds to a source property.

Creating a Directory Structure   An Endeca implementation relies on a specific directory structure for such things as source data, working files, and log files.

Setting Up Your Web Application Server   Follow the vendor's instructions to set up and configure your Web application server. If you are using the same Web application server that you used during the basic Endeca installation, then this step is already completed.

Building and Testing the Data Back End
After making the initial implementation decisions and setting up the environment, the next step is to begin development.

Oracle recommends that you start with developing your data processing back end using the Endeca Information Transformation Layer. The result of transformation development is a running instance of an Endeca Server Engine, populated with indices built from the source data.

Once you have a running Endeca Engine, you can view the engine's data using one of the sample Web applications included with the Endeca distribution. These sample Web applications allow you to view, test, and debug the data processing back end before developing a front-end Web application.

Decoupling the development of the data processing back end from that of the front-end Web application has two major benefits. It allows for early testing and debugging of the indices stored by the Endeca Server Engine. In addition, it increases development efficiency because you can spread development tasks among multiple developers.

Building and Testing a Front-End Web Application

Developing a front-end Web application to an Endeca implementation is similar to building a traditional Web application.

Connecting the Web application to the Endeca Server Engine is a simple matter of making calls to one of the Application Development APIs to request, retrieve, and manipulate the data contained in the Engine.

The Application Development APIs could be one of the following: Presentation APIs, RAD Toolkit for ASP.NET, Content Assembler APIs, or XQuery.

Performance Testing and Tuning   Performance testing and tuning are critical to developing an Endeca implementation that behaves well and provides end users with a satisfactory experience.

There are a number of factors that affect performance, including the design of the Endeca implementation, the infrastructure it is running on, and the way the application has used and configured the various Endeca features.

Oracle strongly recommends that you incorporate performance testing and tuning into your overall development schedule.

For more information on performance testing and performance tuning, please turn to the Endeca documentation on the Oracle Web site.

CHAPTER
12

Big Data Governance

Data governance is critical to getting the most usage and value from the information from data assets at an enterprise that is trusted by key decision makers. Enterprises have gone from being local self-contained organizations to global-complex networked organizations. Often multiple business functions are being performed by partners, so data governance becomes even more critical. And as more digitization has created new data as well as more details for existing data, data governance takes on a whole new meaning in the new world of Big Data with dimensions of extreme volume, wide variety, and high velocity.

The following example highlights how lack of proper governance can create disaster.

This one is a rather well-known case where *Mars Climate Orbiter* crashed and resulted in a loss of $328 million. *Mars Climate Orbiter* began the planned orbital insertion maneuver on September 23, 1999 at 09:00:46 UTC. *Mars Climate Orbiter* went out of radio contact when the spacecraft passed behind Mars at 09:04:52 UTC, 49 seconds earlier than expected, and communication was never re-established. This was due to ground-based computer software that produced output in non-SI units of pound-seconds (lbf×s) instead of the metric units of newton-seconds (N×s) specified in the contract between NASA and Lockheed. The spacecraft encountered Mars at an improperly low altitude, causing it to incorrectly enter the upper atmosphere and disintegrate due to atmospheric stresses. *Mars Reconnaissance Orbiter* has since completed most of the intended objectives for this mission.[1] This illustrates how lack of data governance can result in significant financial loss.

As defined by the Data Management Association (DAMA), data governance is the exercise of authority, control, and shared decision-making (planning, monitoring, and enforcement) over the management of data assets.[2] Data governance involves building the roles, processes, tools, and supported discipline necessary to implement accountability for the management of data assets and resources.

In this chapter we will look at:

■ Key elements of enterprise data governance

■ How does Big Data impact enterprise data governance?

■ Industry-specific use cases

■ How does Big Data impact data governance roles?

■ An approach to implementing Big Data governance

---

[1] http://en.wikipedia.org/wiki/Mars_Climate_Orbiter
[2] "The DAMA Guide to the Data Management Body of Knowledge," DAMA-DMBOK Guide, 2009.

Key Elements of Enterprise Data Governance

The following sections describe some of the key elements of enterprise data governance.

Business Outcome

The most important driving factor in enterprise data governance is to clearly understand business outcome and establish the business value of the data in-scope of governance. This will drive the governance policies that are fit-for-business-purpose as well as implementation of those policies. One should establish the business outcome and value delivered by the data initiatives across four high-level dimensions:

- Revenue

- Cost

- Risk

- Brand

The value against these dimensions can be quantitative, which is preferred, but in case quantitative metrics are not feasible, being able to assess qualitative value is the next best option.

Along with the business outcome and value, one must establish the business owners for the data governance as well. If the data collected has ambiguous ownership of governance, data governance can't be implemented to its full potential. Also, one should establish not only a business owner but also a technical owner who may own the execution of ongoing data governance policies.

Information Lifecycle Management

Information Lifecycle Management (ILM) stands for management of information from the moment it is created, stored, moved, and used until it is erased from all media at an enterprise. The key activities of ILM are

- Acquisition

- Classification/metadata generation

- Storage and retrieval

- Access/distribution

- Analysis and presentation

- Security

- Change control

- Retirement and disposition

All ILM activities and policies need to be developed as part of the enterprise data governance.

Regulatory Compliance and Risk Management

Lack of data governance can pose a higher level of risk for industries that are heavily regulated, such as any Business-to-Consumer (B2C) enterprises (examples: retail, financial services) and Business-to-Business (B2B) enterprises (examples: manufacturing, financial services, defense-related industries, oil and gas industries).

A number of regulations mandate the privacy of consumer data that retailers collect. The retailers must design and control access to and usage of such sensitive data about consumers. If proper care is not taken, privacy laws may be broken, which involves financial risks as well as branding/public relations risks. If a retailer cannot protect consumer data, consumers may not only stop sharing their information with the retailer but also stop doing any business with that retailer. Here are a few other regulations:

- Basel III in financial services

- Health Insurance Portability and Accountability Act (HIPAA) in healthcare

- Sarbanes-Oxley Act for financial reporting, operations, and assets

- Office of Foreign Asset Control (OFAC) published SDN (a list of blocked individuals known as Specially Designated Nationals that companies must verify their customers' identity against

- Federal Trade Commission, 167 CFR Part 210—defines rules for record retention

Metadata Management

Metadata is essential to the success of any enterprise data governance. Metadata serves as a dictionary that everyone uses to make sense of the data that is collected, processed, stored, managed, and used. Metadata is created at every step of the information lifecycle, and all this metadata must be governed properly.

There are various types of metadata that needs to be managed:

■ Business

■ Technical

■ Process

■ Application

■ Metadata model

Data Quality Management

Data quality must be ensured so that the information in reports and the analytics are *trusted* by the business users. The key data-quality dimensions are

■ Correctness (fit-for-business-purpose)

■ Consistency

■ Uniqueness

■ Content in context

Data quality should always be thought of as consistently meeting the needs of running the business effectively—quality of data that is fit-for-business-purpose. There are three types of business rules to solve the data quality issue:

■ Corrective

■ Detective

■ Prescriptive

Master and Reference Data Management

Master data is the business definition of the enterprise that uniquely defines the customers, partners, suppliers, products, units, packaging, and so on, and is critical to running the business. Master data is the data that has been cleansed, rationalized, and integrated into the enterprise-wide "system of record" for all core business activities.[3] *Reference data* is a set of standard internal and external code sets that is essential to standardizing data quality for many entities, including master data.

---

[3] Alex Berson and Larry Dubov, *Master Data Management and Customer Data Integration for a Global Enterprise*. McGraw-Hill, 2007.

Without proper master data management, it would be quite a challenge to run a business.

Data Security and Privacy Management

Securing every piece of sensitive information must be an integral part of data management strategy at every enterprise. Security can be achieved by establishing security standards, classifying sensitive data that needs to be secured, providing administration and authentication of access and usage of the data, and establishing audit procedures to detect and fix any lapse in security.

The privacy of certain sensitive data must be protected to prevent it from falling into the wrong hands as well as to ensure that the policies are established for the permissible usage of such sensitive private data. Privacy is defined as the "right to be left alone."[4] Data governance needs to establish policies for privacy of such sensitive data in the data repository as applicable, and it must conform to established enterprise privacy policies and practices.

Some examples of privacy protection policies are

- The USA Patriot Act's KYC (Know Your Customer) provision

- Gramm-Leach-Bliley Act—protect consumers' personal financial information

- UK Financial Services Act

- DNC compliance

- Consumer Proprietary Network Information (CPNI) compliance

- HIPPA

- European Union Data Protection Directive[5]

- Japanese Protection for Personal Information Act

- Federal Trade Commission, 16 CFR Part 314—safeguarding customer information

Business Process Alignment

The values from data are the insights that can be used to solve ad-hoc one-time problems, such as insights used to refine three-year marketing strategy, as well as insights that can be used on a day-to-day basis, such as online price optimization, driving daily prices and personalization to a customer level. Useful data and insights for tactical and operational activities must be integrated at the business process

---

[4] Louis Brandeis and Samuel Warren, "The Right to Privacy," 4 *Harvard Law Review* 193 (1890).

[5] For more countries, refer to Sunil Soares, *Big Data Governance: An Emerging Imperative*. MC Press, 2013.

level. These values can be used to automate the decision-making process as much as possible using workflow and business rules to reduce human intervention and potential errors. For example, weather data, traffic data, and consumer usage patterns across geographic areas can be used to maximize sales by proactively moving the right inventories to the right geographic area, for example, to move A/C units to forecasted extremely hot regions ahead of time, and automate this process that cuts across planning, forecasting, supply chain logistics, inventory management, pricing, and promotion, saving precious time.

The integration challenges of such insights into business processes are both technical as well as people-related. Data quality and business rules must be governed so that the assumptions as well as the context used to produce the insights are constantly assessed to see if they are still valid. If the context and assumptions are not valid any more, which can happen because market conditions have changed or customer tastes have changed, and so on, the analytics and underlying models will not produce the desired results, and if this problem is not detected in time, it can prove disastrous for the enterprise. The best option is to periodically re-assess the models, and if necessary, redo them.

How Does Big Data Impact Enterprise Data Governance?

Imagine that you reach home and your partner is really angry with you. Before you can say anything, you are shown a marketing letter from your favorite retailer MartForAll and confronted with "Who did you buy the washer and dryer for? I now see they are offering discounts on other kitchen appliances? Who did you buy this for? It wasn't for us." And you have no clue what your partner is talking about. We will see later how this can happen.

Big Data is not a solution; it is not a market, not even a particular technology. Big Data is the *datafication* of everything—every activity in business, government, and even private life is now digitized and stored and can be analyzed. Our thoughts and feelings are captured in Twitter, Facebook, blogs, and status updates; our keystrokes and mouse movements are captured and analyzed; the smallest movements of jet engines and mobile phones in sensor logs, and even fast-changing activities in marketing and product design or stock trading activities every millisecond, are captured. But what is the value of all this data? And how do you capture the value from data and make it work for you? In order to understand this, let's look at the data world we live in.

Modeled Data vs. Raw Data

The world of enterprise data as we have been using and managing it is primarily *modeled data*. For years, we have modeled the data to meet business requirements, using transactional models for transactional business applications such as Enterprise

Resource Planning, Supply Chain Management, Customer Relationship Management, and Supplier Relationship Management. Also we have developed data models for reporting and analytics to implement data warehouses as well as data marts. And accordingly, we have developed governance policies to ensure that this data is trusted and is of high quality and fit-for-business-purpose. When we go through the data-modeling process, we are building certain relationships and business rules into the model as well. Since models are predesigned, we are not able to see data patterns that were not built into the model.

Now there is another data world that has been emerging and growing rapidly; we can call it the *raw data world*. In this world data is captured as it is created and does not go through any modeling process first, thereby providing a faster, flexible, dynamically organized data repository. Such data is stored in Hadoop and NoSQLdb technology using key-value pairs and other flexible data formats to store, manage, access, and analyze this data. This allows storage of many types or varieties of data in the same repository, and this provides huge flexibility, reduces the time to value, and allows for learning through discovery and experimentation at a large scale. In the raw data world, data governance is rarely built in. Since data is in the raw form, data patterns can be discovered and non-obvious data relationships and associations can be found; some call it valuable signals that businesses can leverage. Later we will discuss how we can still implement data governance and preserve the ability to find useful signals in data.

Gartner describes the Big Data world in terms of Volume, Variety, and Velocity. We have been good at handling huge amounts of data in data warehouses, but the Big Data volume is what the conventional technology is not able to handle, due to the other two Vs (Variety and Velocity). Variety refers to structured data plus unstructured and semistructured data. The volumes of data in consideration can't be handled by current architected infrastructure, which is designed to handle modeled data. The following table lists some key attributes of both types of data.

Modeled Data	Raw Data
Standardize, control, and automate processes	Discover, form, and test hypotheses
Information is preorganized and modeled for intended use as defined by business requirements	Information is organized at the moment of use, flexible to use for multiple requirements that are not predefined
Operates on relational and dimensional tables	Operates on key attribute-value pairs
Structured access through predefined language and interfaces such as SQL	Data access is via MapReduce process at the point of use, uses a number of interfaces

Modeled Data	Raw Data
Designed to run the business with stability and predictability, but takes much effort and a long time to change	Designed to provide agile flexible capabilities that have the potential to change the business
Takes a long time for forming and testing hypotheses and experimentation	Faster for forming and testing hypotheses and experimentation
Less noisy data	More noise in the data
Modeled analytics—slice/dice dimensional SQL query, reporting and analytics	Discovery and exploratory analytics using various languages and tools

Bringing these two worlds together is what allows the Big Data world to deliver a unique business outcome. For example, a food company might suddenly ask, "Do the cooking videos we post to YouTube increase in-store sales?" With a raw data technology like Hadoop and NoSQLdb, the company doesn't have to build the model first. Instead, they bring in YouTube viewing and in-store sales data, plus customer demographics and profile data, and begin to experiment with it.

Suppose our food company discovers that when more people watch their YouTube videos, then the company's sales go up. They now want to track this relationship on a regular basis in a marketing dashboard, powered by a data warehouse and/or data marts in the modeled data world. But then, the company wonders, "Is this just a correlation? Did we lower our prices at the same time? Did our competitors raise theirs? Is that the true cause of the sales spike?" Now they want to take marketing campaign, loyalty card, and pricing data from the gold-standard systems in the modeled data world into the raw data world for further exploration. And this allows them to potentially change the way they do business with their customers, partners, and suppliers. Bringing these two worlds together accelerates a company's rise to the next level of best practice, creating competitive advantage and operational effectiveness. These two data worlds are not competing with one another—they are not two ways to do the same thing; they are each part of the way to do something entirely new. So they are complementary. From a data governance perspective, it creates a unique situation.

In contrast, in the modeled data world, one would spend a lot of time building the model for one experiment and analyze the result, and then change the model to do the second experiment, and potentially change the model again for the next one. In the raw data world, the engineering activities such as modeling and ETL/integration/quality processes are done when someone is ready to use the data and do the necessary engineering that is fit for the usage, thus giving flexibility as well as speed to insight and action. This kind of flexibility and fast response dramatically cut the time and effort needed to form and test hypotheses and run hundreds and thousands of experiments in a short period. Months and weeks can be reduced to days and hours. The business benefit is tremendous agility and high-quality business decisions and business outcome. And then a completely new phenomenon occurs—business starts asking new questions and is not afraid that it will take a long time to get an answer, and is not afraid of failure since a new experiment can be done to correct the failure quickly. And business develops this new habit of experimenting and refining decision making quickly through the learning process. That is the game changer in the new world of Big Data—all data is used to make faster and better business decisions.

The two types of data together can provide tremendous value through discovery, analysis, slice-dice, and reporting. It is the discovery process on unfiltered raw data with the right business context that can lead to discovery of hidden new patterns, ideas, anomalies, signals, and reasons for what has happened, and this can lead to predictive analytics to get better business outcome. This discovery can lead to continuous experimentation to validate new hypotheses, and related data transformation can continuously contribute to various interesting and relevant data sets in the process modeled world.

Types of Big Data

What does this Big Data world look like? There are three types of Big Data from the perspective of how it gets created: human-generated data, machine-to-machine (M2M)–generated data, and process-generated data.

Human-Generated Data

Human-generated data represents data created by actions of human beings, such as human-entered data on computers, the Web, social media, e-mails, scans of paper documents, recording of voices, music, transaction data, and big transaction data (utility billing records, call data records, healthcare claims, and so on). Most human-generated data has been structured, but the volume and variety of semistructured and unstructured data are growing rapidly due to the digitization of almost everything.

Human-generated Big Data does need to be governed. Most of our existing data governance policies, governance processes, and governance organizations are designed for structured and semistructured data. We need to rethink how we govern the human-generated unstructured raw Big Data from the point of view of metadata, data quality, privacy, and access rights, internal as well as external security threats, and lifecycle management principles, including retention rules.

Machine-to-Machine (M2M)–Generated Data

M2M data is the data generated by a device that is designed to capture an event and transmit that information about the event over a wired/wireless network to other devices or applications to translate the captured event information into meaningful information that can be analyzed and acted on. McKinsey called this phenomenon the *Internet of Things (IoT)*.[6]

In this article the McKinsey team breaks down this phenomenon into two categories:

- **Information and Analysis**   In this category there are three applications:

  - Tracking behavior: Examples are presence-based advertising, payments based on location of consumers, and inventory and supply chain monitoring and management.

  - Enhanced situational awareness: Example: Sniper detection using the direction of sound to locate the shooter.

  - Sensor-driven decision analytics: Examples are oil site planning with 3D visualization and simulation, and continuous monitoring of chronic diseases to help doctors determine best treatments.

- **Automation and Control**

  - Process optimization: Example: Maximization of lime kiln throughput via wireless sensors, and continuous, precise adjustments in manufacturing lines.

  - Optimized resources consumption: Examples: Smart meters and energy grids that match loads and generation capacity in order to reduce costs; data center management to optimize energy, storage, and processor utilization.

  - Complex autonomous systems: Examples: Collision avoidance systems to sense objects and automatically apply brakes, and cleanup of hazardous material through the use of swarms of robots.

McKinsey Global Institute[7] has estimated the following potential economic impact by 2025 by IoT applications, as shown in Table 12-1.

In all these categories and examples, data governance is a key enabler to achieving the desired business outcome. The Internet of things generates an enormous amount of data which, with other data, analytics, and machines, can yield substantial business benefits. Improper data value, or meaning or tolerance or units or standards or even in the wrong context, can create very different undesirable and costly outcomes.

---

[6] Michael Chui, Markus Loffier, and Roger Roberts, "The Internet of Things," *McKinsey Quarterly* March 2012, https://www.mckinseyquarterly.com/The_Internet_of_Things_2538

[7] Disruptive technologies: Advances that will transform life, business, and the global economy, McKinsey Global Institute, May 2013.

Sized Applications of Mobile Internet	Potential Economic Impact in 2025 ($ in trillions, annually)	Potential Productivity or Value Gains in 2025
Healthcare	1.1–2.5	10–20% cost reduction in chronic disease treatment through remote health monitoring; 80–100% reduction in drug counterfeiting and 0.5–1.0 hour time saved per day by nurses
Manufacturing	0.9–2.3	2.5–5.0% saving in operating costs, including maintenance and input efficiencies
Utility - Electricity	0.2–0.5	2.0–4.0% reduction in demand peaks in the grid, reduction of total load on grid and operating/maintenance savings and shorter outage time through automated meters
Urban Infrastructure	0.1–0.3	10–20% reduction in average travel time through traffic and congestion control, 10–20% reduction in water consumption and leaks with smart meters and demand control, and 10–20% reduction in the cost of waste handling
Security	0.1–0.2	4–5% crime reduction through improved surveillance
Resource Extraction	0.1–0.2	5–10% saving in operating costs from productivity gains
Agriculture	~0.1	10–20% increase in yields from precision application of fertilizer and irrigation
Retail	0.02–0.10	1.5–2.0% increased sales
Vehicles	~0.05	25% reduction in cost of vehicle damage from collision avoidance and increased security

TABLE 12-1. *Potential Economic Impact by 2025 by IoT Applications*

The following types of devices generate this enormous amount of data:

- Smart phones (geolocation data, any sensor data)

- Handheld devices used by various industries such as manufacturing floors

- Robots

- RFIDs

- Geolocation devices

- Sensors used in various industries such as automotive, transportation, oil and gas, and healthcare

- ATMs, vending machines, cameras

- Biometric devices

M2M data is exploding and represents opportunities everywhere to reduce cost, increase revenue, and reduce risks. If governance is not designed into the M2M data lifecycle right from the beginning, the benefits may not be realized. One must assess the type of M2M data that is subjected to privacy laws, such as location data generated by smartphones of consumers or RFID data generated by patient monitoring. Since a lot of M2M data is transmitted over wireless networks, there are security risks if the data is not encrypted and properly protected. If we are dealing with devices that can be programmed over the network, the security issue becomes even more serious. Also, appropriate attention needs to be paid to the metadata of M2M while integrating and analyzing the data, especially to the units and semantics/metadata of what the data is all about. Security must be looked at since this data mostly travels over networks. Any supervisory control and data acquisition (SCADA) network should be protected from cyber attacks.[8]

Organizations should seriously start developing governance process and policies now in order to govern the data generated by M2M interactions.

Process-Generated Data

Data is generated by business processes as well as all subprocesses that are used in enterprises through logs of day-to-day operations. Data is also generated as part of BPM (Business Process Management) and/or BAM (Business Activity Monitoring) applications. Such data has either been just residing in logs or has been looked at minimally. This raw data created via processes holds tremendous insight into how an enterprise runs; sort of a log book of its heartbeats and blood circulation that now, with Big Data technology, can be discovered, analyzed, and benefited from.

---

[8] For more information, refer to Sunil Soares, *Big Data Governance: An Emerging Imperative.* MC Press, 2013.

Applying Data Governance to Big Data

The goals of Big Data governance are to:

- Define, approve, and communicate Big Data strategies, policies, standards, architecture, procedures, and metrics

- Track and enforce regulatory compliance and conformance to Big Data policies, Big Data standards, Big Data architecture and procedures

- Sponsor, track, and oversee the delivery of Big Data management projects and services to deliver the intended business outcome

- Manage and resolve Big Data–related quality issues

- Understand and promote the value of Big Data assets and related governance

The best way to apply data governance to Big Data is to take a look at what elements of enterprise data governance we should focus on and what situations it applies to:

- **Scenario 1**: Access and usage are limited to one data source of raw only.

- **Scenario 2**: One or more sources of data are combined in raw only.

- **Scenario 3**: One or more sources of raw data are blended or integrated with modeled data.

Let's take an example to walk through these three scenarios. Take the case of the Dough family.

Husband and father John Dough:

- Forty-three years old

- College graduate in math and MBA; executive at a bank, making $120K

- Happily married to Jane for 12 years

- Does not use technology gizmos much, shops in person, very little online shopping

- Does not yet have a Facebook account, Klout score is very low, has one valid e-mail address (just one), loves football and no other sports

- Used to be a champion swimmer in college

Wife and mother Jane Dough:

■ Thirty-nine years old

■ College graduate in history and nursing

■ At-home mom now, taking care of 3-year old Matthew and 8-year old Emma, was formerly a nurse at a local hospital making $60K

■ Avid user of technology (smartphone, tablet, video games, and so on), frequent online shopper, has loyalty cards from many stores as well as their credit cards to get the maximum benefit

■ Very active on social networks (Facebook, Twitter, blogs, Yelp, and many others), provides constant feedback on the Web, has many followers due to her honest advice. She is an influencer and has a high Klout score.

■ Has three e-mail addresses, loves many sports, gardening, arts and crafts, and is multidimensional

MartForAll retailer is starting to leverage Big Data to engage with customers like the Dough family at a personal level and sell more via all channels. MartForAll has online as well as physical stores in the United States, Canada, Mexico, and Brazil, and sells many categories of merchandise. MartForAll wants to be price competitive in every market and wants to use Big Data to analyze all pricing information from internal and external sources. The current data warehouse has aggregate-level pricing data and only for one year. MartForAll loads all pricing detail-level data for all SKUs for the last eight years for all the stores, as well as loading raw data on competitive pricing for last eight years for all markets from the archive, which no one had looked at. After analysis of just the pricing detailed data (**Scenario 1**), MartForAll finds out that they are not competitive in all markets, and this finding does not make sense at all. Upon further analysis, they find out that when they were looking at prices over time, they did not factor in SKUs that are retired and then reused for other items in many regions across time. The data warehouse team had coded such business rules and logic approved by business to take care of such SKU reuses across time, so the aggregate report from data warehouse was okay. The team reviews various business rules and quality rules and applies them during their pricing analysis, and the results make sense now. Now they have the advantage to drill down to finer regional details to compete better at the local level.

The team sets up a few experiments in an online store to study price sensitivity to different geography and consumer demographics in that geography. They get all raw-level consumer data and external syndicated data on consumer behavioral classification. Now they combine these various detailed data that they had not analyzed before (**Scenario 2**). Analysis reveals that a combination of income level, family size, as well as the number of cars the family owns, is related to price sensitivity that consumers have. They want to test this out, so they create a cross-sell campaign where if the customer with this profile has bought TVs bigger than 30 inches, they sell this customer a home-theater system, at varying price levels, and the customer can get this price online or in the store. While going through approvals, they learn from the legal team that there might be regulatory compliance issues within their geographic area (federal and/or state and/or local regulation) for setting different price points for people going to the same store in an area. This regulatory compliance could have been a problem had the Big Data team rolled out a new experiment on pricing.

Things get more exciting as the team is able to now leverage the new data as well as existing loyalty card members' data in the modeled data warehouse (**Scenario 3**). They want to identify loyal members who have a high level of Internet and social media presence and run campaigns targeted at the members based on their past purchases. They take the loyal member data from data warehouse and match up the data using a new fuzzy logic–based algorithm (different from the identity-matching routine running on the data warehouse system that has been improved over the last 15 years and can handle all exceptions). Lo and behold, Jane, being an influencer, gets an e-mail for a home theater system at a 40 percent discount, and Jane happily buys the product, uses it, and writes a great review. The mission has been accomplished by using detailed browsing and purchasing activities and new social media information. Now the company can be a player in social networks to improve sales. The new algorithm then identifies the purchase on Jane's husband's credit card of a set of washer and dryer, and decides to send the Doughs a nice card by mail stating that they really appreciate their business and in return are offering a 50 percent discount on a matching kitchen appliances set (refrigerator, stove, dishwasher). The only problem is that they matched the Dough family record to a purchase made by another customer with same name John Dough in the same three-digit zip code, who had purchased the washer and dryer, not Jane's husband. After an uncomfortable argument at home between John and Jane, Jane wants to find the details, and they both go to the store. The store clerk looks up in the new system and checks the full credit card info with John and it does not match, indicating that the discount mailer went to the wrong family.

There are several issues here. Not only has this created an unwarranted situation for Dough's family, but there are legal implications to keep in mind. Sensitive data about customers must be kept encrypted, and can't be used for cross-channel marketing without permission from the customer. It looks as if these governance policies do exist and are being followed in the modeled data warehouse world, but not as part of the new team. Plus the team learns that access to sensitive data is allowed only to employees whose role has the need to use them, such as the fraud prevention team or credit statement/billing team. Encryption needs to be implemented on the new system so that sensitive data is not visible even if it is stolen. Sensitive information should be tagged so that access can be designed properly, and lastly, proper matching standards are implemented so that campaigns are being sent to the right person.

The MartForAll team works jointly with the data warehouse team, the legal team, and governance to review the existing governance policies and extends it to include *all* data—existing modeled data and new raw data.

Leveraging Big Data Governance

In order to fully leverage the new world of Big Data as well as all existing data in enterprise data warehouses and repositories and get the business benefit, one must apply enterprise data governance to *all data* without giving up the flexibility and agility. This can be achieved by creating at least three stages in order to implement governance properly:

1. **Raw Discovery and Analysis:**

   - Load all raw data first into this stage without modeling.

   - Make sure proper security is implemented, and provide limited access to only a few experienced users and data scientists so that risk is minimized.

   - Use this stage of raw unfiltered data to explore and discover/analyze using custom logic as well as tools like Oracle Endeca and Oracle Advanced Analytics.

   - Try to identify the sensitive data in the raw data during this stage.

2. **Organized Discovery and Analysis:**

   - In this stage, blend necessary raw data with modeled data.

   - Apply governance as appropriate.

   - Apply business rules and master/reference data integration and data quality.

   - Privacy and other compliances are put in place as well.

   - Metadata is rationalized across data sets.

   - Further discover and analyze combined raw content plus modeled content using tools like Oracle Endeca, Oracle Advanced Analytics, and Oracle BI.

3. **Experiment and Operationalize:**

   - Use BI tools to operationalize the new nuggets of business insights using tools like Oracle BI.

   - Link to real-time decisioning as needed, using tools like Oracle Real Time Decisioning (RTD).

   - Continue exploring data relationships in the blended raw and modeled data world using tools like Oracle Endeca.

   - Scale and provide feedback to the Discover and Analyze stages.

The key point to keep in mind is that Discovery, Analysis, and Business Intelligence can use *all data* depending on the business situation the data is being applied to, and data governance is essential to keeping the outcome trustworthy.

With Big Data, there is a challenge to figure out the minimum data governance needed. Can one keep getting more business value by applying more data governance? Looking at Figure 12-1, there is always a minimum level of data governance that needs to be implemented with all data, without which there is a negative business impact, such as regulatory compliance–driven governance (security and privacy of sensitive data). There is also an optimal data governance point where one realizes the maximum positive business impact and after which an increasing amount of data governance will have diminishing returns. Every enterprise has to figure where this optimal governance point is in order to get the most out of data governance for all data.

Earlier we discussed key elements of Enterprise Data Governance. Then we went through various use cases of big data. Table 12-2 highlights major governance guidelines for the key elements of Enterprise Data Governance from Big Data perspective.

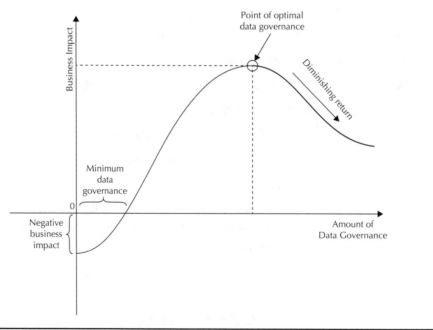

FIGURE 12-1. *Business impact of data governance vs. amount of data governance*

Governance Category	Governance Guidelines
Business Outcome	Document anticipated business outcome for the Big Data initiatives. If such a business outcome can't be established right at the start of the Big Data initiative, set a timeline to establish a business outcome in order to prevent it from becoming a science project with no business value.

Information Lifecycle Management (ILM)	■ Adapt the existing data governance policies and governance processes for ILM to include Big Data.
	
	■ Create a framework to enable how Big Data will be integrated into existing data architecture and infrastructure for ILM perspective.
	
	    ■ Manage retention schedule for local regulations as well as federal and industry regulations.
	
	    ■ Take into consideration legal holds and eDiscovery-related governance policies that might apply to Big Data.
	
	    ■ Social media records must comply with the contract and policy requirement of the data provider—for example, one can access and use a user's Facebook friend's data for a time period allowed by Facebook. Care must be taken to delete it after the business context for using the friend's data is no longer valid.
	
	    ■ Disposition of Big Data must comply with overall data lifecycle for various data types.

Regulatory Compliance and Risk Management	■ Understand federal, state, and local regulatory compliance requirements and assess their impact on the raw Big Data repository. ■ Identify risk levels posed in a Big Data environment in light of these regulatory compliances and mitigate those risks by adapting enterprise data governance to Big Data.

Data Quality Management	■ Review individual data quality from raw sources and establish data quality levels, which will be useful when one data source is combined with another for discovery and analysis.
	
	■ Over time, with a higher level of maturity in understanding new sources, establish new data quality metrics and processes for Big Data in addition to existing ones. Data scientists should play a key role during this process since the new data sources, including streaming real-time data, pose different challenges.
	
	■ Very high volume may drive a need for new ways to audit within a time constraint, and existing tools and batch processes may not be feasible given the amount of time it will take. Probabilistic data quality checks are one of the options to consider so that data quality is fit for the business purpose. This is an emerging field.
	
	■ Use Big Data content to enhance overall data quality.
	
	    ■ Sparse data enhancement.
	
	    ■ Enhance reference/master data to support Big Data quality.
	
	    ■ Use Big Data to enhance reference/master.
	
	    ■ Integrate with sessionized data from social media.
	
	    ■ Text data for adding to reference data.

TABLE 12-2. *Big Data Governance Guidelines for Key Elements of Enterprise Data Governance* (continued)

Governance Category	Governance Guidelines
Data Security and Privacy Management	■ Governance policies for security and privacy for sensitive business data must be applied to *all data*, including Big Data. ■ Access to repositories where unfiltered raw data is loaded into should be restricted until proper governance policies are applied around security and privacy. ■ The governance process needs to establish policies for privacy of such sensitive data in the Big Data repository as applicable. It must conform to established enterprise privacy policies and practices. Privacy applies to almost every industry that deals with personal information as well as other related information protected by regulations. Examples are consumer information, patient information, biometrics data, smart meter data (intervals might indicate subscribers' household activities), social media data, credit data, and so on. ■ While security provided by the new Big Data platforms has improved over time, one must make sure that the enterprise data is secured on the new data platforms with the same seriousness as the existing data platforms. ■ Once the data quality issues of unfiltered raw data are well understood (set a timeline for this), establish business rules and quality processes to improve data quality at the sources, as well as data quality measures when more than one data source is combined and integrated for discover, analysis and reporting.

Metadata Management[9]	■ Extend current metadata management to include Big Data.
	
	 ■ Plan for metadata management right from the beginning of Big Data projects and develop an integrated metadata management strategy. Here are some of the examples of metadata for Big Data:
	
	    ■ Technical metadata of Big Data store (examples: Hadoop, NoSQLdb)
	
	    ■ Operational metadata for data movements for Big Data
	
	    ■ Mappings between data sources, destinations, and business terms, definitions, and tags glossary
	
	    ■ Semantic maps and taxonomies where applicable
	
	 ■ Establish metadata for Big Data; different types of data in value.
	
	 ■ Mark Big Data areas that may contain sensitive data and provide security/privacy for those.
	
	 ■ Collect tags and key terms from unstructured data to enhance metadata search.
	
	 ■ Create a glossary of various industry-specific terms and acronyms and other business terms that might be captured in Big Data key-value.
	
	 ■ Create a glossary of various definitions of business terms that might be embedded in key-value.

TABLE 12-2. *Big Data Governance Guidelines for Key Elements of Enterprise Data Governance*

---

[9] For more detailed coverage, refer to Sunil Soares, *Big Data Governance: An Emerging Imperative*. MC Press, 2013.

Governance Category	Governance Guidelines
	■ Collect technical metadata on Big Data to: 　■ Track data lineage 　■ Impact analysis on changes of Big Data 　■ Automate metadata updates
Master and Reference Data Management	■ During Scenario 2 when raw data is combined with other raw data sources, as well as Scenario 3 where raw data is combined with modeled data, make sure that master data as well as reference data is used to ensure the quality after combination and integration occurs. ■ There can be some usage of master and reference data during Scenario 1, depending on what the raw data is all about and what the usage is.
Business Process Alignment	■ Operationalize and automate experiments and business insights gained from experiments. ■ Identify business processes required and then identify key Big Data elements used during the process. ■ Ensure that governance policies are applied in Big Data repositories as well as integrated repositories. ■ If the business context and assumptions are not valid any more, which can happen because market conditions have changed or customer tastes have changed and so on, Big Data elements, associated analytics, and models must be reassessed and if needed, redone.

TABLE 12-2. *Big Data Governance Guidelines for Key Elements of Enterprise Data Governance*

Big Data governance should be an integral part of an overall enterprise data governance program so that it leverages the existing established data governance capabilities and extends and enhances those capabilities to handle Big Data.

Industry-Specific Use Cases

In order to understand and appreciate the role Big Data governance can play, let's go through various industry use cases[10], described in the following sections.

Utilities

In the utilities industry, with the push for renewable energy, energy conservation, safe energy generation (renewed interest in nuclear energy), and Smart Grid, smart meters as well as sensors are changing this industry. Smart meters generate huge

---

[10] *The Big Book of Big Data*, ebook by Oracle.

amounts of data and this data can be analyzed to improve the usage of energy by consumers. The sensors on utilities equipment can pinpoint problems before they becomes serious, thus saving money and time, as well as lives in some instances. Smart meters capture energy usage data every 15 to 60 minutes for residential and commercial customers and transmit that data for billing and other reporting/analysis. All this machine-generated data will be collected and managed in Big Data environments and needs to be governed properly not only from a security/privacy point of view but also a quality point of view when this machine-generated data is integrated with other data.

The data sources that contribute to the business benefits include structured, semistructured, and unstructured data. Some examples of Big Data sources are

- **Smart grid sensors[11] as well as smart meter readings** While collection of this automated machine data is very useful and can yield many business benefits, proper governance should be put in place to make sure the readings make sense and are within calibration ranges. For example, if a meter reading every 3 hours is 102, 208, 339, and 12032, obviously 12032 is a either a mistake or reflects a massive leakage that should have caused circuits to fuse. Proper governance should catch such spurious readings.

- **Network usage and faults and weather/climate data** Integration of this data with network faults, recovery patterns, recovery time, and other data is very useful in predicting the severity and length of the outage and the level of severity in future. Proper governance must be put in place during integration.

- **Service call records including unstructured comments** This data can be mined to understand customer sentiments as well as key words related to customer satisfaction levels can be extracted. All this can be used to improve customer engagement as well as service quality.

- **Customer data as well as social media** Proper integration of customer profiles as well as social media can provide huge business benefits by monitoring customer sentiments and providing proactive service to improve customer satisfaction. Since social media data can come from various sources, the data quality of stored customer profiles is very important. Also, integration with social media must have proper data quality and privacy governance policies in place.

- **GPS driving data** This data is very useful when combined with grid data and meter data as well as customer outage data. If proper data quality is maintained across Big Data as well as internal master data, this can lead to great efficiency and productivity gains by allocating and tracking the right resources and assets to fix the right problems at the right time.

[11] For more detailed coverage, refer to Sunil Soares, *Big Data Governance: An Emerging Imperative.* MC Press, 2013.

Utilities do have to comply with local, state, and federal regulations, and they need to enforce proper privacy, security, and other governance policies in place to ensure compliance. There is a growing concern among consumers about data that is collected from their smart meters being transmitted over wireless networks, and therefore this data can be vulnerable to data thefts. Also since smart grid enables the electrical distribution network to be controlled digitally over the network, it is also vulnerable to security threats. Governance is crucial not only to provide compliance with regulations but also to ensure privacy and security at every level of data collection, storage, usage, and deletion. Information Lifecycle Management must be carefully designed and implemented so that data is retired at the proper time.

Healthcare

In the healthcare industry, Big Data technology is having a huge impact in improving quality of care as well as reducing the cost of healthcare, including reducing fraud. The healthcare industry represents 17 percent of GDP in the United States and employs about 11 percent of all workers. The McKinsey report suggested that the impact of Big Data on the healthcare industry will be close to $300 billion a year and will provide 0.7 percent productivity gains.[12]

The U.S. Department of Veterans Affairs (VA) has already shown early promise in using Big Data in disease management and performance base accountability and payment. California-based Kaiser Permanente used Big Data with clinical and cost data that led to the discovery of Vioxx's adverse drug effects. There are four primary groups of data that form the pillars of healthcare Big Data:

- **Clinical data**   Owned by providers, has data from EMRs, medical images, and so on

- **Claims and cost data**   Owned by payers and providers. Has data on utilization of care and cost estimates

- **Patient behavior and sentiment data**   Owned by consumers and stakeholders outside healthcare

- **Pharmaceutical R&D data**   Owned by pharmaceutical companies and academia

Integration and analysis of these disparate Big Data islands that contain structured as well as unstructured data have shown a lot of promise, and more collaboration between owners is resulting in various partnerships. In one such partnership, called Aurora, Oracle is providing key leadership and technologies for this project.[13]

---

[12] *Big Data: The next frontier for innovation, competition, and productivity,* McKinsey Global Institute, May 2011.

[13] www.oracle.com/us/corporate/press/301948, www.oracle.com/us/corporate/press/1671436

Because of the highly regulated nature of this industry (HIPPA), core information tends to be well governed, but the integration of data across various data stores needs to be governed well in the areas of privacy (by anonymizing and masking data), data quality, lifecycle management, and security. Proper care must be taken in integrating data across these sources of structured and unstructured data where predictive models are used in order to reduce fraud as well as to predict outcome. Wrong inferences due to improper integration could impact lives and quality of care.

Financial Services

The key services in the financial services area are

- Consumer and commerce banking services
- Credit card services
- Investment services
- Trading and clearing services
- Insurance services
- Research services
- Commodity trading services
- M&A advisory
- Asset-based lending/mortgage lending

While financial services is very much a data-driven industry, it is also a very highly regulated industry as well. The regulations require the financial services industry to store huge amounts of data that they collect about their business for many years depending on the regulations. Examples of these regulations are

- Fair Credit Reporting Act (FCRA) while making credit decisions
- Fair Debt Collection Practices Act (FDCPA) for debt collections
- Anti-money laundering and antiterrorism acts (Bank Secrecy Act, USA Patriot Act, OFAC Sanctions)
- Financial Privacy Act
- Community Reinvestment Act

- Truth in Savings Act, EFT Act, Expedited Finds Availability Act

- BASEL II (capital adequacy to guard against financial and operational risks) and BASEL III (global, voluntary regulatory standard on bank capital adequacy, stress testing, and market liquidity risk)

And there are many more regulations that financial services have to comply with. It is essential that data governance is a key part of data management strategy.

There are a number of Big Data use cases for financial services:

- **Customer insight and analytics** With the internal and external information available about their existing customers, banks can not only target the customers in selling banking products and services, but also extend that to a portfolio of services including investment as well as mortgage and other lending services. Social media data can provide insight into customer sentiments as well as other demographics, helping to micro-target a smaller but highly qualified candidate for a portfolio of services offerings. From a Big Data governance perspective, privacy as well as identity resolutions will be critical to enforce when external data is being integrated.

- **Fraud detection/prevention** Fraud detection and prevention can be helped by Big Data analytics. With all the external detailed insight about consumers, consumer activities on the Web, consumer location during transactions via smartphones, and so on can be used to detect fraud as well as to find the culprit after fraud has occurred. Watch list screening can also be enhanced by Big Data analytics. Identity resolution, data quality, and privacy, as well as master data management, will be factors to consider as part of Big Data governance.

- **On-demand risk analysis** Dynamic risk management is critical to financial services, especially for a global trading environment. It requires near-real-time detection and measurement of risk and then reporting and mitigation of the risks. Add on top of this, the fast-growing data volumes, both structured as well as unstructured. Finding the right signals from the massive data noise will require not only application of new algorithms but also risk model governance to ensure that model assumptions are still valid.

- **Trade monitoring** In order to monitor and detect any rogue trades, financial services companies have to link and connect all pieces of information such as position-tracking data, accounting data, order management systems, and so on from disparate systems globally.

There are many more Big Data use cases that add value to financial services companies, but have to be governed.

Examples of data sources for financial services are

- Call center log/support data

- ePOS data, external syndicated data

- Weather/climate data

- Demographic/census/economic data, residential profile data such as Zillow

- Social network and social media listening data

- Web/click logs

- Competitive data (pricing, promotion, and so on)

Retail

In the retail industry, Big Data plays a major role. Customer acquisition, retention, and growth of wallet share are very important for retailers. Retailers operate customer loyalty programs, and understanding customer behavior and engaging with them on a personal basis requires the use of Big Data. Input to this data consists of not only the customer profile data available internally as well as from data brokers externally, but also all the data generated by customers and their smart devices (such as location data) over the Web and social media. For example, a retailer can provide a customer with personalized shopping experience at the store while the customer is waiting for services like auto-services. Also a retailer can use the geolocation data from smart devices and use geo-fencing to attract customers to the store if they are nearby. Retailers can predict customer propensity to purchase more accurately and in a timely manner by gathering insights from Web site traffic, purchase patterns at the store, social media sentiments, and help desk/support call center data.

Retailers have very thin margins, so their focus is to drive the cost lower and make the operation of the store, online, inventory, merchandising, and supply chain logistics more efficient. RFID, for example, is used to reduce supply chain logistics cost. Based on automotive traffic, weather data, retail POS data, and loyalty data, real-time forecasts can be made on demand, and hence retailers can be proactive in moving merchandise in the right amount at the right time to the right place.

Examples of retail data sources are

- Marketing plans, campaigns, promotions, and coupons

- Customer profile/CRM data

- Product, pricing, rates, exchange rates, risk factors

- Compliance-related metrics

- Inventory and supply chain data

- Order management and billing, shipments

- Consumer call data

- Trade promotions and retail execution

- Retailer POS data, external syndicated data

- Wholesaler and distributor spin data

- Weather/climate data

- Demographic/census/economic data, residential profile data such as Zillow

- Social network and social media listening data

- Web/click logs

- Customer loyalty and market basket data

- Competitive data (pricing, promotion, and so on)

Consumer Packaged Goods (CPG)

The business challenges of the CPG industry are

- Reducing operational cost including commodity and energy cost

- Improving efficiency and productivity in complex supply chain and logistics

- Getting better ROI from investment in sales, marketing, and trade promotions

- Improving the safety of products and of manufacturing processes

- "Direct to consumers" and cross-channel management

- Constantly innovating and adapting to ever-changing consumer demands

Big Data has tremendous potential to address these key challenges by integrating internal and external information and discovering patterns and trends to reduce time to insight and anticipate business challenges faster. Factors to consider as part of Big Data governance are privacy, security, consumer master data management, data quality, and product master data management.

Examples of data sources in CPG are

- Order management and billing, shipments (most detailed level)

- Consumer call and survey data as well as test/panel data

- Marketing campaigns, trade promotions

- Trade promotion, retail execution, retailer POS data, external syndicated data

- Wholesaler and distributor spin data

- Weather/climate data

- Demographic/census/economic data, residential profile data such as Zillow

- Social network and web/click logs

- Retailer loyalty and market basket data

Telecommunications

In the telecommunications industry, the key challenges are customer growth and preventing customer churn. Big Data can play a huge role to uncover patterns of churn faster and with high accuracy by combining call detail records, Web data, social media data, and demographic data, as well as support call center data. Also understanding customer usage patterns better can open up new revenue sources with mobile data. When one combines consumer data from so many places, there are always concerns about master data quality as well as privacy.

Big Data provides many benefits as well as challenges to the telecom industry. Some of the use cases are

- **Multichannel insight** The customer interacts across multiple channels: call center, Web, mobile, retail outlet, service call center, IVRs, and dealers. One must bring all these interactions together in time and combine that data with customer profile data and usage data to derive insights that help personalize the customer engagement. Big Data analytics can play a huge role in delivering the best customer experience. Since data is linked and aggregated across many channels, it is critical that proper governance be in place to ensure that the final integrated picture of the channel interaction is right, which means that metadata and master data, as well as data quality, must be governed.

- **Churn prevention** The ability to create a 360-degree view of customer profile data, cross-channel interaction data, and other social data is a must to proactively detect factors leading to customer churn for every individual customer. Also this can be combined with customer interaction data with TV set-top boxes, pay-for-view usage, Internet bandwidth usage, outage impact, first-time download/use of certain apps, click patterns, and visits to support/ help sections and so on to get signals that can be combined with analytic models to predict customer dissatisfaction with the service. This combined with competitive information will help in taking proactive measures to prevent churn.

■ **Location-based marketing**   Customer location data from smart phones and geo-fencing can be used to understand the movement patterns as well as shopping patterns to help clients deliver customized and personalized offers to consumers. Also one can enable real-time relevant advertisement display by using inputs from various entities in the network and the location information to the consumers. Governance for such applications is important since decisions are made in real time, and if the quality of the data and/or the decision models is not properly managed, the end results could be far from the expected outcome. Data quality, privacy, and proper customer identity are a few areas to consider in Big Data integration.

■ **Customer sentiment analysis**   Customer digital interaction information is valuable to perform sentiment analysis. Telecoms can combine social network data such as Facebook and Twitter, customer purchase history, demographic data, customer psychographic data (interests, lifestyle, and so on), network usage data, relevant sites/blog visit data (if available) to piece together customer sentiment and then use advanced analytics to predict various behavior such as buying more services, buying pay-per-view (send an offer), customer service issues, patterns of certain sentiments specific to some geographic area where major marketing campaign will be launched (assess the likely success or failure of the campaign), and identify influencers (high clout) in a social circle.

■ **Network optimization and monetization**   Telecoms are trying to offer various bundled services to customers and can use Big Data and analytics to analyze network utilization data and data from deep-packet inspection probes, and to understand customer behavior and usage patterns. This will help them keep the customer happy by making sure customers are getting what they paid for by marrying the data with data caps the customer has subscribed to. This ensures that customers are getting what they paid for and are not subsidizing someone else. Telecoms can also figure out which customers should be offered upgrades to their service, or will be good candidates for bundled service.

■ **Clickstream analysis** Big Data can help analyze customer clicks and usage on Web sites as well as mobile data to provide a better understanding of how to personalize Web and mobile interaction with the customer and thereby drive up customer satisfaction. Most clicked options can be offered on the first page as the customer logs in to the online system, so that the customer finds what they are looking for quickly.

Examples of telecom data sources are

■ Call Data Records (CDR), call drop records, and billing data

■ Network usage and outage data

■ Customer usage data as well as profile data, Web log data

■ Session Data Records (SDR)

■ Contracts, rights, and loyalties data

■ Sales and payment data including mobile data

■ Social media data

■ Support logs, systems logs

■ Wi-Fi hotspot usage data

■ Digital set-top box data including customer usage

Oil and Gas

In the oil and gas industry, business challenges are many in both upstream as well as downstream operations. Since drilling for oil and gas is a very capital-intensive operation, high-quality prediction of the potential at a site is crucial. With advancements in sensor technology, it is cheaper to deploy many more sensors, and with improved quality of output from these seismic sensors, accuracy of potential can be improved. Big Data governance plays a huge role. Seismic data purchased from various vendors must have the proper and consistent metadata, or prediction will be useless. Also, improving the efficiency of existing wells is very important. So studying the sensor data for oil wells using Big Data technology can yield high productivity from existing wells. There are a number of use cases for Big Data in this industry.

■ **Downstream** Oil and gas companies deliver their products and services to consumers via gas stations and attached convenience stores, car washes, and car repair shops. Understanding customers and delivering the products and services that customers want is an ongoing effort. Customers also interact with the Web site as well as mobile devices to find products and services. Big Data helps companies perform customer sentiment analysis, pricing optimization, loyalty campaign and offer management, customer engagement, and experience management.

- **Seismic data**   A lot of seismic data is generated by earth measurements and sensors (such as 2D and 3D lines of vector data). This data is either processed by contractors or by the oil and gas companies themselves. Governance of this data is of paramount importance since such information is used in identifying potential fields to drill in.

- **Production data**   This involves capturing sensor information from producing wells and requires real-time data acquisition. Companies use historians to record this data, summarize it, and then transmit it to a central repository. Big Data can enable capture and storage of real-time data without summarizing, thus enabling analysis and discovery of patterns that can help in understanding the leading indicators of production declines, or harmful emissions or equipment failures. This can help companies to take proactive measures.

- **Upstream data management**   Oil and gas companies not only generate their own data that needs to be managed, but also buy data from external sources. There are not many industry standards, and therefore upstream data management becomes quite a challenge. Also, a number of these data sources are semistructured and unstructured. Big Data provides a great platform to manage upstream data.

- **Health and safety**   Health and safety are of paramount importance at the oil well sites, drilling operations, platforms at sea, refinery plants, and oil and gas pipelines. Data is collected in various formats and is stored. Big Data analytics can provide deeper analysis of this data to discover patterns and gain insights that may help improve health and safety.

Governance for oil and gas Big Data must focus on creating and managing a robust metadata repository across all the master data, such as oil well/reservoir data, geospatial data, seismic data, and accounting data. One must govern the data quality of data going into production accounting since the production accounting report is shared with government as well as with partners. Also, health safety and environmental data governance is key to avoiding major accidents as well as regulatory fines.

Examples of the data sources for the oil and gas industry are

- Seismic data
- Sensor data (pressure, temperature, wave state on oil rigs in sea, vibration data, and so on)
- GPS/location data
- Internal oil well data plus external well data

- Land data and earth measurements

- Weather/climate data

- Customer profile data

- Core and rock analysis data

- Refinery operations data and pipeline data

How Does Big Data Impact Data Governance Roles?

Implementing Big Data governance must be undertaken as soon as the business value of the Big Data project is established. That will prevent unnecessary risk due to new sets of data, data management, and data embedded business processes.

Governance Roles and Organization

You should make Big Data governance roles part of the overall data governance roles. Since most of the existing data governance roles will be applicable for governing Big Data as well, we recommend establishing a separate Big Data governance role to map existing data governance policies to various Big Data subject areas and Big Data types, create new governance policies and processes if there are gaps, and be the central point of implementing and coordinating Big Data governance and compliance.

The following points describe key data governance roles and how Big Data impacts these roles:

- **Data owners**   Existing data owners may not be able to understand the full scope of this new Big Data space, hence a Big Data Owner role should be created to manage all Big Data initiatives and own all aspects of all Big Data. This role should be part of the Data Governance Council and should take ownership of the Big Data efforts. This role should come from business.

- **Data stewards**   Data stewards are the champions for the data subject areas. They develop rules, develop processes, and also develop the standards. They are the business interface to the data controllers. Data stewards may be organized by data types and may include subject matter experts (SMEs) in the existing role. Data scientists should play this role for Big Data, and depending on their knowledge, each data scientist can represent one or more Big Data areas.

- **Data manager**   The data manager is from IT and is responsible for technical strategy and architecture, systems and processes, automation, staffing, and projects for existing data projects. This is also a new role for the Big Data space. Skills required for Big Data for this role are different, and one central Data Manager role is recommended for Big Data from IT.

- **Data controller**   Data controllers are from IT and are responsible for most executions such as data workflow, data cleansing, quality reporting, training, support, and automation. This role can handle the Big Data.

Big Data governance roles must be part of enterprise data governance groups as well as the Enterprise Data Governance Steering Group. The Data Governance Steering Group is a centralized governing body that reviews the business case for Big Data governance, and approves the policies, roles, and organization membership. There may be one or more data governance groups reporting into the Steering Group. Big Data governance must be well represented in both the Steering Group and Governance groups.

An Approach to Implementing Big Data Governance

Implementing Big Data governance must be undertaken as soon as the business value of the Big Data project is established. That will prevent unnecessary risk due to new sets of data, data management, and data-embedded business processes. Here are the key steps to implementing Big Data governance:

1. Align with business strategy: Start by defining a clear desired business outcome for Big Data projects that aligns with the business strategy. Also at this point, ensure that there is due diligence in establishing that this is a problem suitable for Big Data and analytics. Next, secure proper executive sponsorship, both from business and IT. Sometimes it may be difficult to assign a specific business value; in that case, establish a timeline to perform discovery and investigation, experiment, and establish the desired business outcome. That will help in getting executive sponsorship and funding as well as necessary support and resources. Always start with a manageable size with a variety of data that can demonstrate the business outcome, and then expand.

2. Establish Big Data governance and incorporate roles into existing Governance organization:

    - Establish a role specifically for all Big Data initiatives. Depending on the industry, you should think about establishing the data steward's role with specific skills in that area such as social media and Web data, M2M data, geolocation data, and clickstream data.

    - Make sure to include the lead data scientist (someone who has knowledge of Big Data initiatives) in the Data Governance Council.

3. Be flexible to change existing governance policies and processes.

   ■ Big Data is relatively new compared to established data management practices, so be prepared to change as you become more experienced with Big Data usage.

4. Embed governance process into Big Data projects:

   ■ As soon as the process of defining and planning Big Data requirements starts, ensure that data governance is an integral part of the Big Data projects.

   ■ Do establish a governance process for the analytics metrics so that it is standardized across the organization in terms of what it means to various organizations/LOBs.

5. Establish key data subject areas in the Big Data space that are linked to high-potential business outcome, such as:

   ■ Real-time machine data

   ■ Web commerce/click data

   ■ Social media data

   ■ External consumer profile and detailed demographic and behavioral data

   ■ Environmental external data

   ■ Unstructured customer feedback data (must capture metadata and tags as available)

6. Establish business as well as technical ownership of Big Data governance.

7. Establish and align Big Data architecture with the Enterprise Information Architecture; consider creating three stages in getting the most out of all data.

8. Establish data quality, master data, and metadata that may be new and unique to Big Data.

   ■ For example, volume and real-time data capture presents a challenge to check everything for data quality. Also, make sure there is correct metadata and context when data variety and source variety are concerned, so that results can be trusted.

9. Clearly establish Information Lifecycle Management components for Big Data governance:

   ■ Retention and disposition

   ■ Privacy and access right based on business usage and intent

   ■ Security

■ Legal compliance depending on industry

■ Backup, restore, and disaster recovery

10. Establish regular meetings between business stewards, data stewards, and data scientists on Big Data that is impacted by regulatory compliance and protection of sensitive data.

As enterprises start their journey into Big Data and analytics, they should include Big Data governance as part of their overall enterprise data governance program, and should integrate Big Data governance into their existing enterprise data governance framework, policies, process, and roles.

CHAPTER
13

Developing Architecture
and Roadmap for Big Data

A s you've read in the earlier chapters, Big Data is characterized by the four "V's": Volume, Velocity, Variety, and Value. It covers a variety of structures and types of data with explosive velocity and volume. The last "V," Value, is also sometimes referred to as "low-density" value. It speaks to the fact that most of the Big Data set is very low in its level of detail. It's not about each of the records. However, the trends and patterns discerned from its aggregated form are where the treasure lies. So the value of Big Data is discovered through a unique set of analytics that includes statistics, semantic analysis, knowledge-based queries, and visualization.

Architecture Capabilities for Big Data

Big Data enables entirely new areas for predictive insights, such as remote patient monitoring, location-based services, and anticipating future consumer behavior based on micro-personalization and detailed past knowledge.

Big Data offers an abundance of opportunities by integrating more granular analyses into conventional enterprise business processes, such as text and sentiment-based customer interaction through sales and service Web sites and call center functions, human resource resume analysis, engineering change management from defect through enhancement in product lifecycle management, factory automation and quality management in manufacturing execution systems, and many more.

Big Data requires an innovative architecture.

As you have read in earlier chapters, all of the four phases of the information lifecycle are part of a Big Data solution: acquire, organize, analyze, and decide.

It takes a lot of Big Data components to deliver a solution. But the opportunity we don't want to miss is the one that exploits the prior investments, investments in infrastructure, standards, Business Intelligence (BI) platform, languages, end-user training and tools, and developer skills. Sometimes, it is easy to abandon all prior standards when embarking or experimenting on something new. Our goal is to help our customers to leverage those prior investments.

And as you have read in previous chapters, Oracle has architected a product strategy that makes it easy to do just that.

New Characteristics of Big Data

So, what are the new information architecture challenges Big Data has introduced?

To answer this question, we need to first look at the new characteristics of Big Data. There are three main categories of new characteristics. They are: new processing of a high volume and variety of data, new analytical methods for highly detailed data, and new ways to associate structured and unstructured data.

Let's start with new processing. It refers to the need to process high-volume and very detailed information that requires hardware and software parallelization and optimization. In addition, the hardware choice needs to make economic sense to meet the size requirement introduced by both storing and processing data. Furthermore, the data model also needs to be flexible. Some of the processing requires write-once and read-many-times. As a result, there's little need for data modeling, and you simply bring in the files as is to be processed. In some other cases, however, there are certain aspects of data modeling that need to be taken into consideration during the overall application design to balance out flexibility and efficiency. Examples of such use cases include customer profile management, personalization, and high-throughput event processing.

New analytical methods are needed to process high analytical volumes and more granular details that in themselves might not be of much value. Statistical modeling has been used in various industries to a different extent in the past. Big Data expanded the use of the statistical approach into new areas. It also poses new requirements for distributed modeling execution due to the large volume of data being introduced. Statistical algorithms need to be adapted to parallel processing. New analyses and methodologies need to take into account the massive volume of data. Visualization and statistical modeling are important to identify trends and patterns that are beyond query capabilities, and the new analytical focus is on predictive and iterative discovery.

New association means aligning new Big Data sets with existing data assets, which requires shared information metadata, leveraging existing skills as well as unified information consumption.

These different characteristics have influenced how we capture, store, process, retrieve, and secure our information architecture. As we begin to work with Big Data, we can minimize our architecture risk by finding synergies across our investments. This allows us to leverage our specialized organizations and their skills, equipment, standards, and governance processes.

So, how do these new requirements impact the existing information architecture of an organization? How do we evolve what we have? What additional investment do we have to make? And, what new skills do we need?

Conceptual Architecture Capabilities of Big Data

Figure 13-1 shows a holistic capability map that bridges traditional information architecture and Big Data architecture.

As various data come in and are captured, they can be stored and processed in traditional DBMS files, in the Hadoop Distributed File System, or in a NoSQL database.

Architecturally, one of the critical components that links Big Data to the rest of the data realms is the integration and data process layer in the middle under the Organize tab in Figure 13-1. This integration layer needs to extend across all of the

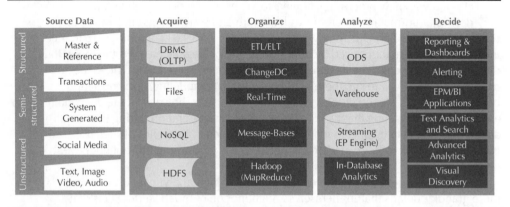

FIGURE 13-1. *Big Data capability map*

data types and domains, and bridge the gap between the traditional and new data acquisition and processing framework. The data integration capability needs to cover the entire spectrum of velocity and frequency. It needs to handle extreme and ever-growing volume requirements, and it needs to bridge the variety of data structures.

We need to look for tools that will allow us to integrate Hadoop/MapReduce with our warehouse and transactional data stores in a bidirectional manner.

To move to the next layer, there we need to be able to load the smaller amount of valuable information from Big Data processing output into our data warehouse. We also need the ability to access our structured data, such as customer profile information, while we process through our Big Data to look for patterns, such as detecting fraudulent activities.

The Big Data processing output will be loaded into Operational Data Store (ODS), data warehouse, and data marts for further analysis, same as the transaction data.

In-database statistical analysis provides a means to analyze data without moving it. The additional component in this layer is the Event Processing engine to analyze stream data in real time.

The Business Intelligence layer will be equipped with advanced analytics and visualization, on top of our traditional BI components such as reports, dashboards, and queries.

Governance, security, and operational management also cover the entire spectrum of data and information landscape at the enterprise level.

And all of this rests on top of the traditional and Big Data hardware platform, able to perform extreme processing and analytics.

Product Capabilities and Tools

Here is a brief outline of Big Data capabilities and primary enabling Oracle technologies.

Storage and Management Capability

Cloudera Distribution of Hadoop (CDH):

- Based on Apache open-source distributed file system, http://hadoop .apache.org.

- Known for highly scalable storage and automatic data replication across three nodes for fault tolerance.

- Automatic data replication across three nodes eliminates the need for backup.

- Write once, read many times.

Cloudera Manager:

- Cloudera Manager is an end-to-end management application for Cloudera's Distribution of Apache Hadoop, www.cloudera.com.

- Cloudera Manager gives a cluster-wide, real-time view of nodes and services running; provides a single, central place to enact configuration changes across the cluster; and incorporates a full range of reporting and diagnostic tools to help optimize cluster performance and utilization.

Oracle Enterprise Manager:

- Oracle Enterprise Manager provides end-to-end Big Data platform management including hardware, network, and software.

- Oracle Enterprise Manager provides a summary view of software layout and identifies the state of services.

- It is also equipped with in-context drill-down to Cloudera Manager for software monitoring.

Database Capabilities

Oracle NoSQL Database:

- High-performance key-value pair database. Key-value pair is an alternative to a predefined schema. Used for nonpredictive and dynamic data for fast predictive response times with a simple API.

■ Simple pattern queries and custom-developed solutions to access data such as Java APIs.

■ Major + Minor key paradigm allows multiple record reads in a single API call.

■ Highly scalable multinode, multiple data center, fault-tolerant, ACID operations.

■ Simple programming model, random index reads and writes.

HBase:

■ Allows random, real-time read/write access.

■ Strictly consistent reads and writes.

■ Automatic and configurable sharding of tables.

■ Automatic failover support between Region Servers.

Processing Capability

MapReduce:

■ Breaks problem up into smaller subproblems.

■ Able to distribute data workloads across thousands of nodes.

Other processing capabilities:

■ **Pig**   Data flow language for data processing

■ **Hive**   SQL-like construct that creates an abstraction layer above MapReduce

Data Integration Capability

Oracle Big Data Connectors, Oracle Loader for Hadoop, Oracle Data Integrator:

■ Exports MapReduce results to RDBMS, Hadoop, and other targets.

■ Connects Hadoop to relational databases for SQL processing.

■ Includes a graphical user interface integration designer that generates Hive scripts to move and transform MapReduce results.

■ Optimized processing with parallel data import/export.

■ Can be installed on Oracle Big Data Appliance or on a generic Hadoop cluster.

Statistical Analysis Capability

Open Source Project R and Oracle Advanced Analytics including Oracle Data Mining and Oracle R Enterprise:

- Programming language for statistical analysis.

- Introduced into Oracle Database as a SQL extension to perform high-performance in-database statistical analysis.

- Oracle R Enterprise allows reuse of pre-existing R scripts with no modification.

Mahout:

- Machine-learning algorithms built on the MapReduce paradigm for clustering, classification, and batch-based collaborative filtering.

- Part of the Cloudera distribution of Hadoop.

Making Big Data Architecture Decisions

Information Architecture is perhaps one of the most complex areas of IT. It is the ultimate investment payoff. Today's economic environment demands that business be driven by useful, accurate, and timely information. And the world of Big Data adds another dimension.

Key Drivers to Consider

Here is a summary of various business and IT drivers you need to consider when making these architecture choices:

Business Drivers	IT Drivers
Better insight	Reduce storage cost
Faster turnaround	Reduce data movement
Accuracy and timeliness	Faster time to market
	Standardized toolset
	Ease of management and operation
	Security and governance

Some of the key business drivers come from the need to derive better, more accurate, and more timely insight for customers, operations, and risk management. For many years, companies have focused on IT-to-business alignment in order to achieve higher business performance. While the main IT objective is to be in alignment with business strategies and drivers, it is also important to keep in mind some of the IT drivers for efficiency, agility, and cost-effectiveness. The IT drivers in the right column of the preceding table are some of the key guiding principles that enable a path to IT-enabled business growth.

For example, new analytical requirements from the business sometimes call for keeping longer and more granular historical data. Different lines of business might need slightly varied ways of data segments and/or aggregation level. It might appear a faster approach for each of the LOBs to acquire and maintain their own data set using their choice of tools and products based on their specific resource strength and preferences. The result of going this route will most undoubtedly introduce complexity of technology infrastructure, redundancy of data, and increased cost for storage and management. Establishing a holistic architecture that incorporates both business drivers as well as IT objectives is the best step forward to enable business agility in the long run.

Architecture Development Process for Realizing Incremental Values

Many organizations have expressed a sense of urgency in implementing Big Data capabilities. However, not everyone is ready to fully commit to a large-scale transformation to embrace Big Data. So what is the best approach to incrementally build up the Big Data capabilities? For that, we are going to first turn our attention to Oracle's Information Architecture and Development Process.

Overview of Oracle Information Architecture Framework

As architects and IT planners, an important part of our job is to simplify, unify, and standardize our solutions. This is especially important when embarking on something new.

Figure 13-2 shows Oracle's Information Architecture Framework and capability model. It's composed of data realms in the middle and management capabilities in the outer ring.

Oracle's Information Architecture Framework contains the following components:

- Data Realms

- Information Architecture Capability Model

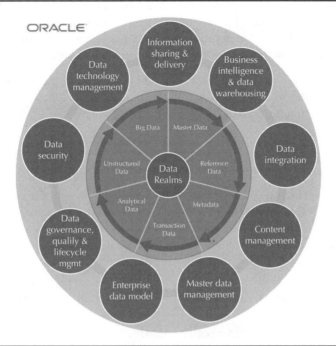

FIGURE 13-2.   *Oracle Information Architecture Framework*

Data Realms

Different types and structures of data exist within an organization. They can be categorized into the following seven data realms:

- *Transaction data* consists of business transactions that are captured during business operations and processes, such as purchase records, inquiries, and payments.

- *Metadata*, defined as "data about the data," is the description of the data. Examples of metadata include the data name, data dimensions or units, definition of a data entity, or a calculation formula of metrics.

- *Master data* refers to the enterprise-level data entities that are of strategic value to an organization. They are typically nonvolatile and nontransactional in nature. Customer, product, supplier, and location/site are some of the common master data entities.

■ *Reference data* consists of internally managed or externally sourced facts to support an organization's ability to effectively process transactions, manage master data, and provide decision support capabilities. Geospatial data and market data are among the most commonly used reference data.

■ *Unstructured data* make up over 70 percent of an organization's data and information assets. They include documents, digital images, geospatial data, and multimedia files.

■ *Analytical data* are derivations of the business operation and transaction data used to satisfy reporting and analytical needs. They reside in data warehouses, data marts, and other decision support applications.

■ *Big Data* refer to large datasets that are challenging to store, search, share, visualize, and analyze. The growth of such data is mainly a result of the increasing channels of data in today's world. Examples include, but are not limited to, user-generated content through social media, Web and software logs, cameras, information-sensing mobile devices, aerial sensory technologies, genomics, and medical records.

Table 13-1 summarizes the data realms and their different characteristics.

Information Architecture Capability Model

Various capabilities are needed in order to manage the different data types and to process different data structures, or the lack thereof. A capability consists of the following dimensions:

■ **Objectives**   The goals and desired outcome

■ **Metrics**   KPI and success criteria to measure the maturity and effectiveness

■ **Processes**   Activities, inputs, outputs, and deliverables

■ **People**   Roles and skillsets required

Enterprise Information Sharing and Delivery   Information Sharing and Delivery addresses how information is propagated directly to its consumers within an organization. Information can be delivered through various channels and devices including desktop integration, alerts, and mobile devices. Recent developments with collaborative technologies have enabled increased user-to-user interaction and thus the need for more access control of shared resources.

Business Intelligence and Data Warehouse   Business Intelligence and Data Warehouse provide users and stakeholders with insights into the health of the business. Rather than delivering rigid or fixed output with outdated information,

Data Realm	Structure	Volume	Description	Examples
Master Data	Structured	Low	Enterprise-level data entities that are of strategic value to an organization. Typically nonvolatile and nontransactional in nature.	Customer, product, supplier, and location/site.
Transaction Data	Structured and semistructured	Medium–High	Business transactions that are captured during business operations and processes.	Purchase records, inquiries, and payments.
Reference Data	Structured and semistructured	Low–Medium	Internally managed or externally sourced facts to support an organization's ability to effectively process transactions, manage master data, and provide decision support capabilities.	Geospatial data and market data.
Metadata	Structured	Low	Defined as "data about the data." Used as an abstraction layer for standardized descriptions and operations. For example, integration, intelligence, services.	Data name, data dimensions or units, definition of a data entity, or a calculation formula of metrics.
Analytical Data	Structured	Medium–High	Derivations of the business operation and transaction data used to satisfy reporting and analytical needs.	Data that resides in data warehouses, data marts, and other decision support applications.
Documents and Content	Unstructured	Medium–High	Documents, digital images, geospatial data, and multimedia files.	Claim forms, medical images, maps, video files.
Big Data	Structured, semistructured, and unstructured	High	Large datasets that are challenging to store, search, share, visualize, and analyze.	User and machine-generated content through social media, Web and software logs, cameras, information-sensing mobile devices, aerial sensory technologies, and genomics.

TABLE 13-1. *Data Realms and Characteristics*

these systems now deliver the capabilities for end users to create the information portals and dashboards they need to expedite strategic and tactical decision making. Subcapabilities in this space include BI foundations, traditional data warehouses and data marts, predictive analytics, data mining, and enterprise performance management.

Data Integration   Organizations are increasingly dependent on data integration to tie together cacophonies of application systems and data stores into cohesive solutions. Legacy sources, merger/acquisition activity, and SaaS/COTS solutions necessitate the need for skillful integration of systems to support business needs. There is a wide spectrum of data integration capabilities that provide coverage from batch-based to real-time integration needs, including ETL, ELT, Change Data Capture, event-driven, message-driven, and real-time integration. Distributed data processing and social media processing are the more recent capabilities to address the volume, velocity, and variety of Big Data.

Master Data Management   Master Data Management consists of a number of subcapabilities unique to the management of the master data for an enterprise. They include

- Ability to specify a gold record definition

- Functions to manage survival rights through rules for merging and matching

- Master hubs such as customer data hub, product data hub, location data hub, and supplier data hub with specific data models for each of the hubs and relevant reference data

- Dimension and hierarchy management capabilities

Enterprise Data Model   Data silos present a significant challenge for many of our customers. The lack of an enterprise data model and ability to connect and correlate data across subject areas (for example, customers with products) reduces the efficacy of an organization's investment in its information. Many opportunities are lost because of the inability to harvest new insights into customers and business activities. The enterprise data model is a key discipline to instill within the organization to ensure that no one solution drives the data model but rather the enterprise data needs. Value chain analysis of core business processes and functions can help draw the boundary of the enterprise data domain and identify key subject areas. The conceptual data model and logical data model make up the next layers of the enterprise data model.

Content Management   The majority of an organization's information asset is unstructured or semistructured. Therefore, content management is recognized in our framework as a key top-level capability to manage content, records, multimedia, and image capture. Adequate search and workflow mechanisms are also required to enable rapid retrieval of pertinent information for decision making and maintenance.

Data Governance, Quality, and Lifecycle Management   No architecture discipline, regardless of domain or subdomain, would be complete without governance, quality assurance, and lifecycle management. Processes and policies are necessary in order to enforce solid discipline and best practices within the organization. Like application systems and other architectural assets, lifecycle management ensures that organizations only retain information necessary to their longevity and legal compliance.

Data Security Management   Data security controls whether the right individuals have access to the right information at the right time. Data is protected while in transit as well as when it is stored. Additionally, continual monitoring is employed to ensure that violations of standards and policies are detected and addressed immediately and proactively.

   With the plethora of information being generated today, organizations face numerous challenges with regard to data security. Information is often distributed across multiple applications and databases, making accessibility/availability of information a challenge. Ensuring that information is connected, available, secure, and reliable across mixed sources and targets is key for enterprises to realize a return on their information investment.

Data Technology Management   Organizations will need to develop or engage core data technology management skills to address the increasing amount of raw information that exists in enterprises today. Organizations are accumulating gigabytes of data every day, and deliberate management of these resources is necessary in order to control costs and ensure agility moving forward. A solid data infrastructure foundation is a critical capability within information architecture. The core of this foundation is the ability of the database management system to effectively store and retrieve various styles and structures of data and information. The ability to manage and operate other infrastructure components in a highly available and recoverable fashion is also essential to ensure the availability of the data at all times.

Why Formalize and Standardize an Information Model?

It's important to have an information model and framework. It isn't just a framework for technical design patterns. It is a framework for success of any new projects or initiatives. There are many benefits from a capability-based framework, as described previously.

First, there are many components to information and data management. This framework helps you to organize all the moving pieces. In addition, it's based on capability instead of components and functions; it helps you to establish objectives, assess maturity, determine gaps between current state and desired future state, and establish a roadmap to drive to that future state vision. Most importantly, it lays out a holistic blueprint to identify gaps and redundancies and enables you to maximize your existing investment with an integrated architecture.

Overview of Applied OADP for Information Architecture

Figure 13-3 shows an overview of the Oracle Architecture Development Process (OADP) for Information Architecture.

Business Architecture

The essence of Enterprise Architecture (EA) is planning, governance, and innovation. The main purpose of the Business Architecture phase is to establish the business context and to understand the business drivers behind the information needs.

The main goal of this phase is to validate our understanding of the business strategies and drivers, to link all the perspectives together, and lay a solid foundation

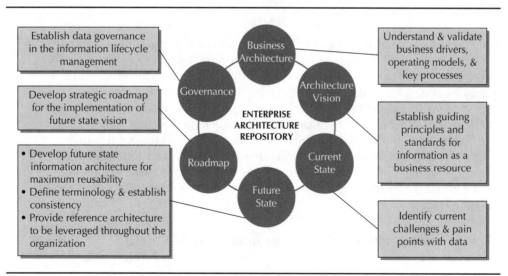

FIGURE 13-3. *Oracle Architecture Development Process for Information Architecture*

for the remainder of the architecture development. Enterprise Architecture is all about alignment of IT and business, and it applies to the information domain as well.

Architecture Vision

All architecture design starts with guiding principles. But it is not just about the principles alone; rather, it is more about the rationale and implications. Why does it matter? Why do we need these principles? What do they do?

The challenges we have seen with our customers in the past where the principles established weren't always well understood or closely followed occurred because two things were missing. First, there are the architectural implications of these guiding principles—what does it mean to the design decisions in your projects and systems? Second, there's a missing link between the principles and business drivers. That's where the principle map comes in. Establishing the linkage and focusing on the business strategy makes clear the importance and benefits of these guiding principles that drive the architecture decisions.

Current State

The main objective of the Current State phase is to capture baseline architecture. Oracle's position on current state analysis can be summarized by two "justs"—Just in Time and Just Enough. Not understanding your current state will "blindside" you. You might establish a future state that is too aspirational and doesn't take into consideration your organization's readiness and maturity level. But at the same time, not all of the current state analysis requires the same level of priority. It is imperative to avoid being overly ambitious, while still having a high level of commitment.

During the Current State analysis phase, it is important to look at data in the context of business processes. What business processes do they support? How critical are these business processes? How critical are the information/data assets to business processes? What are the risks to the business if such data is unavailable or incorrect? That's one of the best ways to capture current state—in the light of business process and context.

Future State

Future state is driven by the newly established business strategies and priorities, and guided by the newly developed or validated principles. Using the same format as the current state but highlighting what will be changed in the future state can help clarify the focus and the impact of the new architecture.

Strategic Roadmap

There are many options to implementation. This adds to the complexity of creating roadmap planning. Comparing and contrasting various options based on cost, risk, time to market, and other factors can help an organization reach consensus and agreement on the approach and associated timeline.

Governance

Another important component in architecture is governance. There is EA governance and data governance. They are both important to consider.

Governance needs to be examined from a variety of angles—people, policies, processes, technologies, and financials. With a clear assessment of the current governance maturity, it is possible to recommend a practical and pragmatic governance model to ensure the success of implementing the future state architecture.

Big Data Architecture Development Process

In this section, we'll walk through the architecture development process step by step for a Big Data use case.

Overview

The case study shown in Figure 13-4 is based on an initiative to achieve a 360-degree view of customers at a telecommunication company. The underlying architecture and framework can be applied to other industries, such as retail, utilities, and financial services.

The overall objectives of this initiative are to increase revenue and profitability through cross-sell and up-sell, to introduce new products and innovations based on deep understanding of the customers and their needs, and to ultimately enhance customer satisfaction through customer intimacy and consistent customer experience across all touchpoints and channels.

Business Architecture

Figure 13-5 illustrates the high-level business architecture of the initiative.

The two main pillars of this architecture are customer intimacy and effective marketing to reduce customer churn and to improve up-sell and cross-sell success. New capabilities are needed in the areas of customer classification, ability to monitor

Increase Revenue and Profitability	Expand Product Portfolio	Enhance Customer Experience
• Improve Cross-Sell and Up-Sell Opportunities • Customer Attrition Prevention • Improve Operational Efficiency and Reduce IT Cost	• New Product Development Based on Social Landscape and Trends • Targeted Campaign and Product Recommendation	• Customer Intimacy with Holistic and Historic View of Each Customer • Customer Satisfaction & Survey Management • Effective, Accurate, and Timely Fraud Detection

FIGURE 13-4. *Telco use case overview*

FIGURE 13-5.   *Telco use case business architecture*

brand reputation and quickly respond to customer sentiment as needed, and the ability to effectively target marketing effort to a specific customer segmentation or even individually.

The focus of the business functional areas includes marketing, sales, network management, transaction management, and customer service. However, the same framework can be applied to risk management and fraud detection, even though these are not the key functions prioritized through the initial implementation.

Architecture Vision

The purpose of the architecture vision as shown in Figure 13-6 is to establish a high-level conceptual representation of the capabilities needed to support and enable the business architecture.

Figure 13-6 illustrates the key components including a data source layer, the Enterprise Data Factory in the middle, and analytics and consumption capabilities.

We are seeing more companies moving away from a monolithic data warehouse and creating a data hub or data factory. The data hub is composed of the following elements: data staging layer for preparation and cleansing as a landing zone, foundation layer as a full history enterprise-level repository, and performance layer with targeted aggregation based on specific subject areas or functional focus. The knowledge discovery layer is a relatively new concept. It enables the iterative nature of data discovery through the ability to rapidly provision a data mining sandbox and a development sandbox.

Another artifact for architecture vision is the guiding principles as shown in Figure 13-7. The main purpose of these principles is to establish a common ground for architecture decision-making. Figure 13-7 is an example of that.

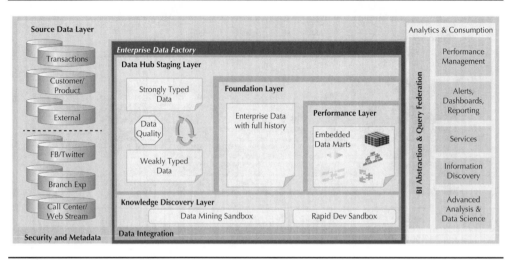

FIGURE 13-6. *Telco use case architecture vision*

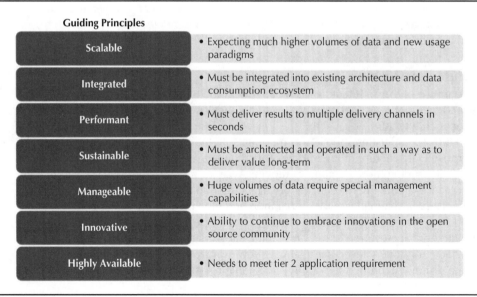

FIGURE 13-7. *Telco use case guiding principles*

Current State Architecture

In the current state summary shown in Figure 13-8, we listed the existing information architecture portfolio and highlighted some of the key gaps. It is not an exhaustive list or depiction of the current state architecture. Instead, it has just enough information to provide a good understanding of the gaps and establish a foundation for the strategic roadmap.

Future State Architecture

Figure 13-9 shows the future state architecture based on the conceptual capability map.

In order to achieve the business objectives outlined in the Business Architecture phase, three main information architecture strategies are in order. The first one is to increase the historic data availability. Instead of having only 6 to 12 months worth of detailed customer transaction and interaction data, all historical transactions need to be made available for analysis. To accomplish this goal, it is imperative to establish a data storage platform that maximizes hardware economics and scalability. The ability to quickly integrate new data sources such as social interaction, branch survey results, clickstreams, and call center logs and transcripts is also critical.

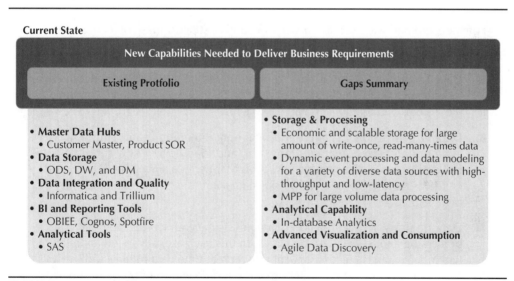

FIGURE 13-8. *Telco use case current state architecture*

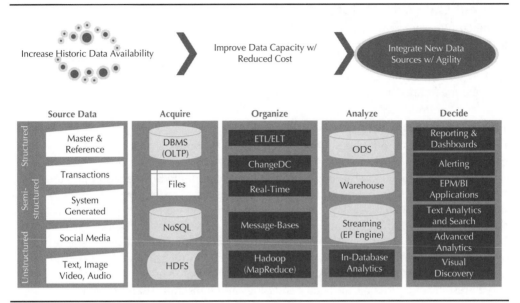

FIGURE 13-9. *Telco use case future state conceptual architecture capability map*

Software and hardware capabilities are needed to support these objectives. They can be organized into the following categories:

- **Data Acquisition** Various data storage options are available to store different types of data including HDFS and NoSQL Database, in addition to existing file systems and relational database systems.

- **Data Organization** While traditional data integration tools still play an important role to extract, transform, and load data, a new set of data integration and processing tools, such as MapReduce, Hive, Pig, Sqoop, and Flume, is required to process various data sources with high volume and high velocity.

- **Data Analysis** New areas of data analysis have arisen including event processing and in-database analytics. In this use case, advanced analytics within the database plays a critical role for real-time data mining and analysis for personalized recommendation and fraud detection of prepaid phone cards. The main advantage of in-database analytics is that it minimizes data movement as it moves algorithm to data instead of the traditional method of moving data to algorithm.

■ **Data Consumption** Advanced visualization tools that can connect to all layers of data factory (sandbox, staging, foundation, and performance) are the glue to enable seamless and integrated data consumption. Actionable data visualization and consumption of the data analytics are aimed to change the business outcome instead of triggering more questions.

■ **Infrastructure and Management** Figure 13-10 illustrates the hardware capabilities of the future state architecture. The three engineered systems from Oracle, including Big Data Appliance, Exadata, and Exalytics, are chosen for integration, optimized performance, ease of management, and quick time to value.

The logical architecture diagram in Figure 13-11 spells out all the software tools in this architecture in the context of the data flow. As master data and transactional data go through the traditional flow into the data warehouse through ETL tools, the Big Data sources are captured and ingested into the Big Data Appliance using Sqoop and Flume. Historical transaction data are also archived into the Big Data cluster as a centralized hub. Big Data sources such as social feeds, call center logs, and clickstream data are preprocessed and cleansed and stored in Hive databases for consumption and analysis. Big Data Connectors will extract aggregated customer data into the data warehouse to be able to correlate with customer profile and demographic information that is already in existence. NoSQL database captures a predefined set of transactions for prepaid calling cards and feeds into Oracle Event Processing (OEP) to detect fraudulent activities. The NoSQL database is also used as a persistent layer for OEP.

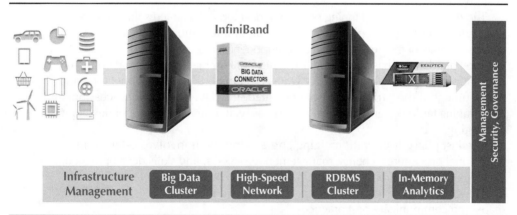

FIGURE 13-10. *Telco use case infrastructure capabilities*

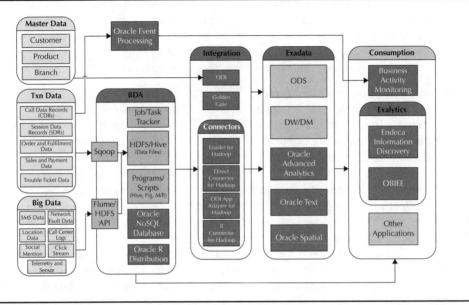

FIGURE 13-11. *Telco use case logical architecture*

Strategic Roadmap

The strategic roadmap is aimed to establish Big Data capabilities in an incremental manner. It is composed of three main phases: Planning, Foundation, and Expansion, as shown in Figure 13-12.

The Architecture and Planning phase will develop the detailed solution architecture and perform a functional prototype to test out all integration points and minimize unforeseen risks of the new architecture components.

The Foundation phase will establish a Big Data architecture foundation including installation and configuration of Big Data Appliance, Big Data Connectors, and development of the various components including data ingestion, processing, and Hive staging table design and development, as well as analytical model development and testing.

The last phase is operationalizing and expanding. It involves establishing operational procedures, change management processes, and skills development and enablement. It is also recommended that we start to build up a Big Data Center of Excellence to develop reference architecture, expand the capabilities, and define, share, and communicate best practices.

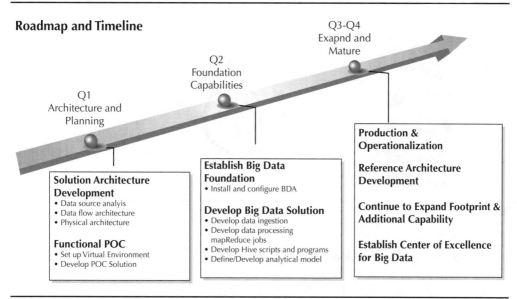

Roadmap and Timeline

FIGURE 13-12. *Telco use case strategic roadmap*

Impact on Data Management and BI Processes

We typically look at capabilities through people, process, and tools. We had a lot of discussion in earlier chapters on tools and products. So let me direct your attention to a few other dimensions of Big Data capability.

First, the Big Data information discovery process is different from the traditional BI process, as illustrated in Figure 13-13.

Traditional BI Development Process

The development of traditional BI and data warehousing (DW) is entirely different from Big Data. With traditional BI, you know the answer you are looking for. You simply define requirements and build to your objective.

Big Data and Analytics Development Process

With Big Data, you may have an idea or interest, but you don't know what would come out of it. The answer for your initial question will trigger the next set of questions. So, the development process is more fluid. It requires that you explore the data as you develop and refine your hypothesis.

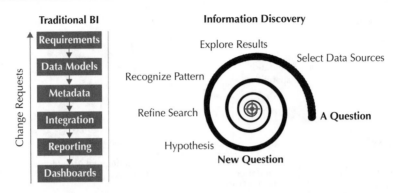

FIGURE 13-13. *Traditional BI process vs. Big Data development process*

So this might be a process you go through with Big Data:

■ You start with a hypothesis, the big idea.

■ You then gather available and relevant data sources.

■ You explore results through various data processing and integration methods including MapReduce, Hive, and interactive query on through search and visualization.

■ You reduce ambiguity, apply statistical models, eliminate outliers, find concentrations, and make correlations.

■ And you interpret the outcome, continuously refine models, and establish an improved hypothesis.

In the end, this analysis might lead to a creation of new theories and predictions based upon the data. In other words, the Big Data development and analytical process is more fluid and iterative compared to traditional Software Development Life Cycle (SDLC) and BI development. Putting aside the differences, we should also realize that the Big Data analytics need to be integrated with the existing BI ecosystem. The value of the analytical results will be limited if it is not easily consumable by business analysts in the context of their day-to-day business operations.

Big Data Governance

Data governance is an integral part of information architecture. However, with Big Data, data governance seems to be forgotten or deemed irrelevant. There's an increasing voice advocating data democracy and it gives rise to a sense of anarchy.

The main reason behind this sentiment lies in the nature and focus of traditional data governance.

Traditional Data Governance Focus

Data governance is the specification of decision rights and an accountability framework to encourage desirable behavior in the valuation, creation, storage, use, archival, and deletion of data and information. It includes the processes, roles, standards, and metrics that ensure the effective and efficient use of data and information in enabling an organization to achieve its goals.

Traditional data governance tends to focus on data standards—common data definition and data integration strategy based on a canonical data model. The focus on data policies, data standards, and overall data strategies is usually the first step when an organization initiates a data governance function. Enterprise initiatives including major business and IT transformations can also benefit from such a program focus.

New Focus for Governance in Big Data

With the rise of Big Data, this focus on data standards and quality no longer takes center stage. As a matter of fact, it is important not to exclude any data elements that are not in alignment with the known definition. One of the main goals of Big Data analytics is to discover outliers.

Does this mean that data governance is no longer relevant in the context of Big Data?

Stephen Hawking once said, "The real enemy of knowledge is not ignorance. It's the illusion of knowledge." With large amounts of data, it's not uncommon to discover false correlations between attributes and datasets. So how do we ensure that the statistical model yields the correct conclusion? How do we know if we can base important business decisions on the models and results of certain analytics? Scientific methodologies have been in existence to provide guidance on the generalizability and validity of research results. The same rigor needs to be applied to govern the statistical process based on the business context.

Figure 13-14 highlights some of the key areas that Big Data introduce for data governance.

In addition, the Big Data conversation is really about bringing higher-quality data to the BI environment. It's coming from new data sources and it needs new techniques to guarantee the quality.

The data governance function for Big Data needs to focus on the balance between the value Big Data brings versus the cost of achieving such value. It needs to be put into the business context. What business processes does it support? How critical is this business process to the overall business capabilities of an organization?

Furthermore, new characteristics of Big Data present your architecture review board with new acquisition, operations, and open source considerations. How do you drive synergies with current investments and maintain alignment with operations?

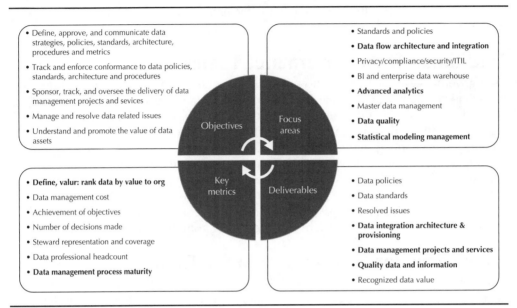

- Define, approve, and communicate data strategies, policies, standards, architecture, procedures and metrics
- Track and enforce conformance to data policies, standards, architecture and procedures
- Sponsor, track, and oversee the delivery of data management projects and sevices
- Manage and resolve data related issues
- Understand and promote the value of data assets

- Standards and policies
- **Data flow architecture and integration**
- Privacy/compliance/security/ITIL
- BI and enterprise data warehouse
- **Advanced analytics**
- Master data management
- **Data quality**
- **Statistical modeling management**

Objectives *Focus areas*

Key metrics *Deliverables*

- **Define, valur: rank data by value to org**
- Data management cost
- Achievement of objectives
- Number of decisions made
- Steward representation and coverage
- Data professional headcount
- **Data management process maturity**

- Data policies
- Data standards
- Resolved issues
- **Data integration architecture & provisioning**
- **Data management projects and services**
- **Quality data and information**
- Recognized data value

FIGURE 13-14. *Data governance focus for Big Data*

And how do you manage standards with regard to open source? You need to know when to adopt open source tools, and how to manage the enterprise requirements when using these open source products, including security, performance, scalability, and high availability.

In summary, data governance is more relevant than ever. The difference is the actual focus areas for Big Data. In the context of Big Data, data governance needs to focus on validity of statistical conclusions. It also needs to focus on data flow architecture to minimize data duplication and ensure efficiency.

Developing Skills and Talent

Three new roles emerge as a result of Big Data. They are data scientist, Big Data developer, and Big Data administrator, as shown in Figure 13-15.

Data Scientist

The Big Data process begs for a special kind of person—data scientist—a new role that has emerged as a result of the Big Data paradigm. This is no longer a back-office function serving the needs of finance or the C-level management. This is a role with extensive industry knowledge as well as deep analytical, math, and statistical ability.

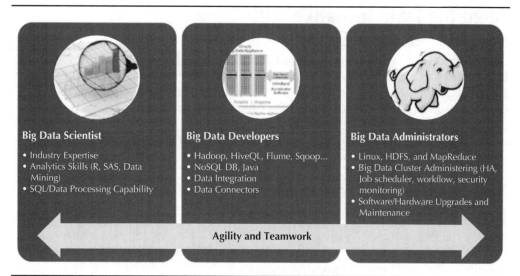

FIGURE 13-15. *Big Data roles and responsibilities*

Data scientists will mine data, apply statistical modeling and analysis, interpret the results, and drive the implication of data results to application and to prediction.

Big Data Developer

Big Data scientists are supported by Big Data developers. From a technical perspective, Big Data developers with Hadoop/Java/NoSQL skills are also going to be in demand. Their jobs are to manage and monitor the infrastructure for security, performance, data growth, availability, and scalability.

Big Data Administrator

Big Data Administrators are similar to traditional system administrators and DBAs, but a new set of skills and tools is needed. These roles can be grown from internal or brought in from consulting services organizations who possess these abilities. Either way, this needs to be a team of individuals who have clear ROI in mind and can function with great agility both technically as well as from a business perspective.

Big Data Best Practices

Here are a few general guidelines to build a successful Big Data architecture foundation.

Align Big Data Initiative with Specific Business Goals

One of the key characteristics of big data is Value—value through low-density and high volumes of data. As we sort through the mountains of low-value-density Big Data and look for the gold nugget, we must not lose sight of why we are doing this. Follow an enterprise architecture approach. Focus on the value it provides to the business. How does it support and enable the business objectives? Properly align and prioritize Big Data implementation with the business drivers that are critical to ensure sponsorship and funding for the long run.

Ensure a Centralized IT Strategy for Standards and Governance

Some of the recent analysts' surveys indicated that one of the biggest obstacles for Big Data is skills shortage. A 60 percent shortfall is predicted by 2018. Address such risk and challenge through IT governance to grow the skill level, to select and enforce standards, and to reduce the overall risks and training cost. Another strategy to consider is to implement appliances that would provide you with a jumpstart and quicker time to value as you grow your in-house expertise.

Use a Center of Excellence to Minimize Training and Risk

Use a center of excellence (CoE) to share solution knowledge, planning artifacts, and oversight for projects. Whether Big Data is a new or expanding investment, the soft and hard costs can be shared across the enterprise. Another benefit from the CoE approach is that it will continue to drive the Big Data and overall information architecture maturity in a more structured and systematical way.

Correlate Big Data with Structured Data

Establish new capabilities and leverage your prior investments in infrastructure, platform, BI, and DW, rather than throwing them away. Invest in integration capabilities that enable your knowledge workers to correlate different types and sources of data, to make associations, and to make meaningful discoveries.

Provide High-Performance and Scalable Analytical Sandboxes

Human beings are very good at solving problems. We do so through a process of exclusion. And often, we don't even know what we are looking for initially. That's completely expected. Enterprise IT needs to support this "lack of direction" or "lack of clear requirement." We need to be able to provide a flexible environment for our end users to explore and find answers. Such sandbox environments also need to be highly optimal in performance and properly governed.

Reshape the IT Operating Model

The new requirements from Big Data will bring certain changes to the enterprise IT operating model. Provisioning of new environments will need to be more timely and user-driven. Resource management also needs to be more dynamic in nature. A well-planned-out cloud strategy plays an integral role in supporting those changing requirements.

Index

Oracle Technology Network. It's code for sharing expertise.

Come to the best place to collaborate with other IT professionals.

Oracle Technology Network is the world's largest community of developers, administrators, and architects using industry-standard technologies with Oracle products.

Sign up for a free membership and you'll have access to:

- Discussion forums and hands-on labs
- Free downloadable software and sample code
- Product documentation
- Member-contributed content

Take advantage of our global network of knowledge.

JOIN TODAY ▷ Go to: oracle.com/technetwork

Reach More than 700,000 Oracle Customers with Oracle Publishing Group

Connect with the Audience that Matters Most to Your Business

Oracle Magazine
The Largest IT Publication in the World
Circulation: 550,000
Audience: IT Managers, DBAs, Programmers, and Developers

Profit
Business Insight for Enterprise-Class Business Leaders to Help Them Build a Better Business Using Oracle Technology
Circulation: 100,000
Audience: Top Executives and Line of Business Managers

Java Magazine
The Essential Source on Java Technology, the Java Programming Language, and Java-Based Applications
Circulation: 125,000 and Growing Steady
Audience: Corporate and Independent Java Developers, Programmers, and Architects

For more information or to sign up for a FREE subscription:
Scan the QR code to visit Oracle Publishing online.